Culinary cultures of Europe

Identity, diversity and dialogue

Presented by

The Directorate General of Education, Culture and Heritage, Youth and Sport of the Council of Europe with the support of the Steering Committee for Culture and its Chair, Roberta Alberotanza, to commemorate the 50th anniversary of the European Cultural Convention, 2004/05, and within the framework of the Portuguese Chairmanship of the Committee of Ministers

Edited by

Darra Goldstein and Kathrin Merkle

With contributions by

Authors from 40 Council of Europe member states, with an introduction by Fabio Parasecoli and conclusions by Stephen Mennell

French edition: *Culture culinaire d'Europe – Identité, diversité et dialogue*

ISBN 92-871-5783-9

The book has been sponsored by the Stellios & Fany Boutari Foundation and the Ursula Lübbe Foundation

Cover photo: Josefa d'Obidos, Still life with cake, pottery and flowers (1676)
Cover design: Graphic Design Workshop, Council of Europe
Layout: Pre-press unit, Council of Europe

Council of Europe Publishing
http://book.coe.int
F-67075 Strasbourg Cedex

ISBN 92-871-5744-8
© Council of Europe, July 2005
Printed in Germany by Verlagsgruppe Lübbe

Table of contents

Preface

There is nothing trivial about food. The study of culinary culture and its history provides an insight into broad social, political and economic changes in society. This collection of essays reflects many of the important transitions through which European societies have passed, and in this sense, it is a history book. It is also a celebration of an enormously rich part of our cultural heritage of everyday life and everyday culture.

The history of a society's food is useful in highlighting the interdependence, delicate balance and, at times, tension over efforts to safeguard cultural identity whilst allowing and promoting cultural diversity. Identity is shaped by differences and its relationship with otherness. So-called local cuisine and products become phenomena only when exposed to new products and habits. However, when closely studied, even local recipes are often the result of cultural exchange. With the unprecedented scale of mass migration during the second half of the twentieth century, historical interactions have gained in significance. Today, global exchanges have become the norm, and they are boldly reflected in our food culture.

This volume is a kaleidoscope of essays describing the food of forty European nations. Each country has approached its culinary culture in its own way, resulting in contributions which range from the folkloric to the theoretical. Taken as a whole, they reflect the remarkable diversity of the European culinary experience.

I wholeheartedly invite you to join me on the "Tour d'Europe" presented in this collection, celebrating the fiftieth anniversary of the European Cultural Convention.

Terry Davis
Secretary General of the Council of Europe

Introduction

Food: identity and diversity

Fabio Parasecoli

*To live together in the world means essentially
that a world of things is between those
who have it in common, as a table
is located between those who sit around it;
the world, like every in-between,
relates and separates at the same time.*

Hannah Arendt, *The human condition*[1]

Meals unite and divide. They connect those who share them, confirm their identities as individuals and as a collectivity, and reinforce their mutual bonds. At the same time, meals exclude those who do not participate in them, threatening and negating their very humanity. Food has always been one of the defining aspects of any given social group, whose members acknowledge each other as such by the way they eat, by what they eat, and by what they abhor. The ancient Greeks used to accuse the neighbouring populations they considered "barbarians" of eating raw meat, of being unable to share food with their own kind in an orderly way, and even of devouring whatever they had at hand whenever they felt the urge,

without waiting for the proper time of day. Centuries later, when their empire was threatened by waves of Germanic populations, the Romans sustained their position as self-proclaimed inheritors of the Mediterranean civilisation by upholding a nutritional model based on wine, olive oil and wheat against the Germanic preference for beer, butter and other cereals.[2]

Food is not only central to ethnic consciousness, it is also paramount to the formation of historical identities. Within the same population, it is not uncommon to think about the past as a time of perfection and happiness, when food was healthier and tastier, or, on the other hand, the past can be remembered as a time of hunger and want. For instance, in the 1960s, when their country underwent major industrialisation and urbanisation, Italians were extremely excited about the increase in their daily consumption, the presence of meat on their tables, and the advertising of new products on TV. They had no nostalgia for a past when most people lived in the countryside and food was scarce. Little did they know that a few decades later their offspring would idealise a previously bucolic world free of genetically modified organisms, mad cows and all kinds of lurking dangers.

Religions rely on food and eating habits as a means of affirming their norms and identifying their followers. In Europe, where the Christian, Muslim and Jewish faiths have interacted for centuries, each religion has also defined itself in terms of diet and food taboos. The Italian word for aubergine, "melanzana", comes from the expression "mela insana", unhealthy apple, a definition given to the vegetable because it was widely consumed in Jewish communities, which had in turn adopted it from the Arabs.

Social classes were often recognisable from what people ate, and how. At different times, sugar, spices, and more recently truffles and caviar, were adopted as symbols of conspicuous consumption, only to lose their fascination as precious and rare ingredients when the changing historical situation made those same ingredients cheaper and easy to purchase.

Gender identifications are also closely connected to food. Some ingredients, dishes or ways of consumption have been sexualised; considered either masculine or feminine. In many cultures women are still in charge of shopping and preparation of meals, if no longer with growing vegetables and breeding animals. The kitchen has at times become an arena of female affirmation and autonomy in male-dominated societies.

Eatymologies[3]

Et à la racine de mon nez
Il y a l'odeur de l'été
C'est le style de ma mémoire.

Piccola Orchestra Avion Travel,
Le style de ma mémoire[4]

All the examples given above reaffirm the fact that food is as exclusive a human behaviour as language. As Lévi-Strauss has pointed out, "Cooking, it has never been sufficiently emphasised, is with language a truly universal form of human activity: if there is no society without a language, nor is there any which does not cook in some manner at least some of its food".[5] In this sense, like any other cultural phenomenon that can be interpreted and understood, food can be considered "an ensemble of texts".[6] Each ingredient, every single dish, the way meals are organised, all the elements of a specific culinary tradition are mutually connected, influenced both by past foodways and by new occurrences, new interpretations or just plain repetitions of a certain dish or recipe.

We may argue that these elements are correlated in systematic, non-casual ways that make up structured codes.[7] Any member of the community that employs a determined culinary tradition is able to recognise dishes, to produce dishes that are recognisable as a specific recipe, to identify most ingredients, and to understand whether a culinary behaviour is acceptable or deviant. Each community is thus able to engage in meaningful action, yet the meanings attributed to food, and to a large extent also its form, can never be completely fixed or defined. On the contrary, the members of the community uninterruptedly negotiate and transform these meanings and values. For instance, for centuries fish was closely connected with Lent and fasting, becoming the main ingredient for many dishes popular at certain times of the year. When the religious principles underlying these specific uses were contested, fish lost its religious connotation to become part of everyday menus. In recent years the nutritional value and low fat content of fish has made it a very popular food, even accepted by some vegetarians.

The different elements that allow us to understand food and to use it in everyday life are also practical tools in a kit acquired through experience in all kinds of cultural, social, economic and political interactions. Each element in a culinary tradition is thus also part of several interconnected networks of meaning, practices, concepts and ideals; the full extent of its meaning and value cannot be grasped without analysing its interaction with other apparently unrelated domains.

We can define these networks as "signifying" because they help us make sense of reality, allowing us to comprehend our cultural environment and to act within its rules and boundaries. The analysis of these various signifying networks is fundamental to an understanding of how food is recognised and interpreted by different actors, whose identities are constructed and performed precisely in their use of these meaningful structures and in their interaction and negotiations with others actors to define them.

In the case of French champagne, for instance, several elements are necessary to recognise it as such and to understand its cultural value. Place and methods of production, ingredients, history, and marketing are defined as distinct or opposed to other sparkling wines – say German Sekt, Italian spumante or even American "champagne". A more or less deep understanding of what French champagne is, how it is produced and where, its cultural and social signification as a symbol of affluent consumption, and how and when to enjoy it, can help define an individual as French or, in different contexts, as a Francophile, as a worldly gourmet, or simply as a snob. These elements affect the image that members of a certain culinary community nurture of themselves and their social position in the ongoing negotiations that define and redefine food.

Here I will focus on how these signifying networks define the key concepts of tradition and authenticity, which play a paramount role in constructing what is "typical", hence defining local, regional or even national identities. Since these qualities are supposed to catch the "essence" of a certain food or foodway, it is precisely around these supposed essences that all the identification and exclusion processes are actually built.

It is necessary to understand that the same signifying networks function in an increasingly abstract way as we pass from the local to the regional and national levels. For instance, the local population of the Basque provinces in Spain could mention many typical elements differentiating, say, traditional foods from Bilbao and from San Sebastian. Nevertheless, for the average non-Basque Spaniards these distinctions would sound irrelevant, and would instead be useful only for understanding the more general elements defining Basque cuisine as opposed to the rest of Spain. So, for instance, Basques could debate the most authentic recipe for pil pil sauce for salted cod, mentioning ingredients, techniques, traditions and so on. On the other hand, the average Spaniard would probably find these same elements too complicated or detailed, focusing instead on the fact that pil pil sauce is totally different from other sauces accompanying salted cod in other parts of the country. To define these differences, non-Basque Spaniards would return to the same set of signifying networks – ingredients, techniques, history – but would use them at a level of higher abstraction. Going from the regional to the national level, a Portuguese would find even more abstract categories to define the typicality or the authenticity of pil pil sauce, opposing its supposed Spanish flavour and character to more familiar sauces used with salted cod in Portugal.

It is possible to individuate various signifying networks that may help define "typical" products, dishes, or eating habits and norms that contribute to a specific identity. We can call these repertoires "eatymologies". Just as etymology deals with the origin and development of words, tracing their diffusion through different places and cultures, eatymology refers to the analysis of the origin and development of specific products, norms and dishes, their spread and hybridisation through commerce, cultural expansion, colonisation, migration, and tourism.

The following paragraphs analyse some of these constitutive components of food-centred identities, not necessarily in order of relevance.

Ingredients. Many ingredients, as we have seen, are important elements in the recognition of a specific dish as "typical", allowing it to be perceived as traditional and authentic. All of them are connected to a determined community with its identity defined by place, geographic elements, time and history, social interactions, and the like. The true Neapolitan pizza, for instance, according to some purists, should only be made using water buffalo mozzarella and San Marzano tomatoes. San Marzano tomatoes need a Mediterranean climate, like that in the countryside around Naples, to grow at their best, and water buffaloes are common in the marshy areas between the regions of Lazio and Campania. Other examples are smoked reindeer manufactured in Lapland, northern Finland, or caviar produced along the coasts of the Caspian Sea. The task of defining a typical ingredient is not always easy. For instance, many European vineyards were grafted with American roots after a phylloxera epidemic raged throughout Europe at the end of the nineteenth century, wiping out most of the local plants. Growers tend to ignore the powerful symbolism of using American roots – the part of the plant that conveys to grapes the character and the composition of the local soil – to make Spanish, Italian or French wines. At the same time, many growers are investing time and money to develop autochthonous grape varieties that had been virtually lost for decades. Such is the case of Sagrantino di Montefalco, in the Italian region of Umbria, which, after near-total extinction, in less than a decade has become a highly appreciated wine. Stimulated by these accomplishments, and by the fact that local varieties can offer wider choices to the educated wine lover who wants to try something new beyond the ubiquitous chardonnays and merlots, many producers are investing in the promotion and marketing of these newly rediscovered wines. Similarly, a few East European countries are trying to change the image of their wines, to raise their profile and give them more international appeal: they include Bulgaria, Romania, Moldova, Georgia and Slovakia. In this case, the rediscovery and promotion of these typical ingredients are the result of recent developments, although their historical origins date to a far, almost forgotten past.

Technique. Many dishes and products are characterised by specific techniques that, in the case of artisan products, are transmitted in very codified ways through generations, constituting a coherent and structured heritage that often plays an important role in the definition of the identity of a local community. To mention only a few examples, this is the case with the production of foie gras in southwestern France, Jerez wine in Spain or lokum jelly in Turkey. At times, ordinary ingredients are transformed into very sought-after delicacies, such as lardo (cured pork fat) in Central Italy, surströmming in Sweden (salt fermented herring), or haggis in Scotland (stuffed sheep's stomach).[8]

In the past the secrets connected with specific products were often protected by guilds regulated by strict rules. Nowadays, many of those techniques are not what they used to be even a few decades ago. The food industry is undergoing an uninterrupted process of modernisation and innovation. For instance, even the most traditional wine producer uses pneumatic presses, or other kinds of time-saving and quality-enhancing machinery. Today, although procedures tend to be industrialised, the production of many handmade products cannot easily be automated without losing certain specific traits such as nuances in flavour and texture. Besides, well-off and discriminate consumers often prefer a traditionally made product, even if it is more expensive. They are willing to pay higher prices for authenticity, or at least for what they assume an authentic dish or product should be (even when this does not necessarily correspond to its perception within the community that actually created it). It is true that excessive industrialisation might ultimately cause the disappearance of certain products which are considered too labour-intensive or not in line with modern hygiene requirements, as in the case of cheese made of raw milk.

Location/place. Unlike Cartesian space where every point is qualitatively equal to the next, place is not neutral. Every point is different because it has been lived and experienced differently by its inhabitants, and still is. Place generates concepts connected with rootedness, such as terroir in France or territorio in Italy, which nevertheless also include traits such as soil, climate and other geographical elements. These ideas yield the concept of "origin", included in the legal definition of "geographical indication", and hence a key element in current international trade negotiations. Besides influencing the character of local products, place is particularly important because it provides a foundation for identities – individual and social, local and national. Yet it is jeopardised by what the literary critic Fredric Jameson defined as the "post-modern hyperspace", which has transcended the fact that the human body is actually located in a specific point of space that functions as the focus for its relation with the surrounding reality.[9] The sameness-of-place on a global scale has its highest and most recent expression in the growing importance of the "virtual markets" created by the Internet, where it is possible to buy products and food from all over the world. Also, many transnational corporations seem to operate in a different space dimension that has been called "glocal", where the global and the local are intermingled so that localities are promoted in the frame of transnationalisation. Many international fast-food chains, for instance, rely on local products to create dishes that are the same all over the planet. This trend has been perceived as the final success of western universalism and cultural imperialism.[10] The very concept of national border, which defines nation-states, homogenising the political space in every continent, is threatened by the expansion of transnational companies that have become the most important agents in the world economy.[11]

Trade/economy. To become "typical", a dish must become part of trade and exchange, thus entering the market. Until a product is consumed directly in the place where it is produced, it is not perceived as specific to that particular place; it is just common food. But when it travels, its local and traditional specific traits become visible, and the producers acknowledge these elements. When it comes to bread, for instance, each type is recognised as typical of a certain place only when it is sold elsewhere, where the common sort of bread is different. "Identity is also defined as difference, as its relationship with otherness. This is evident in the particular case of gastronomy: a local identity is generated by exchange, when and insofar a product or a recipe meets different cultures and regimes... Cooking is the locus of exchange and contamination, besides and more then the locus of origin. If a product can be considered the expression of a territory, its use in a recipe or a menu is almost always the result of hybridisation."[12] The notion of identity moves thus from production to exchange, from point to network. Each community acknowledges certain elements of its culinary tradition as typical and special, hence enhancing its identity only when exposed to other communities that produce different kinds of food.

Time. Time can also be part of many symbolic networks creating identities connected to food. Cosmological time (night and day, seasons, years) determines the growth and the development of many products. Biological time is connected with biorhythms and the phases of human life: different foods are eaten at different ages. Anthropological time determines when during the day, on what occasions, and in which part of the year one eats certain dishes. History – the time

of human societies – influences how the consumption of certain products varies in time. Today's culture seems to be caught up in a new dimension of time determined by necessities of capitalist production, transnational financial exchange and high-speed information highways. The only form of resistance to these phenomena appears to be the construction of a conscious counter-culture that can start at the dining table, as increasingly successful associations such as Slow Food propose.[13] Tradition is often considered in terms of its connections with material culture, labour, territory and human time, as opposed to the obsessive rhythm of modern economies that deprive us of our leisure time. Nevertheless, this approach has sometimes been defined as "culinary Luddism", whose goal would be "to turn back the flood tide of industrialised food in the First World, and to prevent such foods to engulfing traditional ethnic foods elsewhere".[14] This criticism points to the real and present danger that the rediscovery of tradition might be captured within a discourse hinging on conservative moral values and a patriarchal society, reconstructing the ideological myth of a time which knew neither disruptions nor crises.[15] As a matter of fact, the appeal of tradition has already been largely exploited in this sense by the advertising industry: many products are marketed bearing an image of the "good old days".

Media. The growing impact of media on contemporary societies has generated autonomous signifying networks where facts, events and trends are largely determined by the networks themselves.[16] The relevance of a piece of news or of a TV show does not lie in what they refer to, but to the fact that they simply exist, creating a widespread effect of self-referentiality where images and information bear little or no connection to what used to be called reality.[17] Images and information heavily influence other signifying networks. In the case of food, TV networks and magazines affect our perception of what good eating is supposed to be. Recipes created by famous chefs can become so glamorous, being perceived as "high-end", that a middle-class housewife might want to try them to impress her friends. Advertising tries to differentiate foods in order to induce new needs in consumers, to boost sales. The average supermarket-goer is used to choosing among various brands of the same kind of products, each described as "designer food", "family food", "diet food", "organic food", and "luxury food". Similarly, a certain product or dish can become the "marker" of a place or a culture for the media, creating a new perception. Balsamic vinegar was little known in Italy (outside Emilia Romagna, the region where it is produced) until the media connoted it as refined and rare, and famous chefs started using it instead of regular vinegar. Now it is one of the markers for "high-end Italian cuisine", even if one can buy cheap versions. Something similar happened to Prague ham slowly cured in brine, then smoked with birch wood and left to age. Only recently has this exquisite meat gained international renown, due to the increase in tourism to the Czech Republic, and the attention of the media, which is always on the lookout for new products and trends.

Social interactions. Besides those already mentioned (sex, religion, ethnicity, and race), several signifying networks can be listed under this heading, such as age, body image, nationality, social position, and habitus.[18] Cultural studies, anthropology, ethnology, and sociology have focused on foodways and food traditions in order to analyse their connections with rituals, culture, tradition, and social stratification.

Class is probably one of the most relevant elements in establishing what, how and with whom food is prepared, served and consumed.[19] Urban consumption patterns traditionally tend to differ from those adopted in the countryside, influencing the development of diverse culinary habits. Within the urban milieu, middle-class and liberal-arts professionals tend to adopt different manners and taste than blue-collar workers. These differences are particularly striking when analysing public spaces dedicated to the preparation and consumption of food, such as street stalls, taverns, pubs, cafés and restaurants, and in more recent times fast-food and take-away establishments.[20] We cannot forget that the creation of a haute cuisine in many countries, particularly in urban environments, is deeply connected with the same social dynamics that once influenced table manners and etiquette.[21] "Nutritional differences between social classes are not only reflections of manifestations of their economic and cultural inequalities. Such differences, in the form of refined tastes and cultivated preferences, become vehicles for maintaining the distinction between the layers of social hierarchy".[22]

Even more importantly, class structures determine how food is produced and distributed. The culinary habits of certain regions are heavily determined by the kind of food that they had to produce for the higher classes. The development of a "fifth quarter" tradition in Rome was clearly related to the presence of huge slaughterhouses that paid their employees in kind, namely with offal and other parts that were not considered suitable for the most delicate palates. When farmers in a certain area were forced to sell the best part of their crops and herds to city dwellers, they had to develop dishes that made do with whatever was available, and that often became sources of local pride. These traditions are being rediscovered all over Europe by those same city dwellers who a few generations ago would have been horrified by the very idea of ingesting such uncouth foods. Nevertheless, the social role of humble food producers was not only passive: the formation of guilds and other networks charged with the production of certain foods for the more affluent citizens contributed to the renaissance of urban life from the late Middle Ages on. Even the artisans charged with duties considered almost impure, such as the salting and aging of pork meats, played an important role in creating local traditions that still endure. Even now, business associations are paramount in food production and distribution.

Social interactions also determine bodily standards and the nutritional patterns necessary to achieve them. "Each society had its criteria for deciding nutritional values that suits its own needs and self-image, and thus the healthy, happy, well-nourished individual will be quite different from place to place and from century to century… All cultures create a nutritional ideal that reflects their particular values and in turn change their expectations of how their bodies will behave. And bodies do behave differently in different times and places".[23] In modern Europe, ethnic groups from different countries often have differing ideas about what a healthy and beautiful body should look like. If a woman is supposed to be plump and voluptuous to be desirable in a certain community, she will eat more, and with less guilt, than her counterparts in surrounding communities. If religion or traditional mores in a community impose a taboo on a certain ingredient, the members of that community will distinguish themselves wherever they are by refusing that ingredient, and by displaying disgust. If forced to ingest it, they would probably show symptoms of sickness related to what their custom makes them believe would actually happen if they ate it.

Nation-state administrative controls. The rekindled interest in wine and food, in culinary traditions and local produce, as promoted and exploited by the press, is reaching new heights precisely when Europe is undergoing major political changes aimed at increasing integration among the member states, not only administratively but also economically. The theories and practices poignantly illustrated by Carl Schmitt, who centered the definition of political identities on the dichotomy *Freund-Feind* (friend-fiend), are undergoing major transformations: people, territory and

Introduction

government are not so central any longer.[24] The nation-states that in the nineteenth century had become a tool of self-promotion and enhancement for the economically dominant bourgeoisie are renouncing many of their traditional prerogatives in the post-cold war world order, faced with the expansion of transnational corporations and international organisations such as the World Trade Organization. Globalisation seems to grant less and less importance to state borders and controls. The process is not painless, with different countries trying to reaffirm their power and their dominant role against these transformations. Food is not excluded from these phenomena. Many countries are trying to gain advantage from systems that derive from the one France invented in 1855 to exert state control over its agricultural production: a registration that ranked sixty wine makers (or châteaux) on the basis of their wine price and quality. In the 1930s, the system developed into the Controlled Appellation of Origin (AOC, Appellation d'Origine Contrôlée).[25] Each area had to create rules to regulate the production of local wines. Wine makers had to meet specific requirements in order to receive the coveted denomination, which was perceived as a sign of higher quality and had become a very effective marketing device. The system paid off. Wine quality was actually enhanced, and consumers were willing to pay more for wines that had received some sort of recognition from the state. Similar wine classifications were adopted all over Europe. Food manufacturers were aware that a similar system, applied to their production, would increase the value of their goods, and protect them from people selling similar products of lesser quality under the same name, and other types of fraud.

The signifying networks we have analysed are not sufficient to define what a dish or a product or a certain meal signifies for each individual. Various elements might intervene: mere biological instincts (I'm hungry, here and now, or I will probably be hungry in a while), psychology, desire, idiosyncrasies, family habits, and disgust.[26] Besides, taste can be consciously educated.[27]

The elements to be considered appear countless, impossible to assess in their totality. Yet, we know, we feel that we belong to a specific (and not just to any) culinary tradition. We are able to point out many defining elements of our identity as eating individuals. The existence of generally acknowledged "typical" dishes, food customs, and widespread disgusts seems to point to the fact that all the networks we have described interact with each other to form some sort of "nodal points", such as generally acknowledged recipes or food habits.[28] In fact, we know that these may change in time or be interpreted in different ways according to the situation and the context. Nevertheless, the presence of stable clusters of meaning, of solid nodal points, is what allows individuals to share the same information and the same interpretive grids about culinary traditions. If I mention pasta e fagioli (pasta and bean soup) in Italy, or shepherd's pie in England, members of the community that considers those dishes common are likely to understand the reference immediately. Yet, within the same community, the pasta e fagioli could be perceived either as a symbol of long-lasting tradition or merely as a simple, uninteresting, almost vulgar dish. Shepherd's pie is considered by some to be a nutritious, substantial comfort food, by others a cheap pub food. These perceptions are not casual or serendipitous, but they respond to precise and structured interpretations. Within broad limits, the meaning we attribute to food reveals itself as essentially plural, hence subject to interpretation and negotiations. The way codes are structured points to phenomena defined as hegemony,[29] or ideology,[30] in the sense that the signifying networks become the arenas for the affirmation and the fixation of meaning by different and competing agencies. This introduces politics into the communication and practices related to food, where politics is the expression of the efforts in specific instances to articulate the fluid field of food in a way that might be beneficial for their own goals.

Food debates

Once more, quality, that is,
the production of foods that speak to the body
and the imagination, is profitable.

Jean-Robert Pitte, *French gastronomy*[31]

Over the last decade, food-related issues have thus become a relevant part of the political debate both in Europe and the rest of the world. Many global phenomena, such as pollution, endangered biodiversity, food-connected diseases, genetically modified foods, famines, unequal distribution of resources, and solidarity commerce, just to mention a few, seem to threaten not only the social body, but also individuals. The survival of the singular body is at stake, the very body whose frontiers are constantly threatened by fashionable diets, changing standards of beauty, fitness, liposuctions and piercing. At the same time, individuals feel exposed to economic trends they do not understand, ineffable powers that seem to run world politics, and technological transformations that are often too complex to grasp in all their hi-tech implications. In this ever-changing, fast paced reality, transitions and moments of passage of all kinds are uninterruptedly proposed and imposed on subjects who end up finding respite in old and new identification processes. It is not surprising, then, that political instances often recur to identity centred strategies that heed food as one of the hot areas where violent battles are actually waged. In the framework of these debates, typical foods can become nodal points around which opposite partisan forces can condense various elements belonging to any of the signifying networks outlined above. Most of the time, these elements are in themselves politically neutral, but precisely for this reason they end up being used in different, even totally divergent, types of political discourse, acquiring a specific meaning from the context in which they are inserted.[32]

For instance, many organisations and political parties focus their ideology and action on the role of local communities and traditions. Localism has always played an important role in European culture as a reaction against often imposed national identities aimed at making a homogenised whole – a nation – out of a very diverse ensemble of local communities proud of their history, traditions and habits. Over the past few years, bureaucratic decentralisation and a demand for greater local autonomy all over Europe is affecting the institutional structure of many countries. Localism, in a progressive context, has also been connected to multiculturalism and openness to difference. But often it has become the core of federalist or even secessionist demands formulated by many parties throughout Europe. A similar approach to localism can be recognised in the discourse of some conservative parties, which at times consider foreigners and immigrants a threat, all the while emphasizing the importance of cultural identity and of the nation.

For decades, European local and regional food traditions risked disappearing along with local autonomies.

The need for increase in productivity and output to respond to the demands of a growing market, the technocratisation of agribusiness, and the consequent standardisation of production has, on the one hand, allowed most Europeans access to reliable and affordable foods all year round. On the other hand, many typical products are in danger of being completely forgotten. However, in many areas, long-standing rural structures have assured their survival to this day, and they have become fashionable again.

In this context, local and national identities are employed against globalisation, which is considered the new incarnation of international capitalism. As a consequence, it appears necessary to maintain the local by fighting globally. Yet this kind of discourse intrinsically carries an almost contradictory tension. Joseph Bové, the founder of the Confédération Paysanne and archinemesis of McDonald's in Europe, stresses the principle of "alimentary sovereignty", according to which "every country, or groups of countries, must be able to reach the highest level of security – for all citizens – concerning agricultural products, and has the right to establish autonomously its own alimentary necessities and to refuse the imposition of those agricultural practices considered dangerous for the individual (hormones, genetic mutations, patents of living organisms)".[33] At the same time, he acknowledges the necessity for some form of international action to oppose the transnational globalisation of the market. The tension between the global and the local is not an easy matter, since both locality and the global are socially produced. It is necessary to further analyse the simplistic point of view that considers the local as "natural", original, and connected to biodiversity and heterogeneity, and as the last defence against the homogenising, "unnatural" forces of globalisation.[34]

Another issue closely connected with food is ecology, that is, sustainable development and biodiversity, aimed at protecting and revitalising fruits and vegetables that face the risk of disappearing along with the independent farmers who grow them (this is another indirect reference to the importance of small-scale enterprises where labour is the main productive factor versus the omnipresence of super-national companies that adopt capital-intensive industrial methods). A related issue is organic (or biological, as it is called in some European countries) agriculture, a concept whose very definition is already at the centre of heated debates, frequently in the absence of clear laws outlining it. Organic products are becoming so popular that large corporations, as is already happening in the US, may soon start to market organic product lines – the same corporations that are wiping small farmers off the map and that are often responsible for the exploitation of destitute farmers. The critique of globalisation extends to another hot debate: genetically modified food. This is a cause of deep concern among European consumers, and is becoming a point of resistance against globalisation and a catalyst for concrete actions from demonstrations to boycotts of suspect products.

Many European Union member states directly participate in the food politics debate, intervening at times with laws and regulations. When the EU started issuing regulations on this matter, some of them had already created methods of registration for typical products. As a consequence, the existing quality denominations had to be acknowledged and co-ordinated by the European authorities, and rules had to be set on how to establish new denominations. Each country tried to add as many denomination products as possible, making negotiations difficult and long. Finally, in 1992, the European Union issued a regulation, the infamous 2081, that allowed the registration of more than 600 products in ten years under two categories: the PDO (protected designation of origin) and the PGI (protected geographical indication). Other European countries are following this example, creating state-controlled denominations based on local identities and traditions. For instance, the PDO refers to the name of a region, a specific place or a country describing a product originating in that place, whose quality or other characteristics are essentially or exclusively due to a specific geographical environment. This means that production and transformation must be carried out in the geographical area designated by the PDO regulations. The objective of the regulations introduced in 1992 was to add value to specific high-quality products from a demarcated geographical area and, supposedly, to promote the diversification of agricultural production by acknowledging the value of rare or disappearing resources. The new registrations, however, did not automatically mean protection of the products in their most traditional and "authentic" version, if that ever existed. When in 1988 in the village of Genzano, a few miles from Rome, local bread makers decided to found a consortium to define what their bread was supposed to be like and to boost their sales by adding value to its name, some of them decided not to join. The reason was that some of the producers, including industrial bakers, were not willing to follow the old tradition according to which the bread had to be baked in wood ovens, using chestnut wood. When the consortium applied for registration according the European laws, it did not include the chestnut wood oven in the requirements, and the PGI was issued accordingly. An old tradition was thus neglected by a regulation that was supposed to protect it. Similar controversies can be found all over Europe.

The field is ever changing. In April 2003 the European Union issued a law that allows some products to be registered as PDO that were previously excluded from that denomination, such as bread and pasta, biscuits and pastries, beer, wine vinegar, essential oils, cork, flowers and many others. Furthermore, stricter rules are applied to the packaging process, which has to be carried out in the production area. For instance, *prosciutto di Parma* cannot be sliced and packaged anywhere else but in Parma and the surrounding area, in order to better guarantee the quality.

At the same time, the European Union, backed by other European countries, is fighting to get recognition and international protection at the World Trade Organization level for products with geographical indications. At the September 2003 WTO meeting in Cancún, Mexico, the debate centred on the interpretation of the 1994 Agreement on Trade-Related Aspects of Intellectual Property Rights (TRIPs). This agreement defined Geographical Indications (GIs) as identifying "a good as originating in the territory of a member, or a region or locality in that territory, where given quality, reputation or other characteristic of the good is essentially attributable to its geographic origins". While the agreement provided greater protection for wine and spirits, it left space for negotiations when it came to other products. The European Union pushed for the establishment of a multilateral register of GIs, the extension of the protection foreseen for wine and spirits to other products, and the removal of certain GIs whose names are usurped worldwide. To this end, the European Union presented a list of forty-one regional quality products whose name it wants to recuperate. The United States of America and other countries, on the other hand, claim that names such as "Champagne" or "Chablis" are generic terms, and that local producers have already registered them as trademarks.

While this debate goes on at the international level, within the Union a silent battle is being waged over food safety and the establishment of a European Food Authority. In a "White paper of food safety" issued by the Commission – the executive body of the European Union – in January 2000, the establishment of an independent European Food Authority was proposed as the most appropriate response to the need to guarantee a high level of food safety. The mad cow (BSE) epidemic and other worries had become so important in public opinion that the European institutions felt they had to take a clear stand. Right away, the political debate focused on where to locate the new authority, creating a conflict between the different countries that wanted to house it: Italy proposed the city of Parma, while Finland offered Helsinki. The issue embodies the struggle between different conceptions of what food is and what security might entail. The northern European sense of what is edible has been heavily influenced by modern concepts of hygiene: cheese made from unpasteurised milk and aged in natural caves, for example, does not immediately register as safe. Lard seasoned and kept in marble vats, as in the case of the lard from Colonnata, is immediately perceived as unhealthy. Beyond the immediate concerns about mad cow disease and the debate about genetically modified organisms, it became clear that southern countries would accept food policies that value traditions and local habits, while their northern counterparts would push for a more scientific approach.

The result was that when regulation number 178 was passed in January 2002, establishing the European Food Safety Authority, no decision was made concerning the site of the new body. During their December 2003 meeting, the fifteen countries eventually agreed to locate the authority in Parma. The implications of this choice will become more evident in the future.

Body politics

> **The ego is first and foremost a bodily ego.**
>
> Sigmund Freud, *The Ego and the Id* [35]

Why all this interest in food and nutrition from governments and other agencies? It is easy to point to the economic reasons: agribusiness plays an important role in the gross national product, as the heated debates over subsidies given to farmers demonstrate. But there is more. In their material aspects, food habits and behaviours, culinary traditions and identities, are tightly connected with the body, revealing at the same time the nooks and crannies of the material foundations of power and politics. Although the close connections between the body and food are self-explanatory, reflections about food as a political instrument aimed at controlling bodies in their most fundamental and intimate dimension have been rare. As some currents in contemporary thought are trying to demonstrate, the body is far from being an apolitical, natural given. The ways it is conceived, developed, controlled and disciplined, identified and interpreted, are inherently political.[36] The ways we choose, store, prepare, cook, ingest, digest, and excrete food determine how our bodies relate to the outside world and to other bodies. These elements become objects of interest for many agencies of power, which try to use them to reinforce their legitimacy through various narratives – such as identity, diversity, tradition, and authenticity – that structure the transmission of symbols and acts in the public space of communicative exchanges.

Legitimacy of power is successfully reinforced when the ideological manipulation, which is more or less evident and disclosed in the public space, reaches private realms such as the body, sexuality, and the realm of food habits and nutrition. These more hidden forms of control are usually excluded from public discourse, creating the illusion of the political neutrality of the body, whose fluid constitution and whose cultural inscription in materiality become instead the battle-field for cultural, social and political struggles to exert control over the individual. The body, far from being natural, thus becomes the arena where power expresses itself in its more fundamental modalities. While cultural theorists have often pointed to sex as a site of these political struggles, food and ingestion have been left aside, despite their fundamental role in the development of subjectivity.[37]

As shown by the debates over genetically modified crops, globalisation, biological agriculture, presence of hormones in meat, or the increasing opposition to fast food in certain European political circles, food can become a nodal point in political debates. The food battles between the United States of America and Europe often assume a deeper, cultural character than simple wars to conquer larger shares of the consumer markets. Food can actually be used as a metaphor for otherness and, quite often, to affirm cultural superiority. For lack of information, or because of deeply embedded identifications, the food of strangers can be looked upon as barbarian, uncouth, dirty, and even disgusting. An analysis of these phenomena can allow each subject to acknowledge its specific location within its culture, and in relation to other cultures.

In this sense, a deeper awareness of the political, non-neutral nature of all processes defining food traditions can help members of a certain social or ethnic group shift their location not only physically, but also culturally. Having a better grasp of the various signifying networks that allow a dish, a product or a foodway to be perceived as "typical" or "authentic" might help them learn how to understand the subject position of the Other, without losing the awareness of their own location. This would provide effective tools for enhancing diversity and open-mindedness in increasingly larger strata of society. And could there be a better place than the table, considered in many cultures as the locus for pleasure and conviviality, to experience these often troubling and unsettling processes leading to a critical awareness of one's identity?

Yet power structures reveal themselves as omnipresent, coming from everywhere, and not necessarily connected with specific institutions such as national government or multinational corporations.[38] Power and the ideals it promotes – such as tradition and authenticity – are not always imposed on the subject from the outside, but are materialised through norms and regulations in the body itself. No government could convince its citizens that a new ingredient or dish is part of tradition: Dutchmen would not buy into any media campaign trying to impose blue corn as a national product, any more than Belgians could be convinced that reindeer is a common source of animal protein. Tradition and concepts of authenticity, as a cultural construct, cannot be considered a direct consequence of political, economical or social forces. Nevertheless, they are shaped and marked by them. Tradition and authenticity are the result of the reiteration of highly regulated and ritualised practices, norms and processes that respond to an ideal, a cultural model, first made material in the very body of each individual, and only then entering the domain of cultural intelligibility.[39] Russians enjoy vodka and Irishmen appreciate stout because these beverages are part of their habits, to the point of often being employed as negative stereotypes. Nevertheless, the Russians and the Irish can actually recognise different qualities, they know when and how to drink the beverages, they know which foods are best paired with them. Repeating these actions with regularity, and reaffirming their associated cultural values, Russian and Irishmen define themselves and are acknowledged as such. At the same time, they can easily spot foreigners by the way they deal with their traditional beverages.

This means that tradition and authenticity are not artificial and dispensable. They are not a fiction, but constitutive necessities that are constructed together with the subject itself, the conditions of its emergence and operation, of its boundaries and stability. But the production or materialisation of a subject is at the same time its subjection, its submission to rules and norms – including culinary ones – norms that are in turn exposed to negotiation and change. In the above example, teetotal Russians or Irishmen might find themselves the butt of irony or jokes because they do not embody the common ideal of what Russians and Irishmen should be like. Nevertheless, they could respond by showing how excessive consumption of alcohol can be dangerous to the human body, introducing new health concerns in a food discourse that never used to include them.

In this sense, power partly overlaps with the cultural dimension – including language, kinship, ideals, rules, and taboos – which provides a whole body of information about "typical" and "authentic" food and foodways. This information is usually shared within any given social group, reinforcing its identity and sense of belonging, while enhancing the exclusion of outsiders. Tradition and authenticity, although culturally constructed, are perceived as essential, and actually play a paramount role in the formation of the subject. They provide boundaries allowing each subject and each social group to identify itself.[40] These are precisely the boundaries that are threatened by all sorts of rites of passage. It is not by chance that these passages often include elements connected with eating: fasting, introduction to new foods, enduring ingestion of disgusting elements. Now, passage rites can actually be codified by traditions: though menacing for the individual who must go through them, they are actually reinforcing social and cultural identities. Transitions reveal all their destructive potential when they are neither expected nor controlled, undermining the survival of established traditions.

Hungry powers

Everything which is eaten is the food of power

Elias Canetti, *Crowds and power*[41]

Yet, when accepted blindly, without any criticism, tradition and authenticity can become political weapons for discrimination and intolerance. Anything that finds itself outside the boundaries defining identity can be perceived as threatening. This need for a stable, contoured integrity leads subjects and social groups to push whatever they perceive as unfamiliar toward the outside, creating an external space of total difference, which can never be part of the subject and which at the same time defines the subject. "Abject and abjection are my safeguards, the primers of my culture" affirmed the French cultural theorist Julia Kristeva, who also noted that "Food loathing is perhaps the most elementary and most archaic form of abjection".[42] Individuals identify with the norms regulating their eating habits, which, together with sex, plays a paramount role in defining taboo and pollution, as the British anthropologist Mary Douglas demonstrated in her studies about purity.[43] The lack of boundaries and distinctions, fundamental to the smooth functioning of all social structures, constitutes a pending danger for any political body. When individuals or groups share the same desire, or better, when they happen to desire the same thing, they erase the functional distinctions that define them as individuals embodying specific roles. When these boundaries are blurred, violence can ensue, precipitating society into chaos, argues the French philosopher René Girard, who called this phenomenon a "mimetic crisis", a moment of transition where all the players try to copy each other's motivations and actions.[44]

The defence of the subject boundaries, expressing itself in an attachment to identity and a fear of diversity, is often articulated at the bodily level as hunger and desire for incorporation, even at the price of the destruction of the desired object. Of course, these destructive drives and desires are not culturally acceptable, being the negation of culture itself as social interaction and negotiation. Yet, they play a fundamental role in the constitution of power, as the Nobel Prize winner Elias Canetti poignantly expressed it. In a section aptly called "The entrails of power" from his masterpiece *Crowds and Power*, Canetti argues that teeth are "the very first manifestation of order", "the most striking natural instrument of power".[45] More precisely, smoothness and order, which allow teeth to fulfil their task, and their shape so reminiscent of a prison, have become attributes of power. As a matter of fact, power is a form of digestion, often sucking all substance from the subjects it supposedly represents. As happens with the body, if this process of ingestion and digestion is interrupted, the result is death, the dissolution of power. It is not by chance that in the past the king or anyone holding any kind of power had to show their authority by an unusual capacity of consumption, often embodied in full bodies and visible bellies. Now the trend has changed, and power tries to disguise itself in slim and toned bodies that are subjected to all kinds of stress to display eternal youth and fitness. The implicit danger in digestive power is, unconsciously, cannibalism, the fear of being destroyed and consumed by stronger ones.[46] Its antidote, as we already mentioned, is community and the shared meal where bare teeth and hunger do not constitute a threat, where pleasure is obtained from offering food and enjoying the other's enjoyment.[47]

A global restaurant

The alien is always constructed on the familiar

Samuel Delaney, *Stars in my pocket like grains of sand*[48]

The theme proposed for this collection of national essays, food in transitional moments and rites of passage is particularly meaningful. In any kind of transition, be it personal, social or historical, constituted identities go through a process of painful interpolation, if not sheer dissolution. These terrifying moments are nevertheless necessary when adopting or developing new or adult identities. Transitional moments are perfect metaphors for the mass movements that have invested Europe in the last decades, when populations of various origins and cultures have poured in, threatening the traditional perceptions the inhabitants of the continent nurtured about themselves. Every moment of passage intrinsically contains elements of fear and instability. When a child becomes an adult, when a social group enters a new historical phase, or when immigrants reach a geographical area, established identities are threatened by new elements that introduce all kinds of changes.

In the past few decades, human masses have been moving all over the planet, creating unprecedented contacts among different cultures. The modern "technopolis", the updated version of the global village that McLuhan imagined decades ago, creates nomadism, a state that escapes any logic of controlled social construction.[49] Political refugees, immigrants, tourists, global managers, and migrant workers find themselves facing new food habits, unfamiliar dishes, and even unknown ingredients. At the same time, they carry with them their own foodways, recipes and flavours, introducing elements of novelty into the culture that welcomes (or does not welcome) them.

As a matter of fact, all travellers have their own food competence. We all have very clear ideas about what certain recipes should taste like, as Abbé Jean-Baptiste Dubos knew very well in the eighteenth century.

Does one reason in order to know if a ragout is good or if it is bad. Does it ever occur to anyone, after having posed the geometrical principles of flavour and defined the qualities of each ingredient which makes up the composition of food, to discuss the proportions of their mixture, in order to decide if the ragout is good? One never does this. We have in us a sense designed in order to know if a chef has followed the rules of his art. One tastes the ragout, and without knowing the rules, one knows if it's good. It is the same in some respect with the works of the mind and with pictures made in order to please and move us.[50]

We do not necessarily have to know how to cook to tell which dish we are eating, and if it is good.

This food competence can be more or less developed, and more or less conscious. However, it proves very relevant when travellers encounter unfamiliar culinary elements, flavours and textures; it constitutes a loose interpretive grid through which the new experience inevitably gets sifted. This is particularly clear in the case of immigrants, a special category of travellers that undergoes a very intense and prolonged exposure to extraneous gastronomic traditions. Immigrants have to adjust to a new cycle of seasons, foreign calendars, and strange holidays where their food has no part. When they want to prepare their traditional recipes, they often do not find the exact products they are used to: they are compelled to substitute other products as similar as possible to the original ones.

In this sense, food systems – made up of habits, taboos, flavours, recipes – are never closed, but always subject to an ongoing negotiation, often with heavy political undertones. Members of a certain social or national or ethnic group are likely to perceive the new contributions from outsiders either as a development of their own codes, or as an alien element, which in time can be appreciated and become popular. The new food can even end up being slowly absorbed, widening the group's shared experience. In western Europe, no one is nonplussed about eating at Chinese or Indian restaurants. Chilli sauces, exotic fruits like avocados, mangos or pineapples are no longer considered rare. In the past, people initially refused to eat potatoes and tomatoes coming from the Americas; it took decades before they were widely accepted. The fusion phenomenon, which has heavily influenced the restaurant scene all over the world in the past few years, can in itself be considered an example of food systems that have absorbed and transformed extraneous elements to create something new.

Tourists also play an important role in these phenomena, due to the growing impact of leisure travel throughout the world. Yet, when they arrive in another country, or another region of their country, tourists find themselves in a position quite different from immigrants. They don't have to adapt themselves to the new environment if they do not want to; they have paid for their trips, they want to enjoy themselves, they want to have fun. They might experience various feelings: anxiety, elation, curiosity, annoyance, and fear. They can be adventurous, challenging each other to eat whatever seems most exotic and dangerous, ordering from the menu the very dishes they are not familiar with. Or they might try to avoid as much as possible any contact with the unknown, with what does not fit into their food categories and is consequently perceived as polluting or disgusting.

The latter attitude explains the existence of tourist enclaves, where foods from different countries are guaranteed. Claude Fischler has noted how human beings are pulled by two opposite attitudes: "neophilia" and "neophobia": the curiosity to try new food, based on the omnivorous nature of man, and the fear of being poisoned.[51] Human beings are aware that food can be both a source of nourishment (and pleasure) and a very dangerous substance – if taken in excessive quantities, or badly cooked, or just clumsily chosen.[52]

In addition to this basic factor, as well as many others such as social position or spending capacity, two elements affect the attitude of all newcomers toward local food: their knowledge and familiarity with it, and their cultural openness to engaging with otherness. They can situate themselves on a continuum whose extremes are an advanced knowledge of the local gastronomic system and, on the opposite end, total ignorance. In the case of European travellers, these extremes are quite theoretical, and travellers most likely find themselves at some intermediate point. Due to the abundance of information available through the media, the presence of immigrants and exotic restaurants, and the increased average level of education, travellers are likely to have at least a minimal competence consisting in the fact that they expect to find unfamiliar food. The quality of this knowledge and the competence of travellers can vary widely, especially if their experience is based uniquely on the exotic restaurants in their country of origin, which probably offer a choice of dishes selected to please the local patrons, adapted to local taste and habits, and made with the available products.

Although massive exchange of alimentary products has always constituted a very important phenomenon, determining commercial trends and even the rise and fall of empires, in recent years culinary traditions throughout the world are less and less isolated, influenced as they are by increasing levels of globalisation.

In addition to having a more or less wide knowledge of the local gastronomy, all kinds of newcomers situate themselves on another continuum ranging from the total refusal of anything unfamiliar to the total acceptance of whatever might land on their tables: the tension between neophobia and neophilia. The same range of attitudes can be found, as reflected in a mirror, in those who have to deal with the arrival of new fellow citizens.

Immunities and communities

Eu não tenho patria: tenho matria
Eu quero fratria

Caetano Veloso, *Língua*[53]

Newcomers are often perceived as an incumbent threat to the normal functioning of the social body; they are often depicted as viruses or parasites by a rhetoric that literally interprets all these phenomena in terms of infection and immunisation.[54] Groups of foreign settlers are at times compared to wounds that may cause sickness to the whole body.

These rhetorical arguments have invested many different fields, revealing a stubborn pervasiveness and a more encompassing cultural relevance. As a matter of fact, the same discourse can also be found in politics. Certain movements or parties, or even smaller groups, show concern about racially or socially diverse people moving into a certain neighbourhood

or area, and voice their feelings in term of the decay of the social body and the invasion of foreign elements. The physical undertones of such declarations are quite clear, as is also happening in the growing debate over globalisation. In Europe, the growing concerns about genetically modified foods and seeds express the fear that infecting elements might sneak in from outside and affect the core of bodily identity according to the new scientific vulgata, DNA. Many threats are denounced as a menace for ingestion, the most important act of connecting with the external world, as happened with the mad cow scare. The fear of infectious diseases such as AIDS (Acquired Immune Deficiency Syndrome) or more recently SARS (Severe Acute Respiratory Syndrome) has raised the stakes of health safety all over the world and created widespread fear of the approaching bodies of strangers. The same metaphor – centred on invasive elements – is also found in a totally different field: computer science. The world is obsessed with the danger from viruses that infect hard disks and devastate entire networks. It is enough to remember the year 2000 computer virus (Y2K) scare that shook the world at the dawn of the new millennium.

It is interesting that the same rhetoric invests both the body and the field of computers. The sameness and stability of the body are also threatened by numerous elements. New biological technologies can produce clones or create fetuses in vitro. Practices like liposuction and plastic surgery, or an obsessive attachment to physical fitness, aim to exert control over bodily functions and body image. Adopting different diets and nutritional supplements, many western citizens try to counteract the excessive calorie intake that seems to become a problem when food is available and affordable. The growing rate of obesity is the most evident consequence of this alimentary abundance.

In this context, it is maybe useful to consider viruses from another angle. By infiltrating the body, viruses can also enhance the body, making it stronger and connecting it with the external world (hence the use of vaccines to strengthen the body against infection). We know that extreme cleanliness can provoke

the opposite effects, that is to say a certain weakening of the organism. When it comes to food and eating, one must not forget that the bacteria residing in our intestines help us to digest. Moreover, many delicious foods are produced by the action of bacteria: for example cheese and yogurt. The ongoing debate between those who defend traditional cheese-making methods, and those who would implement more hygienic standards embodies this tension between the two conceptions of infectious elements. The French philosopher Michel Serres tackled this theme when he pointed out that the word "parasite" literally means something that eats next to or beside something else.[55] This means that the word not only refers to a presence that consumes food and drink without giving anything back, but also to neutral neighbour eaters, and to symbiotic partners who live in continuous, productive exchange with their hosts. The same ambivalence can be found in the Latin word "hostis", which means both stranger and enemy, and in the Greek word "xénos", which refers to both strangers and guests. It seems that whenever a group finds itself facing elements from outside, blurring the barriers and the boundaries that define its identity, its attitude oscillates between hospitality and hostility.

Yet, against any logic based on dualities and oppositions, parasites introduce dynamics that favour pluralities and transformations, interdependence and innovation, reciprocity and mutuality. The result is a community based not on what unites in a single identity – ethnical, territorial, and spiritual – but rather on a common bond, a mutual gift. Herein lies the origin of the word community: "con munus", where the Latin "munus" means obligation or service – the given gift, not the received one.[56]

If we translate these concepts at the political level, it is evident that outside elements, in other words, diversity, can become positive factors in the process of transformation; diversity should become intrinsic to each body's sense of identity, lest it be turned into an instrument of violence and intolerance.

The fact that the Council of Europe wants to celebrate the fiftieth anniversary of the European Cultural Convention with this volume is already a very important sign to the European public. There is nothing trivial about food. European intellectuals are finally acknowledging this, both inside and outside universities and other cultural institutions. Food is becoming the subject of formal study and research in colleges and universities, not only from the technical or economical point of view, but also in the realm of humanities. The time has finally arrived for the European cultural establishment to acknowledge the role of food in the constitution of local, regional and national identities and their connections in our global era. Yet the renewed interest in food, reflected in its growing popularity in all kinds of media, often limits itself to folklore, to specific products that need promotion and exposure, and to traditions that are presented without any further explanation. A lack of real understanding of tradition and history, and their

connection to the present, can lead some political or social agencies to exploit food-related issues for their own agendas. Defensive discourses built around identities can become very powerful weapons to exclude any elements that might be perceived as unfamiliar, transforming them into a threat or a menace. Diversity is then considered a liability, a force that can increase the perceived instability of society. Nothing could be more destabilising for the future integration of Europe, a continent whose history has been deeply marked by its inherent diversity. Of course, differences among its populations can be cited as the main cause of centuries of wars and misunderstanding. However, we are aware of constant and uninterrupted exchanges among the diverse cultures forming the continental mosaic of today's Europe. For better or worse, the destinies of European local, regional, and national identities are deeply connected, especially in a world where global exchanges have become the norm. Food plays a paramount role in the encounter of different identities. Deeply entangled with man's most basic needs, desires and drives, food resonates in intimate ways in each individual's mental and emotional worlds. Taste aversions and disgusts, unfamiliar smells and challenging textures can undermine the most honest efforts to interact with a foreign culture; or else they can constitute a very effective incentive to explore Otherness. Factors such as personal inclination, education, social background, politics and economics all exert a profound influence on how we approach unusual dishes or ingredients. The powerful impact of food, with all of its bodily and emotional implication, has not yet been fully explored. Precisely when European nations are working to increase their economic, social and political integration, culture in its more material aspects, such as food, must not lag behind. If future assimilation processes were to be limited to bureaucratic or economic aspects, without touching everyday life, their impact might destroy the diversity and the richness of the material cultures that constitute the heritage of centuries of European history. Furthermore, the increasingly close relations with neighbouring countries not traditionally considered part of Europe make this mutual understanding even more necessary.

Meals unite and divide. In both cases, either by inclusion or by exclusion, they connect diverse identities. The table can become more than that: a space for the actual, productive sharing of dishes, traditions, emotions and – why not – food for thought.

Notes

1. Hannah Arendt, *The human condition,* Double Day Anchor Books, Garden City NY, p. 48.
2. Besides ethnicity, race has its food determinations too, although this dimension is probably less visible in Europe, where the perception of race and ethnicity tend to coincide, compared, for instance, to the US, where within the so-called Hispanic ethnicity, different races are individuated, each with its own food habits and traditions.
3. I borrowed this neologism from Salman Rushdie, *The ground beneath her feet,* Picador USA, New York, 1999, p. 61.
4. "And at the root of my nose is the smell of summer. It is the style of my memory" Piccola Orchestra Avion Travel, Poco mossi gli altri bacini, Sugar, 2003.
5. Claude Lévi-Strauss, *The origin of table manners,* Harper Collins Publishers, New York, 1978, p. 471.
6. Clifford Geertz, *The interpretation of cultures: selected essays,* New York, 1993, p. 24.
7. According to Eco "there is a signification system (and therefore a code) when there is the socially conventionalised possibility of generating sign-functions... There is on the contrary a communication process when the possibilities provided by a signification system are exploited in order to physically produce expressions for many practical purposes". Umberto Eco, *A theory of semiotics,* Indiana University Press, Bloomington, 1976, p. 4.
8. For this last case, see Alison Leitch, "The social life of lardo", *The Asia Pacific Journal of Anthropology* 1 (1), 2000, pp. 103-118
9. Fredric Jameson, "Postmodernism, or the cultural logic of late capitalism", *New Left Review* 146 (Jul-Aug 1984), p. 83.
10. "At work, as well in the obscuration of place, is the universalism inherent in western culture from the beginning. This universalism is most starkly evident in the search for ideas, usually labeled 'essences', that obtain everywhere and for which a particular somewhere, a given place, is presumably irrelevant... The Age of Exploration had begun, an era in which the domination of native people was accomplished by their deplacialization: the systematic destruction of regional landscapes that served as the concrete settings for local cultures". Edward Casey, *The fate of place,* University of California Press, Berkeley and Los Angeles, 1997, p. xii.
11. Yves Lacoste, *Questions de géopolitique*, La Découverte, Paris, 1988; Pluriel-Dèbat, *Problèmes de frontières dans le tiers-monde*, L'Harmattan, Paris, 1982.
12. Alberto Capatti and Massimo Montanari, *La cucina italiana,* Roma-Bari: Editori Laterza, 1999, vii-xvi. See also Carlo Petrini, "Le multinazionali del disgusto", in *Micromega* 5, 1999, p. 181: "It is necessary to reflect on the fact that the territorial identity of a product must necessarily coexist with its commercialisation and its exchange of other identities."
13. "We are enslaved by speed and have all succumbed to the same insidious virus: "Fast Life", which disrupts our habits, pervades the privacy of our homes and forces us to eat fast foods... May suitable doses of guaranteed sensual pleasure and slow, long-lasting enjoyment preserve us from the contagion of the multitude who mistake frenzy for efficiency. Our defence should begin at the table with slow food. Let us rediscover the flavours and savours of regional cooking and banish the degrading effects of Fast Food." The English translation of the Slow Food manifesto is available on the Slow Food website www.slowfood.com
14. Rachel Laudan, "A world of inauthentic cuisine", in *Cultural and historical aspects of foods*, Oregon State University, 1999, p. 136.
15. For the semiotic concept of myth see Roland Barthes, *Mythologies*, The Noonday Press, New York, 1972, in particular the analyses of "wine and milk" and "steak and chips". For the emerging of the utopian past as fantasmatic procedure, see also Yannis Stavrakakis, *Lacan and the political*, Routledge, London – New York, 1999.

16. Pierre Bourdieu called this phenomenon "the circular circulation of information" in *On television*, The New Press, New York, 1998, p.23.

17. They become, in the formulation introduced by Baudrillard, *simulacra*. "There is no longer any transcendence or depth, but only the immanent surface of operations unfolding, the smooth and functional surface of communication" Jean Baudrillard, *The ecstasy of communication*, Semiotext(e), New York, 1988, p.12. See also "The implosion of meaning in the media", in *In the shadow of silent majorities*, Semiotext(e), New York, 1983, pp. 93-109.

18. For the concept of *habitus*, as a way of understanding and dealing with the world which one acquires through experience and is related to one's social position and to the environment in which one grows up, see Pierre Bourdieu, *Distinction: a social critique of the judgment of taste*, Harvard University Press, Cambridge, 1984. Bourdieu affirms that the elaborated taste for the most refined objects is reconnected with the elementary taste for the flavours of food (ibid., p. 1). Further on he mentions the tastes of food as "the archetype of all taste", which "refers directly back to the oldest and deepest experiences, those which determine and over-determine the primitive oppositions – bitter/sweet, flavourful/insipid, hot/cold, coarse/delicate, austere/bright – which are as essential to gastronomic commentary as to the refined appreciations of aesthetes", ibid., p. 80.

19. Jack Goody, *Cooking, cuisine and class*, Cambridge University Press, Cambridge MA, 1982; Stephen Mennell, *The sociology of food: eating, diet and culture*, Sage, 1993.

20. Alan Warde and Lydia Martens, *Eating out*, Cambridge University Press, Cambridge UK, 2000.

21. Norbert Elias, *The civilizing process*, Blackwell, Oxford UK, 1994.

22. Alan Beardsworth and Teresa Keil, *Sociology on the menu*, Routledge, London 1997, p. 97.

23. Ken Albala, *Eating right in the Renaissance*, University of California, Berkeley 2002, p. 9.

24. Carl Schmitt, *The concept of the political*, University of Chicago Press, 1996.

25. Kolleen M. Guy, "Wine, champagne and the making of French identity in the *Belle Epoque*", in *Food, drink and identity*, Berg, Oxford-New York. 2002.

26. See Paul Rozin, "Food is fundamental, fun, frightening, and far-reaching", in *Social research*, Vol. 66, No. 1, Spring, 1999, pp. 9-30.

27. "While it is true that humans eat radically different foods, of equal interest is the ability to craft one's taste preferences away from the habitual. We can and often do expand our tastes, and we learn to make subtle discriminations among foods that once seemed all alike. What at first is below the threshold of notice can, with experience and attention, emerge on one's own tongue. The ability to educate one's palate is an almost uniquely human trait". Carolyn Korsmeyer, *Making sense of taste*, Cornell University Press, Ithaca and London, 1999, p. 93.

28. "The impossibility of an ultimate fixity of meaning implies that there have to be partial fixations – otherwise, the very flow of differences would be impossible. Even in order to differ, to subvert meaning, there has to be a meaning... Any discourse is constituted as an attempt to dominate the field of discursivity, to arrest the flow of differences, to construct a centre. We will call the privileged discursive points of this partial fixation, nodal points. Lacan has insisted on these partial fixations through his concept of points *de capiton*, that is, of privileged signifiers that fix the meaning of a signifying chain. This limitation of the productivity of the signifying chain establishes the positions that make predication possible – a discourse incapable of generating any fixity of meaning is the discourse of the psychotic". E. Laclau and C. Mouffe, *Hegemony and socialist strategy*, Verso, London, 1985, p.112.

29. As proposed by Gramsci and later developed by Laclau and Mouffe.

30. I refer to the use of the concept introduced by Althusser and, subsequently, by the Birmingham Centre for Contemporary Cultural Studies. See *On ideology*, Birmingham Centre for Contemporary Cultural Studies, Hutchinson, London, 1977.

31. Jean-Robert Pitte, *French gastronomy*, Columbia University Press, New York, 2002, p.177.

32. Fabio Parasecoli, "Postrevolutionary chowhounds: food, globalization, and the Italian left", *Gastronomica: the journal of food and culture* 3:3 Summer 2003, pp. 29-39.

33. Joseph Bosé, "Yankee (food) go home!", *Micromega*, Vol. 5, 1999, p. 169.

34. "This view can easily devolve into a kind of primordialism that fixes and romanticises social relations and identities. What needs to be addressed, instead, is precisely the production of locality, that is, the social machines that create and recreate the identities and differences that are understood as the local. The differences of locality are neither pre-existing nor natural but rather the effect of a regime of production. Globality similarly should not be understood in terms of cultural, political, or economic homogenisation. Globalisation, like localisation, should be understood instead as a regime of the production of identity and difference, or really of homogenisation and heterogenisation." Michael Hardt and Antonio Negri, *Empire*, Harvard University Press, 2001, pp. 44-45.

35. Sigmund Freud, *The Ego and the Id*, Norton, New York, 1960, p. 16.

36. For an example of this kind of analysis, see Robert Reid-Pharr, *Conjugal union: the body, the house, and the black American*, Oxford University Press, 1999.

37. "Knowledge, to the extent that it is embodied as habitus (Bourdieu), represents a sphere of performativity that no analysis of political articulation can do without. Indeed, if one is interested in understanding the politics of gender, the embodied performativity of social norms will emerge as one of the central sites of political contestation". Judith Butler, "Dynamic conclusions", in Judith Butler, Ernesto Laclau, Slavoj Zizek, *Contingency, hegemony, universality*, Verso, London – New York, 2000, p. 270.

38. "Power must be understood in the first instance as a multiplicity of force relations... as the process which, through ceaseless

struggles and confrontations, transforms, strengthens or reverses them: as the support which these force relations find in one another, thus forming a chain or a system, or on the contrary, the disjunction and contradictions which isolate them from one another; and lastly, as the strategies in which they take effect, whose general design or institutional crystallization is embodied in the state apparatus, in the formulations of the law, in the various social hegemonies". Michel Foucault, *The history of sexuality Vol. I*, Vintage Books, New York, 1990, p. 93.

39. Judith Butler, *Bodies that matter*, Routledge, New York, 1993, pp. 1-23. Butler limits herself to sex, but I do think that also food can be approached in the same way. She wonders: "Given that normative heterosexuality is clearly not the only regulatory regime operative in the production of bodily contours or setting the limits of bodily intelligibility, it makes sense to ask what other regimes of regulatory production contour the materiality of bodies", p. 17

40. "A movement of boundary itself appeared to be quite central to what bodies are", Judith Butler, *Bodies that matter*, Routledge, New York, 1963, p.ix.

41. Elias Canetti, *Crowds and power*, The Noonday Press, New York, 1984, p. 219.

42. Julia Kristeva, *Powers of horrors*, Columbia University Press, New York, 1982, p. 2. She also points out that "it is not lack of cleanliness or health that causes abjection but what disturbs identity, system, order. What does not respect borders, positions, rules. The in-between, the ambiguous, the composite", p. 4.

43. Mary Douglas, *Purity and danger*, Routledge and Kegan Paul, London, 1969.

44. René Girard, *La violence et le sacré*, Editions Albin Michel, Paris, 1990.

45. Elias Canetti, ibidem, p. 207.

46. The same theme often emerges in the writing of Simone Weil, who embodied her refusal of all kind of power to the point of dying of consumption.

47. See also Margaret Visser, *The rituals of dinner*, Penguin Books 1992, p. xii: "Table manners are social agreements; they are devised precisely because violence could so easily erupt at dinner. Eating is aggressive by nature, and the implements required for it could quickly become weapons; table manners are, most basically, a system of taboos designed to ensure that violence remains out of the question".

48. Samuel R. Delany, *Stars in my pocket like grains of sand*, Bantam Books 1985, p. 143.

49. Pasquale Ferrara, *L'Uno plurale*, Città Nuova, Roma, 1990.

50. Abbé Jean-Baptiste Dubos, *Réflexions critiques sur la poésie et sur la peinture*, 1719, quoted in Korsmeyer, pp. 43-44.

51. Claude Fischler, *L'Homnivore*, Editions Odile Jacob, Paris, 2001.

52. "The insulated, safe self, protected by skin from the rest of the world, experiences a material breach of this boundary every day in the act of eating. The world enters the self. This is an act that be exquisitely pleasurable, but also frightening; an act that nourishes, at the same time as it increases the chances of death or illness by toxins and micro-organisms" Paul Rozin, "Food is Fundamental, Fun, Frightening and Far-Reaching", *Social Research*, Vol. 66, No.1, winter 1998, pp. 9-30.

53. "I have no fatherland, only a motherland. What I'd rather have is a brotherland", Caetano Veloso, *Live in Bahia*, Nonesuch, 2002.

54. Roberto Esposito, *Immunitas*, Einaudi, Turin, 2002.

55. Michel Serre, *Le parasite*, Bernard Grasset, Paris, 1980. See also Raymond Boysvert, "The parasite as fundamental ontological category", unpublished paper presented at the conference "Know thyself: food and the human condition", Mississippi State University, April 5th, 2002.

56. Roberto Esposito, *Communitas*, Einaudi, Turin, 1998.

Svetlana Haik Poghosyan

Armenia

Insights into traditional food culture

Because food is one of the most important aspects of culture, national cuisine often serves as an ethnic and cultural marker. Grains, dairy products, meat and fish, vegetables and fruits are all part of the basic Armenian food system which is enhanced with spices, sweets and drinks.

Bread and grains

From ancient times agriculture and cattle breeding have been the main occupation of Armenians, so the predominance of grain and dairy products in the traditional Armenian food system is not accidental. Archeological sources such as mills and remnants of grain in clay pitchers confirm that as far back as the Stone Age the population of the Armenian highlands was skilled in growing and processing beans and grains, including wheat, barley, spelt, and millet. The grains used throughout the year were processed into various types of flour, bulgur (cracked wheat), and pasta (rshta).

Year-bread

Bread has, and continues to have, great importance in the Armenian diet. In regions rich with wood it was baked in large clay ovens in the earth (tonir); it was also baked in stoves. The most widespread and popular Armenian bread – lavash – was baked in the tonir and kept for a long time. After the lavash was baked it was dried and kept in a cool place. The lavash usually lasted for one or two months. Before serving it was moistened with water to refresh its taste and smell.

In colloquial usage the word "bread" often was, and still is, used in the sense of "meal", or even more generally as "food". For example, "an Armenian earns his bread by the sweat of his brow". The word "bread" was also used in the sense of grain field, or harvest. In the traditionally large Armenian family bread was baked by the eldest woman, the mother-in-law, with the help of the eldest daughter-in-law and female neighbours. When baking bread neighbours used to help one another. They shared bread with poor relatives and donated some of the bread to the needy in an example of community support. Bread was a symbol of welfare and prosperity. Sometimes seven lavashes from the winter supply were given to strangers, and during the ritual Easter offering of bread people remembered the axiom "give bread to bring bread".

According to the ancient Armenian value system and beliefs, bread was sacred, a symbol of fertility, fruitfulness, and protection. People worshipped and respected bread; when a piece fell on the floor it was immediately picked up. The fallen bread meant that guests were expected. Children were taught to treat bread with care and respect. Breadcrumbs were gathered and given to the birds and animals. According to folk belief bread was a weapon against evil. When taking a newborn child outside for the first time a piece of bread was put on his chest.

There were different formulas for bread worship – blessings, curses, wishes, and oaths. "This bread is proof!" or "may the bread make me blind!" were typical oaths sworn on bread. For blessings people simply said "blessed is your bread". Bread was sacrificed during a blight like hail or drought, and God was asked to forgive peoples' sins and end the blight.

Tradition called for receiving guests with bread and salt, which had a dual meaning. Bread, symbolising kindness and security, is sacred, and salt is pure.

Loaves were baked in different shapes and sizes, depending on the region – round, oval, flat, flat-holed, round-holed, and long and flat. Round loaves were called pombi. Ancient Armenians used to call this bread pan; they called an identical dough, but made in

Lenten dolma

A New Year's dish

Preparation :
Fry 5 chopped onions in 0.5 litre vegetable oil, add 1 tablespoon tomato paste, 1 spoon each of salt and black and red pepper, 50 g basil, parsley and coriander. Mix 2 glasses of lentils, rice and bulgur which have previously been soaked. Mix everything together, then roll up the mixture in steamed cabbage leaves. Put the rolls in a pot, cover with water, and simmer till tender.

the shape of thick lavash, shaft or shot. In other regions bread was baked in stoves and given the name purnit (pur means "stove" in Armenian). Humsh Armenians called bread that had been baked on a stone "qarehatc" (qar means "stone"). Before a long journey, dried crusts were pressed into a loaf that could be kept for a long time. The older it was, the better it tasted.

Dolma

In the past, after a child had recovered from smallpox, bread was sacrificed by giving it to neighbours and the poor. This bread had no salt or sourdough starter and it was also used at religious ceremonies. Hshkhar(q) (communion bread) was a small, round loaf with a cross on it. Yet another bread was a thin lavash, again without salt and sourdough, which had been blessed by a holy person, a priest.

On the holy day of St Sargis fortunes were told using salty flatbread. Young girls and boys fasted on St Sargis Day, a Friday in Lent. Before going to bed they ate salty flatcakes without drinking any water, so that in their dreams they would see someone who would give them water. This person was predicted to become their spouse.

Another kind of bread with ritual meaning was she-qeliq. When a child was late in taking its first steps mothers used to bake this bread with butter, with a

hole in the middle, and put it on the child's feet, then take the child's hands and raise it to a standing position. Then other children would try to grab the bread and run away with it. Mother would point to the running children to encourage her child to follow the others and bring back the captured bread. It was believed that soon after this ritual, the child would walk.

Dishes made from grains such as bulgur, spelt, and wheat had an important place and were favourites in the traditional Armenian diet. Grains were also prepared with vegetables and meats. Malt, pasta (rshta), boiled roasted wheat flour with butter (atcik), sorrel with bulgur, and edible greens with bulgur are some of the dishes made from flour and dough.

All ethnic regions of Armenia share such rituals as "tooth-grain", which was celebrated when a child cut his first tooth; showering a bride and groom with grains at their wedding; and fortune telling with grains. All of these rituals were connected with

41

notions of sprouting and fertility – the main way to ensure prosperity and well-being.

After grains, dairy products such as milk, butter, cheese, yoghurt, (milk) cream, and curds were very widespread. Cow's, goat's, and sheep's milk were used. Cheese and yoghurt (especially goat's milk yoghurt) were, and continue to be, necessary components of the rural daily meal. Cheese and butter are well loved dairy products, including string cheese, zhazhik cheese, and motal cheese, which has been buried in jars in the ground with different herbs and spices. Dry buttermilk was prepared for winter use by draining buttermilk (lassi) and adding salt. Lassi soup and an onion-buttermilk dish were made with either fresh or dried buttermilk.

Meat

The use of meat products in the Armenian highlands has a centuries-long history. Archeological material proves that as early as the Neolithic Period (8th-3rd centuries BC) meat was used in Armenia. Medieval historians and scribes also attest to the use of meat and meat products. Armenian dishes called for the meat of small livestock – cows, sheep, buffalo, goats, and pigs. Lamb was favoured. Wildfowl such as hens, geese, ducks, partridge, and quail were also eaten.

In the past meat was eaten seasonally. Animals were slaughtered mainly in autumn when they were fat, and in winter when there was little to forage. Meat was also used as an offering (only male animals were sacrificed – sheep, goats, and poultry). Oxen were slaughtered for weddings and funerals.

Meat dishes formed the basis of the Armenian meal. The meat was boiled, baked, grilled and roasted. Dolma, bughlama (steamed meat), khashlama, plav (boiled grains with butter or oil) with meat were all widespread. Harisa (a wheatmeal porridge with chicken), kufta (pounded beef), and khash (a dish of boiled tripe and cow trotters) were holiday and ritual

Harisa

Ingredients :
1 kg chicken, 3 glasses rinsed semolina,
1 glass melted butter, 3 onions,
salt and cinnamon to taste.

Preparation :
Boil the chicken, remove the bones and cut into small pieces.

Add the semolina to the boiling broth along with the chopped meat.
Simmer slowly until the mixture thickens, then beat it hard with a wooden spoon.
Add the salt and stir well.
The harisa can be served with chopped onions that have been gently fried in oil, or with cinnamon and melted butter.

dishes that adorned all festive meals. Today meat is much more in demand and is now the food of choice to offer guests – barbecue, dolma (made of aubergines, pepper, tomato, vine or cabbage leaves stuffed with a savoury ground meat filling), khashlama (stewed meat, usually lamb with tomatoes and spices), kebabs, rissoles, and so on.

Kchuch

The Armenian language distinguishes between the terms "to boil" and "to cook". "To boil" (khashel) refers directly to meat dishes – khash, khashlama; "to cook" refers to everything else prepared for the meal.

Men usually have a monopoly on barbecuing (grilling meat over an open fire meat), and this method of preparing meat in Armenia generally signals a more casual, rather than a ritual, meal.

Food preservation

Over the ages the Armenians acquired great skill in storing and preserving food. Meat was corned and hung in the larder. The most effective way to store meat was thal (cooked meat preserved in fat), which was eaten plain in winter or used in various dishes. Western Armenians cured meat with smoke (basturma) and cured ground meat with different spices. Even today these special meats are an integral part of festive and holiday dinners.

Fish is also a favourite Armenian food. Van herring (corned, with cracked wheat, fried) is highly regarded, and Sevan lake trout or river trout is the queen of all fish.

Armenia is the motherland of many fruit-bearing trees, so fruits and vegetables full of vitamins held an important place in the traditional Armenian food system, even though they were considered of secondary importance to meat. Fruits and vegetables had such a firm position in the traditional food system due to developed agriculture, the early cultivation of vegetables, and the ancient occupation of gathering wild plants and herbs. As early as the Urartu period and in subsequent centuries fruit trees and grape vines were cultivated on the Armenian plateau. Clear evidence of this is found in the big wine jars unearthed in Karmir Blur (Red hill), the remains of carbonised berries, and in the wine presses discovered in Garni.

Vineyards are mentioned on cuneiform scripts (Zvartnoc, second century BC; Van, first century BC), and ancient Armenian cities like Van, Artashat, and Dvin were surrounded by large fruit gardens. Folk art also gives a rich sense of the grapevine and different fruits; the ornamentation illustrates vines, pomegranates and other fruits.

Grapes were widely used for preparing different kinds of sweets. Doshab (thick syrup) was made from grapes and mulberries. A number of sweets were made from this syrup – porridge (with flour made from fried and ground wheat), halva (a paste of nuts, syrup and oil), khavitc (porridge made by boiling fried flour in syrup and milk or water) and others.

A tasty Armenian trout dish

Cultivated fruits and berries include pears, apples, pomegranates, apricots, grapes, peaches, cherries, plums, mulberries, figs, quinces, and walnuts. There are also some wild fruits – apples, pears, medlars, and cornel cherries. Cultivated and wild fruits were used in different states – raw, dried, cooked, pickled and lightly grilled. All fruits were eaten fresh as a dessert and were served at festive meals. Some fruits were added to flavour dishes like dolma, sorrel soup, and bulgur soup. Pears and medlars were pickled. Sweet sujukh (pieces of walnut threaded on a string, then dipped into doshab and dried) was prepared, as were alani (dried peaches stuffed with walnuts, sugar and spices). In the past alani were kept as a delicacy for the New Year's holiday, to be offered to the most honoured guests.

Vegetables were prepared in numerous ways. They were used fresh, roasted, dried, broiled, corned and pickled. Some wild vegetables, like edible greens, were baked into special pies.

Fruits and vegetables were used separately as well as in combination with grains, meat, and dairy products. Fruits were used as flavourings; vegetables could comprise either the main or the supplementary ingredient in various dishes.

Pickles had an important place in the food system as appetizers and also in special dishes. Due to the hot climate Armenian cuisine used many hot, bitter seasonings, for example, pepper, onion, and garlic.

At the beginning of winter and spring the lack of cultivated vegetables was made up for by wild plants, eaten dried or pickled in winter, and fresh and raw in spring. From the end of spring until July or August almost 300 kinds of plants and herbs were gathered – sorrel, black salsify, stinging nettle, hornbeam, and purslane. A number of vegetables were used in salads, soups, and especially with grains. Dishes from all kinds of vegetables were more often prepared during periods of festing and Lent.

Mint, thyme, wild coriander, cumin and other spices were used abundantly. Mint, thyme, and mountain rosehip were steeped in water to make tea and were considered reliable medicines for colds and other illnesses.

Folk skills in fruit and vegetable preservation were developed over the centuries, passing from generation to generation up until our days. Due to these skills it was possible to enjoy a great number of fruits and vegetables throughout the year.

In ancient and medieval Armenia, beer, wine, and vodka were the typical alcoholic drinks. Vodka was flavoured with various fruits and berries – grapes, mulberries, pears, apples, rosehips, and blackberries. A savoury drink, termon, was prepared by boiling wine with syrup made from different berries and honey. It was considered a strong medicine for colds.

The medicinal use of food was common in Armenia. One can find information about the curative properties of food in medical and scientific manuscripts. Ancient authors wrote about the medicinal qualities of the plants that grow in the Armenian highlands. The medieval Armenian doctor Mkhitar Heraci analysed diets for their use against allergies and infectious diseases. He advocated the use of various vegetables, fruits and berries. He advised eating light food, fresh fish, and chicken to cure tuberculosis.

In addition to discussing the curative properties of food, the Armenian doctor Amirdovlat Amasiaci, in his book *Helping medicine* (1469), also described products of animal and vegetable origin and gave instructions for their curative uses. To prevent untimely ageing people were advised to eat thyme, onion, dill, rosehip, figs, honey, animal brains and liver. Pumpkin, pomegranate, plum, quince, millet and barley were useful to cure diabetes, as were watermelon seeds, dill, purslane, and other plants.

Ceremonial meals

Dinners could be everyday, festive or ceremonial. They accompanied weddings, funerals and birth/christening ceremonies. At funerals the sacred element predominated, but birth/christening dinners were more secular, with little religious content. The most characteristic feature of any sacred meal was the communal table. Since food was the main result of social activity, it was believed that everyone should share a common table. All community activities were accompanied by everyday meals that had no sacred or ritual elements. Festive dinners, at which special dishes were served, had both ritual and sacred meaning.

The ancient origins of the communal meal were manifested at the wedding and funeral tables. Following tradition, one representative from each family of the community, usually the patriarch (who came automatically, without a special invitation), was present at wedding and funeral meals. Everyone shared the meal equally. Each family contributed some food, which the women prepared.

Weddings were celebrated with great solemnity and ritual. Sheep were slaughtered before the wedding, for the engagement. Barbecue, khashlama, rice and cracked wheat plav were prepared. Men prepared the barbecue; the meat dishes: dolma, khashlama, and chicken were cooked by the women. An obligatory

element of the engagement ritual was halva. It was placed on a tray, then its surface was smoothed and decorated with raisins in a pattern of crosses. A piece of sugar in the middle ensured a sweet start to a prosperous life. Another custom expressing sincerity, intimacy and harmony was a table near the bridal bed laden with sweets, cakes and fruits, which the groom offered the bride. If she accepted, it meant that she accepted their relationship.

On the third day (or, at a later period, the next day) the wedding participants were offered khash at the groom's house. The most common cake at the wedding was gata (with a filling made of flour, sugar and butter), which was baked in both the groom's and the bride's house; it was also brought by female guests.

The wedding tables for men and women were separate from one another. Seating at the wedding meal was based on gender (men and women took seats at different tables); age (the young people sat with the spouses, while the old people sat separately); and

Plav with trout

Ingredients :
600 g trout, 1/2 glass milk, 3 eggs, 1 glass cooked beans, 1 glass half-cooked rice, 1/2 glass melted butter, salt.

Preparation :
Cut the scaled and rinsed fish into pieces and place in a greased frying pan. Add the milk that has been mixed with the eggs and cook over a low heat until the fish is flaky. Mix the cooked beans with the half-boiled rice. In a separate pan melt the butter, then add the rice and beans. Cook over a slow heat until the rice is tender. Season to taste with salt. Serve the plav with the fish.

Gata

social status (the head of the men's table was the godfather or priest, and the head of the women's was the godmother).

The consent of the community was expressed along the route of the wedding procession, where neighbouring families, friends, and grandparents spread tables with food and wine for the wedding participants. Thanks to this custom the wedding meal acquired a communal nature. The wedding meal began at the groom's father's house and continued at the house of the bride's father. Hospitality was the most important and ancient aspect of the wedding. Moreover, along with such wedding presents as

clothes and jewellery, drinks, sweets and fruits also had an important place.

The funeral table was laid in the afternoon. It was generally prepared by the female relatives. The dishes were very simple, perhaps stewed beef or chicken. This meal referred to the sacred sphere where meat was cooked in this fashion; in the secular sphere it would have been broiled or fried.

The main idea behind the ritual funeral meal and the subsequent meal of mourning was for everyone to partake of the meat offered, in order to symbolically overcome death and encourage rebirth. Only men – or first the men and only after them the women – were present at this meal. The mistress of the house was not involved in the cooking: on the one hand she was considered ritually impure, on the other, her absence in the kitchen provided an opportunity for the women to lend moral and psychological support. The predominance of men at the funeral table was explained by the need to symbolically overcome death.

The birth/christening meal in Armenia was organised on the sixth and seventh days following the child's birth. Men prepared a barbecue, which denotes the secular nature of the meal. The woman of the house prepared dolma, khash, plav, and fish. The godfather or priest sat at the head of the table.

Today, festive meals with a light, entertaining nature have become very common; the ritual-sacred meals, such as the meal prepared when conscripts are about to enter the army are now ritual-secular. This meal was prepared by the mother with the help of her female relatives. Dolma, khashlama, plav, stewed or roasted chicken, salads, smoked meat, and pancakes were served. A barbecue was prepared by the men. The tastiest piece was always the one eaten near the fire.

Sacrifice played a large part in the ritual system; it was the main element of the ritual meal. The offering could come from the community or be private, from a family. Community offerings were made on national holidays (Easter, Transfiguration, Ascension, etc.) and had a specific mythical and ritual nature that aimed to guarantee prosperity and wellbeing. Offerings were also made at chapels along the pilgrimage route. The offerings on pilgrimages or in villages were placed on a common altar. The butcher's preparation and slaughter of the animal, the cooking of the meat and its equal distribution among the people at a common table in the churchyard represented a ritual, and communal, social offering. When people partake of the offering it is accepted by God. Thus the words "may God accept the offering" are uttered as people pass the meat from hand to hand. Occasions for offerings included a preventive offering, made in the hope of bringing good luck and security or an offering of thanks after overcoming misfortune or a bad accident.

The main characteristic of all Armenian church holidays was the communal meal. In this regard the most typical was the New Year's ritual meal, the main feature of which was a rich assortment of dishes, including dried and fresh fruits (pomegranates, apple, pears and grapes), sweet strings of walnuts and alani, nuts, sweet and sour pasteghs (a sweetmeat of fruits and berries).

Aslamazjan, "Still Life"

A number of dishes were prepared on New Year's Eve. The mandatory ones were sweet (honey) soup, harisa, pasutc dolma (vegetarian dolma – different leguminous plants rolled in cabbage leaves), and meat dolma. It was common to prepare a sweet dish, atcik, made from sprouted wheat, raisins, and beans, which symbolised an abundant harvest. The sweet soup was shared with neighbours and relatives to make the coming year sweet.

The New Year's feasting lasted from one to twenty days. The dishes were prepared by the mistress of the house and the entire family, relatives and friends took their places round the table. On Christian New Year's Eve meatless dishes were prepared such as vegetarian dolma and beans. A popular New Year's dish was harisa. Cooking it was believed to ensure a rich harvest in the coming year.

The most popular cake was "year bread" or "new-year bread", a flat bread made from wheat flour and vegetable oil, kneaded with milk or water and divided into twelve pieces. The surface of the cake was decorated with raisins and walnuts. A coin, a ring or some other charm was kneaded into the bread dough. The person who got the piece with this charm would be lucky and happy in the coming year.

An obligatory cake on the New Year's table was gata (with a filling of flour, butter and sugar), which was either round, oval, or triangular in shape. The most well loved desserts were pakhlava ("the queen of cakes"), nazuk (a sweet yeast bread), and sweets with honey and walnuts.

On Christmas and at baptisms and christenings rice plav with raisins and a crust on the bottom of the pot were prepared, as were trout, sorrel and lentil soups, and vegetable and lentil salads.

On St Sargis Day a savoury pastry, pokhindz, was prepared from fried and ground wheat flour and halva. On the fortieth day after Christ's birth He was brought to the church. On this holy day, pokhindz,

Alani

Ingredients :
10 kg peaches, 150 g sulphur, 2 kg nuts, 3.5 kg sugar, 20 g cinnamon, 20 g cardamom

Preparation :
Grind the nuts. Add the sugar, cinnamon, and cardamom and mix well.

Peel the peaches and sprinkle them with the sulphur and place in the sun to dry slightly.
Then stone the peaches and stuff them with with the prepared nut mixture.
Flatten them, thread them on a string and hang in a cool place to dry completely.

aghandz (roasted wheat and hemp), raisins, walnuts and roasted peas were brought out on a tray to a fire that had been built in the yard. The pokhindz was kneaded with honey or doshab right around the fire. After being carried three times around the fire, part of the food was divided among the children present, and the rest was taken back home.

Of all the national holidays Shrovetide was distinguished by the diversity of its dishes, and by abundant meals and entertainment. On this holiday the list of meat dishes was very long and rich – dolma, khash, barbecue, chanakh (lamb) with potatoes, aubergines, bean, tomato and spices cooked in clay pots in the tonir), harslet, khashlama. The best and favourite dish was a kind of haggis – a lamb's stomach was cleaned, filled with cracked wheat and spices, then sewn up and hung in the tonir to roast. A great quantity of halva and gata was prepared. On the last day of the holiday lassi soup and yoghurt and boiled eggs were eaten as people said, "we are closing our mouths with white eggs. May God favour opening our mouths with red eggs", because Lent was about to begin.

During Lent only foods of vegetable origin were prepared, and only vegetable oil was used. Pickled vegetables were used instead of cheese. Typical dishes were vegetarian dolma, rice dolma, atcik, different soups made with greens, and lassi. In the middle of Lent a bread called "middle" was baked without salt and sourdough, similar to the "year bread". Lenten gata and pastries with greens were prepared.

Easter was celebrated in very festive fashion. Eggs were dyed on Holy Thursday. On Good Friday hot and sour spiced vegetables and soups were eaten. On the Saturday fresh vegetables and plants were fried with eggs, butter or oil and gata and pastries were baked. The mandatory components of the Easter meal were red-dyed eggs, fish, plav, greens, and vegetables fried with eggs, with lassi or semolina milk soup at the end. Neither milk nor butter nor cream was used from Easter until Ascension Day. On Ascension Day this ban was lifted, and the main ritual dish was buttermilk soup, which was cooked in each house in the early morning. It was spilled in the gardens and fields to bring a rich and abundant harvest.

The first apple of the season was eaten on Transfiguration Day. On Holy Cross it was common to take food, drinks and fruits to the graveyard and after a blessing to eat and drink them for blessed memory. On this day, too, a kid was sacrificed in memory of the deceased. After the kid was prepared for cooking, it was hung in the tonir. A pot of cracked wheat used to be put under the kid to catch the drippings. Slices of the roast kid were rolled in lavash, then taken to the graveyard to share with the poor and then the relatives.

A well established protocol of hospitality marked Armenian culture and gave shape to a system of receiving guests, paying attention to their place in the house and at the table, offering good wishes, and so on. Traditional Armenian hospitality was natural, spontaneous and voluntary. According to custom, the host was obliged to receive and welcome the guest, make room for him, provide him with food and a place to rest and see him off. In the case of private hosting, the master of the house who received one or more visitors felt obliged to provide food for them as well as for their livestock.

Hospitality is still very important to Armenians, who keep the tradition alive. The guest is offered at least a glass of coffee, cheese and bread or yoghurt. In case he is shy, he is asked a couple of times to help himself. It is not considered acceptable among Armenians to eat standing up, or to discuss practical affairs or work over a meal.

(Illustrations on page 41-48 are reproduced from "Armyanskaya kulinaria", G. Porsughyan/3rd edition of Hayastan, 1985, photographs by R.M. Hambartsumyan)

Armenia

Rainer Metzger

Austria

Contemporary art and the essence of eating

The Phaeacians

One of the most successful Austrian television productions is a celebrity news programme going by the title of Seitenblicke (side glances). The fact that it is only five minutes long is offset by its being broadcast every day, at prime time, after the evening news. Austria is a small country where people are more likely to know each other than in other countries. That, and the fact that celebrities are not as abundant here as in countries with a big entertainment, fitness and leisure-time industry, invests the Seitenblicke show with an immediate promise for the viewers, who feel that in due time they, too, might just make it into the world of glamour and paparazzi. Seitenblicke – and this is what makes the show so successful – is the quintessential medium for the dissemination of societal equality. It owes its egalitarian impact to a considerable degree to the venues roamed by the Seitenblicke team. More often than not the cameras are set up near miscellaneous hot or cold buffets, piled with a wide range of food specialities and regional or exotic culinary delights. They literally garnish any society event and act as background to the socialites who sample them before supplying the Seitenblicke cameras with a telegenic sound bite.

Austria considers itself a country of people who like to eat, and presents itself as such across all social strata and mentality divides. This image is perpetuated with amazing continuity. Largely unfettered by historical developments, the perception of self is informed by unbridled gluttony, the preference for being gourmand rather than gourmet, and the partiality for large quantities of food of the fatty or sugar-laden variety. No doubt, the quality of cooking has improved everywhere. Local cuisine has become open to international influences and, in return, regional specialities have become hallmarks of a new sophistication of taste, rooted in a heightened awareness of lifestyle. But when the focus lies on national identity and illustrative representations thereof, Austrians love what is copious, overabundant and, if need be, unhealthy. They love the traditional that serves as a yardstick for appraising the community one lives in and one's own affiliations to it. Austrians do not perhaps eat heavier food or are more careless about their health than other people, but apparently they feel better represented when portrayed in connection with what is heavy and unhealthy. This image is less to do with cuisine than with the notion of culture in general. While eating is part of culture it may be an Austrian idiosyncrasy to perceive the concrete, sensual and situative, in short the pleasurable attractions of ingesting food, very much in terms of how one is seen by others.

Friedrich Schiller and Johann Wolfgang Goethe, being Germans, Protestants, representatives of a small-states system which had no truck whatsoever with an emperor, were exemplary anti-Austrians. In their Xenien, they included the following distich on the "River Danube": "Mich umwohnt mit glänzendem Aug das Volk der Phajaken/Immer ist's Sonntag, es dreht immer am Herd sich der Spieß." (Around me, bright-eyed, lives the tribe of Phaeacians/ It's always Sunday, there's always a roast in the oven). The topos of ancient Cockaigne which the poets attributed to them seems to suit the Austrians perfectly. Hence they have readily agreed to be related to the Phaeacians, the people who invited Ulysses to a feast when he landed on their shores

after the Odyssey. Probably the most popular Austrian poem on gorging and gluttony was composed by Josef Weinheber. It is entitled *Der Phäake (The Phaeacian)* and its first lines are well known to every child in Austria: "Ich hab sonst nix, drum hab ich gern, ein gutes 'Papperl', liebe Herrn" (I've nothing else, so now and then, I like good food, dear gentlemen); the term Papperl, by the way, like most diminutives reserved for something dearly beloved, is a popular colloquial Austrian synonym for "food". People gladly suffer being related with things epic, Homeric, and legendary, and make a mythical virtue out of the necessity to fulfil a need. Roland Barthes found proof for the French engaging in "mythologies" of that kind in the way in which they deal with "le bifteck et les frites" (steak and chips), and the same principle is reflected in heightened form, even taken to extremes, in Austrian literature. *Kirbisch*, an epic in hexameters by Anton Wildgans, is a case in point. It contains a hymn to a very special national hero, Schweinsbraten or pork roast, described in resounding and untranslatable alliterations: "Brutzelnd, brätend und braun vom prasselnden Brande des Bratherds".

And so on and so forth. If one considers culture's specific area of competency to reside in assessing how one is seen by someone else from the point of view of how well this image fits one's own self-perception, Austria's self-assessment of being a nation of culture is of the utmost cogency. Unlike other countries, Austria considers artists, writers and musicians as national issues for they provide an unbroken flow of images that tell us how to see ourselves. Therefore, five artists will be allowed to speak; visual artists who, through the wide variety of media and lines of work that is so typical of our time, provide formulas for the phenomena and problems associated with eating. In no way the first to do so, these five artists, who were born between 1954 and 1970, represent only a small number of examples in the long succession of Austrian representatives of a culturally transformed eating culture. These artists and their work may, however, serve as representative examples of how art is created in the immediate present: how reality is approached and turned into images. It goes without saying that this article is less concerned with what is trendy or "in" than with what is present and of the present, or what is immediate and of interest to everyone.

Preparing food: Martin Gostner, Dicke Aura Heimat (Thick aura of home), 2001

Over 100 years ago there were dozens of giant Ferris wheels on the globe. Today, if one leaves aside those temporary appearances at funfairs and secondary attractions in leisure-time parks, there is only one of these historical attractions left, the one in Vienna. This may be thought a coincidence, but if one considers that Vienna features a horizontal counterpart to the Ferris wheel's ceaseless vertical rotations, namely the no less ceaseless circling of a centre on the circular Ringstraße boulevard, some kind of logic might transpire. Paris has a finger pointing upwards, the Eiffel Tower, and, translated into the horizontal plane, the straight lines of the boulevards running through the city. Whether they like it or not, cultures live on symbols.

The mechanism underlying the Giant Ferris Wheel is the movement around a centre. In more abstract terms it is a gesture that encloses an inner space, and that might be considered the quintessential Austrian idiom. It must include a perplexive element which precludes any clear statement of what is at the centre of the circling: the inner space or the gesture. Is it, in technical terms, the hub or the rotation? Is it, in urbanistic terms, Vienna's city centre or its imperial enclosure? Is it, in analytic terms, the mind or its analyst? Is it, in aesthetic terms, the interieur or the decoration?

And is it, in culinary terms, the slice of veal or its bread-crumbed coat which make up the Wiener Schnitzel? A wrapping that showcases what is within is the prototypical relationship manufactured by Austrian cuisine and the wrapping can envelop a number of things. In the case of the omnipresent Wiener Schnitzel it is veal, cut against the fibre into slices of no more than six millimetres and well

taverns, two wooden benches and a wooden table, and submitted them to the procedure of a breaded coat. Since it was impossible to follow the usual routine of frying the coated item in a pan, the coat had to be applied – against all culinary wisdom – with an electric iron. Therefore it did not form the undulating ripples one knows from a Schnitzel, but it was a perfect fit. What Gostner performed was more than an eccentric artistic idea inspired by an unusual combination. His work of art is called *Dicke Aura Heimat* (Thick aura of home) and the act of coating actually evokes a homecoming, the golden yellow sheen conveying an aura of motherly protection.

Martin Gostner, Dicke Aura Heimat *(Thick aura of home), 2001. Wooden benches and table, breaded and baked. Courtesy Gabrielle Senn Gallery, Vienna.*

pounded. In the case of the no less omnipresent Backhendl (breaded fried chicken) it is chicken meat, but the wrapping can be enacted on a great variety of comestibles from offal to vegetables, coating them with a crust of flour, eggs and ground white bread. The gesture that divides the inside from the outside: if made by an artist such as Martin Gostner it may even relate to something altogether inedible.

The Wiener Schnitzel is as non-autochthonous as most of the inhabitants of Vienna. The principle was allegedly developed in Byzantium and the gleaming coat of breadcrumbs, or so it is said, is an economy version of the original gold-leaf. Living on, in the nineteenth century, as "Scaloppina alla Milanese", the dish was then brought to the river Danube by Field-Marshal Josef Radetzky who was immortalized in the homonymous march by Johann Strauss. The Wiener Schnitzel was an imported commodity, and a glance into the Viennese telephone directory at the vast number of names of Hungarian, Bohemian, and Croatian origin will reveal that the same goes for

Maybe it took someone who lived in Innsbruck in Tirol and planned an exhibition in Graz, Styria, to illustrate the essence of eating in Austria. Gostner used the typical furnishings of Austrian wine the population. It is little wonder that people tried to compensate by frequently evoking "home", and it is just as little wonder that the method involved was equally imported. As befits a metropolis that was the world's fifth-largest city around 1900, the melting pot worked and still continues to do so in some respects: thus the home has a thick aura and the thick aura has a home. And that is why even cautionary medical warnings against the Wiener Schnitzel are entirely fruitless.

Serving food: Robert F. Hammerstiel, Mittagsporträts (Lunchtime portraits), 1989-1990

"The private dinner table of His Majesty is never short of a good piece of boiled beef, which counts among his favourite dishes." This piece of information about the culinary predilections of Emperor Francis Joseph is to be found in a serving manual of 1912. One does not know whether it was the popularity of the ruler or the emulation effect which has always been a driving force for loyal subjects: what applies to the Wiener Schnitzel equally applies to beef. The voice of authority, be it that of the field marshal or His Imperial Majesty himself, informs the taste of the time. A wide range of Austrian dishes and groceries bear the imperial prefix of "Kaiser-", including jumbled pancakes, pork belly or handmade rolls.

Despite the monarchical preferences, beef boiled in a broth is not among them, which might be due to the fact that Austrian German has developed its very own genuine national idiom in this respect. The Inuit have dozens of words to describe snow, the Aboriginal people have the same for earth- and water holes, and the Austrians have a multiplicity of terms

for beef. Any imperial "Kaiser-" prefix would merely introduce improper uniformity among the splendid variety of names for individual cuts of beef, such as Mageres Meisel, Beiried, Weißes Scherzel, Kruspelspitz or Tafelspitz.

"Mr and Mrs M. and children" are also indulging in a choice piece of cow. Before they started their meal, the Lower Austrian photographer Robert F. Hammerstiel took a picture of the prepared lunch table of the M. family and made it a part of his

Robert F. Hammerstiel, "Herr und Frau M. und Kinder" from Mittagsporträts, *1989-1990*

Mittagsporträts (Lunchtime portraits). The photos present the daily meals of anonymous households with their, usually highly indigenous, attractions. Mr S. and Mrs D. are having pancakes, Mrs Z. dumplings, Mr J. pasta with tomato sauce, while Mrs H. makes do with a plate of fruit.

So there is boiled beef on the M.'s menu, accompanied by the obligatory roast potatoes and a very genuinely Austrian side dish which is called Semmelkren and consists of a mixture of hardened white bread soaked in beef broth and grated horseradish. The children, obviously four of them who share two sides of the table, and the two parents have been served a slice of meat each; the serving plate has already been emptied. Side-dishes are ready for second helpings.

These are the details that invest the photograph with a sociographic dimension. The M. family is obviously part of the less privileged section of the population. The plastic table cloth with its rhomboid pattern with posies that are mirrored on the plates testifies to the dreams of a better life. At the Hofburg in Vienna, a silver chamber was established a few years ago, which features replicas of the imperial and royal dinner tables where the Habsburgs solemnly lived out their majestic rule. Every item on display testifies to the fairy-tale lifestyle that petty bourgeois households then tried to emulate.

A general level of material comfort made it possible for them at least to re-enact the favourite menus of His Majesty: in Austria, the sheer quality of staple foods is extremely high. But when it comes to the tableware – the aspect of eating which is not necessary for survival and thus genuinely cultural – the hierarchy is still overtly manifest despite all democratic endeavours towards equality. You eat with your eyes, says popular wisdom. Ever since eating habits became more sophisticated in the sixteenth century, this appeal to the senses that we consider as "higher", particularly the visual sense, denies any egalitarian approach. He wanted to report "about the state of things and about the people behind them"; says Hammerstiel about his *Mittagsporträts*. His series of photographs has the eye of the camera eating along.

Garnishing: Michaela Spiegel, Schnitzler & Freud, 1996

In the text that marked the foundation of psychoanalysis, the *Interpretation of dreams*, which was first published in 1895, Sigmund Freud describes the situation of Odysseus approaching the Phaeacians. People were "shining in the loveliest colours", wrote Freud, they were "lovely and gracious figures". And

Michaela Spiegel, from Schnitzler & Freud, *1996, inked print on canvas in an iron and plexiglass box*

how did the mythical castaway appear to them? "Ragged, naked and covered with dust". Gone with the wind was any paradisiacal communication and sheer physical nature took its toll. It was in Vienna that such truths about the nether realms of the physical and the psyche emerged. Michaela Spiegel's work *Schnitzler & Freud* commemorates this fact.

The fact that Arthur Schnitzler and Sigmund Freud, the two explorers of the mind, both physicians, one famous as a writer of fiction the other as an author of scientific texts, both have highly evocative names (one evoking the Schnitzel, the other "pleasure"), is the basis of Michaela Spiegel's group of works (equally the bearer of a significant name, the German word Spiegel being "mirror" in English).

The photograph of a dish presented in a highly appetising manner is placed in juxtaposition with a much less appetising image from a porno magazine, the blatant pose of a woman degraded to the level of a piece of equipment. By their second names and by their reputation as thinkers and men of letters, Schnitzler and Freud testify to the close connection that simply exists between eating and sex in human life: as primal needs and objects of obsession, as vehicles of cultural transformation and as objects of reflection.

In one of her image combinations the Viennese artist presents one of the desserts of which Austrian, and particularly Viennese, cuisine is very proud, a cake that bears the name of "health cake". With her very own sense of humour the artist chose as the other depiction a couple engaging in a very particular form of healthy exercise. Eating and love, food and sex are good for the soul, and possible analogies between the photo on the left and the one on the right do not end there, of course. Diogenes the Cynic, when reprimanded for masturbating in public, is said to have replied with the following intriguing analogy: "I wish one could satisfy hunger by similarly rubbing the belly." At any rate, the ascetic and the pleasurable, the inhibited and the unrestrained are available to both regions, the belly and the loins.

In addition, Schnitzler and Freud testify to a predilection for sweets. A cookery book devoted to Freud claims that the great explorer of the psyche raved about an apple tart he called Ödipuskuchen (Oedipus cake). A special tip for preparing it: "The Ödipuskuchen turns out best when your mother is standing by watching you." Here again we have the aspect of obtaining, enveloping, and craving for protection. Sweet food holds the promise of security, and anthropological experience actually tells us that nothing that might harm the body tastes sweet. Sugar is not a poison, but can easily become an addiction. Could this be an explanation for why Austrians identify with what they refer to as "Mehlspeisen" (desserts)? When Switzerland once invited its neighbouring countries to collaborate in preparing a meal for television, Austria was quite naturally in charge of the dessert. And the coverage of an Austrian magazine on a Eurovision cookery programme was entitled "Ein Apfelstrudel für Europa" (An apple strudel for Europe).

Digesting:
Elke Krystufek, Vomiting – eating, 1992

One of the many anecdotes through which Austria's writing guild celebrates the short story has it that when Emperor Francis Joseph and Empress Elisabeth were about to have their wedding dinner, the Hofburg chefs wanted to impress with something particularly delicious. It goes without saying that their ambition was particularly engaged by the dessert, and so they whisked and mixed away until they produced that fluffy batter which is slowly baked in a pan and torn and jumbled with a fork, and which has been called Kaiserschmarren ever since. To their great disappointment the Empress, Austria's beloved Sissi, refused the proffered pudding. The Emperor, however, sampled a sizeable portion, saved the day and gave the dish its name. Once again, a culinary career could be made or broken by the imperial stamp of approval. From the outset it became apparent that the imperial consort suffered from an eating disorder. Elisabeth preserved her famously narrow waist, a purported 50 centimetres, at the price of anorexia.

A completely off-kilter relationship with eating is the frequently overlooked downside to the great boost that cooking and food have received in recent decades. No matter how splendidly aestheticised food has become, how multifarious the refinements and how profound the reflection on food intake and sexuality, there is a further primal human need which consists in processing the fare thus ingested. Digestion is the unacknowledged third party in the polarities of human welfare.

From her beginnings, the Viennese artist Elke Krystufek impressed by her merciless and disillusioned investigation of her own life. Her artwork basically consists in nothing but this exploration of the phenomenon which she herself represents. It relates to her appearance and her love life, and it relates to her body as the *sine qua non* of her physical existence. The body with all its problems. In the one-hour video sequence *Vomiting - eating* of 1992, Elke Krystufek has a camera observe her going through the ritual of an eating disorder. At the time the artist suffered from bulimia, and so she demonstrated what that implied. The video shows her throwing up on the toilet and then, as if compensating for the resulting emptiness, maniacally and relentlessly stuffing herself with food, in an act of pure automatism. A human machine.

In people suffering from bulimia the mechanism of feeling full is unhinged. Obviously this feeling of fullness is linked to experience, for one has the impression of having eaten enough long before digestion has fully set in. The feeling of fullness operates in anticipation. Since bulimics immediately get rid of what they just ate, they do not know what it means to be satisfied. Therefore the anticipatory mechanism does not work and they stuff themselves far beyond the level at which the body usually signals "enough". One of the most significant pieces of literature relating to eating disorders is Franz Kafka's novella *A hunger artist*. A grim reversal of the title applies to Elke Krystufek's auto-focus on video: what she demonstrates drastically is an artist's hunger.

Putting on weight: Erwin Wurm, Jakob-Jakob fat, 1993

Hermann Nitsch, representative of Vienna Actionism since the 1960s, is one of the protagonists of a type of art that approaches eating as a synaesthetic ceremony that involves all the senses. Accordingly, Nitsch stated luxuriously: "A proper pork roast as I like to eat it is not too lean, has some fat and a crust and comes in a golden sauce on which float tiny globules of fat. The sauce is not supposed to be all oily but to contain the wonderful juices of the meat that were released during the cooking.

Served with dumplings. A truly classical dish in my opinion, which I like to compare to a Rembrandt or a Titian. The colouration is strongly condensed. Wonderfully painted pictures that present themselves like a crisp pork roast." Nitsch's superb evocation of an Austrian culinary motif would be suggestive enough even if it did not have a concomitant finale. Nitsch concludes by admitting: "unfortunately it has been my destiny to have problems with my weight ever since I was young. Many of my friends can eat whatever they like and will not put on weight. Without any doubt people who eat and drink and enjoy life without being overweight have easier lives."

Like all countries with a high living standard, Austria has a great number of inhabitants who share the problem of Hermann Nitsch. They are overweight and the probability of surplus weight rises with their predilection for traditions, which involve delights such as pork roast, Schnitzel, or Schmarren. Calories, kilojoules and whatever further sinister terms there are to imply a warning of health risks, are a measure of energy. They are units of measuring heat, and once more one becomes aware of the special biotope character that invades Austrian self-perception and perception from outside. What is comfortable is padded by a layer of subcutaneous fat.

For more than ten years the Viennese artist Erwin Wurm has been exploring the dimensions of what may be considered sculpture. Among the many phenomena that have plasticity, the human body is remarkable for its very three-dimensionality. These were the auspices for Wurm's work *Jakob-Jakob fat* of 1993. One immediately grasps the substance of this work. A young man called Jakob has greatly expanded in girth. Formerly slender, he now looks massive, and this before-and-after is presented in photographs. Admittedly, Wurm's production was realised with the help of garment props and poses and is purely an act. Unlike the famous case of Robert de Niro who gained

Erwin Wurm,
"Jakob-Jakob fat", *1993,*
C-Print on aluminium

Austria

a full 15 kilograms for his part in the film *Raging Bull*. And unlike real life, where such a weight gain would literally carry some weight, the fake is irrelevant for the picture, the large-format photography.

Art and life. The most important of all Austrians according to his compatriots, or so regularly surveyed statistics say, namely Wolfgang Amadeus Mozart, resigned from the service of the Archbishop of Salzburg in 1781 and thereafter lived as a free-lance composer subject to the laws of the market. The courtier turned into an artist as we currently define the term, invested with all the associated liberties and insecurities. What ultimately induced Mozart to escape from the world of the aristocracy was a dinner episode. At a gala dinner given by his master, Mozart had been seated at the servants' table. He had to sit, as he writes, with the cooks and the "confectioner" and felt this to be a great slight. Today we know that this

Further reading

- E. Bakos, *Gaumenschmaus und Seelenfutter. Tausend Jahre Wiener Küche*, Vienna 1996
- H. Bertsch/M. Reckewitz, *Von Absinth bis Zabaione. Wie Speisen und Getränke zu ihrem Namen kamen*, Berlin 2002
- *Essen und Trinken I und II*, special issues of the magazine *Kunstforum international, volumes 159 and 160*, 2002
- *Götterspeisen*, Catalogue Vienna 1997
- L. Kolmer/C. Rohr (Hg.), *Mahl und Repräsentation. Der Kult ums Essen*, Paderborn/München/Wien/Zürich 2. Aufl. 2000
- *Mäßig und Gefräßig*, Catalogue Vienna 1996
- E. Plachutta/C. Wagner, *Die gute Küche. Das österreichische Jahrhundertkochbuch*, Vienna/Munich/Zurich 1993

seating arrangement contains a profound truth which people were unaware of at the time. Chefs and artists give stature to their community, physically and symbolically.

Austria

Tahir I. Amiraslanov

A z e r b a i j a n

A cuisine in harmony

Azerbaijani cuisine is one of the most ancient, rich and tasty cuisines in the world. It encompasses not only meals and their methods of preparation, but also material culture – history, philosophy, psychology, customs, physiology, hygiene, equipment, chemistry, ethics, aesthetics, poetry, and practical skills as they relate to the table, and that have been developed by the people of Azerbaijan in harmony with the surrounding world.

One of the most important factors influencing the creation and development of cuisine is climate. The Republic of Azerbaijan has nine climatic zones, which offer a wealth of flora and fauna that have helped to create a rich cuisine. In addition to the native animals and birds, fish and plants, the development of agriculture yielded a surplus of grain, which meant that complex dishes could be developed. To understand the history of dishes prepared from grain and pastry in the fifth to sixth centuries, BC, we can refer to a cheten (an ancient image of a colander) woven from reeds. This colander tells us about the stable harvests of that period and, accordingly, about the high level of farming that existed. This highly developed agriculture also presup-

poses the existence of irrigation systems and the development of cattle breeding, which was impossible without a settled way of life.

With their high level of farming and their cattle-breeding culture, the Azerbaijanis produced basic materials for cuisines throughout the Caucasus. Over the ages various travellers, scientists, merchants, and diplomats noted that the Azerbaijani population grew a great deal of wheat, oats, rice, sesame seed, soy, beetroot, melons, watermelons, grapes, apples, pomegranates and quince, among other products. These observations are supported by archaeological findings. The local population took advantage of vegetables, fresh and dried fish, caviar, honey, and butter, and exported any surplus to the neighboring countries.

Markets throughout the Caucasus were filled with produce grown by Azerbaijanis. In their book *Old Tiflis*, U.D. Angabadze and N.G. Volkova wrote that "at the Tiflis markets cheese was sold by Ossetians and Azerbaijanis. Cheese was also sold by Borchalints [that is, Azerbaijanis]. Geochay [now Lake Sevan] trout was in popular demand at the Tiflis markets; they brought it from Azerbaijan".

Importantly, Azerbaijan was the main supplier of salt in the Caucasus. Mineral salt was extracted from Nakhchivan Kopiy and sea salt from the Caspian Sea.

The names of many Azerbaijani dishes indicate their method of preparation. For instance, gatlama dolma (grapes leaves stuffed with meat) comes from gatlama (meaning "layer", which refers to a puff-pastry pie) and dolma (meaning "filling", which refers to stuffed grapes leaves). Dogramach (a dish made from yogurt) means "cutting", while azma (a dish of meat mashed with milk) means "pressing". The words gizartma (fried meal), partlama (boiling), govurma (fried), bozartma (stew), and dondurma (ice cream; from the word for "freeze") all refer to types of heat, or lack thereof. Dindili kufta (meatball dindili), nazik yarpag hangal (a dish made with thin pasta), yukha (a thin bread), and lyulya-kebab (minced meat kebab) all have to do with the shape of each dish. Yarpag dolmasi (grapes leaves stuffed with meat), yarma (grain),

Dur

hashil (a dish of thick, boiled pasta), duyi chankuru (a rice dish), sebze-kuku (omelette with greens), and bal-gaymag (honey-cream) indicate the main raw ingredients in each dish. Gatig (yoghurt), sulu hangal (broth with diamond-shaped pasta), and horra (porridge) have to do with texture. Turshu (pickles), shoraba (pickles), and shirin nazik (sweet thin dough) explain the organoleptic features of each dish. Sadjichi (oven hearth), tava kebab (kebab made in a frying-pan), kulfa (a shared village oven), and churek (bread) all refer to different types of hearths. Finally, the names Gandja pakhlava (sweets), Tauz hangal (pasta topped with mashed potatoes), Garabakh basdirmasi (a meat dish), and Sheki halvasi (sweet halva) reflect the regions where these dishes originated. Frequently the name of a dish is generic. For example, there are about thirty variations of dolma (stuffed grapes leaves), about 200 varieties of pilaf, and so on.

A second linguistic feature of Azeri culinary terms is connected with the word ush (pilaf), which is found in such words as ushbaz, (cook), ushichi (professional pilaf cook), ush-hana (canteen), hush (dishes made from leg of lamb or beef), hushhil (flour porridge) and gushig (spoon). The term ush is encountered in many old Turkish written sources, in Orhan-Enisey and on ancient stone tablets.

A third way in which Azeri culinary terms were formed is descriptive and evocative, a feature common to all Turkic languages. In Turkish cuisine we find Imambaildi (the Imam fainted from pleasure);

in Kazakhstan, beshbarmag (five fingers); in Azerbaijan, khangyal (khan, come!), tarhan (young khan-prince); ahsag-ohlag (a lame goat), tutmadj (adj-tutma = don't be hungry), and galadj (be hungry).

Next to climate, a second important influence on cuisine is the hearth. As is well known, a great number of baked, boiled and stewed dishes in Russian cuisine evolved thanks to the possibilities of the Russian stove. The development of Azerbaijani cuisine stems from different sorts of open and closed hearths, such as tandir (a clay oven in the ground, sometimes above ground), kura (a round, carved-out hearth), buhari (an indoor hearth), kulfa (a shared village oven), chala odjag (an in-ground hearth like the tandir), sadj (a flat metal hearth), and mangal (a hearth for preparing kebabs). The oldest known samovar, which is around 3 700 years old, was found in the Sheki region of Azerbaijan. It reveals one of the starting points of cuisine – the transfer of the heat source from outside to inside the appliance, which affected the balance of liquid and air and ultimately affected the taste of dishes prepared in closed vessels.

Dishes and kitchen utensils of various materials also influenced the development of Azerbaijani cuisine. Even today cooks use vessels made of hide, stone, wood, clay, glass and metal. Traditional fuels, still used today, are wood, charcoal, and kizyak (pressed dung). Kizyak is of special interest, as it obviates the need to cut down trees and does not contribute to respiratory illness like other fuels. Indian scientists have

Dovqaz

found that the smoke from kizyak even has some antiseptic features.

An interesting part of people's culinary culture is their attitude towards water, to its purification and use. From ancient times the Azerbaijani people have considered water to be either white or black. Water containing many minerals and metallic elements is hard, or black, while water with few metallic elements and minerals is mild, or white. When Azerbaijani people prepare drinks and food we use only mild, white water. On the riverbanks and ariks (water channels) people always planted weeping willows, since these trees are believed to have antiseptic features that make water healthy. Similarly, to purify water, branches of weeping willow or something silver were put into the water. For further clarification apricot stones and sandstone were added to the water.

It is possible that the first and best natural water cleanser in history, which is still in use, was invented

Dur

by the Azerbaijanis. This is the su dashi, a stone for cleaning water. The su dashi is a hollow pyramid from black and white sandstone, which is put upside-down, on a special wooden stand, with a dish for clean water. People pour water into it and often add willow branches or something silver as filters. The water flows slowly and is cleaned and also cooled by the pressure differential as it drips through the stone.

Another important factor that has influenced cuisine is the geographic location of Azerbaijan and its people. The passing of ancient trade caravans and military roads through the territory of Azerbaijan connected the Azerbaijanis with many other peoples. Long-lasting ties with the Arabians introduced coffee. The Silk Road brought tea from China. Familiarity with Russian cuisine brought shchi (cabbage soup) and borshch into Azerbaijani cuisine, where both soups are called simply borsch. It also introduced Azerbaijanis to a rather distorted "Russian-style" European cuisine. Only at the end of the nineteenth century and the beginning of the twentieth, with the

development of the oil industry, did the process of direct acquaintance with European cuisines begin. The process continues today with the introduction of fast food. However, these western influences are found only in restaurant cuisine; they do not add much positive to the national cuisine, but merely harm health.

One of the most important factors influencing the Azerbaijani national cuisine is religion. Zoroastrism, the fire-worshipping philosophy of Avest and its reflection in the psychology, customs and beliefs of the Azerbaijani people, is also reflected in culinary culture, in our respect for the first helper of the cook, the ochag or hearth. Today's table customs were formed under the faith of those who worshipped white light and fire.

Coexisting with fire worship in the pre-Christian period was tengrianstvo, faith in the Unique Good. Although Christianity did exist in Azerbaijan, the Azerbaijanis have been Muslims for thousands of years, which has greatly influenced cuisine. Proscriptions against using plates made of gold, and against pork and alcohol, reveal the strong influence of Islamic traditions, as do various holidays and customs, such as fasting. The demands of Islam in connection with food are based on scientific principles. For example, Islam advises people not to eat peeled fruits and grains. Recent scientific investigations have shown that most vitamins and minerals are contained in the outer layers of plants.

The meat of cattle has been used in Azerbaijan since ancient times. Although some early sources indicate the use of horseflesh, today Azerbaijanis don't eat horsemeat. Older residents remember the taste of camel meat, especially camel kutabs (stuffed half-moon shaped pancakes). Today, the use of game is prevalent. The meat of young male animals, of shishaks (virgin female goats), and of castrated animals is considered to be milder and tastier. The snow-white meat of animals that graze in pastures, mountains and foothills has great advantages, as the fat content is high. People prefer fresh meat over frozen meat. Offal and the fat of the fat-tailed sheep are also enjoyed. For a long time fresh meat was cut into pieces, fried in tail fat, and put it into wineskins and special clay jugs. Then melted fat was poured over it to seal and preserve it. In addition to preserving fresh meat, people also dried it to make guhudj-at.

The meat of both domestic and wild animals and poultry is widely used. Hunting for wildfowl begins after the first snowfall when the birds' beaks and legs turn red from the cold. The meat of domestic birds – geese, ducks, turkey and chicken – is also used. The birds are confined in special cages and fed with grains that contain a high percentage of oil (corn, sunflower, etc.). Such birds produce rich, mild meat. The fat from birds is considered to be of higher quality than animal fat. Large pieces of meat are cooked whole, separately or with other ingredients, or else the meat is cut up to make such dishes as dolma and kufta.

The Caspian Sea, the Kura River, the Araz and other lakes such as Gey-gel, Djeyranbatan, and Geocha enrich our cuisine with delicious fish, which we fry, stew, boil and stuff. Fish is prepared whole, cut up, or minced. Both red and black caviar are very popular.

Eggs are also widely used, and quail's eggs are especially prized. Egg dishes such as gayganag (omelette), chalhama (fried eggs), kuku (eggs with greens) and chychurtma (omelette with different ingredients) decorate our table. Dairy products are very rich and varied. They include milk, agizsud (milk from a cow milked during the first three days after calving), bulama (cow's milk from three to seven days after calving), karamaz (milk mixed with yoghurt), gatig (yoghurt), pendir (cheese), doog (buttermilk), gaymag (cream), chiya (the top layer of raw milk), ayran (yoghurt with water) and shor (curds with salt). The dishes prepared from them – dovga (a dish prepared from yoghurt), dogramach (raw yoghurt with greens and cucumber), ayranashi (another dish from yoghurt), atilama (yoghurt with water), and syudly sayig (milk porridge) – have enriched our cuisine since ancient times.

Azerbaijanis treat bread with a sense of trembling and respect: yukha (a thin round bread baked on a sadj

Dolma

Azerbaijan

69

hearth), fetir (a bread 1.5 cm thick), lavash (a thin bread baked in a tandir), sengah (a thin bread baked on river stones), hamrali tandir-churek (a small round bread 12 cm in diametre) and other breads of different shapes, thicknesses and methods of preparation are set on the table. Azerbaijanis begin meals by paying respect to bread, because they believe that there is nothing better. We traditionally have sworn at the hearth on mother's milk, bread, and the Koran.

Pastry occupies a special place in Azerbaijani cuisine; the combination of meat and pastry is typical for all Turkic peoples. In his book *Ogoozi* historian Farig Sumer states that in order for the Seljuksto to prove they were Turkish, they ate tutmadj (a dish of pastry, meat and beans) and hangal ("pasta topped with minced meat and served with different sauces"), sulu hangal (broth with diamond-shaped pasta), and yarpag hangal (diamond-shaped pasta with minced meat). Goorza (a dumpling with boiled meat), dushbara (soup with dumplings), hashil (boiled flour with honey or grape sause), horra (milk porridge) and other flour-based pastries are prepared mainly in winter.

When the weather gets warmer, fewer dishes are prepared from flour and meat and more from plants, both wild and cultivated. Kyata (dough stuffed with greens and cheese), siyug (a dish of greens and rice), dovga (a dish prepared from yoghurt with greens) adjab-sandal (a layered dish of different vegetables) and a variety of salads are prepared from wild greens (about 400 kinds), spinach and beetroot greens, mint, eggplants and tomatoes.

Grain and beans occupy a special place on the table. Favourite dishes include suyig (porridge), pilaf, chilov (pilaf with green beans or pumpkin), govurga (fried grain), and hadiy (boiled grain). The most delicious dish is considered pilaf. In Azerbaijan, a country that can be surely be considered one of the motherlands of rice, there around 200 different kinds of pilaf. Rice even replaces bread in some areas of Azerbaijan. For example, the Lenkoran people never used to eat wheat bread; they ate rice bread instead.

Dovqa

Because Azerbaijan produced sugar; sweets, confectionery and halva hold an important place in Azerbaijani cuisine. Sugar was refined in Azerbaijan as early as the tenth century. By order of Catherine the Great, Prince Potemkin brought sugar cane from Azerbaijan to Russia. Such sugar was called tahtagyand. Later, sugar was manufactured from beetroot as well.

In addition to sugar from sugar cane and beetroot, the Azerbaijanis prepared fruit sugars, or nabat. Honey and fruit juices were boiled into thick syrup to make bekmez and doshab (different sorts of boiled fruit juices), which contributed to the variety of desserts.

Such sweets and baked goods as paklava (a sweet made with walnuts), shakerbura (another sweet with nuts), rahatlukum (Turkish delight), richal (thick fruit juice boiled with flour and fruit), sudjuk (yet another sweet with nuts), peshmek (cotton candy), peshvenk (sweets), ter halva (fresh halva with rice), guymag (a sweet made from flour, honey and butter), gatlama (puff-pastry pie), and juha halvasi (sweet dough) are the pride of Azerbaijani housewives and master bakers. Using honey, sugar, bekmez and fruits, people could create delicious jams, compotes, marmalades and other sweets from cornelian cherries, quince, cherries, figs, nuts, and rose petals.

Vegetables (tutma) were preserved with the help of a sour base (turshular) and salt (shorbalar).

Azerbaijani cuisine pays attention to the nutritive and medicinal properties of such dishes as umadj (pastries eaten when one has a cold), hash (leg of lamb or beef, eaten when one has broken a bone), horra (porridge to heal a sore throat), and guymag (a dish made of fried flour, butter and sweet water, which is eaten for energy). All of these have traditionally been used as home remedies for ailments. Thanks to a healthy kitchen, Azerbaijanis live for a long time.

Ritual and holiday meals occupy an important place in Azerbaijani cuisine. Dishes made from semeni (live wheat sprouts) are prepared only during Hidir Nebi holiday, which is celebrated on 10 February to mark the arrival of spring. People also prepare govud

Levengi

(fried grains with sweets shaped into balls). Hedik (grain porridge) and gouvurg (fried seeds) are prepared when baby's first tooth appears, or when 100-year-old men get a set of new teeth. During the winter women's holiday Little Chillya, special watermelon is served.

We have a wide variety of beverages. Arag-vodka prepared from mulberry, cornelian cherry and other plants is used mainly for medicinal purposes. Arag (vodka) means "white drink" (ag = white, ar = drink). In another context, ar can also mean "pure, clean, without impurities" (from the word aranmish, free of impurities). Different medicinal and alcoholic extracts and arags are prepared by means of distillation, such as mint aragiz (vodka with mint), gulyabi (rosewater), ovshara, gyandab (sweet water), mushmuli (berry) and chal arag (mixed-herb extract).

Buza (beer) has been brewed in Azerbaijan since ancient times. As in other Turkic cuisines, there are

71

many drinks from milk and sour-milk products, such as ayran (yoghurt with water), atilama (another sort of yoghurt with water), and bulama (cow's milk from three to seven days after calving). Sherbets are prepared from fruit juices and various plant extracts mixed with sugar and saccharine. They are served with pilafs for holidays and ritual celebrations.

Different drinks not only decorated the table, but are also medical.

It is impossible to imagine the Azerbaijani table without tea. Coffee and cocoa are used more rarely. In the morning warm boiled milk and milk drinks are served. The mineral waters of Azerbaijan – Istisu, Badamli, Sirab, and so on – are served when people are thirsty or ill. People consider bekmez drinks (called doshabs), boiled to the consistency of thick syrup from mulberry juice, watermelon, sugarcane, beetroot, grapes, wild persimmons, and other fruits, to be very nutritious. When people are especially thirsty and in need of something substantial, iskend-jebi is served. It is prepared from a mixture of honey and vinegar (in some sources, it is called vinegar-honey). Sometimes sugar is used instead of honey. Thickened fruits, made into compotes (hoshabs) and puddings (paludi), are also grouped among liquids in Azerbaijani cuisine. But the best natural drink of all is ice-cold spring water.

As for snacks (kalyanalti), yahma (open-faced sandwiches, from the word for "cover") and durmeks, prepared by wrapping foods in bread, are popular. Yukha (thin bread) and lavash are shaped into rolls; tendir-churek is often sliced, while sandwich hamrali (a small, round bread 12 cm in diametre) and other breads are made into pockets that can hold fillings. Accordingly, durmeks are called either bukme (wrapped) or jibbi (pocket). Durmeks are served both cold and hot.

Meze salads are also popular light meals. Fruits, dried fruits, and nuts (known as charas) are served at the end of the meal, as are sweets.

Sauces and zvars reveal the level of richness, variety, and development of the Azerbaijani kitchen. In the seventeenth century the famous Turkish traveler Evliya Chelebi wrote about Azerbaijan: "Here more than twelve kinds of sauces and zvars are known". Sauces from sour milk (katig) and garlic, garlic and vinegar thickened to the consistency of honey or sour cream, and fruit juices are mainly used. Sauces based on pastila and lavashana (different sorts of dried boiled fruit juice) are added to various dishes. Narsharab (sauce from pomegranate juice) or a sauce based on it is usually served with fish.

The traditional Azerbaijani menu takes into account such factors as season, weather, place, traditions, and who the diners are. There are several different types of meals: aran (lowland) meal, diet meals, meals for women in childbirth, meals for fiancées, meals for children, for young people and for old men.

Azerbaijani cuisine is very varied, with around 2 000 dishes. The sixteenth century English traveller Anthony Jenkinson wrote that "Abdulla-khan from Shemakha was given 150 types of dishes, after those 140 types of dishes were brought at once". Such variety called for specialists, who in turn helped to create and maintain the variety. Evliya Chelebi writes of twelve cook shops connected with twelve imams, where thousands of people worked, including bakers, chorekchi (churek bakers), yukhasalan (yukha makers), shatir (bread bakers), ashchi (pilaf cooks), pitichi (piti cooks), kebabchi (kebab cooks), chaychi (tea masters), halvachi (halva makers), confectioners, sherbetdar (sherbet makers). Even today, similar specialists work at our food enterprises. This division of labour increases the variety of each kind of dish. For instance, 200 types of pilaf, thirty types of dolma, and twenty types of lyulya-kebab are known.

The culture of the Azerbaijan kitchen allows for eating with the hands. Our thin types of bread (yukha, sangah, lavash) are used as a spoon to scoop up the liquid part of a dish. The solid parts of the dish are wrapped into this thin bread. Eating with the hands has many advantages.

Each finger has very sensitive nerve endings. Hands can feel and appreciate the warmth and consistency of each dish.

When food is brought to the mouth with a spoon or fork we can burn or freeze our mouth. When eating with the hands, the food is brought to the mouth at nearly body temperature, at which taste receptors and salivation work better. Food eaten with the hands is not rushed, but savoured slowly and chewed carefully. That's why Islam forbids hot foods and recommends eating food warm, at a more normal temperature.

The metal elements in forks and spoons destroy fluoride and iodine, causing teeth to decay.

Eating with the hands forces everyone to observe high standards of hygiene, because you must wash your hands thoroughly. All of these steps make the process of eating something like a little holiday, because it prepares you psychologically to receive the meal. According to tradition, after thoroughly washing your hands, you should dip your fingers into rosewater.

One last important note: in Azerbaijani cuisine what is most important are not particular dishes, pleasant drinks, or fruits. The most important part of our kitchen is the guest, who stands at the heart of the Azerbaijani kitchen.

So, welcome! Be our guest!

Marc Jacobs and Jean Fraikin

Belgium

Endives, Brussels sprouts and other innovations

The official version of history recounts in its own way how modern nations were created. A recent study has pertinently shown that the modern nation is "born" as soon as a given number of individuals determined to prove its existence declare that it does exist.[1] Since the eighteenth century, the modern state has been viewed as a broad community united by links no longer characterised by a policy of dynastic succession (marriage and inheritance) or by armed conflict between princes and kings.

Under the old system, for instance, a state of Burgundy was created in the fifteenth century under the dukes. This was a mosaic of independent principalities brought together as minor local dynasties were extinguished, land was purchased, marriages were entered into and favourable circumstances prevailed. When the Duchy of Burgundy first came into being, successive monarchs put together a powerful state comprising *la Comté* (Franche-Comté) and, with the exception of the episcopal principality of Liège, the territories which currently comprise Belgium and the Netherlands.

With the death of the last Duke, Charles the Bold (Charles le Téméraire), at the gates of Nancy in 1477 during a battle against a coalition from Switzerland, Alsace and Lorraine led by René II of Anjou, the fate of the provinces of the Somme, Artois and Burgundy was sealed: they were seized by the King of France. By marrying Maximilian of Austria, one of the Hapsburgs, Charles the Bold's heir managed to save the rest of his inheritance. However, "by taking the hand of Maximilian in marriage,… Mary of Burgundy left Belgium without a dynasty of its own until the contemporary period".[2] Their grandson Charles Quint, who had been born in Ghent, in the south of the Low Countries, inherited Franche-Comté, fulfilling the wish expressed by his aunt, Margaret of Austria, that these two provinces should be kept together so that the name of the house of Burgundy was not lost. It was the first region of

75

Europe to experience the (dis)advantages of remote government from "Brussels", although it did preserve a certain amount of autonomy. Franche-Comté was attached to France under Louis XIV, and it is almost impossible now to imagine that the two Burgundies were not always part of France.

Large numbers of nations emerged during the nineteenth century. Their successful formation was described by Thiesse as depending on certain vital ingredients: "a history which establishes continuity with their great ancestors, a number of heroes who were paragons of the national virtues, a language, cultural monuments, folk traditions, [historic] sites and typical landscape, a particular mentality, official symbols (anthem and flag) and picturesque identifying features: dress, culinary specialities or an emblematic animal".[3]

While food-related identities are not of vital importance, they do still have a role to play. It has been observed that there is a complex relationship between national emergence and modernisation: according to Bruegel and Laurioux, "founding a new national state also means creating its cuisine, but not necessarily on the basis of the ancestral traditions just referred to. When such a state emerges by chance, the cuisine created to go with it is shaped as much by other people's view as by a re-evaluation of these traditions, and the case of Belgium is illuminating in this respect".[4]

Belgium is a federal state made up of communities and regions.[5] The "community" concept refers to the persons therein and the ties which bind them, that is their language and culture, and this extends to their cuisine. Belgium straddles the Germanic and Latin

Irène Sweijd, "Moules-titude", installation at the exhibition "A table?", Galerie de Prêt d'Œuvres d'Art, Bruxelles, September 2003. ©Irène Sweijd, Photograph © by GPOA

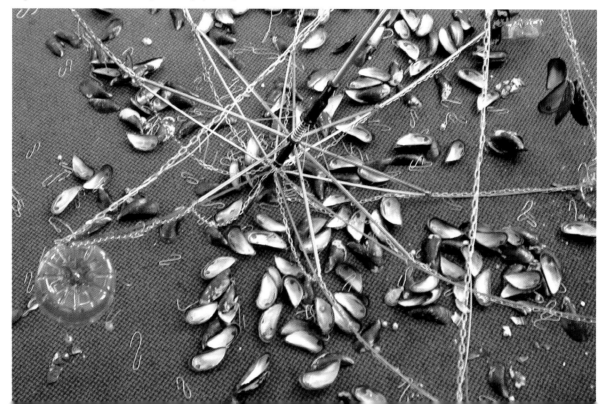

cultures and has three official languages, Dutch, French and German. It therefore has three communities: Flemish, French and German-speaking, each representing a population group. In theory (these two small words are important), as the communities' governments are responsible for culture, they must be responsible now, in the twenty-first century, for a culinary policy, connected with (the building of) a regional identity. The questions which arise are: is there such a thing as Belgian, Flemish or Walloon cuisine, and is there a "Burgundian" (bourguignon) style of cooking?

Belgian cuisine

Once the 1830 Revolution had put an end to the union with the Netherlands created under the Treaty of Vienna in the aftermath of the fall of Napoleon, newly independent Belgium embarked on the process of creating for itself a national feeling and a national identity. Initially, it was highly successful. Not because of its language, but thanks to the majority of its elite groups, which were keen to live in a modern, liberal state which was neither France nor the Netherlands. Through the nineteenth and, in particular, the twentieth century, language and a feeling of being "different" played a significant part in the division between French and Flemish speakers.

Now we come to the question of cuisine. We realise the extent to which chips are identified with Belgian cooking (except in America, where they are known as "French fries"). One of our top culinary history experts drew up a list of food-related identities and raised the question of whether this "dish" had the same status as goulash in Hungary, a national symbol since the 1870s, and now an indicator of patriotic identity. Although chips have become omnipresent in fast food establishments worldwide, Belgians are aware of their own reputation for the consumption of chips. Belgian cuisine, however, as featured in numerous books published recently both in Belgium and abroad, rarely includes chips. The authors have preferred to focus more on the originality of Belgian specialities, on refined Belgian cuisine, on Belgians' love of food, on the generous portions served, on the country's fine chocolate and on its small breweries' beers. All these mean that Belgian food and drink undeniably deserve to be described as "rich".[6]

A culinary revolution took place in the eighteenth century, suggesting "a return to the natural, without too much cooking", thanks to La Varenne's famous work, *Le cuisinier françois*, published in Brussels in 1697, followed by his *Le cuisinier familier*, describing two specialities of Brussels, fricadelles and carbonnades.[7] Since then, Belgium's upper middle classes have been very keen on French cuisine, particularly as served in the restaurants of Paris. As soon as Belgium became a state, many French chefs and restaurateurs moved to Brussels, where their celebrated gastronomy became the norm. Proof of this situation was provided by the 1880 Exhibition marking Belgium's fifty years of existence, where the absence of references to traditional dishes typical of Belgium showed that such dishes lacked any influence on patriotic feeling and, more prosaically, on gourmet restaurants or their popular counterparts. The 1910 Baedeker, a German guide, said that the great restaurants of Brussels (by then imitating such celebrated chefs as Carême and Escoffier) served "excellent French cuisine, accompanied by good Bordeaux and Burgundy wines".

It was on the occasion of the 1910 Universal Exhibition that a major shift became evident, with the invention of what may be called Belgian cuisine,

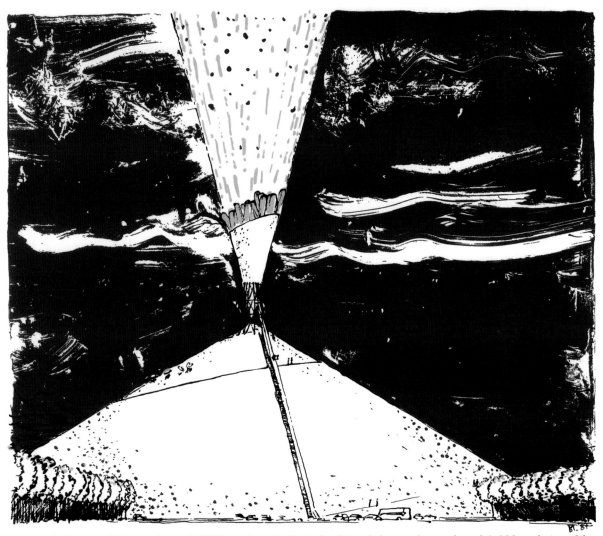

Bernard Maquet, "Frites géantes" ("Giant chips"), limited edition lithograph, numbered 1-100 and signed by the Concours Terril et l'Exposition Mines, Faculté Polytechnique de Mons, Ecole des Mines, 1987

consisting of regional dishes widespread in the early years of the century. This developed further after the First World War, when, in particular, the terminology used for advertising, on menus, in tourist guides and in specialist publications changed. These innovations stemmed from an expansion of middle-class culinary culture at popular restaurants and from the development of a more sophisticated cuisine. During the first half of the twentieth century, the names of Belgian regions and cities proliferated on menus, as did local specialities on dining tables. Waterzooi à la gantoise was a typical example reflecting the situation in Belgium, with a Flemish speciality (à la gantoise = Ghent-style) being given a French-sounding name. Between the two world wars, restaurants served huge numbers of regional dishes with patriotic connotations, but this did not stop French influence from continuing to dominate.

After the Second World War, the culinary synthesis between Belgium and France grew, although local traditions were maintained. The 1957 Michelin Guide noted that "regional food has put up heroic resistance, and the Walloon and Flemish provinces are proud of their specialities". This culinary medley – a rich regional cuisine coexisting with a deluxe international cuisine – has given Belgium its image as a country characterised by diversity and abundance in its food and drink. There is no dish identified with the Belgian nation as a whole.[8]

Inventions

Since early 2004, the federal government's official website[9] has encapsulated and presented Belgium's culture under seven headings, one of which is its gastronomy. This last-named category encompasses six key words: gastronomy (a brief survey), gin, frites (chips), waffles, pralines (Belgian chocolates) and speculoos (biscuits). The five sub-categories covered are regional specialities, the endive, chocolate, personalities (chefs who hold three Michelin stars) and beer.

This presentation has its entertaining side, as well as being educational, showing that, at an advanced stage of the state formation process, the stage at which federalisation has already taken place and a large number of central government responsibilities have been transferred to the regional and community tiers, food-related identities have taken on some importance. A good example is that of the endive, also known as the witloof (literally: white leaf), for its discovery is reputedly directly linked to the key date of 1830. "There is some mystery about the origin of the endive. The traditional belief is that this Belgian vegetable was discovered by chance during the period when Belgium was acquiring its independence. During the upheaval of the September 1830 Revolution, Jan Lammers, a farmer from Schaarbeek, fled from his land, and, when he returned to the farm, noticed with amazement that white leaves had grown from the chicory roots which he had left in his cellar under a layer of earth." Se non è vero…The story, headed "Witloof or Belgian endives, Belgium's white gold", is a typical example of fiction giving rise to a kind of national folklore connected with the myths about the origins of a state. Sometimes the farmer's name is different, that of Jean Brammers, and several variations on the story have been circulated to give it greater local colour, showing that Belgium's white gold also has an explicit link with the concept of "invention". As though we were in the realms of literature, the same source mentions the "invention" of the endive in the mid-nineteenth century in the cellars beneath the Botanical Garden in Brussels, where Mr Breziers, chief horticulturalist, managed to produce white or yellow leaves related to wild chicory. Having placed the roots vertically side-by-side, he covered them with a mixture of earth and manure before watering them. The first shoots of endives are reported soon to have come through. Other foods which people associate with Belgium have also fallen victim to similar accounts, mixtures of historical facts and fable, which can also be found on websites and in tourist guides. The history of the Brussels sprout provides another example. It is part of Belgium's "heritage". In the second half of the twentieth century, the heritage concept was extended to monuments and sites, and another extension to include the intangible (ethnological) heritage has occurred in the early twenty-first century. Legends, know-how and recipes have come to be regarded as parts of the intangible heritage.

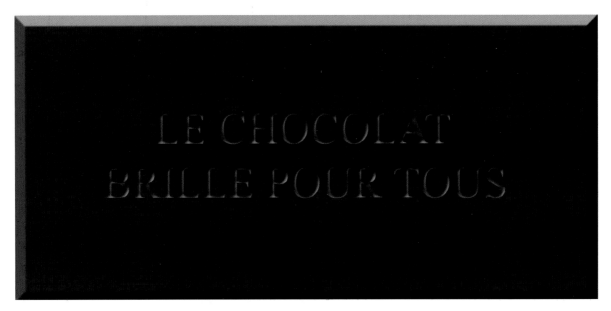

Jean Lucien Guillaume, Série "les tablettes virtuelles" ("Virtual tablet" series), numbered 1-10 and signed, ENBA pôle estampes, 2003. ©Jean Lucien Guillaume

Ancient and more recent traditions which can be traced back are now regarded as forms of intangible heritage. Attention can be drawn here to another dimension of the subject: the great importance, if we wish to understand the food-related identities of the regions of Europe and the world, of rituals marking the cycles of life and the times of year, of rites of passage and of festivals held at certain moments of transition. Food and drink often play a central role in devised ("invented") customs both ancient and modern.

The concept of "invented traditions" first saw the light of day in one of the most famous works of social history and ethnology published in the past twenty years, Eric Hobsbawm and Terence Ranger's

The invention of tradition. It was not by chance that 1 May was declared to be Labour Day, the first modern Olympics were held, and the first F. A. Cup Final and Tour de France took place before the First World War. The period 1870-1914 in Europe may be regarded as one in which traditions were "mass-produced". These innovations stemmed from the style of government and control practised by states and the holders of political and social authority in the face of social change. New ways of governing and instilling loyalty had to be found. The ensuing invention of "political" traditions became conscious and calculated once institutions of political scope had largely come to accept that deliberate invention in accordance with public expectations was guaranteed to be successful.[10]

Living the "Burgundian" life in Belgium

The invention of traditions, drawing on the national and international, local and regional influences and customs which shape food culture in the broad sense, is a process which has continued in the twenty-first century. Research in this sphere is only just beginning, but has already opened up some interesting possibilities in terms of identities, practices and other food-related behaviour.

In Brussels, Wallonia and Flanders, tourist offices are currently running an active campaign centred on gastronomy, which nowadays draws tourists. Noticeable differences are sometimes found, clearly connected with linguistic sensitivities and language.

Advertising material issued by the Wallonia/Brussels Community tourist office, which focuses on the capital city, highlights its restaurants. Wallonia is better known for its nature, with its gastronomy taking second place. The wording used makes you feel quite hungry: "Make no mistake, the good life in the Ardennes means eating and drinking well. Some parts of Wallonia, both within the capital city and elsewhere, could be compared to the Milky Way, so many stars do their restaurants have in their galaxy". The third characteristic emphasised is the human warmth which helps to give the Ardennes their reputation: "Excesses at carnival time accurately reflect the conviviality of the Ardennes. Our hoteliers in both town and country make every effort to translate this conviviality into unfailing hospitality. It is not a Wallonian habit to offer a cold, severe, impersonal welcome." Thus references to the concepts of tradition and heritage are highlighted, alongside the aspects of well-being and the comforts of life.

The agencies responsible for promoting tourism in the Flanders region, provinces and cities issue some quite outstanding advertisements. The region's attractions are marketed mainly to its neighbours in the Netherlands. A special word has been coined for Belgian cuisine and, by extension, for the Belgian way of life. The word is bourgondisch. This is rendered in French by bourguignon, which means Burgundian, or Burgundy-style, but the alternative translation into French means "abundant", and, when applied to a person, it implies that he or she knows how to live well and is a *bon vivant* comparable to the people of Burgundy. But the thing which amazes Dutch speakers is that most French speakers, even in Belgium, are unaware of this association between "Burgundian", meaning abundant, and "Belgian". Belgians' way of life, especially their way of eating, is often described in the Netherlands as Burgundian, which is the adjective preferred by the Dutch press and people when they refer to their neighbour's cuisine.

The Flemish tourist offices do not miss the opportunity to cultivate this image. The province of Antwerp has published a tourist guide entitled "Bourgondisch genieten" (savouring Burgundian delights). Even the Wallonian government has issued Dutch-language material using the same word. In September 1998, for instance, a tourism fair called Bourgondisch Wallonië was held in the Nekkershal in Mechelen.

The Flemish newspapers have readily taken up this term, which has become an integral part of the region's culture. It crops up regularly. One example was an article under the headline Bourgondisch België (Burgundian Belgium) published in a business daily (the Financieel-Economische Tijd) on 17 August 2001, which said that the country's typical Burgundian culture was an important asset for attracting firms and investors, making business people aware that Belgium was an unparalleled gastronomic paradise at prices bearing no comparison with those of Paris and London. It also pointed out that it was not all beer and chocolate. Political circles unhesitatingly took up the term, with the Flemish Minister for Welfare proudly stating: "I am a Burgundian. The only regular feature of my diet is a beer from a Trappist brewery accompanied by peanuts".[11] Similarly, an animal rights campaigner has confessed to living "Burgundy-style" and to having, in spite of being a vegetarian, bones covered by more than just the skin some people expect vegetarians to have.[12]

The Belgian expression, a "Burgundy-style government", refers to one very far removed from the Dutch governments which confine themselves to egg salad rolls or ham or cheese on toast. "Burgundian" is a term which also means copious, or can be applied to

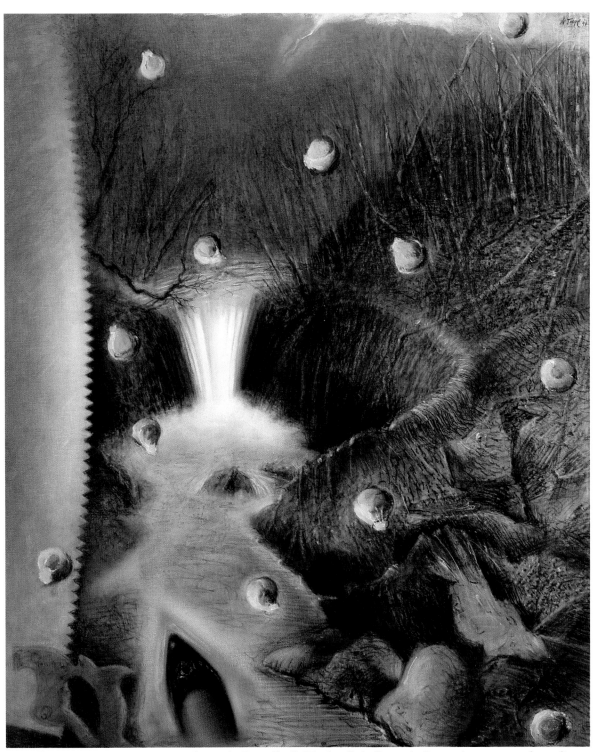

Camille De Taeye, "Douze petits choux de Bruxelles" (Twelve little Brussels Sprouts), crayon and acrylic on linen, 100 x 81 cm, 1994

people with a good appetite. There is no confusion between this concept and that of "haute cuisine, with a piece of meat hidden behind a single pea".[13] The metaphor is applied even to the royal family: in 1998, when Prince Philippe went to the Netherlands and visited an Albert Heyn supermarket in Purmerend (North Holland) which had organised a promotional week featuring Belgian products, the local people said: "He needs a bit of weight on him, your prince. He's so thin that he is not a good advertisement for Burgundian Belgium".[14] Less certain is whether to agree unreservedly with a well-known photographer who traces the links with Burgundy back to the union of Marguerite de Male and Philip the Bold (Philippe le Hardi) in 1369, which sealed the alliance between Flanders and Burgundy, amidst much rejoicing during which Beaune wine flowed freely.[15] The uncertainty relates to a long-standing ally of France, the former principality of Liège, the capital city of which was sacked and laid to waste 100 years later by its implacable enemy, Charles the Bold (Charles le Téméraire).

A few years ago, a Flemish newspaper food critic wrote an article headed "A cuisine without a label. Eating with the true Burgundians". The article compared the culinary art of the French province of Burgundy with "family cooking based on recipes handed down from mother to daughter". One expert from the region[17] did not approve, disputing the Burgundian origin of the best-known dishes, saying that wherever there were cows, boeuf bourguignon

was served. In contrast, the wines of Burgundy (Chablis, Côte d'Or, Chalonnais, Mâconnais and Beaujolais) have an excellent reputation and are well marketed. Flanders is taking a more romantic look at its past, remembering historical Burgundian exploits, opulent feasts given by the Dukes who had ruled the greater part of Belgium, and the "golden age" of Charles Quint.

Such reminiscences of times long past do not prevent people's mindset from changing. Things are changing

Philibert Delécluse "Etre mangé?" ("Be eaten?") created for the exhibition "A table?", Galerie de prêt d'Œuvres d'Art, Bruxelles, September 2003.
© Philibert Delécluse, photo credit GPOA

before our eyes, and our attention is drawn to the future behaviour of Flanders and Wallonia, where innovations tracing identity proliferate every year. Many lessons will be able to be learned from the way in which the concept of intangible heritage develops and the fate which will befall it as a result of an affirmed policy of cultural identity. There has been a glimpse of this developing tendency recently. Numerous popular events take place in Wallonia, with impressive processions, picturesque carnivals and traditional shows being converted into vehicles for the promotion of local products to tourists. Yet the festivals of Wallonia and of the French and German-speaking communities do not offer platforms for identity-based nationalism, and even less so for inclinations towards greater independence or a stronger attachment. Without forgetting to celebrate the centuries-old popular festivals, Flanders has brought culinary culture into the political world. Steve Stevaert, a chef who had moved from his post as a regional minister to the chairmanship of the Flemish socialist party, published a cookbook in 2003 entitled *Koken met Steve* (*Cooking with Steve*), in which he also expressed his views about the importance of cookery in contemporary society. The "national day" of Flanders, 11 July, was chosen by reference to the Battle of the Golden Spurs, in which the French cavalry was defeated on the plains of Courtrai in 1302, a century before the period of domination of the Duchy of Burgundy. This day was successfully commemorated in 2002 with a "celebration vouchers" campaign and with street barbecues financed by the Flemish government, providing evidence of the emergence of a new tradition.

1. Thiesse, A-M., *La création des identités nationales*. Europe XVIII-XXe siècle, Paris, Seuil, 2001, p. 14.
2. Pirenne, H., *Histoire de Belgique*, Vol. III, Brussels, 1907, p. 23.
3. Thiesse, A-M., op. cit., p. 14.
4. Bruegel, M. and Laurioux, B. (eds.), *Histoire et identités alimentaires en Europe, Introduction*, Paris, Hachette, 2002, pp. 9-19.
5. <www.belgium.be>
6. Scholliers, P., *L'invention d'une cuisine belge. Restaurants et sentiments nationaux dans un jeune État*, 1830-1930, Bruegel, M. and Laurioux, B. (eds.), op. cit., pp. 151-168, p. 153.
7. Plouvier, L., "D'Anthime à Pierre Wynants. Mille cinq cents ans de gastronomie dans la Communauté française", *Vu d'ici*, No 13, Brussels, Ministère de la Communauté française, 2004, p. 29.
8. In the words of Peter Scholliers, Professor at the Vrije Universiteit, Brussels.
9. <www.belgium.be>.
10. Hobsbawm, E., "Mass-Producing Traditions: Europe, 1870-1914", in Hobsbawm, E. and Ranger, T. (eds.), *The invention of tradition*, Cambridge University Press, Cambridge, 1999, pp. 263-308.
11. *Het laatste Nieuws*, 16 February 2002.
12. *Het Belang van Limburg*, 19 January 2002.
13. *Het Belang van Limburg*, 24 April 2002.
14. *De Standaard*, 10 November 1998.
15. Michiel Hendryckx, in *De Standaard*, 16 August 2003.
16. *De Morgen*, 4 November 2000.
17. Alain Franck, from the Ecole du vin de Beaune.

Nenad Tanović

Bosnia and Herzegovina

The mouth is small but it can swallow a mountain

If the eyes are the windows of the soul, then the food people eat is an image of their character. There are dishes that fill our stomachs but do not satisfy our hunger, and those that satisfy our hunger but do not overly fill our stomachs. There are also dishes that fill our soul and those that make us happy. And if in most cases character is destiny, then the cuisine of a people tells the true history of its creators.

The cuisine of Bosnia and Herzegovina mirrors our character. If we ascribe human characteristics to ingredients used in dishes, as is sometimes done in fairy tales, than a dish can unerringly describe the people who prepare and eat it, the geography of the area they inhabit, the breath of the mountain and the speech of the river, the silence of the prairie and still-ness of the forest, the glow of the sun, the bite of winter and the sound of rain. There are few countries like Bosnia and Herzegovina that have both mountains and the sea, pastures and forests, a multitude of lakes and rivers, prairies and canyons all within a 200 km

radius. It is incredible that rivers with springs on two sides of the same mountain travel to different seas, the Adriatic and the Black Sea. In Bosnia and Herzegovina, grapes and figs grow on the southern side of mountain ranges, while the northern side is covered with thick evergreen forests full of game. In this country grow oranges and lemons, pomegranates and olives, laurel trees and peaches, potatoes and cabbage, wheat, rye, corn, plums and apricots, apples and kiwi. Here, in the summertime, the sun leaves its traces in the fragrant plants and flowers. One thing is certain: here beauty does not abide in one place alone. There are more than twenty types of honey here and three types of milk (cow's milk, sheep's milk, goat's milk), a multitude of cheeses, and bread made out of wheat, corn, oats, beans and rye.

In Bosnia and Herzegovina there is no national cui-sine, but rather a traditional one. You will never see a restaurant bearing a sign that proclaims it to be Bosnian, Croatian, Serbian, Hungarian or Turkish.

Many dishes that did not originate in Bosnia and Herzegovina, whose oriental or western origin is undisputed, have over time acquired characteristics that differentiate them from the same dishes prepared in the East (Persia, Turkey) or in the West (Austria, Italy, Hungary). The cuisine, or, to be more precise, the traditional culinary art of Bosnia and Herzegovina is based on the culinary skill of the people of Bosnia and Herzegovina, which combines their own cultural elements with foreign recipes, thereby endowing them with a specific stamp characteristic of Bosnia and Herzegovina.

Because the culinary art of the medieval Bosnian kingdom was confined to the noblemen's castles, we can say that the year 1462 marks the birth of traditional cuisine in Bosnia and Herzegovina. That was the year when the first aščinca, a restaurant for the townspeople, was opened. We do not have precise evidence about the contents of the menu at the time. However, we do know that 400 years later the variety of meals available throughout the year in an aščinca in any larger town in Bosnia and Herzegovina spanned over 200 different dishes. The common characteristics of these dishes are:

– Bosnian cuisine contains an abundance of vegetables, meat, fruit, milk and dairy products;
– the dishes are not made with a browned-flour base (roux), and strong or hot spices are not used. When spices are used, only very small amounts are added to the food so that the taste of meat is not diminished;

– cooked dishes are light because they are prepared in small amounts of water and cooked in their own natural juices, without a roux. The resulting sauce thus has a minimal amount of oriental spices. As a rule, quality dishes are not prepared in fat but are boiled in the juices of cooked meat, which is rich in proteins, and the juices of vegetables;
– roasts and many pies, both sweet and savoury, are popular;
– broths and soups are practically compulsory;
– a wide range of sweets are available.

The function of the traditional large hearth (measuring 2-4 metres in length, 1.20 metres in width and 1.5 metres in height) in the aščinca, as well as in the bakeries where most dishes were prepared, was twofold. New dishes could be quickly prepared on the hearth and other dishes could finish cooking, so that that area also served as a kind of visible menu. The dishes were laid out on plates on the hearth, for which only wood or charcoal was used, so that they were kept continually warm and the customer could choose which dish he wanted and in what quantity.

The hearth in an aščinca consists of three parts. The first is a burner with very hot fires. There are three troughs 20 cm to 30 cm wide and 20 cm to 40 cm deep into which embers are poured or charcoal is burned. Some dishes are quickly prepared here, while others finish cooking and are kept warm. In addition to the dishes there are sauces which are mixed in for flavouring. The skill of a chef is measured by the

©Zlatan Filipovic

quality of these sauces and the way he uses them in different dishes.

The second is a compartment for plates. The hearth also serves as a warming table because all of the plates are warmed there at a steady temperature. Here the dishes are also arranged into individual servings.

The third is a cauldron. It is used for cooking soups and broths and for keeping them warm.

The kitchen of the aščinca was situated behind the room where food was served. It consisted of an area where the dishes were prepared and the kitchen hearth where the fires were kept burning and the final touches were added to the dishes. Above the hearth were pothooks from which cauldrons hung, while on the hearth itself was a small clay oven for preparing roasts and pies. One corner was designated for the making and drying of pastry dough; next to it was an area for brewing coffee. Since most towns in Bosnia and Herzegovina had running water, the kitchen also had a separate area for the washing and drying of dishes. Apart from these rooms the aščinca also had a

place for drying, smoking and curing meat, adjacent to a room containing the butcher's tools. There was usually a cold storage room located in the cellar where food was kept and preserved. The bakery, which was separate from the aščinca, was used for the baking of different types of pastries, as well as cakes and pies and dishes prepared in pots. Once the bread and pastries were baked the fire in the bakery hearth was kept burning so that other dishes could be cooked on this low heat.

Larger aščinca as well as karavansarajs (hotels) had large trays with small samples of the dishes and many spoons so that the guest could try each dish. A different spoon was used for the sampling of each dish, and a bowl of water was provided for the immediate disposal of used spoons.

Surviving historical data tells us that during celebrations, weddings, gatherings and picnics all ethnic groups used the same rich and varied menu consisting of twelve to thirty different dishes.

Let us have a look at some of these historical menus.

Sarajevo feast

1. Poached eggs with minced meat and a side dish of soup with dumplings
2. Broth (Sarajevo broth, Bay's broth etc.)
3. Stuffed turkey with a side dish of beef stew with bread
4. Sarajevo baklava and cakes
5. Okra
6. Spinach pie
7. Minced meat pie
8. Fruit gelatine
9. Stuffed grape leaves
10. Noodles served with olives or radishes and sour cream)
11. Pilaf (meat with rice and yoghurt)
12. Stewed fruit, rice pudding with cinnamon, saffron and nuts, coffee, nargilehs (water pipes)

Holiday meal in Sarajevo

1. Lamb broth
2. Stew
3. Minced meat pies served with yoghurt
4. Stuffed grape leaves
5. Sweet noodles
6. Okra
7. Spinach pie
8. Stuffed onions
9. Cake
10. Minced meat patties in sauce
11. Chicken pilaf
12. Rice pudding with honey
13. Stewed fruit, coffee, nargilehs and tobacco

or

1. Iced rose juice, cherry preserve, Travnik cheese, almond cakes
2. Broth
3. Poached eggs with minced meat
4. Cakes
5. Okra
6. Stew served with quince
7. Spinach pie
8. Noodles with cream
9. Stuffed vegetables with meat
10. Cold vegetables stuffed with cheese
11. Nougat
12. White pilaf
13. Iced stewed cherries, nargilehs, tobacco and coffee

Travnik, a city in central Bosnia and a long-time seat of the Vizier, had a somewhat different order of dishes. Here are sample menus for a wedding and a holiday in Travnik:

Wedding menu

Soup served with bread or pastry
Travnik dumplings
Travnik stuffed lamb roasted whole in a bakery
Travnik stuffed grape leaves
Bean stew with meat
Stew or "Bosnian pot"
Travnik stuffed peppers
Bošaluk, a minced meat pie specially shaped
for each guest
Okra or Travnik stuffed onions (after minced meat
pies a dish served in a sauce is compulsory).
Baklava (sweet noodles were not usually served in
Travnik as they were considered too simple a dish).
Spinach pie prepared with sour cream or milk
Rice pudding or stewed fruit, coffee, tobacco and nargileh

Holiday menu

Rice soup with dumplings
Veal shank with bread
Spinach or cheese pie
Okra
Travnik minced meat pie
Stuffed onions or Travnik stuffed grape leaves
Baklava or other sweets
Beef stew with prunes
Travnik stuffed peppers
Pies
Pilaf prepared with meat and served with yoghurt
Rice pudding or stewed fruit

Preserved manuscripts reveal to us that these menus were not confined only to the cities and their wealthy population. The menus of wedding celebrations in villages usually consisted of many more dishes (over thirty). The number of dishes is so high because all sorts of pies were prepared in addition to dishes customary in that part of the country. Thus, there are a number of dishes prepared from turnip and pumpkin which are not present on the city menus.

In the rural areas of Herzegovina the menu is somewhat different. Brandy, fruit, cakes and coffee are served at the beginning of each meal and not at the end, as is customary in other parts of the country.

Herzegovina feast

1. Vine brandy, cakes, fruit

2. Coffee

3. Broth

4. Stuffed grape leaves

5. Cooked meat

6. Roast and salad served with Herzegovinan wine

Today, the modern pace of life has suppressed the values of traditional cuisine and imposed, as a standard, readymade meals, microwave ovens and fast-food restaurants. However, in Bosnia and Herzegovina housewives still, at least on weekends, prepare some

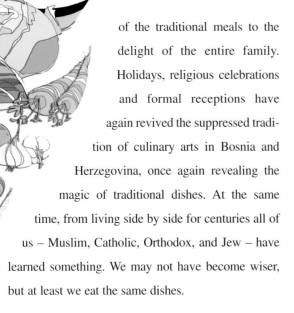

©Zlatan Filipovic

of the traditional meals to the delight of the entire family. Holidays, religious celebrations and formal receptions have again revived the suppressed tradition of culinary arts in Bosnia and Herzegovina, once again revealing the magic of traditional dishes. At the same time, from living side by side for centuries all of us – Muslim, Catholic, Orthodox, and Jew – have learned something. We may not have become wiser, but at least we eat the same dishes.

One of the few dishes from the treasury of traditional cuisine that is actually named after our country is the so-called "Bosnian pot". Both the name and the dish are full of meaning. The tastiness of the dish depends equally on the ingredients used and on the amount of time spent preparing it. Today, all over Bosnia and Herzegovina there are many variations of the "Bosnian pot", which use different meats, vegetables or spices characteristic of different regions of the country. There is, for example, the "butcher's pot", in which the proportion of meat is greater and in more variety than in the traditional dish. Cinnamon sticks are also added for flavor. The "Semberian Bosnian pot" is prepared with mixed meat, that is mutton and pork, a spoonful of grease or butter on the bottom of the pot, peas in addition to the standard vegetables, equal amounts of wine and water, and bay leaf as an extra spice. The "Mostar Bosnian pot" contains mutton, lamb or veal, butter or grease. After a few hours

of simmering, vegetables mixed with rice are added, and the dish is left to simmer for another hour and a half or two. The "spicy Bosnian pot" is prepared with much fattier meat, more garlic (two to three more cloves) and more onion, as well as vinegar mixed with water. The "carp Bosnian pot" is prepared using carp (1 kilogram) and 100 grams of fat. The carp is cleaned, cut diagonally into steaks, salted and left to stand. After the pot has simmered for four to five hours it is taken out of the oven, the upper layer of vegetables is pushed to the side, and the carp is added to the centre. The fish is then covered by the vegetables, and the pot is returned to the oven to bake for another fifteen minutes. The "hunters' Bosnian pot" is prepared using various types of marinated game. There is also the "Bosnian pot with kebab", when the traditional dish is served in an aščinca accompanied by two kebabs.

The origin of this stew is Bosnian. Bosnia is rich in ores, and the medieval miners who worked hard to extract these ores had to prepare their own food. Their workday lasted twelve or more hours, and so at least six hours would pass before they could have their first meal. The mining was mostly done on the surface, so the miners would make a common hearth close to the work site. Marking their individual pots, they would leave them on the hearth. Since the dish did not require too much attention, each individual or group of miners simply had to keep their eye on the pot. It is also important to point out that this dish is good when reheated, so the miners would not only cook for a number of people but also for a number of days.

The "Bosnian pot" has kept its original simplicity and "philosophy" to this day, a philosophy that is important to understanding this most basic dish of Bosnian cuisine. The hot pot more or less cooks itself, simmering on a low fire. It is a communal dish, whose taste and aroma are better when the dish is prepared for a larger group of people, not just for one person. The "Bosnian pot" is all about sharing.

By providing you with this recipe we wish to share with you the joy of good food. We know that our parents' genetic code will determine the colour of our hair, whether we will be tall or short, or have blue or brown eyes. However, we also know that the food we eat will determine our health and our happiness. Let this dish be a pearl of happiness in your necklace of health.

The "Bosnian pot"

Ingredients (for four persons):
800 g quality beef (entrecote steak or meat from the shank, breast or flank),
600 g of potatoes, 20 g salt
1 dl quality white wine (or half a decilitre of wine vinegar), 1 dl water,
150 g onions, 200 g string beans
8 cloves garlic (approximately 20 g),
a few tomatoes, 16 grains pepper,
100 g carrots, 30 g parsley leaves,
20 g celery, 12 cloves, gauze and string (or parchment paper and string)
(In the winter when there are no fresh vegetables, uveā [pickled vegetables] are used along with potatoes, dried parsley and other available vegetables.)

Preparation:
All of the vegetables are thoroughly washed and cut into cubes, except for the garlic that will be used in whole cloves. Large onions are cut diagonally and smaller ones are chopped. The meat is cut into pieces weighing from 80 to 100 grams. The potatoes are peeled and cut into halves or quarters depending on their size. Smaller potatoes are used whole.
Layers of vegetables and layers of meat are arranged one on top of the other in the pot, making sure that the vegetable layers contain all of the vegetables as well as the spices.

The pot is never filled to the brim, leaving the upper part of the pot free so that the ingredients can simmer. If we do not want to put the spices (garlic, peppers and cloves) directly into the dish we can place them into the gauze, which serves as a bag and allows us to remove the spices once the dish is cooked. Once the ingredients have been placed in layers, white wine is poured over them and chopped tomatoes are added. In the winter when there is a shortage of tomatoes tomato concentrate diluted with water and vinegar can be added. If vinegar is used, then water must be added instead of the wine.
After the ingredients have been arranged the pot is covered with parchment paper or cloth fixed in place with string. The pot is put into the oven, or sometimes the bakery hearth, to be cooked at a high temperature. The heat is later lowered and the pot is left to simmer for the entire night, or for at least four to five hours. During the cooking process, the dish must not be allowed to boil but only to simmer. The rule is simple: the longer the dish is allowed to simmer, the better and tastier it will be.
If the dish is prepared with baby beef or veal (fatter varieties of meat), then only one decilitre of white wine is added, and the bones from the meat are put onto the bottom of the pot.
The dish is best served in individual small clay pots for each person, or in a sahan (a copper dish with a lid).

Rayna Gavrilova

Bulgaria

Golden fruits from the orchards

Once upon a time, there was a man who had three sons. He was a not a rich man, but he had one priceless treasure: an apple tree, which bore one golden apple each year. And each year a vicious dragon stole the golden apple the moment it was ripe. Finally, the man ordered his three sons to take turns, stand watch by the apple tree, and guard the precious fruit.

This is the beginning of one of the most popular Bulgarian folk tales, *The three brothers and the golden apple*. The unfolding of the tale is predictable: failure and success, horrors and heroic exploits, competition and friendship, betrayal and loyalty, upper and nether worlds. By the end, the dragon is slain, the golden apple shines on top of the tree, and the youngest brother marries the princess. An attentive analysis of the tale reveals worlds of meanings and offers a shortcut to the heart of Bulgarian popular mythology, traditional ethics and appreciation of beauty. And the golden apple stands as a strong and clear symbol: it is the incarnation of well being.

The text that follows is an attempt to present a glimpse of Bulgarian culture and identity as reflected in the consumption and perception of fruits. The choice is not arbitrary and some rationale will be provided below. We can note at the outset that for a land with 8 000 years of tradition in growing crops, the fruits of the earth have acquired a very special place not only in the Bulgarian diet, but also in our culture in general. This story could be told about different crops: wheat, for instance, or grapes, or the humble cabbage, the life saviour during long vitamin-less winters. But I have chosen to select a few golden fruits: the apple, the apricot and peach, and the tomato for their rich symbolism and appealing taste, as well as for the fact that they also tell another story: the story of change, of the historical movement of people, ideas and objects; the story of difference and integration, of openness and adaptation.

The apple is by far the oldest member of this group. The apple tree is indigenous to south-eastern Europe, and even today one can see dwarf-like wild apple trees with their dark crooked twigs and lush green leaves in many parts of Bulgaria. The wild fruit is small with a tart, even bitter, taste and a wonderful aroma. The seeds of the apples are too small to be preserved in the archaeological sites, yet it is certain that even prehistoric man fed on wild apples, among other fruits and berries. The apple tree was cultivated with the beginning of agriculture, and over the centuries a number of local varieties were developed.

In traditional Bulgarian cuisine, the apple is consumed primarily raw, as a desert or between meals. Before industrial preservation, refrigeration, canning, waxing and ethylene treatment, apples were stored for the winter in barrels or buried in straw. Many elderly Bulgarians jokingly complained, "We were eating rotten apples during the entire winter", since the good housekeeper would regularly check the stock and pull out the fruits that had begun to spoil. The fact remains, however, that pre-modern man escaped scurvy only thanks to the apple, along with other preserved fruits and vegetables, such as grapes, onions, cucumbers, carrots, and cabbages.

A tastier way to preserve and consume apples outside of the growing season was drying. Nowadays, in almost every Bulgarian village on a serene and sunny September day one can see trays with apples, plums and pears drying under the mild sun. Here is the way to prepare and eat this specialty.

To make Oshaf: on a nice and sunny late summer-early autumn day, cut ripe, flawless apples into wedges without removing the seeds or the peel. Spread the wedges on a tray and expose them for a week to direct sunlight. The pieces will turn brownish-yellow, shrink and become very hard. Store them in a container. On a cold winter evening, put a cup of dried fruits in one litre of water and boil until soft. Add honey and cinnamon (optional). Let it cool and drink by the fireplace.

The apple did not appear in recipes or fancy preparations. It had a beauty of its own, standing out as something much more complex than merely something to eat. In the rather prudish style of Bulgarian folk songs, the most daring erotic moment occurred with the symbolic mention of an apple, which united gustatory and sexual pleasures. The longing for the beloved was compared to the pleasure of tasting a fresh and juicy apple. One might speculate that the Biblical story about the primordial sin involving an apple and temptation influenced the perception of the apple as something standing meaningfully between man and woman. Elements of the Bulgarian matrimonial cycle seem to reaffirm this relation. The traditional wedding in Bulgaria included three separate acts: the "asking" of the maiden, the official betrothal, and the wedding ceremony itself. Although there were some regional variations, invariably the apple had some role to play – the matchmaker and the parents of the groom offered an apple and a golden coin during their visits to the house of the bride, which can be read as a symbolic request for being granted the love of the bride in exchange for an official matrimony. On the wedding day the procession from the groom's house to

Bulgarian girl

Bulgaria

the bride's and then to the church was led by a person carrying a banner with an apple stuck on the shaft.

The late nineteenth and the twentieth centuries brought a lot of change to the apple: the Viennese strudel and the American apple pie; canned apple pectin and commercially sold dried apples were among the new ways of bringing this fruit to the table. The apple acquired some powerful rivals, among them the orange, the new golden fruit known to Bulgarians as "portokal", the fruit from Portugal. For quite some time the orange was regarded as an interesting gift to bring from abroad as souvenir. After a century of change, in one of those strange twists in culinary development, the most popular brand of apples on the Bulgarian market today is the "Golden delicious". The circle is closed, the golden apple of the fairy tales returns to our tables every day.

In 1396, the Ottoman Turks conquered the Bulgarian Medieval Kingdom; a century and a half later, all of south-eastern Europe was under Ottoman rule. The existing Greek and Slavic Christian Orthodox world was incorporated into an empire stretching over three continents and ruling over dozens of different peoples. The Ottoman social and cultural system itself was the product of the mingling of several traditions: Turkic nomad culture; Islamic culture; late Byzantine tradition. The Ottoman Turks demonstrated astonishing capability in adopting and adapting different elements into their system and the Ottoman

Empire became a crossroads, the place where East met West and North met South.

Part of this cultural interaction had, of course, to do with food: products, cooking techniques, table manners, recipes and tastes. Rice pilaf and yoghurt, shish kebab and rose-petal jam became part of the local food repertoire. Influences and exchanges were so intense that in some instance it became impossible to ascertain who invented what. (One might recall that half of the Balkan nations call the thick coffee brewed in small pots "Turkish coffee", while Greeks insist on calling it "Greek coffee".) The transformation of the culinary culture in south-eastern Europe starting in the fifteenth century was impressive. As a result, Bulgarian cuisine, in marrying the Slavic, Greek and Turkish traditions, became a treasure of tastes and possibilities.

The Ottoman Turks, great lovers of green gardens and sweet treats, brought to the Balkans many new fruits or better varieties of existing local crops. The melon and the watermelon, the cherry and the sour cherry, the apricot and the peach became so much part of the national cuisine that few would believe they had not belonged to it forever.

The apricot and the peach (in Bulgarian, kaysiya and praskova) came with the Ottoman Turks to find a new home in Bulgaria. They are believed to have been originally cultivated in China and then in Persia, whence the word praskova is derived. Both fruits were (and are) considered primarily a dessert. The dried apricot was a delicacy, offered in the past very much in the same way we offer chocolate truffles today, stuffed with almonds or other nuts. The peach was mostly eaten in season and was difficult to preserve (except rarely in jams or preserves). The peach, however, developed as a powerful aesthetic symbol: its exquisite aroma and delicate texture, the fine down on its pastel-colored skin, reminiscent of the face of fair maidens were probably the reasons why peaches became associated with youth, innocence and beauty. "Fresh as a peach" is a common Bulgarian saying. This "imported" fruit came to be associated with the intrinsic, inherently "Bulgarian" beauty and femininity. The greatest Bulgarian artist, Vladimir Dimitrov the Master, left a series of paintings depicting young Bulgarian women against a background of peaches. The colours, the rhythm, the atmosphere, the calm beauty of the woman and the peach are without a doubt the most extraordinary artistic expression demonstration of the union between the land and the people.

Apricot preserve, a trademark of the good Bulgarian housekeeper during the late nineteenth and the twentieth century, offers a more sensory experience. Carefully prepared up to highest standards of texture, colour and taste, it was offered to afternoon guests on a small crystal plate and eaten with small silver spoon and a glass of water.

Apricot preserve: the apricots used to prepare the preserve should be fully ripe yet firm. Peel the skin carefully. Remove the stone without breaking the fruit into two halves (something like a pencil or a grandma's hairpin should do the job). Soak the small, hollow balls for ten minutes in two litres of water in which a piece of hydrated lime, the size of a walnut, has been dissolved (this helps to firm the flesh and prevent it from falling apart during cooking). Meanwhile, break the stones of the apricots and extract the kernels. Dip them in boiling water for a few minutes, then peel the skin. (Some of them might have a bitter taste, but this is part of the surprise for the palate). Take the apricot out of the lime solution and insert one nut into each fruit. In a large pan, bring to a boil 1kg of sugar and 600 ml of water (per 1 kg of fruit). Put the apricots in the boiling syrup one by one and cook until the syrup thickens. Flavour with a few leaves of geranium or, if you prefer, vanilla.

During the twentieth century, the two golden fruits became a trademark in the commercial sense of the word as well. Bulgaria became a major exporter of peaches and apricots, of peach compotes and apricot brandy. Huge gardens have been planted in the northeast corner of the country (apricots), in the south-east and in the south-west (peaches). The apricot brandy of the region of Silistra is simultaneously mild and fiery and has become a brand name. The peaches of Petrich, a town close to the Greek border, are huge and sweet and last only a month, as does youth. These newcomers have become part of the country's economy and culture. The same as the Turks who live in Bulgaria today and make up nearly 10 % of its population: foreign by origin but unquestionably belonging here.

The tomato came to south-eastern Europe late and last of the group, by the mid-nineteenth century. Originally it was regarded as decorative plant – its small red fruits were mistakenly believed to be poisonous. For a while they did not even have a name of their own. Some called them "frenk patlidjan", which meant "French aubergine". It took a few cookbooks

Red peppers

recommending their usage and a few daring home cooks to convince the urban population that the new fruit could be regarded as a vegetable and used to improve the quality and variety of dishes.

The history of the introduction and the evolution of the usage of the tomato is a good case study of modernisation, its directions, vehicles and effects. We can firmly state that in 1850, for instance, the tomato was entirely unknown. A century later, a cookbook on Bulgarian national cuisine, published in 1984 and based on extensive ethnological research, lists 567 main courses, including vegetarian, rice and pulse dishes, egg and cheese preparations and all kinds of meat, poultry and seafood dishes. Out of these, 224 require the use of tomatoes or tomato products. Obviously, the tomato has become a staple food.

The acquaintance started in Istanbul – the capital of the Ottoman Empire had marked taste for testing new foods and all "American" foods found their way to the East via Turkey. Then, a few Europeans working in Bulgarian towns and a few Bulgarians trading with "Europe" brought some seeds and the news about the interesting new plant. Once Bulgaria was re-established as an independent state, the new mass press started publishing household advice and recipes for cooking with tomatoes. Then a few restaurants opened that served tomato salads and sauces. Then smart tradesmen started importing seed. Finally, Bulgarian peasants started planting tomatoes. And everyone started liking and eating tomatoes.

There are several explanations for this phenomenon. For one thing, the tomato grows well in Bulgaria – this is an understatement. Bulgaria produces a great variety of superb tomatoes. The climate, the soil, the water, the availability and widespread use of manual labour come together to produce excellent quality and quantity. Secondly, the type of cuisine preferred by Bulgarians mixes and matches well with the tomato. The extensive use of onions, garlic, vegetable oil, pulses and vegetables stimulated natural affiliations between different foods and produced, as in Italy or Spain, a sort of a Mediterranean cuisine. Moreover, Bulgarian drinking patterns seem to invite the tomato: the preference for plum and grape brandies as aperitifs rather than digestifs calls for some kind of accompaniment that would not spoil the appetite for the main dish. Tomato salad, especially with white sheep cheese, is an excellent starter. Wine, which is well loved in Bulgaria, goes well with spicy tomato sauces. Even the smallest restaurant carries Shopska salad (Shopska belongs to the region roughly coinciding with the district of Sofia). Should a foreigner ask for advice as to which Bulgarian starter to choose, the first answer would be the Shopska salad. Shopska salad is the taste of summer in Bulgaria. Every family eats it regularly all summer long; very few make it in winter. It should be consumed with a shot of ice-cold fruit brandy (apricot is a good choice).

Shopska salad: Take half a kilo of ripe but firm tomatoes (the best are the ones called oxheart, sweet and pale purple in colour) and cut them in cubes. Peel and cut into cubes one cucumber, preferably the long slim variety, not a gherkin. Chop a small onion, salt it, squeeze out the juices, and rinse it with water. Mix the vegetables together. Add a generous amount of chopped fresh parsley, season with vegetable oil, salt and vinegar. Arrange the mixture on plates and top with grated white cheese (feta, preferably not too salty).

The third factor that contributed to the success of the tomato was the fact that it lends itself well to preserving. The canning industry developed in Bulgaria almost at the same time as the introduction of the vegetable itself. Stewed or pureed tomatoes (first known in Bulgaria under the name salsa, from the Italian – pointing once again at the origin) became available year round.

In a word, the tomato proved to be tasty, cheap and convenient, with universal appeal; it entered all European national cuisines, including Bulgarian, to a different degree. Curiously enough, in Bulgaria one can discern two distinctive waves of its diffusion. The first occurred during the late nineteenth and early twentieth century, when the tomato became an important element of salads and main dishes and spread from the urban areas to the countryside and home gardens. The second wave can be regarded as part of the process of globalisation, when certain originally ethnic foods became available worldwide.

In the case of the tomato, ketchup and spaghetti sauce exemplify this trend. The introduction and spread of ketchup, a condiment originally unknown to the Bulgarians, demonstrates how a culinary item can colonise a country twice: at present, there is no restaurant or fast-food joint in Bulgaria where a bottle of ketchup is absent. Spaghetti sauce (or pizza sauce) is another newcomer to the culinary scene. Riding the wave of popularity of Italian food, the Bulgarian canning industry has swiftly put on the market numerous prefabricated sauces, which sometimes bear very faint resemblance to their Italian original.

The tomato, then, tells the story of the modern epoch: starting with the discovery of the New World, colonising the east, and ending, so far, with the new global and post-modern situation where no one seems surprised by a sauce Bolognese, produced by a factory in a town with an impossible-to-pronounce name in Bulgaria's countryside, and proudly poured on traditional Bulgarian chicken stew. Think global, act local. If we asked a Bulgarian to name three kinds of fruits and vegetables typical of Bulgarian cuisine, chances are great that the apple, the peach and the tomato would come first. This short study of their origin has attempted to emphasize once again that food is culture, and that Bulgarian food reflects in a very appealing way what Bulgarian culture is. Something old and local, something old and foreign, something new and already local. The mixing, the metissage, of food and cuisine is one of the greatest arguments for encouraging diversity and local quality at the same time. The golden fruits of Bulgaria might be of different origins, but they have found a land where they thrive. They are much more than a symbol of well-being; they are part of it. Bulgarians are skilled fruit growers and avid fruit eaters. We will never know what the father and the three sons did with their golden apples. However, we Bulgarians do know quite well what we do with ours: we offer to share.

Veljko Barbieri

Croatia

From myth to authenticity

As recorded by the ancient historian Theopomp, the sea god Poseidon seduced the beautiful nymph Dachomar, the favourite of his brother Zeus, and fled with her to the Hadrian Bay, the Adriatic. After a sumptuous feast, at which particularly attractive fish and sea plant dishes were served, they engaged in passionate lovemaking. Furious and jealous, Zeus caught up with the lovers after hot pursuit, and struck the embracing couple with a bolt of lightning. However, Poseidon saved himself and Dachomar by diving into the sea just as their passion climaxed. The seed of pleasure and fertility released by the sea god was burnt by Zeus' lightning and turned into a stony archipelago. They say that vessels dating from that ancient feast can still be found glittering amidst hardened rock in secluded coves and pine groves of the Adriatic archipelago.

Even earlier than Theopomp, Apollonius Rhodius in his *Argonautica* described the return of Jason and Medea from Colchis and their flight with the Golden Fleece from the mouth of the Danube to the island of Cres in the Adriatic. The Argo's crew was already waiting for them at the estate of Medea's aunt, the enchantress Circe. If Robert Graves' version is to be trusted, Odysseus in his wanderings ended up in the land of the cruel Laestrygonians, somewhere in what is today northern Croatia, where he suffered terribly. In periods of reprieve he feasted on their thick soups, after which he enjoyed Circe's love and hospitality. Before his return to Ithaca, he lived seven years in leisure and abundance, lavishly fed and caressed by the nymph Calypso on the island of Melissa, present-day Mljet.

These mythological stories are followed by historical records from Pseudo Skylax to Pseudo Skymno, from Ephor to Diodor, from Apianus to Caesar, all equally exciting and fierce. These tales tell of revelry at the tables of mythological beings and enchantresses, deities, heroes and demons, and of cruel but great lovers of wine and food like the Illyrians or the Illyro-Celtic tribes along the eastern Adriatic coast to the present Gorski Kotar and Pannonia. In these impressive descriptions, myth and legend rub shoulders with dishes of supernatural

103

Slavonian fish stew

properties: game which transmits the elixir of the ancestors to brave hearts and heroes; vegetables capable of restoring lost strength or courage; soups increasing amorous power like aphrodisiacs; and freshwater and sea fish swimming in incredible dishes, satisfied because their extraordinary flavour has pleased the mythological and historical voyagers. Through stories and legends, this fantastic gastroinventory blends different peoples and their menus. Symbolically – but also actually, at least as far as their heterogeneity is concerned – these foods resemble those of present-day Croatia and identify Croatian cuisine as a combination of many indigenous sources along with migratory and historical influences.

Considering the small area involved, nowhere in Europe is there likely to be found as pronounced a mingling of central and southern European, Mediterranean and partly Balkan traditions as in present-day Croatia. Of course, just as anywhere in these continuously volatile parts of Europe, moments of peace and leisure compete with periods of war, after which, as a rule, there emerges new knowledge, but also new culinary techniques and ingredients. Thus, what we consider traditions are actually the outcome of lengthy historical and intellectual restratification. Luckily, these new gastronomical expressions containing all the inherited – and sometimes imposed – aromas and flavours comprise an identifiable corpus of dishes and techniques, which can convincingly be termed Croatian cuisine. Although this cuisine has often been on the brink of yielding to the power of superior influences, more often it has imposed its own gastrononomic personality on the newly introduced ingredients and techniques – at least to the extent that a small country, with a population of less than 5 million can act independently within such a rich heritage.

Two basic gastronomic spheres can be distinguished in present-day Croatia, with each divided in turn into several distinct areas. The first is the central European and Pannonian region encompassing the north-western, northern and north-eastern parts of the country. The second, Mediterranean one has ancient, even archetypal roots. It includes the Croatian coast and islands, and the hinterland from the Istrian peninsula to the Boka Kotorska fjord. Despite Croatia's diversity, history did leave certain common traces in its culinary traditions. Following the Neolithic period, there emerged hunting, fishing and farming cultures like the Vučedol culture in eastern Slavonia, where grains and seeds of early cultivated plants have been discovered in cooking and ritual vessels, as have the first European astral calendar on an earthen jar and the well-known symbol of fertility and heaven, the Vučedol dove. In the south, on the Dalmatian islands, in a somewhat different intellectual and geographical context but also dating approximately from the sixth millennium BC onwards, painted bowls and vessels, fragments of pottery and remains of shells, fish and animal bones reveal the beginnings of farming and gastronomy among the ancient island cultures. They also reveal early contacts with the Pelasgian and Cretan Minoan worlds, and with later archaic Greece, up to the more developed Hellenic poleis and Illyrian states from the late first millennium BC

The culture of migratory tribal communities, which has influenced Croatian cuisine up to the present day, developed in the north and north-west. In the south, according to the latest carbon dating, olives and vines were being cultivated along the Adriatic belt by the eighth century BC, that is, even before the foundation of the Hellenic colonies so renowned for the quality of their oil, wine and food. Simple dishes, mainly prepared with fish and seafood, of the newly

founded outlying Greek poleis like Issa and Pharos (the present-day islands of Vis and Hvar) and their colonies on the Dalmatian coast, mingled with spit-roasted lamb offal (vitalci in the local language), the culinary analogies of which are found today only on Rhodos and Crete. This relative simplicity was soon replaced at sea, on land and at the table by the Illyrian monarchs, thanks to the triumphal feasts they held regardless of who had won in battle.

The northern region was soon swallowed up by Rome in its initial expansion. After the first millennium the Empire gained full control over the entire coast and the interior and imposed new gastronomic standards. With its dominant military, plebeian but

Pogača (unleavened bread) with salt fish from the island of Vis

©Marko Čolic

Croatia

also patrician customs, the distinction between the metropolis and the backwoods was abolished, at least as far as the palate was concerned. This was especially true in colonies like Siscia (present-day Sisak), the large city of Salona (Solin near Split), and municipalities like Mursa (Osijek) in the north, and Iadera (Zadar), Narona and the still-Greek Epidaurus in the south. The standards and culinary knowledge imposed by the Romans lived on after the collapse of the ancient world in the southern cities of Istria, the Croatian Littoral and Dalmatia, and in the free Dalmatian municipalities. In the north they persisted in the fortified towns and castles, burgs and Carolingian monasteries, which secretly tried to save the knowledge, flavours and culinary techniques of the ancient world from extinction. Even when, in the late seventh and early eighth centuries, the Croats gained control of their new homeland from the north-west and north to the southern borders and the sea, this Mediterranean-Pannonian, Illyro-Roman culture survived. It was only after the fall of the independent Croatian kingdom in the eleventh century that the two civilisational and gastronomical spheres went their separate cultural and culinary ways.

Across the lowlands to the mountains

Because of this split, the gastronomic identity of the northern part of Croatia is still distinct today. Its two culinary threads complement each other in flavour and fragrance. Of course, the desirable juxtaposition of flavours and traditions that generally distinguishes Croatia serves both to unite and divide. The north-west remains under the strong influence of the culturally developed western and central European spheres, from the Frankish empire through the Carolingian state, the Croatian and Croato-Hungarian kingdom and the Austro-Hungarian monarchy. Despite important indigenous accents dating from the days of the early medieval Croatian princedom, the cuisine still reflects features of Mitteleuropean cooking with its mainly gentle flavours. On the other hand, Slavonia and the eastern, Pannonian part of the Croatian north inherited a pre-ancient migratory character and preserved, in a more sustained and pronounced way, the cooking of the lowlands, which resembles that of the Hungarian steppes and pusztas, with an occasional Ottoman feature thrown in from the centuries of Turkish occupation. However, both the lowland and the Ottoman influences yielded over time to the culture of Slavonian pork and dried meat, to adopted but improved pungent dishes of lowland meat or fish from the great Slavonian rivers, prepared in pots and kettles. Thus Pannonian Croatia belongs to the rim of central European gastronomy with its mixed techniques of preparation and flavours, resembling the armies and the peoples that came and went like the huge herds in the lowlands. In such cultural and, therefore, gastronomic circumstances the ancient culinary fire was extinguished at an earlier date, allowing the Croatian south – Istria, the Croatian Littoral and Dalmatia – largely to maintain its transformed ancient character to the present day.

Therefore it seems fitting to begin this story about Croatian gastronomy at the southern rim. Although regional flavours are discernible only when they are all assembled into a whole, it is impossible here to list the major dishes of every Croatian region. Nevertheless, the outstanding dishes presented here are sufficiently representative to convey the essence of each region and its heritage.

In eastern Slavonia an essential dish is the čobanac or pastirac (herdsman's stew), which owes its name to shepherds (čoban, pastir = shepherd). This stew has its origins in Hungarian and Pannonian goulashes, tokanys, stews and pörkölts, but the Slavonian version thickens the soupy style of the more northerly regions. Also in contrast to the earlier versions, paprika and meat do not predominate. Instead, bits of beef and pork are added to a series of vegetables that have been stewed in fat and sauce, then simmered and seasoned with bay leaf, white wine and sour cream. Although čobanac originated in eastern Slavonian towns like Vinkovci, it has become the hallmark of Slavonian cuisine in general and is also favoured in the western part of the region.

If čobanac is the hallmark, then the highest-quality Slavonian product is undoubtedly kulen. In Slavonia there is no match for this piquant sausage made from the best cuts of pork and seasonings, predominately paprika. The meat is stuffed into casings, pressed, slightly smoked, and dried for about six months. Slavonian hams, sausages and dried meats of

Pašticada

Pašticada is the most well-known Dalmatian dish, a true mirror of eastern Adriatic gastronomic skill. Like the Venetian pastissada, it has common Roman and Byzantine roots and was highly appreciated in Italy and the Austro-Hungarian Empire. Prepared for special occasions, this aged beef or veal dish stewed in wine, wine vinegar, nutmeg, bacon and vegetables has long been the source of heated arguments among Dalmatian gourmets about the proper way to prepare it, how it should taste, and where it originated. Of course, everyone praises a well-prepared pašticada, but each individual keeps the secret of the best, most authentic version for himself.

Preparation :
Marinate a bacon-dressed beef or veal rump in diluted wine for 24 hours. Then braise with 300 g of chopped onion, 100 g of chopped carrot and celery root, and baste with the marinade. After the meat has browned on all sides, add 2 spoonfuls of tomato concentrate, a glass of red wine, a glass of prošek (prosecco), salt and pepper, a couple of cloves and some nutmeg. Simmer for 2-3 hours until the meat is tender. Remove the meat, slice it, and keep it warm. Boil 15 prunes in the sauce, then pour the sauce over the meat. Serve with gnocchi and grated Pag or Livno cheese.

various kinds are also worthy of mention. Đakovo, renowned for its stud-farm, offers pork roulades, roasted, like all Slavonian roasts, in lard in the oven after marinating in seasonings and garlic. The champion of Slavonian roulades is undoubtedly stuffed suckling pig. After the ribs have been carefully removed, the stomach of the pig is stuffed with choice fresh or dried meat, veal, chicken, pork and vegetables, and then roasted for several hours in the oven or on the spit until its skin turns golden brown and crisp. It is served cold, cut into coils like a large roulade.

Gregada (fish stew) from the island of Hvar

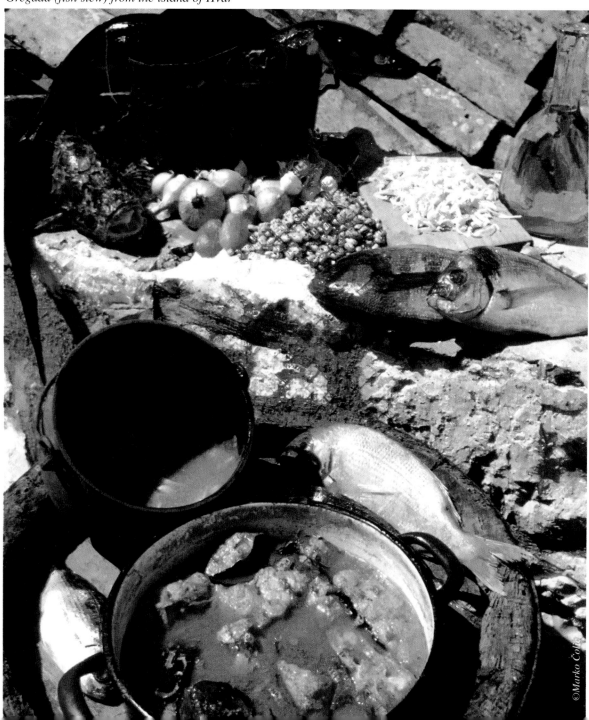

©Marko Čolić

The largest Slavonian town of Osijek is also the capital of pork, poultry and veal that has been stuffed or, most often, prepared in kettles on an open fire. Capon, goose and duck stews, braised in goose fat, are the outstanding specialities. However, owing to the two large rivers in the area, the Drava and the Danube, fish occupies a special place on the local menu. The fish stews are thicker and more aromatic than the Hungarian originals; breaded carp, catfish stewed with vegetables, and, in Baranja, thick fish soups are also enjoyed. Somewhat further to the south, in the Croatian part of Srijem, fried fish is sometimes laid on đuveč (meat and vegetable stew with rice), clearly reflecting the Ottoman influence; otherwise it is fried the Slavonian way with bacon and potatoes. Fish salads, dried fish and fish sausages are also typical of the vast lowlands and large rivers. No genuine Slavonian wedding can be imagined without the dozens of cakes that are prepared, as many as thirty or even forty. Their sweet fragrance mingles with that of stews, roasted or stuffed suckling pigs, geese and ducks, fish and dried meats. At the banquet table kulen, like a swollen cloud strewn with ground paprika, exudes its rosy and fatty tears. It gives off a pleasant smell of smoke and precious mould, suggesting the secrets of the lowlands.

Western Slavonia is an area of wooded mountains and hills rising from the lowlands, with the Vallis Aurea, the Golden Valley, famous since Roman times, and Slavonska Požega in the centre. It boasts excellent wines such as graševina (a variety of Riesling) and klikun. The local cuisine is a blend of indigenous Slavonian practices and culinary traditions of the ethnic minorities that settled here mainly in the eighteenth century during the reign of Empress Maria Theresa. The source of many dishes is easily recognized: roasted and stuffed poultry with quince compote is of Czech provenance; some bean and grilled dishes originate from Serbia; ajvar (seasoned chopped aubergine and pepper) and the Slavonian sarma (stuffed sauerkraut/cabbage rolls) are of Ottoman and Bosnian origin; the unique horse-meat sausages and dishes reached this area from Italy; the frequent use of flour and cream reflects Germany and Austria; and the goulashes and stews are Hungarian. There are many other, more marginal influences and cuisines. Nevertheless, through centuries of blending with the culture and customs of the original Croatian population, the traditions of these seemingly disunited worlds were assimilated into west Slavonian dishes and culture, which, at least at the table, mitigated the ethnic differences. Thus, in this region of forests with a long hunting tradition, the shared culinary experience has been recorded continuously in the charters of towns and noble houses since the Middle Ages.

The repertoire includes suckling pigs roasted on spits, poultry or fish baked in the ovens, kettles of Slavonian goulash or seasoned poultry soup, pheasant, hare, venison haunches and boar, thick sauces, wines and forest fruits. To the north, the large fish ponds between Daruvar and Bjelovar offer carp to roast on forked branches and pike-perch to cook in wine and cream – in its gastronomic simplicity and harmony of flavour one of the refinements of west Slavonian cooking. Eating this magical fish from a clear west Slavonian stream entices us with its unique flavour and leads us to believe that one of our dearest wishes might come true.

The flavours of pastures, mountains and towns

To the west, en route to central Croatia, lies the region of Moslavina with its boiled legs of pork, roasted chicken, bean and vegetable soups. The old kettles – actually large plates with a hollow for cooking over fire – lent their name to kotlovina (kotao = kettle), an umbrella term for prepared sausages, meats and, in recent times, vegetables. Posavina and Turopolje are the home of fat geese, goose liver, of a very old and tasty breed of Turopolje pigs, pork liver dishes, roasts, and carp from the fish ponds and streams around Sisak. The cooking of Banovina and Kordun has a more pronounced Orthodox influence, and a somewhat greater presence of lamb, various cheeses,

kajmak (cream) and sour cream. Podravina offers legs of pork marinated in garlic, wrapped in bacon and fried in their own juice and white wine.

Pork tenderloin in a sack with hashbrowns, roasted in the oven, is a well-known dish of Međimurje, Croatia's fairy-tale region. Here, in the mists creeping through the willow groves and across the pastures, hills and rivers, you can still hear the chants of the nymphs and the squabbling of the dwarfs. This enchanted scene is permeated with the aroma of štrukli (boiled cottage cheese strudel), native to Međimurje and Zagorje and prepared from flour, eggs, butter, and cottage cheese. In Međimurje štrukli also can be filled with boiled buckwheat, apples or nuts. Ducks, the symbol of the region's rivers, are roasted in the oven and basted with white Štrigovo wine. Behind the façades of the baroque town of Varaždin on the river Drava, game and poultry stews have been seasoning the air ever since the town was the administrative seat of Croatia.

The region of Zagorje resembles a large scattered village, with old forts and burgs, sites of many crucial historical events that left a lasting central

©Marko Čolic

Strukli (boiled cheese pastry) from Zagorje

European imprint on north-west Croatia. In every small town and village one can enjoy breaded chicken, poultry consommés with home-made noodles, stewed beans, marrows, sauerkraut and nettle, češnjovke (sausages seasoned with garlic) and the well-known Zagorje krvavice (blood sausages). An outstanding dish is the Stubica roasted tenderloin, stuffed with prunes and stewed in lard and wine, then basted with sour and sweet cream and a tumbler of plum brandy. According to historical records, this original Zagorje speciality was prepared and served in noble families beginning in the sixteenth century, along with the famous Zagorje turkey with mlinci (a type of baked and then boiled dough) and, in affluent homes, game with mushroom sauce, baked boletes and stewed chanterelles and beech-staffs. Less well-off people had to content themselves with maize porridge and milk, and soup with Zagorje štrukli.

Although a number of old-fashioned dishes have disappeared, many are still present on the menus of Zagreb, Croatia's capital. Its central European features are visible at every step – in the mentality of the city and in its gastronomic and cultural traits, which are distinguished by its competition with Vienna in a charming but unequal desire to assert itself. In Zagreb this competition is not marked so much by the number of indigenous dishes as by the menus that follow their own gastronomic expression. The tables of Zagreb are full of classic central European dishes like Wiener Schnitzel; but the provincial, Zagreb version of cordon bleu, breaded veal stuffed with ham and cheese, is really more interesting, in gastronomic terms, than its Viennese model. The Zagreb menu includes a variety of poultry and game pies, meatballs, liver dumplings in soups, roasted chicken, and Zagorje turkey or Turopolje goose with mlinci for special occasions, oxtail soup, tripe, wine goulash and ričet, an old dish prepared with boiled beans and barley, bound with meat stock and browned flour, with boiled pieces of dried meat. Chicken, duck and veal ragout soups, thicker than their Austrian counterparts, occupy a special place. Although pigeon and partridge, crayfish and frog dishes have not survived over time, stuffed breast of veal has, as has apple strudel, which is said to have originated in Zagreb kitchens and then travelled to Vienna. Finally, there is fresh cottage cheese, a dish of rural origin but now firmly established in the city. It is sometimes eaten as an hors-d'oeuvre, topped with thick sour cream.

Time stopped on the coast

West of Zagreb lies the town of Samobor, also an old baroque settlement, which is renowned for its cutlets, custard slices and the Samobor muštarda (grape mustard) that arrived, as did the digestif bermet, with Napoleon's soldiers. To the south lies the military town of Karlovac, girded by octagonal walls and rapid, clear rivers, home to perhaps the best trout in Croatia.

Here, in the courtyards of Lika and Gorski Kotar, you can smell the aroma of lamb and suckling pig on the spit, once prepared for solemn occasions both by Croatian soldiers in the Austrian army and by Orthodox Serbs along the military border with Turkey. You can savour Lika lamb under a lid, pickled Lika soup and sauerkraut, dried bear paws and basa, a rather bitter pickled cheese spread, one of the gastronomic features of the area. The regions of Lika and Gorski Kotar with the national parks of the Plitvice Lakes and Mount Risnjak are breathtakingly beautiful. Here you can enjoy dishes still popular from the past such as game on a spit, stewed venison with polenta, all sorts of mushrooms (baked on a hot plate or breaded) and smoked cheese.

However, to feel that time no longer exists, that you are one with nature, you must go to to Istria, the largest Adriatic peninsula, thrusting into the sea like a flint arrow. With the possible exception of Dalmatia, Istria is the most enclosed ethnic environment. Although this region drew upon the cultures of its models and occasional masters, from the Franks to the Venetians, Istria always managed to reinforce its own identity through these external influences. The result is a highly eclectic cuisine. In the coastal part of the peninsula, fish and seafood dishes predominate, such as fish fillets, lobster with truffles, shellfish in sauces over pasta, white fish baked in the oven, Istrian brujet (fish stew), and scorpionfish in white wine, which is first fried, then braised, and then boiled with onions, garlic, parsley and tomatoes. From Poreč to Rovinj, and onwards to Pula, Lovran, Opatija and Rijeka, coastal Istria and Liburnija weave a necklace round the interior. Not to be missed along this route are the chestnut festival in Lovran, the wild asparagus feasts offering fritaje (asparagus omelettes), and the annual cherry festivals. The Istrian interior offers soups prepared from heated Teran wine and a little olive oil, cinnamon and cloves, direct descendants of the seasoned medieval wine, hypocras; thick soups with bobići (maize), beans, vegetables and dried meat; and jota, a thick soup prepared with beans, potatoes, sauerkraut and dried meat, of Venetian provenance but with a pronounced Istrian touch. In this region lamb, game and poultry are most frequently stewed "na žgvacet": the meat is first stewed before the other ingredients – vegetables, fruit and occasionally wild asparagus, another Istrian mainstay – are added. The well-known Pazin turkeys are baked in the oven with apples. Dried pork tenderloins sizzle on the grill, while boiled salt cod and creamed cod await winter days. Ravioli and fuži (spindle-shaped pasta), risottos and pasta with meat, asparagus and seafood sauces expand the menu. Yet no sauce or dish compares to the dishes prepared with truffles. Throughout Europe these white (more expensive) and black (somewhat cheaper) kings of Istrian cooking have spread the fame of the rich black soil under the crowns of Istrian oaks. With the start of the truffle season the entire gastronomic continent is focused on Istrian pointers, a breed of dog specially trained to detect this aromatic mushroom.

Dalmatia, the land of living heritage

On the Kvarner islands, the archipelago stretching south-east of Istria, indigenous tradition blends with the Venetian in dishes prepared with local scampi, said to be the best in the Mediterranean. The range of specialities is extensive: dried and baked or boiled sausages; lamb stew Vrbnik style; exquisite fish; dishes prepared with olives; dentex or gilthead, and sometimes poultry, baked in coarse salt; shellfish in wine sauces; sweets prepared with honey; fig jam and ground almonds.

Dalmatia is the epitome of a sustained heritage, a culinary kaleidoscope of ancient sea urchin dishes, raw fish salads, meats roasted under a lid, ancient doughs and breads, Byzantine sweet-and-sour sauces and Saracen vegetables like stuffed aubergines. These vegetables were introduced by desert horsemen and seafarers from Asia along with many other foods and seasonings, and ancient culinary techniques spread through Sicily and Apulia to the kitchen gardens of the Adriatic. Dalmatian cuisine abounds in dishes prepared from lamb offal, seasoned with blood and stewed in vegetables and tomatoes. Dalmatia boasts perhaps the best Mediterranean dried and smoked product – the Dalmatian pršut (ham). Cookery books offer old recipes for unleavened bread (pogače) stuffed with salt fish, onions, and parsley, like that baked on Vis, the ancient Issa, from which Dionysius of Syracuse ruled the Adriatic. Other ancient dishes include pašticada, marinated and dressed veal or beef rump cooked in a slow-simmered vegetable sauce that exudes the aromas of Rome, Byzantium and Venice. A number of fish casseroles are prepared on Dalmatia's millennial fires, such as the lešada and popara (boiled fish) of the island of Korčula, and the gregada (fish stew) prepared on the island of Hvar (the name reveals its Greek ties). These dishes are accompanied by the best Mediterranean fish stews, above all the Dalmatian brujet, whose flavour assimilates the strength of the sea, kitchen gardens, olive groves and vineyards, and surpasses that of its culinary cousins,

Gregada (fish stew) from Hvar

Preparation :
Boil 1 kilogram of sliced potatoes,
1 kilogram of sliced onions and 5 cloves of sliced garlic. Add a sprig of chopped parsley and 1 whole tomato. When the vegetables are cooked, add 2 kilograms of fish – dory, gilthead, scorpionfish and conger eel. Use a strainer to remove some of the cooked vegetables, mash them and return to the pot. Add a good quantity of olive oil, salt and pepper to taste, and simmer until the fish is cooked, and the gregada is as thick as a cream soup.

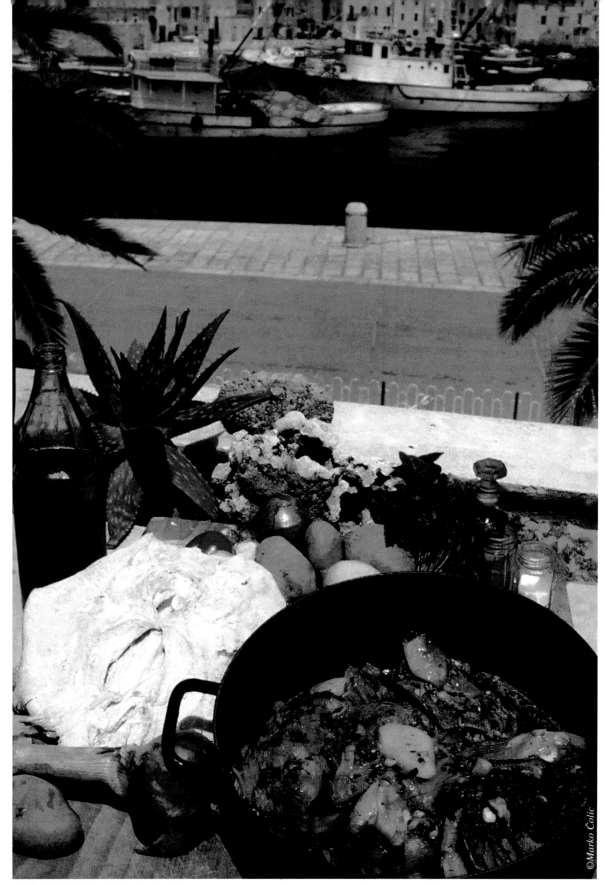

Dalmatian brujet (fish stew)

the Portuguese caldeirada, the Provençal bouilla-baisse, the Italian brodetto, broeta or burrida. Dalmatia also treats fish in ways common throughout the Mediterranean: grilling, spit-roasting, frying, and marinating it. From the Kornati archipelago to the Dubrovnik littoral, octopus, squid and cuttlefish stuffed with their own flesh and, occasionally, Pag cheese, smoked ham, and a variety of shellfish buzare (stew) swim in the flavours of the sea, wine, vegetables and spices. Cities like Split, Zadar and Šibenik look to the past in their traditional risottos, pasta with fish or meat sauces, dressed, salted and pressed tongue boiled with cloves and coriander, and game prepared Dalmatian-style with wine, olive oil, lemon juice and rosemary. Cabbage, which the emperor Diocletian grew in Aspalathos, present-day Split, is especially prized; chard, wild cabbage, and legumes are also widely used. The river deltas of the Krka, the Cetina and the Neretva, comprising the area of the old Croatian kingdom, offer eel and frog's leg casseroles, baked eels and frogs with smoked ham, and stewed crayfish seasoned with wild mint; in springtime, vineyard snails, grilled or cooked in a piquant sauce with fresh shallots and wine, are served.

Dalmatia's hinterland is a region of exquisite mountain lamb and kid, spitted fresh and dried meats, lamb and veal casseroles with peas, and boiled meat with the ubiquitous tomato sauce. When the famous Plavac grapes are harvested, mutton patties are fried with baked grapes. Islamic flavours crept through the mountain gorges and ravines, bringing the flavours of the sea and of ingredients acquired in coastal towns, and giving birth to unusual dishes such as the arambašiši of Sinj, a Dalmatian variant of the Bosnian-Turkish sarma (stuffed cabbage or vine leaves). For this specialty, instead of the ancient fig leaves, cabbage or vine leaves are stuffed with meat or fish. The Turks guaranteed the independence of the Dubrovnik Republic, which impressed foreign visitors with the Bosnian and Ottoman flavours of its thick green soups prepared with several varieties of cabbage, dried mutton and smoked ham. This small state and its cookery are equally renowned for the shellfish from Mali Ston Bay – the farmed oysters are considered the best in Europe. The Dalmatian story ends with ravioli, cheese cakes, crisp kroštule and pašurate (fritters), which travelled there from the carnivals in Venice. Other sweets include rožata (caramel pudding) prepared from egg yolks and sugar; hibovi, small loaves made from pressed dried figs; herbal brandy and fennel; Konavle mantale, cakes prepared from cooked and pressed grapes; and, not least, torta macarana, the famous cake from the Makarska Littoral of almonds bathed in maraschino, the equally famous Dalmatian liqueur praised so highly by Giacomo Casanova.

The varied menu of Croatia has been cooked in the kettle of time, which still simmers on the horizon of our awareness. The pleasure it brings binds seas and mountains, rivers and lowlands, peoples and beliefs. The known history of Croatia is only one small part;

from recorded recipes we can recognize the ingredients, seasonings and dishes that comprised the original Croatian cuisine. Perhaps it is less original than distinct, with all sorts of influences blended with its own traditions in the pot and on the palate. Croatian cuisine reflects the traditions of its neighbours and conquerors, the historical epochs that have come and gone like waves or flocks of sheep. Croatian cuisine is simultaneously dependent and free, at least in the choice of its own flavours and aromas, in that it contains, boiling and burning on the great hearth of time, our common heritage.

Slavonian čobanac

Croatia

At the end of the eighteenth century, during the reign of Joseph II of Habsburg, stories circulated about the visit of his mother, the Austrian Empress Maria Theresa, to the commander of her brave troops, the popular Baron Trenk.
As the story goes, they sat alone, in a small salon lit by flickering candles, as a pungent smell stimulated their already heightened senses. "Baron, you always surprise me, this dish is truly irresistible…" "This is Slavonian čobanac, shepherd's stew, your most gracious Majesty". "But it tastes like goulash… stew… pörkölt…?" "Indeed, just like goulash, stew and pörkölt together! " On that tumultuous night, they say, Maria Theresa ate all the čobanac, and Trenk also helped himself several times from the copper kettle, until he felt strong enough for a long and sweet vigil. The horses, or so the story goes, kicked in the stables until morning, while the fragrance of čobanac graced the Baron's bed-chamber.

Preparation :
Lightly brown in oil 200 g of chopped onions, 100 g of chopped carrots, 50 g of chopped parsley root and one minced clove of garlic. Add 300 g each of chopped pork and veal, salt, two spoonfuls of sweet paprika, one hot pepper, one bay leaf, and some warm water. When the meat is half cooked, continue to braise by adding water or meat stock. At the end add dumplings that have been prepared with eggs and flour. After everything has simmered for 15 minutes, add a spoonful of ajvar, 1 decilitre of cream and 1 decilitre of white wine.

Slavonian čobanac (pork and veal stew)

Savvas Sakkadas

Cyprus

Culinary traditions throughout the year

Greek-Cypriot cuisine is an important part of the history and civilization of Cyprus. The earliest evidence of human presence on the island is associated with food. At the "Episkopi-Aetokremmon" site, remains of pygmy hippopotami, which must have been eaten, have been found in association with crafts dating back to around 8500 BC. Most of the information concerning food on the island of Cyprus in ancient times is secondary and deals mainly with the raw materials – the animals and plants – that were used for food, rather than with the preparation of dishes. The earliest records indicate that few ingredients existed in the region, and those available were of poor quality.

The first permanent settlers did not appear on the island until around 7000 BC, at the beginning of the Neolithic Period. Archaeological remains indicate that their main occupations were cultivating the land and making pottery. Arrows and clay bows reveal that

people also engaged in hunting and fishing. Charred seed remains from prehistoric sites show that by this time the Cypriots were already cultivating or using a relatively wide variety of foods, including einkorn and wheat, barley, lentils, peas, chickpeas, mulberries, figs, pomegranates, grapes, olives, carob, pistachios, and capers. Birds also were part of the ancient Cypriots' diet, and the remains of fish and mollusks are common in most archeological sites. The Greek historian Strabo mentions that Cyprus was self-sufficient in grain, and it would seem that when need arose, the island was able to supply grain to other countries. Shipping, journeys, wars, colonies, conquerors and expeditions eventually brought the Greek-Cypriots into contact with new civilizations, and as a result new ingredients and techniques were introduced. By the end of the second millennium BC Cypriots were using aromatic leaves in their cooking. Many herbs were used, mainly for sauces, main dishes and to flavour drinks.

For many centuries bread, oil and wine constituted the basic trinity of the diet. The Mycenaeans cooked food well with olive oil. The main products they used were lamb, kid and pork, wheat and barley bread, cheese, milk, and beans. In the middle of the Geometric period (900-700 BC) spits (ovelos) were imported to prepare warriors' meals; at the end of this period, imported Greek pottery such as amphoras and kraters point to new systems in eating, and especially in drinking. There is strong evidence that vineyards have been cultivated since the Neolithic era. Homer writes that in symposia and at royal meals, drinking wine was a must. In his *Deipnosophistae* (Banquet of the learned)

Athenaeus provides culinary sources and elaborate recipes reflecting foods from the twelfth to the second century BC Cyprus's glory period lasted from the Classical (709-332 BC) through the Hellenistic (325-58 BC) eras. In comedies from the third century BC the Greeks accuse the Cypriots of living a sensual life and of having strange recipes and tastes. In the Roman era (58 BC-330 AD) Cypriots enjoyed "Lucullan" dinners with shellfish, snails and mushrooms; these foods were also served after funerals.

In the Byzantine period (330-1191) the various regional cuisines of Cyprus – those of the northern

House of Dionysos mosaic floor: Dionysos, Akne, Ikaros. Pafos, Cyprus

and southern coasts, of the mountains and of the cities – merged. Thanks to the trade routes, spices, sugar and new vegetables found their way to the Cypriot market, motivating Cypriot cooks to experiment with them. As the years passed, two new culinary tendencies developed: the elaborate eastern, or Byzantine cuisine; and the leaner Cypriot cuisine, based primarily on local traditions and relying less on the exchange of foreign products. Even in Cypriot cuisine, however, the use of spices can be seen in such dishes as split peas with nutmeg for fast days and fresh figs with salt, which were an important component of daily nutrition.

Sugar was introduced into Byzantium at around the same time, as early as the twelfth century, leading to the production of liqueurs and sweets, including puddings, rice pudding with honey, marmalades and fruit-based sweets made of quinces and pears. Wines flavored with aniseed, mastic and resin – the precursors of today's liqueurs – were popular.

Most culinary innovations in the Cypriot cuisine occurred during the Byzantine era. Even so, the basic diet continued to consist of fish, meat and dried meat, which had only recently been discovered. During the twelfth century caviar, fish roe and dried herrings were imported from Britain. Aubergine and bitter oranges were new ingredients; likewise, the production of koupepia using vine leaves instead of fig leaves was an innovation (the leaves are stuffed with rice and minced pork or lamb, and seasoned with olive oil, salt and pepper). Experimentation with dairy products resulted in the now-famous halloumi and feta cheese.

Cypriots were also influenced by the Franks and the Venetians, who were very impressed with the local products and the abundance of game and meat. The small birds boiled in water and preserved in salt and vinegar with aromatic herbs were famous, and only the Cypriots knew at that time how to cook with wine.

With the Turkish occupation of the island in 1571 poverty became widespread in Cyprus. The preservation of food enabled people to have good food year round, including pickled vegetables, smoked meat, dried pulses and sweets. It was at this time that Turkish and Arabic influences began to be felt, in such dishes as tavas (lamb or goat with potatoes and herbs stewed in a clay pot in the oven) and sheftali kebabs, small, spicy skewers of ground meat grilled over charcoal.

In more recent history, following the collapse of the Ottoman Empire in the early twentieth century, the cuisine of Cyprus became more cosmopolitan as people from all over the world introduced their foods, such as English Christmas cake, Italian pizza, and the now-ubiquitous potato chips. Indian chapati was adopted from the Indian troops stationed in Cyprus during the Second World War.

After the British Colonisation in 1960 urbanisation brought new recipes and new ways of presentation to

Cypriot cuisine along with processed foods. Cypriot cuisine today is the result of both local traditions and foreign influences, which are, however, no longer seen as foreign. For instance, modern Cypriot cuisine relies on ingredients that were unknown until the Middle Ages, such as the potato, tomato, spinach, bananas, coffee and tea, many of which came to Cyprus after the discovery of America. The main

herbs used nowadays are basil, oregano, mint, menta (wild mint), and thyme. Yoghurt is valued both as a main ingredient and as a side dish.

With the rapid changes in Cypriot society, technological advances in food production, preparation, cooking and service are causing people to look at the culinary arts in new and critical ways.

The calendar of Cypriot cuisine

Throughout the year the cuisine of Cyprus can be experienced through local customs, religious ceremonies and family celebrations involving traditional foods. The modest life of the simple Cypriot led to the evolution of Cypriot cuisine based on a magnificent blend of Greek Orthodoxy and Byzantine culture. For such a small island, the culinary culture is fantastic. Seasonal and religious festivals take place all year round in Cyprus, each with its own special foods.

New Year's Day is known in Cyprus as St Basil's Day. This is a day for optimism, when Cypriots hope that the coming year will be fruitful. A special cake, Vasilopitta, is baked, and when it is cut, whoever finds a coin in his slice is assured of luck in the coming year. Another custom calls for a person in love to sing "St Vasilis show me if…loves me" in order to find out if the love is, or will be, reciprocated. Then an olive leaf is thrown into the fireplace. If a crackle is heard the lovers will soon be together.

Epiphany, celebrated on 6 January, is a holiday when all Cypriots go to church to ask for a prosperous new year. To symbolise Christ's baptism a cross is thrown into the sea, river or lake. Epiphany is also the last day when evil spirits are said to dwell on earth. Families gather to share a feast of mixed dishes, at the conclusion of which they go to the roofs of their houses to bid goodbye to the evil spirits. Loukoumades – fried dough with honey – is the popular sweet of the day.

Carnival involves two weeks of fun and feasting prior to the great Lenten fast. During Carnival Cypriots really let down their hair to prepare the body for this frugal time. Carnival begins on a Thursday, when the Cypriots grill meat. Although many towns and villages celebrate, Lemesos is especially famous for its carnival celebrations and processions. The last week of carnival is "cheese week". It ends on "green Monday", the first day of Lent, when Cypriots pack a picnic and head for the

Grape harvest

C y p r u s

countryside. They eat vegetables, olives, bread and salad and drink village wine.

Lent is still taken seriously by many Cypriots; no meat, fish or dairy products are consumed during this period. Instead, pulses, vegetables and fruits are eaten, particularly edible greens from the countryside; and a variety of pies is prepared, including kolokopitta, made from pumpkin, raisins and cracked wheat; tahinopitta, made with tahini (sesame-seed paste); and spanakopitta, spinach and egg wrapped in filo pastry.

Easter is the major religious celebration of the year, when all family members come together to celebrate. Avgolemono soup (an egg and lemon broth) is traditional Easter fare, as are flaounes, savory Easter tarts baked in every household. They contain a special Easter cheese, eggs, spices and herbs (often mint), all wrapped in a yeast pastry. People crack eggs one against the other as they proclaim "Christos Anesti – Alithos Anesti" ("Christ is Risen – Truly He is Risen"). The main Easter dish is souvla, large chunks of lamb threaded onto skewers and grilled, and served with potatoes and salad. Singing and dancing, breaking eggs with one another and turning the Easter lamb on the spit are all part of the celebration.

Summer. During the summer industrious Cypriot housewives make orange-blossom water and rosewater to cleanse their faces and flavour their pastries and the fruit preserves known as glyko. These necessary sweets are served to guests along with coffee in summertime.

Weddings. Popular in the summer, the whole village turns out to celebrate these happy events. Resi, a rich pilaf of lamb and wheat is prepared, and special little shortbreads, loukoumia, are served to the wedding guests.

September. The making of souzoukos begins with the wine festival in Lemesos. Souzoukos is a chewy sweet made by dipping strings of almonds into fresh grape juice. Cypriot wine producers offer visitors the opportunity to sample Cypriot wines, and they demonstrate the use of wine presses and stills. Traditional harvest dances are held, and there is a fine array of foods to choose from.

Harvest time. This is the busiest time in rural Cyprus. Before the autumn rains begin the harvest must be taken in. Harvesting begins in late August with almonds, carob, wine grapes and olives. Cypriots celebrate the harvest with grape festivals, preparing souzoukos and palouzes, a pudding made from the juice of unfermented grapes. After the carob harvest people enjoy pasteli, a honey candy with sesame seeds or nuts, and syrup made from boiled carob pods, which is spread on slices of fresh bread. Finally, the new wine is made. Koumantaria is one of the oldest known wines in the world.

Christmas. Many people in Cyprus still observe the Advent fast before Christmas. In the past every family slaughtered a pig and salted, cured or smoked the fresh meat to last through the winter. Nowadays many families still make and smoke loukanika sausages for Christmas. Cypriot Christmas cake is basically a British recipe that has been adapted to local ingredients – and jolly good it is too! In the past, traditional Christmas baking got underway only a few days before 25 December, when crumbly kourambiedes (shortbread biscuits covered in icing sugar), melomakarouna (spicy buns drenched in honey syrup), and koulouria (traditional sesame bread) were prepared.

Food and music

Love and food, music and song are linked with the important Cypriot tradition of hospitality, and an important part of that tradition has always been wine. Gastronomic feasts of the ancient kingdoms involved the consumption of huge amounts of game and meat as well as of grapes, other luscious fruits and spices. The feasts were accompanied by flutes, string instruments, cymbals, rattles and song.

Since these ancient times, the constant invasion and occupation of Cyprus by foreign powers, including the Egyptians, Romans, Franks, Genoese, Venetians, Turks and British, have brought a variety of influences to the native music of the island as well as to its food. One of the main elements of Cypriot music is the tsiattista, song competitions held at weddings or on other feast days. They are still heard sometimes. A special melody accompanied the preparation of the pasta served with boiled chicken and grated halloumi cheese.

In the first half of the twentieth century, before the age of refrigeration, irrigation systems, quick transportation and economic growth, the average Cypriot ate a good deal of salted and pickled foods, and some preserved in sugar, according to regional variations. But over the past twenty years, according to Dr M. Tornaritis, a historian of Cypriot cuisine, a revolution in eating habits has taken place, and the traditional diet is nearly a thing of the past.

Food from the countryside

Today, most cooking and eating remains focused on the food of the villages. Food is entirely seasonal on the island, and flavours are enhanced by the use of wild mountain herbs, oregano, thyme, mint, sage and lavender. Olive oil is widely used; in ancient mythology, Zeus challenged the gods by saying that the god or goddess who brought him the most useful invention would win the coveted land of Attica, and olive oil proved the most useful.

Although olive oil is still central to cooking, it is used more sparingly than in the past. Even in Cyprus, times are changing; as machines help to reduce the amount of hard manual labour, diets have been modified. However, many old recipes are still in use, such as those for national soups, which are quite popular, especially in the mountains and the countryside during the winter. They are prepared and served in the same way they were hundreds of years ago, with either grains or milk products such as trachanas (sour-milk pasta) and halloumi. Avgolemono, lentil, fish and vegetable soups are also traditional.

One term that confuses foreigners is "salad". Cypriots call many different types of dishes "salads". On the meze (appetizer) table, for example, where a meal is comprised of numerous small plates that are usually accompanied by ouzo or wine. These include preparations like roasted aubergine, melitzanosalata (puréed aubergine) and yoghurt, garlic and cucumber tzatziki, all of which are considered salads, perhaps because they are served cold. Other salads in the Cypriot kitchen include boiled greens, served at room temperature or chilled, and dressed with lemon juice or vinegar, salt and olive oil. Many salads are served warm or at room temperature. The classic salad known as "village salad", or simply as "Cypriot salad", consists of vine-ripened tomatoes, olives, raw onions, peppers, cucumbers and herbs such as dried oregano, mint and thyme. It is usually topped with a wedge of feta cheese.

©Cyprus Tourism Organization

Meze (appetizers)

Meze

For centuries the Cypriots have accompanied their alcoholic drinks with meze – delicacies consisting of many small dishes containing small quantities of delicious foods. Meze are a traditional feature of religious feast days, birthdays, weddings, name-days and funerals. Feasting means endless eating, singing and joking, accompanied by wine and ziva-nia, a strong spirit similar to vodka.

Meze are served all over Cyprus, and they offer the true flavours of the island. Up to thirty dishes can be served. First come black and green olives, then tahi-ni, skordalia (potato and garlic dip), taramosalata (fish roe dip), and tsatziki, which arrive with a bas-ket of fresh bread and a bowl of village salad. Octopus in red wine, snails in tomato sauce, brains with pickled capers, kappari (capers) and cauli-flower moungra (pickled cauliflower) are some of the unusual meze dishes that may be served today. Bunches of greens, some raw, some dressed with lemon juice and salt, are also served, as are fish, grilled halloumi cheese, loutza (smoked pork fillet), keftedes (minced meat patties), sheftalia (pork ris-soles) and loukanika sausages.

Toward the end of the meal, kebabs as well as lamb chops and chicken are brought to the table. The last dish to be served is fruit or glyko prepared from fruit, or sometimes small vegetables, cooked in syrup. Glyko is found in every home and is the first thing to be offered a guest, along with a glass of water.

Cypriot women follow the old tradition of preparing glyko as their mothers taught them, and they offer it up with great pride.

The bread of Cyprus

One of the main agricultural products of Cyprus since ancient times has been wheat. Because the island's climate favours the growth of grains, the inhabitants turned to agriculture, and early on they recognized the nutritional value of wheat, which became a basis of their daily diet.

Using traditional methods which have remained intact throughout the ages, wheat is processed to yield products of exquisite quality for which the Cypriots are known.

Many ancient writers and poets describe the excel-lence of Cypriot breads. The poet Efvoulos said that it " is difficult to pass the breads of Cyprus by even if you were a rider, because they draw you like a magnet". And the Greek historian Strabo said that as early as the sixth century BC the breads of Cyprus

Making village bread

were praised by those who had tasted them, especially the breads made from wheat.

Although foreign foods have influenced the Cypriot table, the Cypriots have kept their own traditions and their original dishes remarkably intact and alive throughout the centuries, passing them on from generation to generation.

Works Cited

1. Amaranth, S. (1968). *Kopiaste*. Limassol, Cyprus
2. Davies, G. (1998). *The Taste of Cyprus, A seasonal look at Cypriot Cooking*, Nicosia, Cyprus
3. Evangelatou, F. (2000). *Traditional Recipes from the Village*, Nicosia, Cyprus
Food and the Traveler. Migration, Immigration, Tourism and Ethnic Food, Nicosia, Intercollege Press.
4. Hadjioannou, A., (1999). *Customs of Cyprus*. Nicosia, Cyprus
5. Hansen, J., (1991). "Palaeoethnobotany in Cyprus: Recent research", in J.M. Renfrew (ed.) *New Light in Early Farming*, Edinburgh.
6. Held, S.O., (1991). *Colonization and Extinction on Early Prehistoric Cyprus*. On the mammals of early prehistoric Cyprus.
7. Ioannou, T. (1978), *Culinary Art through our History and Culture*. Nicosia, Cyprus
8. Ioannou, T. (1989). *The Tastes of our Kitchen, A Heritage of 3300 years*. Nicosia, Cyprus
9. Karagiorgis V., (1996) The *Coroplastic Art of Ancient Cyprus. The Cyprus Archaic Period. Monsters, monsters animals and Miscellanea*, Nicosia, Cyprus.
10. Lysaght, P., (1998), *In Cyprus Traditional Food Makes a Visitor*,
11. Masson, O.,(1994). "Kypriaka" XVIII: Amargetti, un sanctuaire rural pres de Paphos *"Bulletin de Correspondance Hellenique"*
12. Prince, T. (1998). *Food from the Village*. Thanos Press, Paphos, Cyprus
13. Simmons, A. (1992). " Preliminary Report on the Akrotiri Peninsula Survey"91, *Report of the Department of Antiquities Cyprus* 1992, Nicosia, Cyprus.

Else-Marie Boyhus

Denmark

Nation-building and cuisine

Chronology is the historian's way of organising the enormous number of facts in human history. Traditionally history has been categorised in terms of the prehistoric period, the classical world, the middle ages, the early modern period, the modern period, and contemporary life. Art historians use a different system of classification, dividing history into the Roman, Gothic, Renaissance, Baroque, Rococo, Classical and other periods; political historians analyse the flow of events according to dynasties or governments. Yet, none of these categories works for the history of cooking, for which a new chronology is needed.

On the basis of Danish sources I have identified three main periods in the history of cooking:
– the first period: from prehistoric times until the mid-nineteenth century
– the second period: from the mid-nineteenth to the mid-twentieth century
– the third period: from the mid-twentieth century to the present.

The first period

The first era comprises the long pre-industrial period that lasted until the middle of the nineteenth century. This was the epoch of the self-sufficient economy whereby a farm was expected to produce enough to make a living but nothing more; the goal was not profit, but continuation. Large amounts of food were put up for the so-called storage household in which people lived off of what could be grown locally and stored for a long time, such as rye for bread and barley for

Freshly dug potatoes

129

porridge and malt to brew beer. Dried pies, salt pork, pickled herring and cured dried fish – cod being the most important – were also part of this economy. During the winter kale was the only fresh vegetable. Later on Dutch cabbage, carrots and other root vegetables were introduced, but potatoes were not yet available.

Cooking was done over an open fire at the hearth. Only wealthy households had several hearths and appliances like spits and jacks for roasting. Ordinary households had only one hearth, so cooking was limited to one-pot or one-pan dishes. Bread was baked once a month in a large bread oven. Rye bread and small beer formed the basis of the diet. There were vast regional differences in the food that was eaten. Local dishes from this period are still enjoyed today, although now only Bornholm and North Schleswig have regional cuisines of any significance. In the rest of Denmark the regional differences disappeared in the nineteenth century.

The second period

The second period can be called the age of the cast-iron stove. During this era modern Denmark was born and along with it, a Danish cuisine.

The wood-burning cast-iron stove was introduced in the mid-nineteenth century, and by the end of the century one was to be found in nearly every house. The cast-iron stove made it possible to cook several dishes at the same time, and food could be roasted and baked in the oven.

This revolution in the kitchen took place at the same time that Denmark was transformed from a group of separate regions into a united nation. Physically the country was connected by new roads, railways and steamships. Mentally there was a similar unification through education, spiritual and national movements, and the struggle for democracy. Populist movements were organised as farmers formed co-operatives that restructured farming along with the production and sale of agricultural goods. As Denmark became an export country, prosperity and self-confidence came to the rural areas even as the urban middle class gained power and influence and the labour movement grew strong. Social inequalities existed, but they were less pronounced than in many other countries.

This nation-building coincided with a change from the self-sufficient economy to a market economy. The old storage household was replaced by a consumer household based mainly on purchased goods. As retail trade expanded, fresh food became available to all. This transformation of the Danish cuisine was defined by the norms and eating habits of the urban middle class, namely daily menus of two to three courses: a first course of sweet soup with fruit, gruel or porridge; a main course of meat or fish with boiled potatoes and gravy; and on Sundays a dessert.

Denmark was prosperous enough to support the development of the culinary arts, which reached their climax between 1880 and 1910. Social life was important, so the well-composed meal became a matter of prestige. This environment created favourable conditions for full-time and occasional female cooks, producers and suppliers. Although advanced international and French cooking became known in Denmark, the country also created its own unique cuisine. But in contrast to other European countries, where the great international hotels and restaurants were the trendsetters, the Danish bourgeois cuisine was created in the home.

Fisherman on a trawler

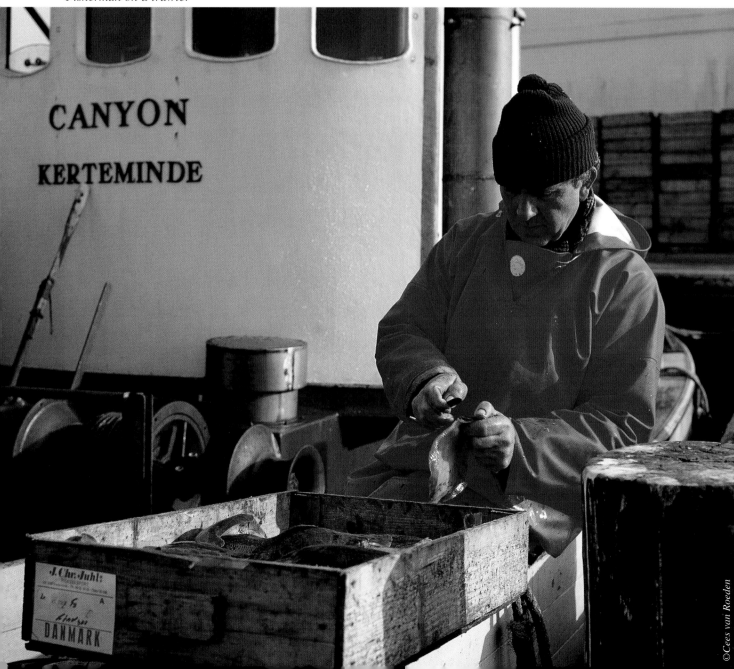

Dishes from the age of the cast-iron stove

Roast meats with gravy and potatoes became standard, as did consommé with flour and meat dumplings followed by boiled beef in a sweet and sour horseradish sauce with currants. The sweet and sour flavour was generally characteristic of this period. For instance, pork, goose or duck was roasted with apples and prunes and accompanied by brown gravy, sweet and sour red cabbage and caramelised potatoes.

Milk, which had previously been in short supply, was now plentiful, and the quality of butter in particular increased considerably. The basis of the diet was now milk and potatoes, instead of rye bread and beer as it had been in the previous period. Milk sauce with parsley was – and still is – a very popular accompaniment to such dishes as roast bacon, eel and herring and all sorts of boiled and cured meats.

The variety of fresh vegetables grew enormously, with potatoes becoming the most important. The Danes, especially the men, preferred vegetables like white cabbage, Brussels sprouts, kale, green peas and carrots served in a milk sauce. A beloved early summer dish is "ruskomsnusk" – small new potatoes, green peas and carrots boiled in milk thickened with butter and flour and seasoned with chopped parsley, and accompanied by crisp slices of roast pork breast.

Game had previously been the preserve of a small upper class, but it was now also eaten by the middle classes. It too was prepared with milk or cream. The meat was roasted, then braised in a milk or cream sauce and served with apple compote and redcurrant jelly. An everyday dish was mock hare – a roast of minced pork and veal shaped to look like a hare, larded like real game, and then prepared with milk sauce.

The advent of the meat-mincer in the late nineteenth century was an important innovation. Mincemeat became widespread, and classic Danish dishes found their form, such as meatballs of pork and veal either fried to make "frikadeller" or boiled for "boller" in curry or celeriac sauce. "Dansk bøf" (Danish beef) – minced beef fried and served with braised onions – is a very popular dish, and one that should be distinguished from "engelsk bøf" (filet of beef with onions). These dishes are served with gravy and potatoes and garnished with pickled gherkins or beetroot or a special Danish version of cucumber salad, for which thin slices of cucumber are cured and then pickled in a sweetened marinade of vinegar, black pepper and water.

In the second half of the nineteenth century it became possible to obtain fresh fish; fish from the cold northern seas are excellent. A dish fit for kings is super-fresh cod, boiled and served with potatoes, melted butter, chopped hardboiled eggs and mustard or mustard sauce. Boiled plaice served simply with melted fresh butter and chopped parsley is another example of simplicity grounded in the excellence and freshness of the fish. Unfortunately, this method of preparing plaice is no longer common; today plaice is almost always served fried.

Smoked fish is another specialty from this period. The heavy old-fashioned style of curing disappeared, as did cold-smoking as a means of preservation. These methods were replaced by light curing followed by hot-smoking solely in order to enhance the taste. This technique is used to make such specialties as smoked herring, smoked mackerel and smoked salmon. The Danes also enjoyed bay shrimp, which are bought alive, then boiled, peeled and served on a slice of buttered bread.

With the introduction of sugar beets, sugar became less expensive, and sweet starters such as apple soup and "sødsuppe" (fruit soup) became common. The range of puddings was expanded with such dishes as "rødgrød" (thickened stewed red fruit) with single cream and apple charlotte, for which cooked apples are layered with breadcrumbs fried in butter, then baked in a tin, turned out and decorated with

Newly smoked herrings, rye bread, egg yolk, radishes and chives

©Henrik Stenberg

133

whipped cream and redcurrant jelly. The combination of red and white foods was very popular, in imitation of the Danish national flag; it is also found in the Christmas Eve dessert "risalamande". Though the name sounds French, it is pure Danish, a sweet mousse of short-grained rice boiled in milk and mixed with whipped cream, vanilla and almonds, served with warm cherry sauce.

With the cast-iron stove, home baking really took off. At the same time, professional bakers and pâtissiers gained importance. Two Danish specialities are "wienerbrød" and "kransekage". Danish pastry is called "wienerbrød", Viennese bread, in Danish, though it is completely unknown in Vienna. This pastry is made from enriched dough rolled out and layered several times with butter, like puff pastry. It is

Kranskekagehuset (pastry shop)

filled with flavoured pastry cream or various sweet confections. "Kransekage" is a special treat made of a marzipan, sugar and egg white dough that is shaped into rings of varying sizes so that the baked rings can be placed one on top of the another to form a cone. The cone is decorated with stripes of white icing, crackers, small Danish flags and a crowning figure to mark a special occasion such as a wedding or confirmation. "Kransekage" is also eaten on New Year's Eve, at which time it is formed not as a cone but as a horn of plenty.

A cold parallel to the warm stove-age cuisine is "smørrebrød" (open sandwiches), which have been around since the 1880s. Smørrebrød is a festive version of the standard lunch. The classics include buttered rye bread with either pickled herring salad, smoked herring, smoked salmon, smoked eel with scrambled egg, corned beef with pickles and horseradish, veal tongue with carrot and pea salad (called Italian salad), roast pork with apples and prunes or red cabbage, liver paste with pickled gherkins or strong cheese with jelly and rum.

The cold buffet is another Danish phenomenon from the late nineteenth century. It is presented in several stages. The first part consists of fish: pickled herring, fried herring in vinegar, smoked salmon, warm fish fillets with remoulade, shrimp and other shellfish. Then follow cold cuts such as sausage, smoked pork fillet, ham, roast beef and liver paste, as well as warm dishes such as "frikadeller" (fried meatballs),

medaillons of pork loin and, at Christmas time, roast duck and roast pork with red cabbage. Then come cheeses and finally a selection of puddings and fruit. Everything is accompanied with rye bread, white bread and butter.

A meal of special importance in the nation-building period was "fÆlles kaffebord", the communal coffee table, which was a notable feature of the populist meetings where people sang together and listened to speeches. After the proceedings coffee was served along with buttered currant buns, Danish pastries, sponge cake, layer cake and a rich variety of small cookies and biscuits. This coffee meal was particularly important at the Danish national meetings held in North Schleswig following Denmark's defeat by Prussia in 1864. Even well into the twentieth century the coffee table was indispensable at political and popular meetings all over the country, and it still exists today, albeit in a reduced form.

The first half of the twentieth century was not an auspicious time for Danish cooking. The cuisine of the cast-iron stove age was neither renewed nor developed, and greater emphasis was placed on nutrition, hygiene and cost than on the culinary arts. As households grew smaller, only a few could afford to employ a full-time female cook or other professionals. At the same time, the burgeoning food industry offered cheap substitutes such as margarine, stock cubes, flavour additives and essences, resulting in an over-stretched and unneccessarily heavy cuisine.

The third period

Beginning in the 1960s great changes took place. An increased number of women went to work outside the home. They still had a lot to do at home, but it was no longer their main career. The kitchen was equipped with electric stoves, refrigerators, freezers and other work-saving appliances. Cooking on weekdays was reduced to only one dish.

Self-service in the retail trade and overall globalisation meant that new and international foods were introduced. The American influence is obvious in such dishes as salads, pasta, baked potatoes, barbecues, turkey and ready-to-eat chicken dishes. Italian cuisine has also established itself with pizzas, several sorts of pasta and a widespread use of tomatoes.

Increased affluence has made it possible for everyone to have access to everything – the whole world is in our hands. Our choice of foods is both individual and national. For instance, from Mediterranean cuisine the Danes have incorporated creamy dishes such as moussaka and lasagne, which are closest to the milk-based cuisine of the stove age.

Eating habits die hard, though, and the potato and gravy cuisine of the stove age is still on the scene, despite its rejection by gourmets and the number of new foods and dishes that have been introduced from abroad. In Denmark Christmas Eve is the greatest feast of the year, as it has been since the mid-nineteenth century. That evening all Danes eat dishes from the second culinary period, the stove-age: roast duck or pork with red cabbage, brown gravy and caramelised potatoes, and the dessert "risalamand" with red cherry sauce. In the pre-industrial society, Christmas Day was the most important, and even today Danes get together then for a family lunch. On this one day of the year, Denmark reappears as it was before the nation-building era as people serve dishes from the various regional cuisines and from the first culinary period.

All cuisines contain elements that are not contemporary. In Danish supermarkets you can now by fresh pasta, an innovation from the 1990s, alongside ready-made split-pea soup, a dish dating back to the Middle Ages. In my home, dinner tonight might be an Asian wok dish, introduced around the year 2000, while yesterday it was mock hare with potatoes and gravy, a stove-age dish. Next week I will serve green kale with cured pork, a dish from the pre-industrial first period.

Every cuisine contains layers from different periods, some strong, some weak. In Danish cuisine the impact of the nation-building era is so strong that even restaurants that try to appeal to a young public by offering American spareribs and other international dishes also offer the traditional Danish buffet or "stegt flÆsk med persillesovs" – roast pork breast and milk sauce with parsley and potatoes.

Christmas buffet, Hotel d'Angleterre

©Henrik Stenberg

D e n m a r k

Maire Suitsu

Estonia

Pleasures of the palate

No description of Estonia can avoid mention of its favourable location, which, over the years, has largely determined the fate and customs of the country and its inhabitants: for ages, important trade routes and diverse peoples have crossed this territory and unavoidably moulded the local traditions. Thus a dish that has a familiar name and look can turn out to

be something quite different from what you expected. For instance, a cutlet is a fried meat patty, whereas the piece of meat called "cutlet" elsewhere is referred to as carbonade here.

Estonian cuisine has some simple pleasures of the palate that you cannot find anywhere else. Thus an Estonian who has moved abroad will forever miss leavened rye bread and sauerkraut. Even those who have lived abroad for dozens of years still do not forget its characteristic taste. Black bread is a symbol of survival. In olden times, if you dropped a piece of bread, you picked it up and kissed it, for bread was considered sacred. It still is – communion wafers in Estonian are called "communion bread". The importance of rye bread on an Estonian dinner table is such that all other food is known as "something to go with bread".

Another dish that the Estonians regard as their very own is brawn, prepared from pork or veal and trotters with herbs and spices. Pork has always been the favourite type of meat, usually accompanied by

Brawn

©Jaan Heimann, Studio Filmari

Estonia

139

potatoes and stewed sauerkraut. One speciality is mulgikapsad: stewed sauerkraut with pearl barley and pork fat.

The famous sprats of Tallinn, prepared with twelve different spices, is one of the delicacies of Estonian cuisine, and something quite unique. There must be thousands of different methods for preserving and preparing sprats. As early as the seventeenth century it was written that the sprats of Reval (that is Tallinn) were "especially sweet". Preparing sprats was such a refined activity that even aristocratic ladies did not turn up their noble noses at it – they even prepared the dish themselves.

Estonia is a Nordic country, which has a lot to do with its native eating habits, foods, and preparation methods. The rather sharp contrast between seasons, quite unusual for the south, is also reflected in the rhythm of life of the people, who are closer to nature than the average European. An Estonian tends to be slow and introverted in autumn and winter, and much more energetic and communicative in summertime. How, what, and where an Estonian eats seems largely to be determined by the length and warmth of the days. Darkness and frost bring to the table sauerkraut and roast, brawn and black pudding, thick soups and stews. In summertime, on the other hand, it seems that people are able to survive on little but the warmth and sunlight, accompanied by everything light and fresh that gardens and forests have to offer.

When the first signs of autumn appear, in August, a sudden change of mood overcomes Estonians who have so far been enjoying a carefree summer. Clouds of steam and delicious smells emanate from our kitchens until the late hours; cellars, fridges and larders fill up with jams, preserves and pickles. Late summer inevitably means weekends in the forest, often several hours' drive from home, and a triumphant return with basketfuls of berries and mushrooms.

Herring in sour cream

Estonians have always regarded Atlantic herrings as a delicacy.

Ingredients:
4 slightly salted herring fillets
3 small onions
30 cl of fairly thick crème fraîche
3 hard-boiled eggs
dill

Preparation :
Cut the herring fillets into 2 cm strips and place on a small elongated dish. Cut the onions into rings and place them on the herring. Add a little salt to the cream, and spread it on the herring and onions.
Separate the whites of the hard-boiled eggs from the yolks and break up with a fork. Sprinkle onto the cream and garnish with dill.
Serve with black bread or with boiled potatoes.

Leib

Nowadays, gathering and conserving the fruits of the forest carries mainly ritual significance, though an instinctive desire to face the winter with a full larder is undoubtedly also important. A major motivation is probably the Estonians' strong attachment to the forest as a provider and protector. At times of trouble, people hid themselves there, and the forest has always offered herbs for healing the sick, as well as everyday food. Thus, hunting and fishing – adventure and entertainment for the modern city folk – still provide a significant amount of extra food for country people.

In the past, islanders and coastal people, living on poor, stony land, mostly ate potatoes and salted, dried or smoked fish with their bread. Inland farmers raised cattle, of which only the milch cows and breeding animals were kept over the winter.

The fatal day for rams was Michaelmas on 29 September; St Martin's Day on 10 November always boasted a goose on the table, and on 25 November, St Catherine's Day, a chicken was served. Before Christmas, a fatted pig was killed. After the festive food was prepared, the salted meat and lard were supposed to last until the following autumn. Seasoning was mostly done with salt, as only urban artisans and the landed gentry could afford expensive spices. Honey was used rather than sugar; it was viewed as a medicine as much as a foodstuff.

On weekdays, a farmer would sit down to pearl barley porridge with sour milk, or boiled unpeeled potatoes with curd or salted Baltic herring; on festive days, he could also enjoy butter, meat or egg porridge. On more prosperous farms, where the purse strings were not so tight, farmhands and maids ate at the same table with the farmer and his wife. Farmhands at a stingy farmer's table had only potatoes, bread, thin gruel and salt herring, and occasionally porridge; the same food was given to cottagers.

The most popular drinks were light malt ale in north Estonia and light ale made from barley and rye in south Estonia, or of birch sap in spring. Beer has been the traditional beverage for all occasions, having displaced mead, its ancient rival brewed from honey, several hundred years ago. Ale brewing, especially on our larger islands, has always been a serious and important business for the local people. The islanders' secret tricks of the trade remain a

mystery to mainlanders even today. The beer, served in large wooden piggins, is all the more lethal for its mild taste.

The cultivation of potatoes, a crop introduced into manorial kitchen gardens by the 1740s, finally took root during the nineteenth century. By 1900, potatoes had become a staple of regional food, competing with pearl barley porridge – competing so successfully, in fact, that only recently Estonia came second in the world (after Poland) in per capita potato yield! Spices, and various new dishes such as semolina and rice porridge, gradually made their way from manor and city kitchens to the tables of wealthier farmers. On market days, village boys could treat their girls to a sweet, golden-white bread, which indeed was long known as market bread. Grocers' shops began proudly to offer salt herring, which, despite the wide variety of local fish, became instantly popular and remains a favourite on the Estonian table today.

As with potatoes, getting used to coffee, which arrived in Estonia as early as the late seventeenth century, took a long time. But by the end of the nineteenth century Tallinn had several cafés of quite the same standard as those in central Europe. At the same time, the habit of drinking coffee also spread amongst the farmers. In the country, people drank home-roasted and hand-ground coffee on Sundays, as well as on festive days and when guests arrived. On weekdays, a simpler "coffee" made from roasted grain and chicory was regarded as good enough.

Over the past century, Estonians' everyday food has inevitably changed. To Estonians who have moved to the cities over the last few generations, the cuisine of their mostly country-based forefathers of the late nineteenth century has become rather unfamiliar. Regional distinctions, sharply defined a hundred years ago, have now become fairly hazy.

The traditional dishes and customs are still in use on the more significant festivals of the folk calendar, the most important being the pagan Yuletide (Estonian jõulud), celebrated long before the arrival of Christianity. The previously more frugal Christmas dishes became rather lavish during the 1930s and have not changed much since. Whether in the city or in the country, even an Estonian who might normally be constrained to tighten his belt must have his Christmas brawn, roast pork or goose, sauerkraut and black pudding, followed by apples, mandarins, nuts and gingerbread.

Despite increasing similarity, there are still some differences between the everyday meals of Estonians living in the city and those in the country. Hard work in the fields even today requires substantial peasant dishes, like pearl barley porridge with bacon or pearl barley and potato porridge, thick flour or bacon sauce, kama (roasted mixed grains) with fermented milk and

Estonian-style sauerkraut

Ingredients:
1 kg sauerkraut, 500 g pork loin,
10 cl pearl barley, water, salt, sugar

Preparation :
Cut the meat into small pieces and place it with the sauerkraut in an ovenproof dish.

Add the pearl barley and approximately 50cl of water. Bake slowly at a low temperature for 1.5 to 2 hours, until all the ingredients are tender, adding more water if necessary to keep the mixture from drying out.
Season with salt and a little sugar.

Rossolye

Rossolye was at its most popular in the first half of the nineteenth century. Since then, this uncrowned king of the Estonian holiday table has lost ground to Russian salad, which is easier to prepare.

Ingredients:
700 g cooked beetroot , 400 g cooked potatoes,
200 g cooked carrots, 2 herring fillets,
2 large Russian-style pickled gherkins,
2 sour apples, 200 g boiled pork or veal,
3 hard-boiled eggs, 50 cl thick crème fraîche
1 tablespoon salt, 1/2 tablespoon of strong mustard, a little sugar

Preparation :
Chop all the solid ingredients except the eggs into small pieces. Make the sauce by mixing together the cream, mustard, salt and sugar. Stir the ingredients into the sauce and refrigerate for approximately one hour. Garnish with pieces of egg white and slices of yolk.

sugar, milk soup with barley-flour dumplings, home-made rye bread and griddle-bread. With their lower energy consumption and their greater interest in slender waists, townsfolk try to use less fat and flour and more fruit and vegetables. Milk and all sorts of dairy products like fermented milk, yoghurt, and various tasty dishes made of curd are solid favourites.

An Estonian farmer's family always ate at home and the whole family would sit down to their meal together 100 years ago. Eating was a serious, even sacred activity. The meal was accompanied by numerous customs, to be strictly observed lest the household be plagued by hunger or other misfortunes.

For instance, placing a loaf of bread on the table with its top down forebode the death of the hostess, and wiping the table with the bare hand threatened poverty.

Even at the beginning of the last century, meals were still largely determined by the rhythms of farm work. Modern Estonia has no fixed times for meals. Breakfast is usually eaten at home before hurrying off to work, but coffee shops open their doors early to save people the trouble. Those who fancy porridge have oatmeal or a quick bowl of cereal, while coffee-lovers choose sandwiches to go with their favourite beverage.

Vahutav

After midday it is time for lunch. For the average office worker this means a cup of coffee at the office accompanied by sandwiches brought from home, or a light meal at a nearby fast-food outlet. Successful businessmen, following the western example, have business lunches at restaurants. Schoolchildren waste their pocket money on junk food, chips or trendy sweets.

Only about ten years ago, an Estonian family still usually sat down to dinner together; sadly, nowadays everyone tends to eat separately and at different times. The family meets only for Sunday dinner, and often not even then.

But changes in Estonian cuisine have not been limited to mere ripples on the surface, in the form of new eating habits. Staggering innovations and changes in society have created strong undercurrents which have raised eating – something that was previously done quietly at home within the family circle – to the status of unflagging public interest. Every respectable paper or magazine prints an obligatory food column, every slightly longer interview tackles the respondent's opinions about food and cuisine. The public also avidly wants to know who dines with whom and where, and, of course, what exactly they eat and drink. Wining and dining places are regularly reviewed and compared, and rankings drawn up. Estonian cuisine, as a trade, has no objections to all this: it is a well-known fact that whoever or whatever is continually in the spotlight has no choice but to offer the best.

Rhubarb cake

Rhubarb is the first fruit in the garden each spring, so it is widely used in desserts of every kind. This cake is made from two different mixtures.

First mixture:
250 g butter or margarine,
10 cl sugar, 1 egg, 60cl flour

Filling:
600 g rhubarb,
4 tablespoons sugar,
1/2 tablespoon cinnamon

Second mixture:
4 eggs, 4 tablespoons flour, sifted
4 tablespoons sugar

Preparation:
Cream the butter and sugar, then beat in the egg and continue beating with a whisk until the mixture is fluffy. Add the flour and whisk until the mixture is smooth. Roll the mixture out with a rolling pin on a floured surface to approximately 1.5 cm thick. Fit the dough into a cake tin.
Peel the rhubarb, cut it into 1 cm long pieces and spread them evenly over the dough. Sprinkle with a mixture of sugar and cinnamon. Bake at 175° for 10 minutes.
Meanwhile, prepare the second mixture: mix the egg yolks with the sugar and gently stir in the sifted flour. Beat the egg whites until very stiff and carefully fold them in. Spoon this mixture onto the rhubarb and bake for about another 10 minutes, until the cake is golden. Once the cake has cooled, sprinkle with icing sugar.

Johanna Mäkelä

Finland

Continuity and change

The modernisation of the Finnish diet

The way a society structures its eating habits is a microcosmic reflection of that society at any given moment in history. This is especially true in the case of Finland, where the processes of industrialisation and urbanisation rapidly and radically changed the social structure after the Second World War. These changes have left their mark on Finnish eating practices, and most Finns are now consumers, not producers, of food. The consumption of grain and starch products has declined while the consumption of animal products has increased, along with a steady rise in the consumption of vegetables and fruits. Shopping baskets are filled with foods imported from all over the world as globalisation materialises on the supermarket shelves. The supply has broadened significantly, so that products that once were luxuries have rapidly been transformed into everyday goods (for example, kiwi fruit). Influences from different ethnic kitchens have been tamed and made appropriate for every home (for example, pizza). The Finnish people have access to better, safer and healthier food than ever before. The problems of the diet have changed from scarcity to excess.

The Finnish diet and eating habits began to modernise when food rationing ended after the Second World War. Coffee was rationed until 1954. Recovering from the war, the nation enjoyed fatty and sugary foods. But the joy did not last for long, since several campaigns, especially against animal fats, were launched in the late 1960s. The Finns have dutifully decreased their fat consumption, but this has not prevented the increasing problem of obesity.

During the twentieth century, the differences in food use among social groups have diminished in western countries. Along with the rise in income and living standards, the percentage of total expenditure on food has declined, and food consumption habits have changed. However, although the differences among social groups have diminished, they have not disappeared. On the level of nutrients, different social groups eat quite similarly, but some differences still exist on the level of individual foods. Cultural preferences and choices vary. People with higher education and better income consume more meat, cheese, vegetables and fruit, while people with lesser means eat more sausage, grain products, butter and potatoes.

The social organisation of eating has also changed. The high proportion of women working outside the home has created a need for alternatives to the home-cooked meal prepared by the mother. A significant proportion of meals are eaten outside the home. At the same time, the development of household appliances has made the preparation and preservation of food easier at home. The introduction of refrigerators

and freezers changed the provisioning of Finnish food, since the growing supply in grocery stores could be more easily stored.

Despite these remarkable changes that have had an effect on every individual in Finland, the meaning of food to the Finnish identity has not vanished – on the contrary. This is nicely epitomised in the wish lists Finns living abroad send to their fellow countrymen. Rye bread, milk chocolate, salted liquorice and xylitol chewing gum travel across the world to those who long for these Finnish specialties.

However, the changes in Finnish food habits have also provoked concern over the future of Finnish eating. Some feel that the original, authentic Finnish

Finnish lunch

foods and food habits are disappearing. Yet Finland has received, accepted and remoulded influences from both East and West for centuries. In an era when culinary influences and trends travel faster than ever, the interest in regional foods and dishes is increasing. In some cases, historically rather local foods have been transformed into national dishes and emblems that serve almost as ambassadors of Finnish food culture. A good example is karjalanpiirakka, the Karelian pasty, which was recently awarded the EU's Traditional Speciality Guaranteed label (TSG).

According to the TSG product description, "the karjalanpiirakka is a small, open, flat pasty, comprising a thin crust and a filling. The filling is usually a purée of barley or rice or mashed potato. Instead of these, cooked mashed vegetables (for example,

swede, carrot, turnip or stewed cabbage or mushrooms) may also be used. It is usually between 7 and 20 cm long. The karjalanpiirakka is mainly elliptical, but can also be round. The crust is open on top. The sides of the crust are drawn up over the filling and crimped. The karjalanpiirakka has a crispy crust. The crust usually makes up about a third of the entire product and the filling accounts for about two thirds."

People have become distanced from the production of food and rely on the supply offered by the food industry and national or international retail chains. As the quantity of food is no longer the most important issue, it is possible to ponder questions concerning the origin, quality, healthfulness, safety, ethics and politics of the food eaten.

A Finnish meal

The basic structure of the Finnish meal, that is, a staple with meat or fish, has remained relatively similar over the last decades. Common everyday main courses today are minced meat sauce, meatballs, macaroni casserole and other pasta dishes, pizza, fried chicken, meat and fish soups, and meat stews. The most significant addition is the idea that a proper meal should also include fresh, that is, uncooked, vegetables. This "salad" can be anything from lettuce to grated carrots, as long as the vegetables are uncooked. Of course the main dish can be complemented with cooked vegetables as well. However,

the content of the Finnish meal has changed. Whereas the generation born just after the Second World War had boiled potatoes and meat stew for their dinner, their grandchildren now enjoy rice with Thai curry. Globalisation is encountered at the table.

The Finnish weekday meal typically consists of one main course, which on Sundays is accompanied by a dessert. During annual celebrations like Christmas, several courses are served. Christmas-time is considered a traditional feast in Finland. It may be the most important one, as the Finns celebrate it for a full three days. In making a proper Christmas, the role of food is vital. The Christmas evening meal is a mixture of new and old dishes. The meal starts with cold fish like pickled herrings and salmon with boiled potatoes. A baked ham is served with casseroles made of root crops like carrot, turnip and potato. The meal is finished off with a dessert, commonly based on prunes, to be followed with coffee, gingerbreads and mince pies. Still, even though the menu is considered to be very stable, with the same dishes cooked year after year, newer influences have made their way into Finnish kitchens. When Finland joined the EU in 1995, unified Europe was introduced through European baked specialties of the season, such as Stollen, Panettone and Bûche de Noël.

Convenience in eating is also appreciated in Finland. The selection of ready-made dishes has broadened remarkably during the last decade and also includes some of the traditional Christmas foods. However, Christmas foods are seasonal and not available throughout the year. Still, consumers can choose between classics like liver casserole (produced industrially since the 1950s) and chicken with white wine sauce. Semi-finished products like marinated meat strips or frozen vegetables have made cooking easier and faster. Yet, the most important task is left to the home cook: the actual process of cooking, that is, transforming prepared but raw ingredients into a hot meal.

At the same time, the number of hot meals eaten daily has declined. The majority of Finns nowadays eat only one hot meal a day. However, it is quite common to have both hot lunch and dinner. Hot meals still play an important role in Finnish eating habits. The debate over waning family meals and individualisation tends to overlook the fact that the traditional family – Mum, Dad and children – is no longer the representative household pattern in real life. The number of single-person households is increasing. Eating patterns and life phases are related to each other. Within the commonly acknowledged Finnish food culture, there is variation according to gender, generation, social group and family situation.

Family dinners, fast food outlets and canteens

A typical feature of Finnish everyday eating is the mass catering system. About one-third of all Finns use mass catering services daily. Since many women are now employed full-time outside the home, there has been a need to revamp the social organisation of cooking and food provisioning. Today, meals are eaten outside the home in day-care centres, at schools and workplaces, as well in institution like hospitals, the army and prisons. Since 1948, school canteens have provided meals for children free of charge, and many employers subsidise their employees' meals.

Mass catering meals have also acted as a healthy and nutritious model for home cooking. In particular, the

Salad bar in a canteen

idea of the above-mentioned "salad" has been promoted by these meals. Today it is common to have a salad bar, at which customers can put together their own salads from a variety of uncooked vegetables. Besides lettuce and the like, the selection includes cucumber and tomatoes, but grated root crops are also typical.

Cooking has been and still is a female chore even though a growing number of men take part in or are responsible for cooking. The new opportunities for eating outside the home or for buying convenience foods and take-away foods affect the division of labour at home. Family meals are not the only way to feed the family. It is important to bear in mind that family meals are actually only one type of meal. A lovers' dinner at a restaurant, a teenager's hamburger meal at a fast-food joint, and a lunch with colleagues at the workplace canteen are all meals, but they take place outside the home.

In the 1950s, restaurants catered mainly to urban upper-class men. Eating in restaurants democratised slowly. The pizzeria boom started in the 1970s. The pizzerias represented a new type of restaurant. They were more informal and appealed to the younger generations. Eating in restaurants was no longer reserved for special occasions. Today, Finns have a wide variety of possibilities for eating outside the home. On the one hand, it is possible to grab a hamburger or a kebab from a fast-food outlet. On the other, the interest in fine dining is increasing. In 2003 the first Finnish restaurant gained two stars in the Michelin Guide Rouge.

Fear of fat

As the relation between nutrition and health grows stronger than ever, it is obvious that eating is not only a question of national or personal identity but also of well-being. A diet with lots of sugar and animal fats was attractive to the post-war generation who still had food rationing fresh in their minds. Since the beginning of the 1970s, the high rate of cardiovascular mortality has triggered different types of health and nutrition projects and educational campaigns. In Finland nutrition education has been relatively successful: for example, the consumption of butter and high-fat milk has decreased rapidly. By and large, changes in eating habits have followed the direction presented in nutrition recommendations, even if there are some differences between men and women and social groups. However, despite these changes the proportion of obese Finns is increasing.

The quest for healthy eating has also influenced the product development of new foods. First came different light products with reduced fat, salt or sugar content. The latest addition is functional foods that try to improve the user's state of health and reduce the risk of disease by affecting certain target functions in the body. One of the most successful products has been xylitol chewing gum to prevent cavities.

The Northern Karelia project that began in 1972 has been one of the most influential studies and campaigns. Since the late 1970s, the National Nutrition Council has issued nutrition recommendations. The message of nutritionally correct eating did not reach the Finns by itself. Nutrition education has been provided by the public administration, NGOs and extension organisations, and also by the food industry and trade. Women have often acted as intermediaries for this message, and the education of women in particular has traditionally been seen as essential. Women learned new recipes and ways of cooking at school, in courses, from cookbooks, newspapers and weekly magazines. Home economics for girls has been on the school curriculum since the beginning of the twentieth century. The reform of comprehensive schools in the 1970s introduced home economics to boys as well. Television has played an important part in the education project. In the 1970s, TV chefs really were educators providing tips for healthy eating. Later the emphasis shifted from education to entertainment with programme formats like "Ready, Steady, Cook", known all over Europe.

Meatballs old and new

The history of Finnish eating is interesting. In spite of the wide range of changes that have deeply affected the structure, content and social organisation of eating during the last century, the core of Finnish eating is still the same – or is it? It is rather difficult to take a still picture of any food culture. A food culture is constantly on the move, but the question is, how slow or fast is this movement and the changes

Meatballs 1938

Kotiruoka (Home food) is the one of the most popular Finnish cookbooks. It has been modernised several times. Its first edition was printed in 1908. This recipe is from the 1938 edition. The latest edition was published in 2001.

Ingredients
700 g boneless beef
1.5 dl cream
2 dl water
1.5 dl rusks
1-2 eggs
1/2 onion
2 tablespoons margarine or butter
1 tablespoon salt
1/2 teaspoon white pepper
margarine or butter for frying

Method
Mince the meat in a meat grinder three times. Cover the rusks with cream and water and leave for a moment. Add the bread to the meat along with the beaten eggs. Mix well.
Cook chopped onion in margarine or butter, cool slightly and add to the meat mixture together with the spices. Form into small balls and fry in a frying pan/griddle with margarine or butter.
Serve with cream sauce.

Meatballs 1999

This recipe comes from *Herkkuja Martan keittiöstä (Delicacies from Martha's kitchen)*, the 1999 cookbook of the year. The Martha Union is an extension organisation founded in 1899, which specializes in household issues. Developing new recipes with a respect for tradition is one of their trademarks.

Ingredients
500 g minced lamb
piece of white bread
1 dl water
2 dl chopped nuts
2 onions
2 garlic cloves
oil
2 eggs
thyme
rosemary
white pepper, salt

Method
Cover the bread with water and leave for a moment. Add nuts, chopped and cooked onion, garlic and spices. Mix. Add minced meat and mix well. Form mixture into small balls and put them on a baking tray. Preheat the oven to 225°C. Cook meatballs in the oven until they are nicely browned. Serve with mashed potatoes and herb-cheese sauce.

it causes? Finnish food culture changed rapidly and visibly after the Second World War. Yet, it is possible to trace a continuum in Finnish eating. Porridge and other foods based on grains were the staple of the Finnish diet a century ago. The societal, cultural and economic changes that have occurred since then can be seen in the variety of present-day eating patterns. However, the Finns still eat porridge in the morning. It might not be as common as it used to be, but still the typical breakfast of Finnish toddlers is porridge. But porridge has entered the era of healthy eating. The ingredients may basically be the same, but now the traditional oats are spiked with bran flakes in order to give an extra kick of fibre. The relation between health and diet has been established by many studies. Therefore, there is a growing interest in healthy eating and developing new foods for health.

Finnish food culture is vivid and proud. It is obvious that the children of the new millennium eat foods unknown to their grandparents. Still, the pizza boom, for instance, would have been impossible had it not been for the rich tradition of various pies in the Finnish food culture; Italian pizza fit in well. The original concept has been developed even further to suit Finnish palates and foodstuffs. Thus, reindeer pizza can be found on menus in northern parts of Finland. This is a perfect example of how foreign influences have been assimilated into the Finnish food culture.

Another common and well-known dish in Finland, as well as in other Nordic countries, is meatballs, which provide a good example of the cycle of food habits, traditions and new influences. In the late nineteenth century, meatballs were a novelty, the preparation of which required a special appliance – a mincemeat – that was first available only in the kitchens of wealthy households. In the 1920s meatballs were still food for a feast. They were served especially in western Finland. Gradually, mincemeat became standard kitchen equipment, but even in the 1950s meatballs were served only on Sundays. Slowly meatballs began to appear in weekday meals. The grinder got dusty because the meat could be purchased minced. Soon traditional "mother's meatballs" could be bought ready-made from the nearest shop.

Meatballs are still a favourite. Today they can be spiked with spices from ethnic cuisines or made of other types of meat than the traditional beef or pork. They can even be served as a trend-conscious retro dish with cream sauce in a restaurant catering to young, urban adults. There are two meatballs recipes on page 153 that nicely tell what has happened in the Finnish food culture over the past sixty years. The first recipe begins with grinding/mincing the beef. Then the meatballs are fried. In 1999 the meatballs are health-consciously cooked in the oven. They are made of lamb, and the recipe is spicier.

The younger generations are well aware of global trends in eating. They have travelled, they have

Meatballs – a Finnish favourite

Finland

tasted new foods and they want to cook these dishes at home as well. Still, their roots are in the Finnish food culture, and they return to it quite often. Even though their meatballs might be spiked with spices, they still cook oatmeal porridge for their children. The interplay of food traditions and innovations goes on.

Literature

Heikkinen, Sakari – Maula, Johanna (1996): *Finnish food consumption 1860–1993. Publications 1*. Helsinki: National Consumer Research Centre.

Kjærnes, Unni, ed. (2002): *Eating Patterns. A Day in the Lives of Nordic Peoples*. Rapport no. 7:2001. Lysaker: SIFO.

Lahti-Koski, Marjaana – Kilkkinen, Annamari (2001): *Ravitsemuskertomus 2000 [Nutrition report]*. Helsinki: Publications of the National Public Health Institute B1.

Mäkelä, Johanna (2002): *Syömisen rakenne ja kulttuurinen vaihtelu [The structure of eating and cultural variation]*. Helsinki: Kuluttajatutkimuskeskus.

Mäkelä, Johanna – Viinisalo, Mirja (1997): *Maitoperunoita, lihapullia ja voileipäkakkua – syömisen arki ja juhla [Milk potatoes, meatballs and smorgastart]*. In Kotikaduilla – kaupunki – laiselämää 1970-luvun Helsingissä (ed. Maria Koskijoki). Helsinki: Edita.

Prättälä, Ritva – Helminen, Päivi (1990): *Finnish meal patterns*. Bibliotheca Nutritio et Dieta 45, 80–91.

Roos, Eva (1998): *Social patterning of food behaviour among Finnish men and women*. Helsinki: Publications of the National Public Health Institute A 6.

Sillanpää, Merja (1999): *Happamasta makeaan. Suomalaisen ruoka- ja tapakulttuurin kehitys [From sour to sweet. The development of Finnish food habits and customs]*. Vantaa: Hyvää Suomesta.

Croatia

Jean-Pierre Poulain

France

French gastronomy, French gastronomies

Modern French gastronomy is a skilful mix of haute cuisine and the cuisines of France's regions. However, this was not always the case. For many years haute cuisine kept its distance from what was eaten by ordinary French people, and the native, rustic cooking of France, or "cuisine du terroir", as it is conceived today, is but a recent invention, dating back scarcely further than the mid-nineteenth century.

How, following the Renaissance, did France become the country synonymous with gastronomy? To understand how this movement attaching aesthetic value to the act of eating came about we must look at the social context in which it developed and identify the social functions it fulfils. What role do the arts of the table play in the civilising process described by the German sociologist Norbert Elias? How does gastronomy relate to Catholic religious morals? How do traditional French chefs perceive culinary inventiveness? How did this form of cuisine and the accompanying table manners impose themselves as the standard of excellence recognised by western elites? At the same time, taking an interest in French gastronomy entails a sociological rereading of French and European history.

The second part of this essay deals with the rise of regionalism in French cuisine and the export of the concepts of nouvelle cuisine, which allowed the decolonisation of haute cuisine and the development of new gastronomic movements all over the world.

A driving force for social differentiation

It all began in 1530 when the term "civility" was first used in a text by Erasmus of Rotterdam entitled *De civitate morum puerilium*. This concept was to become the "backbone of court society"

F r a n c e

©Cliché Bibliothèque nationale de France, Paris

Le foyer, Tacuinum Sanitatis, XVᵉ siècle. Paris, BNF, Département des manuscrits, Latin 9333 fol. 97v

(Elias, 1939). It corresponded to a way of portraying oneself aimed at enabling a distinction to be drawn between the upper and the lower classes. Table manners were to become governed by extremely strict rules. By the Renaissance the movement had spread to a majority of countries in Europe and reflected a degree of European social unity. However, it was in France that the conditions were conducive to its

158

taking a particular form. The establishment of the French court at Versailles in the late seventeenth century, in line with the centralising logic initiated by Henri IV, marked the beginning of a number of key social changes. To be nearer to the centres of decision-making the provincial aristocracy moved to the court, neglecting its political role in the regions. Confronted with the resulting local political power vacuum, the bourgeoisie, whose economic strength was growing, began to copy the manners of the aristocracy, adopting an attitude denounced in Molière's *Le Bourgeois Gentilhomme*. The copied members of the nobility then hastened to commission their artists, cooks, clothing, perfume and wig makers to invent new social practices designed to denote their difference. This led to the "civilising process" described by Elias. Fashion in clothing, the art of perfume-making and gastronomy thus became distinctive systems, means of asserting social differences and of recognition. The "French way of life", rapidly imitated by Europe's elites, was based on the growing sophistication of these practices, which ensured that the up-and-coming classes were kept out of touch and guaranteed the superiority of the elites. It was from these games of recognition and differentiation, from this hiatus between the true followers and those who merely copied, that fashion derived its vitality. As early as 1691 culinary literature began to serve this social process. The first explicit reference to the bourgeoisie appeared in the title of Massialot's book *Le Cuisinier royal et bourgeois*. Henceforth the chefs of the aristocracy would write books targeting this social category, with the aim of educating the upwardly mobile middle classes about "good taste".

Far from bringing an end to this movement, the French revolution breathed new life into it, since it gave the bourgeoisie the social standing it had aspired to for the past 200 years. This was because, although the French revolution was a popular uprising, it was the bourgeoisie which chiefly benefited from it. Commercialisation of gastronomy via the restaurants opened by chefs who now found themselves unemployed gave a greater number of people access to the experience of fine food. Apart from its role in differentiating the social classes, the French gastronomic model, which progressed through society in a top-down movement, helped to shape the French identity.

Taste as a vector of development

In medieval and Renaissance cooking spices played a key role in marking social differences. When, in the late sixteenth century following the discovery of the New World, the bourgeoisie began to make ostentatious use of spices, which had become both less expensive and more commonplace, the cuisine of the aristocracy turned away from them. Abandoning the use of spices, as a sign of disregard for such needs, sophisticated French gastronomes switched to taking an interest in the taste of food. In 1654, in a fundamental work *Les délices de la campagne*, Nicolas de Bonnefons established a revolutionary concept: "Cabbage soup must taste of cabbage, leek soup of leek, turnip soup of turnip, and so on … And I intend what I say about soup to become a common precept, applicable to all food." This laid down the basic principle of what was to become French gastronomy. A cuisine where the taste of food was masked by strongly flavoured secondary elements was replaced by a cuisine where the combination of ingredients became an art governed by rules very similar to that of musical harmony or pictorial balance. A new culinary category came into being: the sauce base, or "fonds", which enhanced the taste of food. Unlike mediaeval sauces, which closely resembled our current mustard or Vietnamese nuoc mam, the sauce became a genuine base in the pictorial sense. It was used to bring out the savour of the food it accompanied. Massialot, for instance, proposed not less than twenty-three different "coulis", each with a dominant flavour and all with specific uses (1691).

It was along these lines that French cuisine developed – from Marin to Carême, from Beauvilliers to Escoffier, from Gouffé to Robuchon. This quest for flavour must be understood in a dynamic sense. Starting from the mediaeval culinary concept, in which spices covered the taste of food, it resulted in an ever-more subtle combination of the savours of a dish's ingredients.

It has been shown that the thinking of eighteenth and nineteenth century chefs, pursuing this quest for flavour, was influenced by alchemic theory, which concerns the relations and symbolic interdependence of humans and nature. Aware that there was something magic about their ovens, equated with the alchemist's athanor, they began their quest to produce edible gold. In their writings the great chefs of the time express their desire to improve their sauces and sauce bases in genuinely alchemic terms. For the eighteenth century cook, the quest is not just for the most perfect sauce – by improving his cuisine he believes that he is perfecting himself, and also contributing to human progress. That is Menon's viewpoint: "Would it be going too far to say that the skills of modern cuisine are among the physical reasons that, when barbarism reigned, caused us to return to an age of courtesy and of the talents of the mind, the arts and the sciences?" (1849). It was in even clearer terms that Favre, the founder of the culinary academy, illustrated the magic of the principle of incorporation: "By consuming these sublime sauces, this 'liquid gold', humanity is transformed. It is because of these sauces that France is at the forefront of gastronomy. Sauces constitute the basis of good cooking, and it is their excellence which makes French cuisine superior to that of other nations." (1883). In sum, by eating good food the French became even better – human beings are in fact what they eat. However, for the sensuality peculiar to French gastronomy to emerge, there had to be a religious context which allowed pleasure to be seen in a positive light. This was provided by Catholicism.

Catholic morals and the gastronomic spirit

The arguments I wish to advance here are partly inspired by and constitute a counterpoint to Max Weber's still debated theories on "The Protestant ethic and the spirit of capitalism". The hedonism characteristic of the gastronomic spirit was able to emerge and to thrive solely in the Catholic religious environment of the early modern era.

Is enjoying life's pleasures a sin? From the sixteenth century the answer to this question was linked to the divide between the Reformation and Catholicism. The first was synonymous with an anxious asceticism, in the hope of spending eternity in paradise, which attached little value to the body and its crudest senses; the second glorified God in an aesthetic perception of life on earth and in the company of others.

Similar theories have already been mooted on several occasions. In a romanticised form this thinking is at the heart of Karen von Blixen's *Babette's Feast* (which Gabriel Axel turned into a film). This is doubtless one of the best introductions to the aesthetics of French gastronomy. The film is extremely well-acted, and the tense faces which gradually relax, the convivial atmosphere – in the strong sense of the term, that of "living together" – which the food and drink create, say a great deal about the role of fine dining in French culture.

It is to the geographer Pitte that we owe the most detailed analysis of this theory. He concludes by saying "the possibility of making food sacred, of attaining something of God by eating good food, an old animist concept which Christianity had more or less tacitly made its own, thus vanished in the world of the Reformation". In a study of how happiness and sexuality were perceived by the English puritan theologians better known as the "Cambridge Platonists", Leites questions the idea that they renounced all that was worldly and shows that their ideal was a mix of sensual pleasures and spiritual joys (Leites, 1986). It is accordingly doubtless more reasonable to seek the differences between Catholics and Protestants in the break with the "cycle of sin/confession/penitence/pardon instituted by the church" (Valade, 1996) which the Reformation brought about.

I myself believe that gastronomic aesthetics owe something to Catholic morals not only in their original approach to pleasure but also, and above all, in the special relationship between food and the sacred in Catholic thinking. Three examples serve to illustrate the imagery underlying the relationship of Catholicism to food and the pleasures of eating. Christianity as a whole has made Communion, based on the tangible act of eating and drinking, the prototype of man's relationship with God. In the process it utilises the two components of the imagery of incorporation – "I become what I eat", meaning what I eat changes my very substance, and the idea that by consuming a food valued by a social group and sharing

France

the act of eating with that group, the individual becomes part of that community. This imagery was also relied on by very many religions predating Christianity.

However, although Christianity made use of the mental associations that these images of incorporation aroused, it was to attach considerable importance to distinguishing Communion from the sacrificial rituals of both animism and Judaism. By achieving the transition from sacrifice to a god (or gods) to commemoration of the sacrifice of the "son of God made man", rendering any other form of sacrifice pointless, it fundamentally departed from sacrificial reasoning. The sacred dimension of the Eucharistic meal erases its food and drink components. Détienne shows how Christian theorists who studied the Greek ritual of sacrifice denied the bodily nature and the eating and drinking dimension of the Eucharistic sacrifice: "To prevent confusion between the gross rituals of the nature-worshippers and the spiritual mystery of the Eucharist in the only true religion, a distinction is drawn within the concept of sacrifice between instincts led astray to the point of practising the abject display of bloody flesh and, on the other hand, the noble tendencies of a purely spiritual exchange where the forms of manducation are negligible and the eating and drinking aspects are obliterated, as in a manner of denial." (1979)

Among Christians the Eucharistic ritual became one of the most contentious points of divergence between Catholics and Reformers. There is no doubt that, in accordance with the biblical message "This is my body … This is my blood" and "Do this in remembrance of me", during the first millennium Communion was most frequently taken in the two forms – bread and wine, respectively representing the body and the blood of Christ. The wine, which symbolised the blood, had to be red and the bread leavened, which was both a reference to the metaphoric description of Christ as the "leaven of faith" and a means of differentiation from the Jews who consumed unleavened bread in memory of the exodus from Egypt (Dupuy, 1986).

In the late Middle Ages the rituals of Communion underwent a first change, with the separation of Communion in the two forms, reserved for the clergy, and Communion solely with bread, for the laity (Loret, 1982). This showed the increasingly hierarchical nature of the Catholic community, with a distinction between ordinary worshippers, allowed to partake of the Eucharistic meal only via the bread, and the ecclesiastical ranks, receiving Communion by eating bread and drinking wine. Wycliffe, Huss, Luther and Calvin – representing all the different tendencies within the Reformation – called for Communion in the two forms to be restored, so as to place all believers on an equal footing before God.

The second change came with the rise of the Reformation. It consisted in the replacement of the leavened bread with the unleavened host, and of the red wine with white. The switch from red to white wine corresponded to a symbolic differentiation between the blood and the wine, a euphemisation of the image of the blood. The substitution of the host for leavened bread, strongly identified with the early Christians who sought to distinguish themselves from the Jews, is intended to make the bread less real a food. Behind these apparently harmless changes of ritual, which make the Eucharist more remote from a real meal, a change in the relationship between the sacred and the profane can be perceived.

To grasp these changes' full importance, they must be relocated in the context of the theory of transubstantiation. The Catholic theory, reasserted even in the latest version of the Catholic catechism of 1992, is that during the sacrament of Communion "the fundamental substance of the bread and the wine is wholly converted into the body of Christ risen from the dead". It is therein that the mystery of the Eucharist lies – the bread and the wine change their nature and ontologically become the body and the blood of the son of God made man.

As far back as the twelfth century Berengar of Tours challenged this "sacramental materialism", which, he maintained, lent credence to the theory that Christ was really present in the Eucharistic bread and wine. He thereby initiated a debate, which was to assume growing importance until the Reformation and drastically divide Christians. The Reformers denied the change in substance and defended concepts that can be classified in two main approaches: on the one hand, Wycliffe and Luther proposed the idea of "consubstantiation", whereby the "body of Christ is in, with and under the bread and the wine, which entails the permanence of these natural substances"; on the other hand, Calvin rejected both transubstantiation, which he considered an annihilation of the bread and the wine, and consubstantiation, which he regarded as too spiritual a position. He accordingly envisaged a spiritual yet real presence, where bread and wine are such strong symbols that the truth is joined to them. "Here the emphasis is on faith and faith alone, without which there is no presence, since there is no ontological link between the body and blood of Christ and the bread and wine: if one eats and drinks with faith, one also receives the spiritual gift."

With the discovery of the New World and the revelation of the cannibalistic practices of certain of its inhabitants, the clash between these theories worsened and became a true rift at the very heart of Christianity. The Reformers accused the Catholics of being God-eaters and denounced this "God of flour" and the "butcher priests disjointing the body of Christ" (Lestringant, 1981 and 1994). It was in reaction to this criticism that the ritual was changed and the bread and red wine were replaced with the host and white wine. To preserve what they regarded as the essence of the Eucharistic ritual, that is to say the divine presence, the Catholics accordingly desubstantiated the Eucharist, separating the secular consumption of food and drink from the sacred incorporation

(Poulain and Rouyer, 1987). This desubstantiation was based on three forms of dematerialisation of the Eucharist: rejection of the alcoholic nature of the wine and the drunkenness it causes, replacement of the red wine (too representative of the blood) with white, and replacement of the leavened bread (a real food) with the host.

Catholic ritual accordingly became more remote from the process of incorporation of food and drink, which had too magical overtones and was above all too cannibalistic, since it was indeed a question of consuming the body and blood of a man, albeit the son of God. This led to the emergence of a fundamental division between the sacred and the profane in the field of eating and drinking: on one hand the Eucharist, an encounter with Christ and the related incorporation of the partaker of Communion into the community of Christians; on the other hand, ordinary day-to-day food with real bread and wine, synonymous with the human condition. The distinction between sacred incorporation and profane incorporation made daily eating and drinking an area which escaped the Church's supervision, one over which it exercised little control. However, gluttony remained a cardinal

sin, and it took the extraordinary means of release from guilt offered by confession, the theories of repentance and of purgatory and even the practice of granting indulgences to enable Catholic society to set store by the "here and now" and to dare transgress the commandment forbidding gluttony and its transformation into an aesthetic art. Gastronomy was then set to become a celebration of all that was worldly.

Gastronomy can be seen to be a key to the development of French society, which, apart from marking differences, helped to build the national identity. For example, after the revolution, when part of the aristocracy had been driven out of France and the king had just been guillotined, the bourgeoisie, which was now giving the orders in culinary matters, took delight in dishes such as "bouchée à la reine", "poularde royale", "fruits condé" and "potage conti"... In this way it metaphorically cannibalised the aristocracy so as to incorporate one of its characteristics – "class", which was to lend it the legitimacy it had lacked for centuries. At the same time, when a chef named a dish after one of these new power mongers, they raised him to and incorporated him in the aristocratic "pantheon".

The food critic: a mediator between two worlds

The bourgeoisie's position, both close to power and still seeking legitimacy, encouraged the emergence of a new figure in society – the food critic. It was the food critic who determined what constituted

fine food, because the bourgeois food lover could not really tell what was good for lack of criteria. This new role was to be pioneered by individuals straddling the dividing line between the two

ALMANACH
DES
GOURMANDS
pr 1862
PAR CH. MONSELET

AVEC LE CONCOURS
DE

LÉON GOZLAN, FERNAND DESNOYERS, J. DE GONCOURT
ARMAND BARTHET, ÉDOUARD FOURNIER
BERNARD LOPEZ, ACHILLE ARNAUD,
CHARLES JOBEY, VICOMTE LOUIS DE DAX, ARMAND LEBAILLY,
CHARLES COLIGNY, J. RÉGNIER, ANTOINE GANDON, ETC.

PRIX : **50** CENT

PARIS
E PICK, DE L'ISÉRE, ÉDITEUR
5, RUE DU PONT-DE-LODI, 5

worlds – the aristocracy and the bourgeoisie – such as Grimod de la Reynière and Brillat-Savarin. The first had a very surprising social career. The son of a farmer general and the daughter of a noble French family, he was born into the highest level of the aristocracy. His parents owned a mansion on the corner of rue Boissy d'Anglas and place de la Concorde, a building which now houses the United States Embassy. However, Grimod was a difficult child. Following a number of episodes of misbehaviour, his father obtained a "lettre de cachet" from Louis XVI so that he could have him confined to a convent near Nancy. He was released a few years later subject to the proviso that he stay away from Paris and the court. He thus found himself banned from frequenting the aristocracy. When the Revolution took place, Grimod de la Reynière was not in Paris and escaped the upheavals of the terror.

On his return some years later, he became aware of the emerging social movement and published a book *L'almanach des gourmands* (1802), which set itself the express objective of "guiding the bourgeoisie through the jungle of new food shops, restaurants, caterers, etc." as well as inculcating in them the precepts of gastronomy. Several issues of this book were brought out between 1802 and 1812, and it became a genuine guide classifying the restaurants, etc., and distributing seals of approval. De la Reynière's *Manuel des amphitryons*, published a few years later, was intended as a "book of lessons … in the art of good living and entertaining" targeted at "the new

rich of the Revolution", which "by redistributing wealth, had placed riches in the hands of people who, so far, had been strangers to the art of the noble use and enjoyment of wealth" (la Reynière, 1808, 315). In view of his intermediate social position, as a descendant of the aristocracy but simultaneously excluded from it, aware of the behavioural codes but not taking them entirely seriously, la Reynière was to play the role of mediator. He simultaneously invented gastronomic literature, the guides and the quality seals, which are all still important means of legitimisation in modern-day gastronomy and eating.

Anthelme Brillat-Savarin, the second major contributor to the codes of good eating and good manners of the aristocracy and the post -revolutionary bourgeoisie, was of more humble origins. A forward-looking provincial aristocrat, who was a practising lawyer and a member of France's Constituent Assembly, he left France for the United States in 1793 following the vote condemning Louis XVI to death, in which he refused to take part. His *Physiologie du goût*, published in 1824, adopted a position very close to that "invented" by la Reynière. If it is Brillat-Savarin who is mentioned first and foremost in the history books, that is because he is more presentable and more in conformity with the Republican ideals and, doubtless, with good morals. Grimod de la Reynière was in fact a shady individual, who was quite disreputable and whose love life was shared between a mistress in Lyon and his own aunt, his mother's sister.

The guides, periodicals and books on cooking and dining were of huge benefit to professional chefs. By listing good cooks and speaking of their work in a manner which legitimised it, they conferred unhoped-for renown on them. However, what is of interest here is above all the social position of these critics, who were neither cooks nor maîtres d'hôtel but intermediaries. They served as a link between a rising social group and the groups which already had high standing, enabling the former to make fine cuisine a means of asserting their new social status. When in 1960s France the new managerial class emerged – half-way between the entrepreneurs and shareholders, who delegated authority to them, and the workers, whose status as employees they shared – Gault and Millau were to play the same role, helping them to use "nouvelle cuisine" to legitimise their status (Aron, 1986).

The emergence of gastronomy in the seventeenth century and its subsequent development in France can be seen to be the outcome of a social context resulting from the fact that gastronomic theories and literature became an independent branch of knowledge, from the social impact of the drive for differentiation, from the quest for flavour as a vector of development of the culinary arts and, lastly, from the Catholic ethic.

All of these social factors were individually necessary preconditions but not enough in isolation. For gastronomy to come into being they also had to be linked together, forming a specific social context. It is possible to offer an answer to the question "Why is gastronomy French?" France was the place where these various factors were combined.

From discovery of regional cooking to "nouvelle cuisine"

In 1923 and 1924, in the context of the autumn arts fair, Austin de Croze organised a regional gastronomy week, at which chefs from all over France were invited to present their regional dishes. Four years later, with the assistance of the tourist boards, an inventory of French regional cookery traditions was produced (Croze, 1928). This led to the gradual emergence of a regional gastronomy, extolled by Charles Brun in the following terms: "Although one can dine in Paris, the real eating goes on only in France's provinces.

The delicious variety of dishes and wines … the tasty recipes religiously passed on from one generation to the next constitute a treasure for each region of France, of an entirely unsuspected, incredible diversity. ..." (Brun, 1928).

The golden age of gastronomy had made Paris the centre of culinary inventiveness, but the twentieth century was that of the discovery of France's regional cuisines thanks to a partnership between tourism and gastronomy.

In 1970 gastronomy took a new direction. Tired of repeatedly producing Escoffier's classic dishes, chefs adopted a creative attitude. Food critics announced the birth of "nouvelle cuisine". The idea behind this new concept of cooking was that there was a dual gastronomic heritage: the haute cuisine and table manners of the elites and the local, regional gastronomic cultures founded on popular tradition. Leading French chefs' taste for the cuisines of exotic places and for fusions between styles of cuisine has its origins in the same movement that led them to turn to the rustic, native cooking of France's regions. After some teething troubles, characterised by the desire to break free from the values and ideas of traditional nineteenth century gastronomy, French "nouvelle cuisine" accepted as its sources of inspiration both traditional haute cuisine and popular, regional cooking. In the 1980s it was with this concept of gastronomy that the great French chefs swept through the entire world. They were invited abroad to promote French cuisine, and the best known names were asked to serve as consultants for major international hotel chains or big agro-food groups. Verger and Blanc in Bangkok, Robuchon, Gagnaire, Loiseau and Bras in Japan, Guérard in the United States and Bocuse worldwide … today followed by Ducasse.

The leading European, North-American and Asian catering colleges were visited by flagship French chefs. Those awarded the distinction "meilleur ouvrier de France" and the happy possessors of the famous three Michelin stars came to spread the good word of French "nouvelle cuisine" and its rediscovery of French cooking's regional roots.

It must be said that an interest in foreign cuisine is not entirely new in French gastronomy. Dubois, one of the great nineteenth century masters, published a book entitled *La cuisine de tous les pays* (1868). His standpoint was nonetheless rather colonialist and, to say the least, decidedly ethnocentric, since he did not hesitate to rethink these cuisines, deemed "lacking in gastronomic qualities", according to the rules of "true" cuisine – that of France.

What distinguishes contemporary French chefs from their predecessors is that they have ceased to regard other culinary traditions as "sub-cultures" that need civilising and now find new sources of inspiration in them. Their encounters with other food cultures have firstly contributed to the development of local forms of haute cuisine and enabled the birth of the "new cuisines" of Quebec, Japan, Australia, California, Germany and Spain, in which many young chefs are now revealing their talents.

In return, these cuisines have influenced French cooking itself. The outcome is a new fusion cuisine, enriched by the use of exotic products and techniques. The most visible sign of this lies in a dish's presentation. Modern plates of food are arranged in a way that owes much to Asian, in particular Japanese, decorative skills. From a culinary standpoint, among the many changes mention can be made of the use of a broader range of spices, formerly present in virtually homeopathic doses but now more widely used to the point where they are sometimes ingredients in their own right. Another revolution has taken place with the diversity of cooking techniques.

Interest in the local heritage of native cooking is becoming international and can nowadays be observed throughout the western world. With the European Union's assistance, the gastronomic heritage inventory programme was extended to the whole of Europe in 1996. In a context of growing international travel the tourism industry now treats the gastronomic traditions of tourist areas as a heritage to be turned to account and a means of promoting local development (Bessière, 2000, Tibère, 2004). The values attached to popular traditions, native cooking and "authentic" produce can be seen against the background of concern about the increasing industrialisation of food production and distribution and the risks of a dilution of local and national identities in globalisation or within larger areas, such as Europe.

The emergence of leading chefs all over the world was a natural consequence of the attitude of the adepts of "nouvelle cuisine". The new focus on local food cultures has engendered conditions conducive to gastronomic decolonisation, which can only be welcomed. It will not harm France's great chefs that there is less French ethnocentrism in gastronomy, and this cannot but be a healthy trend for those who are less skilled. The talent of one chef does not in any way diminish that of the others.

France

Bibliography

Albert, Jean Pierre, 1991, "Le vin sans l'ivresse", in Fournier, Dominique, and D'Onofrio, Salvatore, *Le Ferment divin*, Paris, MSH, 1991.

Jean Paul, Aron, 1976, *Le mangeur du 19ᵉ*, Paris, Laffont.

Bessières, Jacinthe, *Valorisation du patrimoine gastronomique et dynamiques de développement territorial*. Le haut plateau de l'Aubrac, le pays de Roquefort et le Périgord Noir, L'Harmattan, 2001.

von Blixen, Karen, *Babette's Feast*, New York, Random House, London, 1958.

Michael Joseph de Bonnefons, Nicolas, *Les délices de la campagne*, Paris, 1654.

Brillat Savarin, Anthelme, *La physiologie du goût*, 1824, republished by Herman, 1975.

Brun, Charles, "Gastronomie régionaliste", in de Croze, Austin, *Psychologie de la table*, 1928.

Corbeau, Jean-Pierre, "Socialité, sociabilité... sauce toujours !" *Cultures, nourriture*, Internationale de l'imaginaire, Babel-Actes Sud, No. 245, 1997.

de Croze, Austin, *La psychologie de la table*, Paris, Au sans pareil, 1933.

de Croze, Austin, *Les plats régionaux de France, 1400 succulentes recettes traditionnelles de toutes les provinces françaises*, Imp Ramlot, 1928, reprint Morcrette 1977.

Daumas, Jean-Marc, "La cène dans la conception de l'église réformée" in Rencontres de l'Ecole du Louvre, *La table et le partage*, Paris, La Documentation Française, 1986.

Détienne, Marcel, "Pratiques culinaires et esprit de sacrifice" in Détienne, Marcel, et Vernant, Jean-Pierre, *La cuisine du sacrifice au pays grec*, Paris, Gallimard, 1979.

Elias, Norbert, *The civilising process: the history of manners, 1939.*

Favre, Joseph, *Dictionnaire universel de cuisine*, Paris, 1883.

Fischler, Claude, *L'Homnivore*, Odile Jacob, Paris, 1990.

Flandrin, Jean Louis, "La distinction par le goût", *Histoire de la vie privée*, edited by Ariès, Philippe, and Duby, Georges, Volume 3, Seuil, 267-309, Paris, 1987.

Garine (de), Igor, "Les modes alimentaires: histoire de l'alimentation et des manières de table" Jean Poirier *Histoire des moeurs*, La Pléiade, Gallimard, Paris, 1991.

Grimod de la Reynière, *Écrits gastronomiques*, UGE, Paris, 1978.

Leites Edmund, *The puritan conscience and modern sexuality*, Yale University Press, 1986.

Lestringant, Frank, *Le cannibale, grandeur et décadence*, Perrin, Paris, 1994.

Lévi-Strauss, Claude, *L'origine des manières de tables*, Plon, 1968.

Loret, Pierre, *La messe. Du Christ à Jean-Paul II, histoire de la liturgie eucharistique*, Novalis Salvator, Ottawa, 1982.

Massialot, *Le cuisinier royal et bourgeois*, Paris, 1691, republished by Dessagnes 1982.

Menon, *La science du maître d'hôtel cuisinier*, Paris, 1749.

Menon, *La cuisinière bourgeoise*, Paris, 1774.

Moulin, Léo, *Les Liturgies de la table*, Albin Michel, Paris,1988.

Pitte, Jean-Robert, *Gastronomie française, Histoire et géographie d'une passion*, Fayard, Paris, 1991.

Poulain, Jean-Pierre, and Neirinck, Edmond, *Histoire de la cuisine et des cuisiniers, techniques culinaires et manières de tables en France du moyen âge à nos jours*, Lanore, Paris, 2004, first edition republished in 1988.

Poulain, Jean-Pierre, "Le goût du terroir à l'heure de l'Europe", Paris, *Ethnologie française*, XXVII, pp. 18-26, 1997 -1.

Poulain, Jean-Pierre, *Sociologies de l'alimentation*, PUF, 2002.

Soler, Jean, "Sémiotique de la nourriture dans la Bible", Paris, *Annales ESC, 1973/ 2, 1973*.

Valade, Bernard, *Introduction aux sciences sociales*, Paris, PUF, 1996.

Weber, Max, *The protestant ethic and the spirit of capitalism, 1905.*

France

Mary Ellen Chatwin and Zaal Kikodze

Georgia

Foodways in rapid transition

The muffled, occasionally strident sounds of crying women seated around a military camp bed filled the mountain air. In July 2003, a small Georgian village in Khevsureti, in northern Georgia, was the scene of a farewell gathering for a young villager who had died several months before. The young man, in his twenties, had taken his own life. It had been winter then, and in November no one travels to such remote areas to comfort the family, to finally put the deceased soul at rest. His grave, outside the village, was not where his family and friends had gathered. A camp bed stood in an open space before his home, and slowly the villagers gathered around within the space, the women grouped seated and crying, the men standing silently or speaking in low tones.

Traditional beer locally made from barley stood in plastic bottles near a small table laden for the guests, which was placed next to the camp bed where the young man's shoes, clothes, and other

Village ceremony

©Z. Kikodze

G e o r g i a

personal articles were laid out carefully. His shoes were lined up at one end of the bed, and his portrait, framed, propped up at the head. Here a whole village's identity was at stake, and his soul hovered near. The ceremony that would ensue would bring peace to the family, the young wife, the father, and close clan members gathered together. The man's young wife, as tradition has it, did not cry, but saluted the deceased man's horse quietly. Her late husband's steed, his "soul horse", would soon take the young man's soul to the "other side". The mount stood saddled, colourful blankets and woven bags fixed to the saddle, his tail braided; even the blue sleeping bag of the deceased was carefully folded and tied behind the saddle, ready for the long journey.

Several other young men, friends of the deceased, led their brown Tushetian mountain horses up to a gathering place in a nearby clearing. As the ceremony of drinking and traditional toasting continued, they passed in turn by a large wool coverlet placed on the ground where barley had been strewn. Each horse would partake of the symbolic grains before the race

The race begins

to come. Partaking of a common food, just as their human masters shared a common drink, the community of interdependent beings would contribute as a whole to ensuring that the young man's soul arrived at its destination.

When the wild race began, most horses were ridden bareback. They would cover several kilometres of rugged mountain trails. The soul horse, however, had a different mission. It would be ridden by a respected man of the village, and though accompanied by the racers at first, would not compete. Instead, he would gallop at his own rhythm, running the same trails, carrying the soul to its destination before returning to the village.

Drinking traditional village beer prepared from barley (keri), eating and toasting, the villagers would raise many a glass to the deceased. Then the father would finally present the clothes, shoes and other objects to his son's closest friends, those he had grown up with and loved.

This ceremony, called saknari, evokes other burial traditions in the mountains and the lowlands of Georgia, yet the strong representation of cohesiveness and integration of traditional community remain today as an acknowledgment of the country's ancient origins as well as of the pre-Christian rituals of the Caucasus – a continuity that weaves a thread of identity through transitions over ages past.

The impact of migration is centuries old

On the highway that leads over the Greater Caucasus, through Georgia up to the Kazbegi region, then on to Vladikavkaz in the Russian region of North Ossetia, visitors today remark on small signs of a growing commercialisation. Basic tourism often begins with local foods. When local populations have been praised for unique or unusual dishes, these are the first to be offered in a commercialised form to outsiders. It isn't the staples of bread and cheese that mountain villagers eat everyday that are offered to outsiders. With the Mongols who entered Georgia from the north in the thirteenth century, meat dumplings were introduced and became a specialty of the southern Caucasus. These dumplings took

other forms and incorporated various ingredients according to the populations that adopted them.[1] Called khinkali in Georgia, they are increasingly common in lowland areas as well, and have entered all regions of the country.[2] The meat stuffing varies and every cook has his own recipe.

A recipe that uses two types of meat follows; alternatively, only one type of meat can be used, and sometimes mutton is substituted for pork.

Indeed, it is men who traditionally make this dish. Men who rarely cook otherwise often pride themselves in making khinkali, seeking the perfect form

Georgia

173

and texture. These dumplings are eaten by hand and usually accompanied by vodka, or Georgian tchacha, made from grape skins, or jiptauri, a wonderful-tasting eau de vie distilled from wild pears. As in other cultures, men's cooking is frequently limited to meat dishes, grilled, roasted and boiled.

Men continue to butcher meat in local contexts, and to eat in the outdoors. Along the road, shish kebabs, (mtsvadi in Georgian), are served to travellers. There is no more appetizing meal than a picnic in the forest, sitting around the fire with mtsvadi roasting and drinking white Khakhetian wine accompanied by the long, flat, tapered Georgian bread called shoti that is baked in earthen ovens.

In small cabins or makeshift restaurants along the highway where no commercial food had ever been offered, signs offering khinkali have sprung up in Russian – not in Georgian. In Georgia one addresses "the foreigner" in the Russian language, whoever they may be. It is true that rarely does a foreigner speak Georgian. The new "eateries" that began appearing along the most likely tourist routes after the year 2000 were sometimes simple lean-tos, and offered travellers what were traditionally home-made, family-only foods of the simplest kind. One sign reads "khinkali, shashlik, khadjapuri",[3] with a note at the bottom of the same sign stating that tea and coffee are "free of charge". The beginnings of a market economy, these strategies are also a simple

Khinkali

Adapted from Taste of International Cuisine, International Women's Association, Tbilisi, Georgia, 2003.

Dough :
1 kg white or semi-white flour
1/2 cup warm water, 1/2 tablespoon salt

Filling :
1 kg minced pork/beef mixture, 2 large onions finely chopped, 2 tablespoons herbs: cilantro, parsley, 1 small red chilli pepper, salt and pepper 2 tablespoons water

Preparation :
1. Sift flour and pour in some warm water to moisten. Add salt and lightly knead the dough until smooth and not sticky when pressed.

2. Roll out dough in a thin layer, about 20 cm thick. Cut out round pieces about 20 cm in diameter
3. Mix the meat, onions and other filling ingredients well in a large bowl.
4. Place a spoonful of prepared stuffing on each piece of dough.
5. Carefully enclose the filling by gradually gathering the dough in folds in a circle around it and forming a little topknot of dough to seal it together.
6. In a large pot of salted boiling water, drop the dumplings in one at a time, making sure that they have room to cook. Stir from time to time with a wooden spoon to keep them from sticking to the pot. Boil for 5 minutes or until meat is cooked and the khinkali start to float on the top.
7. Remove them with a flat skimmer with holes, Place in a serving dish and serve with black pepper.

recognition that tourists – rare during the first post-Soviet years – again climb the highway north to the majestic peaks and slopes of the Caucasus.

More recently new roadside restaurants offer Elitaruli khinkali, or "elite khinkali"… another step in marketing, integrating references to a growing upper class that now dares to admit class differences. Unmentionable terms in a socialist totalitarian system have now surged to the forefront of salesmanship as a new capitalism takes its first steps. Formerly the most modest food, khinkali is becoming a dish promoted through tourism to a higher status both in rural and urban areas.

Regional differences

Georgia today is made up of eleven administrative regions, demarcating approximate areas where ethnic groups have lived for centuries. Mountain regions of eastern Georgia, such as Khevsureti and Tusheti, developed centuries-old political and social relationships with the lowland areas of Kakheti and Kartli. One example is the seasonal system of sheep herding between the highlands of Tusheti and the Kakheti lowlands along the Alazani River, based on an historical interdependence between the lowland nobles and the mountain villages that supplied soldiers and manpower during former centuries.

What were formerly considered Caucasian minorities speaking languages within the Kartvelian[4] family became ever more assimilated under the communist regime, and today these groups are considered "Georgian", both ethnically and nationally. However, even among these groups, distinct political and social divisions still dominate local village identity, foodways and even language. Other ethnic groups such as Azeri Georgian, Armenian Georgian and Georgians of Russian descent make up 30-40% of the population. Some are integrated within urban areas and speak Georgian. Others live in enclaved settlements in different areas of the country and speak Azeri, Armenian, Russian, Turkic and other languages.

Food remains an important marker of cultural differences for these groups as well. For example, in the southern region of Kvemo Kartli, there are many minority areas, as well as villages that remain "enclaves within enclaves": a village of ethnic Georgians will be situated within an enclave of Azeri Georgians, who are Muslim. Driving along a main road will take you from one cultural area to the next. Road signs will not always let you see the difference in cultures you are passing through, yet along the roadside meat is sold, hanging from makeshift wooden frames. It is striking to see a pig's carcass for sale as the road leaves a Muslim settlement and leads into the Orthodox, ethnic Georgian village.

In Kvemo Kartli, Georgian Azeri populations cultivate most of the high-quality vegetables that the country boasts, as the earth is rich and fertile. Here villagers – some quite wealthy – produce the lettuce, spinach, tomatoes, aubergines, herbs, carrots, potatoes, beans and other staples that the entire country calls "traditional foods". Yet this semi-arid zone depends on water management upriver from a region where Azeri Georgians are not a majority. This "vegetable basket" of the country has made a different kind of transition than the mainstream groups of Georgian populations. Production and sales of food products are heavily dependent on female labour, both in the fields and in the market. Girls and women – the backbone of the agricultural system – are today less likely to finish school and choose their destinies than under the former socialist system. Girls drop out of school as young as 14, some staying home to keep house and others to work in the fields. Very often marriage is earlier than in other regions. The lawlessness and lack of infrastructure that came to characterise much of the country during the previous decade still threatens the girls, according to local elders, who fear they will be "snatched" as a bride on their path to school. Educational and legal infrastructures and law enforcement cannot prevent this from happening today, while under the former Soviet system young women ran little risk of not finishing secondary education.

Economic development tends to privilege the men in these regions who, for example, are supported by international agencies to build better infrastructures for their fields and irrigation systems, while too little attention is paid to the fact that women are walking ever-longer distances carrying clean drinking water for their families.

Today, without a centralised authority dealing with minority issues, groups that are not Georgian-speaking are disadvantaged, for example in the case of representation in parliament, or when the children begin school. There are no preparatory classes for young children entering school to give them the same chances as Georgian ethnic groups.

Georgia's identity and tamadoba

Symbolically, regional family identity, as well as hospitality, is represented by food, while group values and personal identity – including honour – are represented by drink. Drink carries social meaning and is not taken lightly by those who participate in the repasts it structures. Food, often abundant, always aesthetically prepared and varied, takes second place to drink during special meals.

Feasts and the large supra[5] remain a central symbolic food moment for all major rites of passage in Georgia. Even in Muslim areas of the country, and

Mtsvadi grilled over an open fire

where no pork is consumed, the essence of Georgian identity – wine or spirits offered to guests – remains an important marker of hospitality. Such occasions may be celebrated with different foods, in different languages or dialects, and even the major marker – drink – may change, but this "cultural fact" remains.

The system known as tamadoba is recognized in all the Caucasus, and specific expressions can be seen in neighbouring countries. Yet Georgians have a particular reputation for the distinctiveness of their conviviality at table. The tamadoba process has regional variations that are familiar to most Georgians.

The feast and its social importance

Ostensibly proscribed for economic and political reasons under the former communist system, feasts created in fact still another point of social resistance, as large repasts with wasteful consumption not only illustrated the existence of an independent economic system, but provided a constant local reminder of who owed social debts to whom, links which were to prove stronger within the country's shadow economy than the Soviet state itself.

Such socio-economic aspects are indeed essential to understand the tamada's (or "toastmaster's") role. Another important facet of this role is closely linked with the tamada's personality. Usually someone from the host family with a certain gift for speaking, a tamada must provide the guests with a group identity. He (and by far most are men, as women shun the "heavy role" that the tamadoba imposes[6]) should possess psychological characteristics that create empathy between him and the guests. He must know how to exclude all forms of animosity and quarrelling at table. It is unusual indeed at the Georgian table to hear any unpleasant statement. From a psychosocial point of view, one could perhaps interpret this aspect of the tamada's role as a process of controlled drinking, since alcohol intake from such occasions rarely – if ever – results in conflictual interaction, even after several hours of consumption.

It is up to the tamada to "open" the feast with a first raised glass, joined by all at the table, and to continue this process with successive (and expected) statements at frequent intervals throughout the entire meal. An average supra lasts several hours, and wine consumption varies from two to six litres of wine per person during that time. Unless the tamada calls for a sadhregrdzelo,[7] no wine will be sipped outside of these toasts. This social control of alcohol consumption has meant that Georgia rarely sees uncontrolled drunkenness in public; a good tamada keeps his eye on each person's mood and behaviour, and takes into account quantities consumed and the flow of emotion during the meal. A guest does not propose a toast without permission of the tamada, nor does one change the theme of the toast proposed (an important difference from anglophone toasting behaviour).

A gathering

No wine is drunk without the tamada's sadhregrdzelo uttered first – and even then, in turn.

When guests are seated, foods are immediately served in small dishes. Guests help themselves right away; there is no "bon appétit" to encourage one to begin, and it is understood that once seated, the group partakes immediately of the dishes in front of them: salads of carrot, red beets or cabbage rolled with walnuts, cold meats, cheeses and greens such as parsley, cilantro or dill, tomatoes and the soft sulguni cheese, similar to Italian mozzarella. Later will come steaming hot khadjapuri, or cheese pie, made according to local traditions. There are many regional variations: Imeruli khadjapuri (named after the large Imereti region) is most common in east Georgia, prepared with cheese curd and sometimes yoghurt-based dough that encloses the tasty melted cheese in a plate-sized pie form, while the megruli khadjapuri (from Samegrelo) is covered with butter and cheese which becomes crusty on top. A distinctive khadjapuri from the Ajara region takes a boat-like form with pointed ends, and the cheese in the middle of the dough is topped by a fresh egg. Eating this type of khadjapuri is a full meal and not usually possible during a supra, where the simpler forms of khadjapuri are served.

In South Ossetia, an autonomous region of Georgia, a similar form of cheese pie is served, called khabjini, considered the national dish. In addition to cheese, there are often potatoes and green herbs. In the Caucasus, potatoes are a common addition to mountain dishes.

In western Georgia, meals will include corn bread, or mchadi, as well as traditionally baked wheat bread. In eastern Georgia meat is often boiled in different forms, for example flavored with tarragon and many other spices. Western Georgian feasts most often finish with a flourish of long roasting sticks with mtsvadi, pieces of grilled beef or pork. Within the last five years, however, there has been a very distinct "invasion" of west Georgian foods and dishes to the detriment of boiled meat dishes. Georgians living in the eastern regions have also acquired a taste for the hot ajika,[8] which was almost unthinkable ten years ago. Spicy foods seem to be going global, and it is interesting that to escape globalisation and increase the consumption of traditional foods, Georgians are, in a sense, joining much of the world in a heightened taste for hot pepper.

The commercialisation of Georgian foods might also lead to a banalisation of "taste principles" such as the distinction of hot and spicy in western Georgia, and the type of red or green wild plum sauce called tkhemali that each family has kept as its own guarded recipe over generations. Today, the sauce can be found in different forms, marketed to the Russian and other world markets that have come to appreciate Georgian food.

An assortment of present-day labelled and marketed Georgian foods that were formerly only found in a traditional context, including wild plum sauce (tkhemali), frozen versions of khinkali and ready-to-fry chicken breasts are now widely available. Mineral waters, Georgian tea (sometimes packaged in bamboo containers from western Georgia), and even Coca-cola company products from the factory in Tbilisi accompany family meals when parents come home tired from work and cannot count on the long preparation time they enjoyed before. The humble khinkali that arrived with the Mongols travelling across the Caucasus has become a fast-food for hurried Georgian families who can keep a meal on hand when the traditional breadwinners can no longer take the care and time to make the real thing.

Yet only the "real thing" will be offered on important occasions. An important birthday will still mean days of preparation in advance, as these occasions are a path for the lives of those who participate. These paths lead to the future of the family, the

Megruli khadjapuri

Adapted from Taste of International Cuisine, International Women's Association, Tbilisi, Georgia, 2003. Megruli indicates a dish from the western region of Mingrelia.

Dough :
1 kg flour, 100 g butter,
2 eggs
1/2 tablespoon baking soda,
1/2 tablespoon salt
1 tablespoon lemon or citric acid,
1 tablespoon yeast mixed with 1 cup of warm water

Filling :
600 g soft cheese (cottage cheese, mozzarella, etc), 1 egg,
250 g melted butter

Preparation :
1. Mix all the dough ingredients after sifting flour.
2. Knead thoroughly and leave for approximately one hour to rise.
3. Break cheese into small pieces if necessary. Mix with egg and butter.
4. Roll out the dough in a thin layer.
5. Cut out 2 round pieces of the dough around 20 cm in diametre.
6. Place the cheese stuffing in the middle of one half of the dough and cover with the other half to enclose it.
7. Place the khadjapuri in a pan that has been heated, with 1 tablespoon butter, and bake for 10 to 15 minutes or until brown.
8. When done, cover with cheese and butter on top and return to oven for 5 minutes before serving.

region, the country. Such meals do not "close" an event, but rather celebrate or "open" new directions. One leaves a supra or even a funeral meal not with a feeling of closure, but of social bonding, even with those who have gone before. Significantly, during the recent political upheavals many keipis or festive meals[9] – usually celebrated on special occasions – were held; they encouraged the participants to continue their actions towards a new type of government. The word used to greet your neighbours at the table as you raise a glass in Georgia is "gaumardjos", wishing success. Both for the afterlife and through present changes, Georgians cherish hope, which is fed by hospitality at table. They raise their glasses and voice this key word: "victory", or gaumarjos!

The supra: a Georgian feast, with khadjapuri in the foreground

1. Food and globalisation has been with us for centuries. It is interesting that scholars today study the thirteenth to fourteenth century Mongol historical, political and religious philosophies and are finding that the theory of "Heavenism" was a cohesive Mongol theory justifying the world's largest land empire, and perhaps one of the first examples of planned globalisation. It is thus no wonder that such foods as the Chinese type of ravioli (later transported to Italy), dumplings, Russian pelmeni and khinkali are still found throughout this former Mongol empire.
2. Khinkal, spelled slightly differently in the Azeri Georgian regions, is a different speciality. Served in the morning, this unctuous dish is composed of flat flour pasta, boiled, and topped with brown gravy and fried onions.
3. Shashlik is shish kebab – meat cooked over hot coals on long skewers. Khadjapuri is traditional Georgian cheese bread/pie, whose style varies according to region.
4. Kartvelian languages include Georgian, Svan, Mingrelian, and Laz, of which only Georgian has a written alphabet.
5. From the Arab for cloth spread with food.
6. This role includes drinking quite heavily and holding one's drink – several litres of wine per person at a sitting – and a strong voice that will resound over the many directions that a Georgian feast takes as the meal goes on, sometimes for several hours.
7. "Toast" in Georgian, the term could actually incorporate something of a prayer-like attitude towards the subjects being evoked.
8. Ajika is a hot red pepper paste or sauce, depending on the recipe.
9. A word derived from an ancient Persian word for joy.

Gunther Hirschfelder and Gesa U. Schönberger

Germany

Sauerkraut, beer and so much more

The sauerkraut problem – a story to start with

"Sauerkraut", John Miller asks, "where can I get sauerkraut?" That is a good question. John is in Königswinter, a little town on the banks of the Rhine. Overlooking the town is the ruined Drachenfels castle, which for over 200 years has made Königswinter one of Germany's most popular tourist attractions. John has set his heart on sauerkraut. His real name is not John Miller but Hans Müller. He has lived in America since his childhood, however, and is convinced – without quite knowing why – that sauerkraut with sausages or some other typical dish is served everywhere in Germany. His explorations of the restaurants in the city centre prove disappointing. He finds two Turkish restaurants, three Italian pizzerias and one Chinese restaurant. Everywhere the food smells appetizing, but definitely not German. Finally he discovers the Restaurant Krone, with its wood-panelled interior, heavy tables and long counter. The menu offers dishes catering to its customers' tastes, for example Schnitzel, pork escalopes broad and flat as a hand,

A restaurant in Germany

dipped in a flour and egg batter before being fried and served with a thick mushroom sauce, chips (French fries) and a small green salad. You can also have Schnitzel plain, without the sauce, or marinaded herring with diced apples and onions in a cream sauce, or roast venison served with kraut – at long last – but this kind is called Rotkohl (red cabbage), not sauerkraut. John samples everything and washes it down with the local red wine. It is all delicious, a trifle heavy perhaps, but not spicy. He wonders how people can eat this sort of food in hot summer weather! John has enjoyed his meal, but the sauerkraut problem has still not been solved. The proprietress of the Krone comes to the rescue: "Tomorrow I'll cook sauerkraut especially for you! Our customers don't want sauerkraut when they eat out, that's something they often get at home. On restaurant menus you'll see more joints and fried dishes, which in restaurants, anyway, are rarely served with sauerkraut. Certainly not here in the Rhineland, the westernmost part of the country. But my husband comes from eastern Germany and there's nothing he likes better than boiled sausages with sauerkraut and mashed potatoes!"

Regional - national - international

What do Germans in 2004 eat? Every day some 82 million appetites are satisfied, but what people eat varies considerably: there are all kinds of different seasonings, ingredients and ways of cooking as well as different types of cuisine. And different eating habits, too. Why is this? One reason is certainly Germany's long federal tradition dating back to the Middle Ages. A dominant ruler or capital was the exception rather than the rule; political and social life was shaped by a complicated patchwork of smaller units – principalities, petty kingdoms, cities, counties and bishoprics. Consequently, German cuisine is essentially regional cuisine. People in the south-west, for example, eat more white bread and noodles, while people in Mecklenburg on the Baltic Sea coast eat more potatoes and use different spices and seasonings.

As elsewhere, geography is, of course, an important factor. Even today fish is very popular along the Baltic and North Sea coast, while people in Bavaria tend to eat more meat. Many Bavarians shudder at the very thought of eating fish – an attitude unthinkable in the north!

Another thing that distinctively shapes Germany's eating habits is our nine neighbours, each with their own typical cuisine. Hence in Aachen, just across the border from Belgium and the Netherlands, shoppers can choose from a great variety of fish or cheeses, while in Frankfurt an der Oder you can buy Polish delicacies such as pickled forest mushrooms or piroggen, a type of ravioli with a sweet or savoury filling. In the Erzgebirge near the Czech border Bohemian dumplings known as Knödel are very popular. These differences are also reflected in regional preferences for particular spices and flavours: the sweet-sour combination that northerners relish in liquorice sweets, for example, or Himmel und Erde – a dish made with potatoes, onions, apples and bacon – southerners find peculiar and not at all to their taste.

In the first half of the twentieth century what people ate still depended largely on where they lived, there was nothing that could be considered typical German fare. The more standard diet that exists today is the result of three fairly recent developments. One factor has been the trend to mechanisation and the more widespread use of chemicals in agriculture, especially since the 1950s. This has meant not only more abundant supplies but also a similar choice of foodstuffs throughout the country. Another factor was the spread of supermarkets from the 1960s onwards, which completely revolutionised shopping. Brand names and standardised products from a handful of suppliers soon dominated the market, making it increasingly difficult for small regional noodle manufacturers, for example, to compete. The third factor is globalisation, although where tastes in food are concerned "Europeanisation" is perhaps the better word. It is against this background that the current boom in magazines and television programmes on the subject of food and eating should be seen. Clearly they play a key role in determining tastes and fashions in food.

What impact has globalisation had on Germany's meals? Will the Germans soon be consuming only some kind of standard European fare? Before answering that question we should first investigate the contents of Germany's cooking-pots and take a closer look at its eating habits.

Rotkohl - red cabbage

(Recipe from the *Dr Oetker School Cookery Book*, 13th edition, 1963, Bielefeld)

Ingredients:
1 kg red cabbage, 60 g lard or goose dripping, 1 large onion, 1 laurel leaf, a few cloves, a little salt, a little sugar, 1/8 l water, 3-4 cooking apples, 1 teaspoon cornflour or equivalent, 1 dessert spoon vinegar

Preparation :
Remove from the cabbage the coarse outer leaves and stem. Cut the cabbage into quarters, wash the pieces and either finely chop or grate them. Melt the lard or dripping and fry the chopped onion gently until it turns a light golden colour. Add the chopped or grated cabbage and heat it gently. Add the laurel leaf, cloves, a little salt and sugar, 1 dessert spoon vinegar, water and the chopped apples. Cook everything over a low flame for 65-75 minutes.
At the end add the cornflour dissolved in a little water in a cup and season with salt, sugar and vinegar.

Breakfast in Germany

Seven o'clock in the morning, breakfast-time. Here at least there does exist a typical drink: coffee. Coffee consumption amounts to 160 litres per capita per year, which means that statistically every German drinks four cups a day. So coffee, taken with milk or sugar or both, or simply black, is a must on almost every breakfast table. Tea is less common and more often drunk in northern areas. Among health-conscious people there is an increasing tendency to drink coffee surrogates, unsweetened fruit juice or mineral water at breakfast-time. For the first meal of the day most Germans prefer something savoury like cheese and cold cuts or sausage, sometimes even pickled cucumbers or fish. Bread or rolls, too, belong on virtually every breakfast table. Most bread is made from a combination of flours – usually wheat and rye – and sold as Graubrot. There is a huge variety – maybe even hundreds – of different kinds. Wholemeal bread and bread containing nuts, seeds or potatoes used to be the standard fare of the poor in former times, but today these coarser and more nutritious types of bread are popular with the growing number of health-conscious consumers. There are countless small bakeries that offer a large range of different breads, including white or brown rolls. Only about half of Germany's daily bread comes from the supermarket, which also sells do-it-yourself baking mixtures and special sliced bread for toast. If there is anything Germany can claim as typical besides coffee, it is undoubtedly bread.

Bread is not only an essential part of breakfast but also supplies the sandwiches for the schoolchild's breaktime or the office worker's lunch, and it is often an important component of the evening meal. Whether eaten as closed or open sandwiches, the method is the same: a pound or kilo loaf is cut into finger-thick slices and spread with butter or margarine; then comes a layer of jam or jelly, sometimes also honey or a chocolate-flavoured spread or – as a savoury alternative – cold cuts, sausage or cheese.

But there is more to breakfast than coffee and bread. Muesli is increasingly popular and now appears on 10% of German breakfast tables. Those with time for a leisurely breakfast may also eat an egg, often with a glass of fruit juice.

Breakfast is clearly quite a substantial meal, especially when eaten in the family. The trend toward one-person households, however – today some 40% of Germans live alone - is undermining such traditional habits. Over 30% of students report that they breakfast on whatever is at hand – biscuits and orange juice, a bar of chocolate and milk, or the previous day's leftovers.

Breakfast is followed by a long morning – so to keep hunger at bay people often have a mid-morning snack, a cup of coffee with a sandwich, fruit or a bar of chocolate.

The land of the lunch

Snacks should not be too substantial, however, as Germany is a very lunch-minded country. Until a few years ago lunch was by far the most important meal of the day. While there is a trend now to make dinner the main meal, it is still rare to have only a light lunch in the middle of the day.

Lunch in Germany is a substantial affair and always hot. Since the nineteenth century it has consisted of meat or fish and two side dishes – potatoes or, less commonly, rice or noodles, and a vegetable. In restaurants, hospitals and canteens soup is served before the main course and the meal is rounded off with a dessert. Most young people, however, find the traditional soup at the start of a meal boring and old-fashioned.

Where lunch is concerned, Germans prize variety. Escalopes, cutlets, fish dishes and regional specialities that are now popular all over the country regularly appear on the menu. A good example of such a regional speciality is Königsberger Klopse – mince meat balls with capers in a white sauce. Around the year 1900, when Königsberg – now the Russian city

Germany

Maultaschen – a typical Swabian ravioli-style dish

©CMA

of Kaliningrad – was still a German town, a whole generation of German housewives learnt their culinary skills from cookery books designed to promote more modern, varied and healthier family fare. Recipes such as that for Königsberger Klopse were adapted from dishes popular among local burghers and soon became a national favourite. Up to the 1960s meat dishes – mostly pork or beef – were made from just about every part of the animal – trotters, lungs, heart, kidneys and of course joints – cooked in a variety of different ways. Meat arrived on the table stewed, roasted, salted or smoked in ever larger quantities. By the turn of this century Germans were eating on average 60 kg a year! However, now that virtually every household has a refrigerator, many traditions – conserving food by pickling and smoking, for instance – seem to be on the way out. New trends have made their appearance, and since the 1960s the popularity of chicken and other poultry dishes has soared.

New fashions are apparent in the side dishes as well. Around a generation ago Germans were still eating some 175 kg of potatoes a year – mostly for lunch, often in the evening and sometimes even at breakfast – cooked peeled or unpeeled, mashed or fried, in soups or in salads. One cookery lexicon lists as many as 160 different ways to prepare potatoes. Today, with consumption down to 75 kg per year, variety has given way to a few standard recipes and there is greater use of processed products such as frozen chips and croquettes, air-dried potato dumplings or instant mashed potatoes.

On the vegetable front much has changed, too. Cabbage – a vegetable that keeps well and is highly suited to cooler climes – has lost its former dominance. Being difficult to digest, it needs a lot of cooking – and for that people nowadays cannot spare the time. Germany's favourite vegetables are cauliflower and tomatoes.

Lunchtime – the ideal and the reality

An idyllic scene: a German family, father, mother and two children sitting down to lunch either at home or in the traditional kind of restaurant known as gutbuergerlich. There is soup, a main course and a pudding, accompanied by polite conversation. Yet this traditional ideal exists mainly in people's heads. Only a proportion of older women still produce such meals, usually at weekends or on special occasions. The dictates of working life, mobility and school as well as lack of time and culinary skill have all contributed to this demise. Another important factor is television, which people often prefer to conversation – if they lunch at home, that is, rather than elsewhere.

On the subject of eating out: for many that means the canteen rather than a restaurant. On average Germans eat away from home four times a week.

Indeed, young working men tend not to eat at home at all. Nevertheless, canteens cannot take their customers for granted. How they compete for their favour reveals a lot about German tastes in food. While male customers prefer high-fat foods such as meat and chips, women are partial to vegetables and salads. In an effort to counteract the trend to bland, standardised fare, many canteens offer seasonal dishes much appreciated by their customers. Here, too,

however, the traditional main course is the rule – meat and two vegetables all served on the same plate. This typical lunch is eaten relatively quickly by European standards – according to one study, men finish their meal in just seven and women in nine minutes. In other ways, too, hospital and canteen caterers reflect and reinforce people's eating habits. On Fridays, for example, a fish or pasta dish is usually served, since for centuries Friday was a fast day.

Germany

German fast food

The German lunch is certainly not on the way out. Neverthless, over 60% of what 19- to 25-year-olds eat is consumed between meals, in front of the television or out and about and above all at snack bars. This segment of the market is shared between international fast-food chains, local bakeries, takeaways and food stores, which offer savoury snacks, sweets and drinks to suit all tastes. Here, too, there are firm favourites such as the döner kebab, which arrived with the first Turkish immigrants to Germany, whose

descendants now number some 3 million. The döner kebab – a special kind of bread roll filled with spit-roasted lamb – is universally available and a highly popular alternative to German food and even the fare offered by the fast-food chains. Yet for most snack-bar customers there is still nothing to beat bratwurst or currywurst – grilled sausage and its curry-flavoured cousin – and chips, often with mayonnaise. Much too fatty and definitely unhealthy, so what is the secret of its success? It is quick, tastes good and is a hot meal. Another reason – a relic of former times – is the prestige traditionally attached to grilled, roasted and fried foods. Meat stews and soups that preserved every precious gram of fat were long considered poor people's fare. In food as in so much else, old habits die hard. The Germans and the sausage – on that a whole chapter could be written! Yet how did the sausage team up with the chips? The potato has been a staple food in Germany for around 200 years, but for much of that time fat was in short

Urban takeaway

supply. From the 1960s onwards many West Germans spent seaside holidays in Holland and Belgium where they acquired a taste for the chips long popular with the locals. Soon chips were being produced and eaten in Germany as well, especially since in the 1950s and 1960s the economy was growing rapidly. With road and housing construction and the car industry booming, people wanted to eat well, too – which typically meant eating large quantities of high-fat, cheap food. That was the dominant pattern – albeit somewhat delayed in East Germany – right up to German reunification in 1990.

Special cakes for tea-time

A snack or treat between meals is not always savoury. Especially in the afternoon people like to indulge their sweet tooth. And because Germans are so fond of cakes and pastries, there are bakeries everywhere. They all sell a range of cakes and cookies, in particular small, palm-sized pastries iced or with a crumbled topping, and filled with custard cream or cooked fruit. There is a wide range of regional specialities: Streuselkuchen – crumble cake – originally from central and northern Germany is now a national favourite. Cakes filled with pear confit are popular in Hunsrück, and in eastern areas poppy-seed cake is a winner. Doughnuts strewn with sugar and with a jam filling – known variously as Berliner, Pfannkuchen or Krapfen – are sold in winter virtually everywhere. In addition to the bakeries, albeit not quite so common, special pastry-shops sell more elaborate tarts and gâteaux. In the days when several generations used to live under one roof, when mobility was more restricted and most women worked at home, the Sunday tea table laden with cakes was an institution. On all festive family

Himmel und Erde

(Recipe from the *Dr Oetker School Cookery Book*, 13th edition, 1963, Bielefeld)

Ingredients:

1 1/2 kg potatoes, 500 g apples,
3/8 l water, a little salt, a little sugar,
a little vinegar (optional),
100 g unsliced bacon , 2 onions

Preparation :

Put the peeled, diced potatoes and the peeled, quartered and cored apples into a pot of boiling water with a little salt and sugar and cook till soft. Drain and season with salt, sugar and vinegar. Chop the bacon into lardons and fry gently. Add the sliced onion, fry till golden brown and then scatter the lardons and sliced onion over the potatoes and apples.

Sausages, cold cuts and bread

occasions such home-made creations were the proud centrepiece – but nowadays they are more likely to be bought from the pastry-shop. Elderly German ladies are particularly fond of their cake – for as the saying goes, a slice of cake in the afternoon makes every day a Sunday!

Dinner – Germany goes European

No one who has had a substantial lunch, tucked into coffee and cake in the afternoon and snacked in-between on currywurst or döner will have much of an appetite in the evening. And of course hardly anyone eats that much – by European standards Germans are of about average weight. Eaten generally between 6 p.m. and 7 p.m., the evening meal bears no comparison with dinner elsewhere in Europe, since traditionally it was much less important than lunch. Most elderly, and indeed many young, Germans eat a supper of open sandwiches topped with cheese, sausage or cold cuts, sometimes with gherkins or other pickled vegetables or soup.

Owing to greater mobility and more people working outside the home, around a third of German households now have their main meal in the evening – often the only one they have they time and leisure to enjoy. Not that Germans take that much time for food – on average only 1 hour and 23 minutes a day, which makes them pretty fast eaters by European standards.

New trends are influencing not only the time when the main meal is eaten but also its contents. Hot evening meals are more likely than hot lunches to consist of processed food and ready-made meat products. A whole range of Italian-style noodle and pasta dishes – a great favourite, quick to prepare, cheap and filling – have been created for the German market.

Sharing a meal is an experience that forges bonds. One way in which people manifest friendship, for example, is to eat together. This is a universal phenomenon and the Germans are no exception. It is customary to invite family and friends to festive meals celebrating special occasions such as christenings, weddings, silver and golden wedding anniversaries, birthdays and Christmas. However, Germans do even more drinking together than eating together – for example, when they celebrate birthdays or go out to the pub with friends and colleagues.

Eating out in restaurants has become increasingly common, not just on special occasions but also simply to enjoy conversation and good food in a relaxed atmosphere. Home fare and the food served in restaurants differ in a number of ways. Restaurant menus offer not only more courses but also much greater variety, including dishes with a Mediterranean, Asian or South American flavour. At least when they eat out Germans like to linger over their meal. They have now also acquired a taste for the kind of refined, light cuisine popularised by star chefs like Eckart Witzigmann, whom Gault Millau in 1994 hailed as the best chef of the twentieth century.

The Germans and their drink: Prost!

In other countries drinks are what people have with a meal. But in Germany there is one drink that is drunk in its own right: beer. One reason for its popularity is the low taxes (by European standards) on alcohol, a mere €2 per litre of pure alcohol. But by far the main reason is the key role beer and wine have played in daily life since the Middle Ages. As important beverages but also as status symbols and luxury items, they are considered part and parcel of German culture.

It is hardly surprising, therefore, that there is less debate in Germany than in many other countries about the negative effects of alcohol consumption. Only 5% of German men and 10% of women drink no alcohol at all.

Beer is the most widely drunk alcoholic beverage. Whether Bavarian Weissbier, Kölsch from the Rhineland, Berliner Weisse or Pils, whether drunk at a restaurant, takeaway, disco or at home, beer is a food, an image-maker, a thirst-quencher and much else besides. With average beer consumption now at 120 litres per year, Germany is in the European top league – a fact that explains the cliché of the beer-bellied Germans and worries the medical profession.

While for many years beer consumption rose steadily, sales now seem to have peaked. Presumably today's performance-oriented society rules out still higher consumption. There is clear evidence, however, that some 5% of Germans have an alcohol problem.

Doctors complain that people drink far too little ordinary water. The leading non-alcoholic beverages are coffee and carbonated mineral water, of which the average German drinks 160 and 150 litres a year respectively. Especially mineral water is seen as indispensable at mealtimes. Germans are also very fond of orange and apple juice, but less keen on lemonade and Coca-Cola-type drinks than their European neighbours.

Food in Germany – conclusions

According to the figures, some 327 million meals – or 2.9 meals per person – are eaten in Germany every day. What comes on people's plates is the product of centuries-old economic, scientific, cultural and political traditions, traditions that are not static but constantly evolving in response to new developments. Seen in this light, is it possible to arrive at any valid and final conclusions about German food? The answer is bound to be "no".

What people eat and how they eat it is a reflection of how they perceive themselves, both as individuals and as a nation. From this perspective at least some general statements appear warranted. First of all, food has acquired a whole set of new meanings. We no longer eat just to keep alive. Over the past thirty years food and nutrition have become hot topics in the context of health reform, the situation of agriculture, sustainability and individual quality of life. To a greater extent than their European neighbours Germans are also concerned about the quality and content of what they eat and by and large are well informed about such issues. They know – at least in theory – what the relevant national organisations recommend as a healthy diet, although acting accordingly is another matter. Cooking is nowadays not just a chore but one of the most popular leisure-time activities. In the arts world, too, food plays an important role.

Food, Europeanisation, globalisation, national identity and local roots – all of these concepts are interlinked. In our grandparents' day a huge variety of different dishes were served all over Germany. Often it was tradition that dictated what was served when.

Maultaschen, a typical Swabian ravioli-style dish, was originally eaten on fast days and every village had its own particular recipe. Smoked eel was a favourite on the Baltic coast, and in the Advent season every region had its special spiced cookies, cakes and biscuits – even today Nuremberg is famous for its Lebkuchen and Dresden for its Christstollen. Nowadays, however, sales of frozen pizzas have soared, fast-food chains have spread all over the country and supermarkets stock the same standard fare – spaghetti or Alsatian onion tart – with the same standard taste.

So in twenty years' time will there be any regional cuisines left for tourists visiting Germany to discover? The answer is reassuring. In Germany, as elsewhere, people prize their identity. Local and regional specialities will continue to be eaten and even become more popular, now that other ways of expressing identity are in decline – in today's mobile society dialects are less widely spoken than in the past and traditional regional costumes have virtually disappeared. But regional cuisines are experiencing a renaissance – every German appreciates good food, after all! Just come and try!

Eleonora Skouteri-Didaskalou and Evie Voutsina

Greece

A well-tempered culinary experience

A piece of bread baptised in the eternity of an exquisite wine

The essence of Greek cuisine might be found in a choice cut of spit-roasted lamb or kid – if it is Eastertime and spring is bursting forth. But couldn't the same be said for a panful of fried pork at Carnival time, or a tempting dish of stuffed cabbage leaves at Christmas? Or for the aroma that rises from a festive pot, for a little grape-must pudding, a glass of wine, a spoonful of trachanas (handmade noodle soup) or fasoulotava (baked beans)? Or even for the cheese pies or milk pies or others filled with every kind of garden vegetable and wild herb? Or for just a handful of memorial kollyva (boiled whole wheat berries) or a piece of communion wafer from the Sunday mass?

All of these foods constitute an inclusive culinary identity that has withstood the test of time, and that can still arouse the senses of Greeks today with their riot of tastes. The meanings of these foods are registered not only in the Greeks' own history but also in experiences and attitudes deeply rooted in the history of Europe,

©Takis Tloupas 1971

Ambelakia Larissa, Thessaly. Examining the new wine

195

the history of the Mediterranean, and that of the region that was the cradle of the Old World. Thus, whatever might be called the "Greek table" is more than particular dishes or foods; it reveals a longstanding and well-tempered cuisine (like Bach's clavier) as a topos of cultural production and reproduction, a frame in which the hands that perform the cooking activate an experience that is lived and acquired over many generations.

Festive pots for the day of St John the Prodromus on 29 September, St Prodomus village, Halkidiki, northern Greece

The Greeks wine and dine while talking. They talk while eating and treat one another by drinking. Companionship means conversation, symposium means dialogue. One who eats alone is not only a miser but refuses the community of the table. The Greeks eat while celebrating and celebrate while eating. Every "let's eat", every "savouring" (life itself being measured "until one's oil runs out"), every piece of bread "that wards off evil" presents food as an index of social status and identity revealing both an everyday routine and a festive, ritual ceremony that revolves around the table.

The word phai/phagito (from the Ancient Greek verb phagein of bibrôskô/ esthiô/ trôô), literally meaning what is edible or already eaten, also denotes bread, the most essential, blessed and sacred food. Anything else, even a little garlic, onion or radish, is prosphagi or symphagi, something to complement the bread and extend it further: fish, meat, cheese, pulses and everything eaten with bread, the opson of the ancients. Whether skilfully made prosphagia ("pepoiêmena technê tini") or plain supplement, these foods signify something extra, a sought-after distinction, even a luxury. By contrast, bread is unique, the absolute measure of life and living: Poverty means not having bread to eat.

If the Greek table effectively sums up Greek identity, the language of cooking reveals deeply rooted habits and tastes that are recorded in generic terms, such as phagito (food), chorta (potgreens), ladera (cooked-with-olive-oil). In culinary practice the language also denotes particular dishes, such as mageirefta (cooked), psita (roast), vrasta (boiled), or mageiritsa (the Easter offal soup). The names of utensils can designate food, for instance, the kazania (pots, festive pots and food). Simple in its essence, Greek cuisine reveals itself through archaeological and historical research as a culinary synthesis that has been confirmed ethnographically by cooking techniques and eating practices that remain alive today.

Accordingly, in Greece there is no vegetable, herb or plant above or below ground that has not been named, tried and immortalised in one or more recipes. Side by side with the cultivated crops – dominated by the Mediterranean trinity of wheat, vine and olive, those "treasures of the world" – wild plants have enriched the Greek table with their distinctive flavours. The fact that Greek cuisine comes in limitless variations does not contradict the ever-present sense of proportion and balance (as in Greek Byzantine and folk music), whether in the blessing of Mediterranean olive oil drizzled over oregano and thyme (the crowning glory of a slice of well-baked bread); or in the memory of a dry crust baptised in the eternity of an exquisite wine.

A moderate cuisine

The Modern Greek dietary standard is based not only on the ancient Greek "mêden agan" (moderation in all things), as redefined by the strictures of the Eastern Orthodox Church, but also on enduring culinary techniques and foodstuffs. One can easily trace dishes that have been cooked the same way since antiquity, through the Byzantine period and into our own time (such as squid cooked in its own ink, fish simmered in vinegar and raisins, or various pies like plakountes with sesame). Many foodstuffs have kept their

Plakous entyrites or tyropsomo (bread with cheese)

A recipe based on ancient Greek and Byzantine sources and contemporary ethnographic evidence provided by Evie Voutsina.

Ingredients:

500 g durum flour, 1 level tablespoon dry yeast, 1 level teaspoon salt, 1/2 teaspoon mixed cinnamon and cloves , 1/2 cup (100 ml) olive oil, 1/2 cup (100 ml) white wine, 100 g anthotyro (light white cheese), 100 g grated Gruyère-type cheese, 3/4 cup coarse-chopped walnuts 1 tablespoon sesame seeds, 2 tablespoons poppy seeds (preferably ground)

Preparation :

Mix the flour, yeast, salt and cinnamon-clove mixture. Add the oil and wine and knead, gradually adding lukewarm water until the dough is smooth and elastic. Continue kneading and add the two cheeses, the sesame seeds and poppy seeds, and then the walnuts. Knead until everything is well mixed. Cover the dough and leave for 15 minutes. Oil a round baking pan (28 or 30 cm diametre) and place the dough in it, spreading it with wet hands. Cover with a folded towel and let it rise until it is double its original bulk. Score the surface in two or three places and bake in a preheated oven at 175°C for about 15 minutes or until done.

ancient names, like the myxinari fish mentioned in Athenaeos as ichthys myxinos, and culinary techniques have stood the test of time, the best example being sykomyzêthra (full-fat cheese made with fig sap). Exotic spices known from antiquity are still used today in dishes that combine local foodstuffs and flavours such as wheat, cheese and saffron (krokos) with exotic spices, from the "artoi tryphôntes dipyroi" of Alkaeos (seventh century BC) made with "tyros, peperi, cinnamômon and krokos" to the modern Eastertide kitrinokouloura (yellow rolls) of Astypalaia in the Dodecanese, similarly prepared with cheese, pepper, cinnamon and saffron.

Greek cuisine developed along two paths that intersected now and then: that of the ordinary people, the folk and the peasants – a cuisine divided into daily and festive meals and transmitted orally and by example from generation to generation; and that of the wealthier classes, also in distinct everyday and celebratory versions, which produced richer, more complex and more innovative dishes, plus an interest in haute cuisine that led to specialisation in food supply, production and consumption. The two culinary traditions, the one definitively urban and the other rather provincial, centred respectively in the great cities of Hellenism where trade flourished and wealth accumulated, and in the countryside, where local culinary habits were marked by frugality combined with inventiveness in exploiting to the utmost all locally available products and edibles.

The history of modern Greek cooking is one of innovations alongside continuities. For instance, the Greek Orthodox Christian culinary tradition, which redefined, codified and classified into a structured dietary canon the Mediterranean, Neolithic and ancient Greek diets without overturning either their material basis or their rationale or symbolism, existed symbiotically – albeit at a safe distance – with other religious and/or ethnic culinary traditions. In a similar way this tradition survived the West European culinary invasion during the nineteenth and twentieth centuries, which led to the formation of a new bourgeois cuisine: Greek in substance, even though rather French in appearance, and with an Italian touch.

The similarities with and differences between modern, Byzantine and ancient Greek cuisine reveal deep-rooted relationships in the techniques, habits and symbolism associated with cooking and eating, as well as in a number of basic

"At the table", Book of Job

foodstuffs (pomegranate, apple, wheat, meat, honey, salt, vinegar), utensils and appliances (pot, hearth, oven, knife, salt cellar, jug, oil dispenser, oil lamp, plate, plough, sickle, basket). The persistence of both basic meals (bread and prosphagia, pies, vegetables cooked with oil) and ceremonial ones (pork, lamb, goat, honey, wheat, oil, wine) also exhibit age-old connections. Prolific grains and fruits like wheat, rice, pomegranate, nuts, and sesame, long recognised for their taste and nutritional value, similarly connect back to ancient times in their symbolism. Sesame is used on everyday bread or rolls to heighten taste, or in sweets such as pasteli (sesame bars with honey and almonds) or halvas (sweet curd) to give pleasure; it is spread on ritual breads or incorporated into kollyva for its deep meanings (abundance, life, birth, continuity, fecundity, strength). Tahini (sesame paste), mixed with honey or plain, constitutes a basic Lenten meal, while sisamozoumo (roasted sesame soup) is a fortifying meal for those working in the fields. Last but not least, sesame oil is used in everyday cooking and in pastries in northern Greece (in areas where olive oil was once a luxury, olive trees are not cultivated, so sesame was, and still is, a basic crop), coastal Halkidiki being the only exception. However, a historically concrete interpretation of such symbolic uses of food especially in rites of passage remains problematic, despite its importance.

Greek cuisine may be seen as both an array of coexisting realities and a single reality with many versions. Local dishes or foodstuffs that seem different

Late-spring grape leaves at the open-air market in Athens

or that have various names are in fact either the same or else they represent equivalent variants or complementary, if disparate, versions. They might even be new combinations. Late nineteenth and twentieth century urbanisation and migration spread culinary techniques and tastes beyond the confines of their original locale. Networks established between the homeland and the place of settlement facilitated the transfer of essential local products (oil, wine, poultry, wheat or flour, homemade pasta and pickles), thus favouring the crossing of borders and the diffusion of local culinary traditions. At the same time, the professionals of Greek cuisine set the tables of Greek restaurants and tavernas at home and abroad with roughly the same typically Greek dishes.

To comprehend the range of culinary variety in modern Greek cuisine it would be sufficient to observe how many ways there are to cook, for example, lamb: koukoulôto, that is covered with a yoghurt egg-mixture, apricot or lettuce; baked with vegetables; prepared in a casserole with tomatoes and spices; roasted in the oven or spit-roasted; simmered in a soup (especially the offal) or fried, to name but a few. Roasting meat over an open fire (spit roasting) – a simple but outstandingly ceremonial way of cooking – has a long history. And one need only list the fish and shellfish available in order to appreciate the endless local variations of a cuisine that exploits to the fullest the produce of sea, lakes and rivers. Every fish dish with its local identity is closely related to either the recent past or a more distant one: bakaliaros skordalia (codfish with garlic or onion relish), served throughout Greece; whitebait bourdeto in the Ionian islands; gambari (prawns baked with potatoes, garlic and parsley) in Preveza in Epirus; garoufa and saltsisto with lake or river fish in Kastoria in western Macedonia.

The Greeks eat according to their culture, sometimes tenaciously holding out against the natural flow of products but also paying the price of sticking to social and religious rules. For example, the domesticated pig fed all year long on leftovers and peelings was for several days fed on acorns and chestnuts to improve the flavour of its meat before being sacrificed for the Christmas table. For the same reason the Christmas turkey was fed whole walnuts. Discipline was in complete harmony with the frugal use of available foodstuffs. Greek cuisine displays a deep knowledge of how to exploit both the wild and cultivated environment, as well as the available market; it also attests to a considered relationship not only with the product but also (perhaps even more so) with the leftovers.

A. Tassos, Peasant wedding, *woodcut*

To eat or not to eat? Fasting and feasting the Greek way

The traditional Greek diet is based on a recurring annual cycle of feasts and fasts. The Greek Orthodox Church conceived of the idea of fasting as a discipline for body and soul and established it as a canonical rule that is expressed in eating arrangements for the faithful to follow the year round. These arrangements, discussed below, remain essentially unchanged today.

Fasting means abstinence from animal products and fish, apart from shellfish and snails. That is, no meat, eggs, milk or dairy products are allowed, and on certain days no oil. Protein is replaced by carbohydrates. For example, instead of eggs and cheese, raisins, honey, grape-juice syrup, nuts or light compotes are served. Non-Lenten fare consists of animal products with vegetables.

The basic Lenten foods are "white", that is bloodless: wheat and bread, pulses, fresh and dried fruits as well as retselia (vegetables and fruit preserved in epsima, a sugarless thick grape syrup), shellfish, mushrooms, and, last but not least, pantosynanchta chorta (all kinds of greens). The principal non-Lenten foods are ceremonial and are used in all the major feasts and individual, familial and community rites of passage. Ceremonial foods are combinations of bloodless and sanguinary foods. Pride of place goes to bread and wheat, moulded into special shapes, decorated with special designs, and heavy with symbolism: wedding bread at weddings, pancakes with honey and pastry at births, memorial and festive kollyva for the dead.

Sterea Ellada (Roumeli) Easter in Arahova

Spring, harvest (summer), autumn, winter

The presence of oil and wine sanctify the ritual from oil decanter to plate or votive lamp, from oil lamp to baptismal font, from wine bottle onto the grave, from cup to chalice. First among animal products is meat, the mark of festive fare, which is served at weddings (for instance, the gamopilafo: into the wedding pot go chicken, goat or kid, or all three, slaughtered "to bloody the marriage", to be boiled with rice) and at births (nursing mothers eat chicken and drink chicken broth to increase the flow of milk). However, meat is forbidden at funerals (the mourning meal consists of fish, vermicelli with cinnamon for dessert, and bitter coffee and strong spirits).

Ceremonial preferences mark the ritual table of the great feasts: at Christmas, during the Twelve Days, and during the Carnival Kreatini (meat week) pork is served, stuffed in cabbage leaves or as a vegetable stew, roasted, or made into sausages, or syglino (preserved in its own fat). At Christmas poultry is served stuffed or in soups; at Easter, spring lamb or spit-roasted kid are offered, and their offal is presented with spring onions and aromatic plants in mageiritsa soup or roasted over an open fire as kokoretsi. Sacrificial lambs go into the holiday pot for all the saints' days and for the Assumption on 15 August. The ceremonial consumption of wine and bread is frequently required, from the Christopsomo, the round, decorated, egg-rich Christmas bread, to the lazarakia, small breads in the form of a shrouded

Fasolada nistisimi
(fat-free bean soup)

A recipe from western Macedonia provided by Evie Voutsina.

Ingredients:
300 g beans (preferably a mixture of large, red, small white and others) , 1 medium onion,
2 small carrots, 1 small potato,
3-4 sprigs celery,
1 level teaspoon sweet paprika, salt,
200 g crushed walnuts

Preparation :
Wash beans, put in a saucepan with ample water and let them soak overnight. Rinse soaked beans thoroughly and put in saucepan with double their volume of water. Boil for 1/2 hour. Add some salt, the diced vegetables and the paprika. When beans are boiled, add walnuts and cook while stirring for 3 minutes. Check for seasoning, adding salt to taste. Cover and allow to stand for about an hour before serving.

Lazarus; from the unleavened Lenten lagana to the egg-rich Easter bread kouloura, round or braided and topped with a red egg.

The annual dietary cycle involves not only acceptance but also daily observance of the church year, with its fixed feasts and holiday periods, and its incorporation into the national political and economic life in the form of an official calendar regulating work days and holidays. This yearly cycle gives 171-190 days of nominal or actual fasting, grouped into the following periods: 49 days (7 weeks) of Lent, 40 days of the Christmas Fast, 1 to 28 days for the Holy Apostles, 15 days for the Assumption, and also every Wednesday (partial fast) and Friday (oil-free fast). Of this total, 100 + 4 days are those of the strict, oil-free fast observed by monks, priests, the elderly and the very religious. Regardless of how faithfully this basically religious dietary regime is adhered to, it affects all aspects of personal, family and social life. Even those who do not fast are careful to show some respect for the symbols of dietary prescriptions and proscriptions. For example, on the eve of the great feasts, such as Christmas or Epiphany, fasting is strict, though only on Good Friday is the restraint and abstinence total, when "the pot should stay away from fire, the table remain unset". On the day of a funeral the family abstain from "red foods" (particularly blood and meat); St Barbara's Day means varvara, a polysporia mixture of grains and seeds. On her wedding day the bride must eat nothing but three bites offered by her mother-in-law; and on the

Annunciation fish must be eaten (even if it is "cod from the grocer", salted and long of northern provenance). Even the poorest family must roast some meat on Carnival Tsiknopempti ("fat Thursday"), and "red food" is also eaten on Kreatini (meat) week and Apokreo (Carnival) Sunday. "White food" – makaronia (pasta) and cheese – is served on Tirini (cheese) Sunday, while Katharodeftera ("clean Monday"), the first day of Lent, requires Lenten fare and lagana. Resurrection midnight calls for red eggs and mageiritsa, Easter Day for spit-roasted lamb or kid. At Christmas there must be pork, cabbage,

Octopus drying in the sun by the sea

chicken, pies, and syrup pastries – baklava and saragli made with layers of phyllo (dough) with nuts and honey syrup, spread or rolled.

Foods are classified into "ours" and "foreign", not according to some uncertain identity but according to a definite order and hierarchy of the ingredients by availability, season and environment. Most of all they are categorised according to what is Lenten fare and what is not, what is daily and what festive, what is eaten when and by whom, what has symbolic value and what has none.

The winter holiday season from Christmas to Carnival centres on pork; the spring, on lamb and goat. Bread is omnipresent. The three-month period from winter solstice (Christmas/New Year's Day) to spring equinox (Annunciation) anticipates the nine-month (spring, summer and autumn) period, binding together the agricultural and the ecclesiastical calendars, thus connecting the annual cycle of seasonal dietary custom with Christian cosmology. Both fasting and feasting are linked to archaic Mediterranean customs and flavours and to ancient Greek dishes spiced with special symbolism. It is in this sense that we should read the symbolic metaphors of the sealed, stuffed, wrapped and covered Christmas fare (sausages, stuffed chicken, stuffed cabbage leaves, wrapped saragli, layered baklava – they are all references to the swaddled Christ-child). The pierced, chopped and torn foods of Eastertime represent the Passion of Christ – an innocent lamb, supreme gift and sacrifice, is roasted whole though pierced through. All of its parts are consumed; even the intestines are "torn out and chopped up". The ritual cracking of red eggs symbolises the breaking open of the tomb and the crushing of death at the Resurrection.

Conquering time

In addition to its Christian content this dietary cycle reveals the traditional farming community's preoccupation with its "triplet" crop of wheat, wine and olive oil, and its concern for the rest of nature, whether wild or domesticated (animals and plants). All of nature is subject to the rule of the seasons and to environmental limitations regulated by human skill and inventiveness. In the same way, the poets of the larder and kitchen skilfully overcome the restrictions of seasonal conditions and conquer time using natural mediators and processes. Salt, vinegar, wine, honey, grape must, syrup or sugar preserve and heighten flavour (salted meat and fish, sausages, dried greens and herbs, fruit and nuts dried, pickled or in syrup, or simply and masterfully stored in their natural state; potatoes re-buried in the earth, meat in its own fat; olives in oil with aromatic herbs, or preserved in vinegar and honey with coriander and bitter orange, the Byzantine sêraion). For vine-leaf dolmades it is necessary to preserve the tender spring leaves for use in the summer with rice, and in winter with minced meat and rice. Stuffed cabbage leaves require both the compact winter cabbage and cabbage leaves pickled in brine. Beans and other pulses are Greek staples because they keep when dry, and pork preserved in various ways allows meat to be eaten in the winter. Traditional Greek cuisine is especially rich in preserved foods. Jams, marmalades, retselia fruits and vegetables, grape-must puddings, rusks, sausages, casseroles, pasta, pickles, dried garlic and onions, dried greens and fruit, nuts and aromatic herbs for teas (mountain tea, camomile, linden, sage and mint) all have a place in the housewife's larder.

The collective awareness of want and the customary habits and practices that ensure prosperity, or at least the promise of prosperity, define the Greeks' approach to food. The fear of scarcity and lack, the fear that there will not be enough bread, continues to rule attitudes toward the provision, storage and cooking of food. In an essentially peasant society the fear of hunger is ever-present, even though most products come through the market, scarcity combined with high prices and inflation is a recurrent threat, famine a grievous danger engraved in the collective memory. The rites of passage that signify the pivotal points in the farming year aim to symbolically ward off hunger and want, and help bring plenty and prosperity. Just before the June harvest and July threshing in high summer, the "joining of the two breads" – one made with the remaining seeds that empty the basket, the other with the new crop – is a telling metaphor for the precarious line between plenty and nothing at all. The first roll (koulouri) from the new harvest is presented to a passerby or offered to the village fountain so that "blessings will flow like water". Wishing "a good year" (kalochronia) refers to a good harvest and brimming granaries; wishing a "good day" (kalêmera) means a prosperous day and fine weather.

The diet of the poor and needy is mostly vegetarian and makes full use of the environment with surprising

Gambari fournou

A recipe from coastal Epirus and the Ionian Islands provided by Evie Voutsina.

Ingredients:
750 g gambari (grey prawns),
3 large potatoes,
1 bunch parsley,
8 cloves garlic,
finely-chopped,
salt, pepper,
1 cup olive oil

Preparation :
Clean and wash prawns well. Trim the long antennae, place in a sieve and salt carefully. Cut potatoes in round slices and arrange in baking pan. Add salt and pepper and cover potatoes completely with mixture of garlic and finely chopped parsley. Arrange prawns on top, sprinkle with pepper and pour the olive oil over them. Bake in preheated oven at approximately 180°C until potatoes become soft and shrimp turn pink, about one hour.

inventiveness (gruel made with cheap flour, pies filled with every imaginable vegetable growing in the most unlikely places, watery boiled pulses flavoured with red pepper and aromatic plants). It also makes the most tasty meals out of leftovers. The gaps are filled with dreams and stories about destitute heroes and heroines, hungry people who managed to fill both their pockets and their bellies, or about magic tables that at the snap of the fingers produce a spread of all the good things one could desire. A careful system of ritual redistribution of staple foods leaves no one hungry, at least not in a community-based society. The traditional dietary system just about permits communication between its two extremes: holidays and festivals, on the one hand, and food donations on the other. Ritual treats given, for example, for carol singing or kollyva offerings, allowed, and continue to allow, both the haves and the have-nots to eat and also to communicate. The sacrificial animal donated by the economically and socially powerful was distributed to all households, and the wedding banquet was open to all. Every holiday was an excuse to distribute food and provisions such as eggs, fruit, grains. Houses were open during the name-days, and the "virgin's table" and "Christ's table" laid out symbolically in every household with its nine or twelve dishes on Christmas Eve constituted "the poor man's table".

This customary attitude and behaviour reveals historical, cultural and social continuities. For example, the hondros or bulgur (cracked wheat) passed from the Neolithic cooking pots of Crete and the islands, and from those of the Peloponnese, Thessaly, Epiros, Macedonia, Thrace and Asia Minor to the pots of the Greece of yore, retaining its flavour as well as its sacred and everyday characters. A medley in the form of the ancient Greek panspermia offered for the dead on chytroi, the third day of Anthestêria, is connected to the Byzantine and modern Greek kollyva or stari, the symbolic food based on boiled whole wheat berries, pomegranate seeds, raisins and currants, white almonds, sesame, spices such as cumin, coriander, cinnamon, nutmeg, and decorated

Hippocras

A recipe based on ancient sources provided by Evie Voutsina.

Ingredients:
1 lt dry red wine, 1 medium whole nutmeg, 1 small cinnamon stick, 4 whole cloves, 5-6 sprigs lemon verbena, 3 sprigs marjoram, 1 small grain of pure frankincense, 2-3 tablespoons grape-juice syrup or honey (or even sugar)

Preparation :
Put the wine in a glass vessel. Break the nutmeg with a hammer and put it in a small saucepan along with the cinnamon, cloves, marjoram (one might also add lemon verbena) and 2 glasses of water. Boil until reduced to 1/2 cup of liquid. Before removing from heat, add the frankincense and then pour the mixture into the wine. Cover with film wrap and leave for 24 hours before filtering. Serve at room temperature or warmed.

with powdered sugar and silver bonbons, each decorations and ritual gesture laden with symbolism. Kollyva in the form of pikrokollyva (bitter and inedible half-boiled plain wheat) is spread on the grave on the third day after the funeral, while at memorial services it is offered as an elaborate, sweet dish of well-boiled wheat with accompaniments. It also appears as the yortasimo stari (festive wheat or kollyva of the living) made on the name-day of the head of the household to ensure a good harvest and individual and family prosperity. Finally, it shows up as the stari of St Theodoros (replaced today by sugared almonds from weddings) that girls put under their pillow on the first Saturday of Lent to dream of the man they will marry.

The seasonal and Orthodox diet is still fundamentally Neolithic (cereals, nuts and greens, honey, fruit and herbs, milk and eggs, meat) and Mediterranean (bread, oil and wine). The wine plays the dual role of a nourishing food supplement and – in moderation – an exquisite drink.

This simple diet in which foodstuffs are eaten either in basic combinations (bread with oil and/or wine, bread with oil and oregano, bread and olives, bread and cheese, butter beans with aromatic plants), elaborate compositions (pork with quince or prunes in a sweet-and-sour sauce, leeks or onions with prunes, tomatoes with raisins), or in larger syntheses at meals and banquets, is accompanied by new and foreign foodstuffs, either through trade (sugar, rice, spices,

Cappadocian Greeks baking kete (butter breads)

coffee, cocoa, various flavourings and vegetables) or by introduction into the local production (sweet corn, potatoes, various cereals, nuts, fruits and vegetables, with pride of place going to potatoes, peppers and tomatoes). Certain foodstuffs such as rice, coffee, sugar and tomatoes have dramatically altered the daily diet as well as the dishes associated with rites of passage, successfully replacing older ones embedded in ritual life. For example, rice or potatoes replace cracked wheat in the festive pot of meat; sugar is used instead of honey. They have also led to culinary innovations that range from the fully incorporated exotic aubergine cooked in the most familiar ways, to such an unsuitable mismatch of flavours as kolokythia or kolokythia me tin rigani ("marrows plain or with oregano") – an expression that is nonsense.

In their hands

Both as reality and as possibility the identity of Greek cuisine is in the hands of those who take a handful of beans and boil them for just the right length of time before "matching" them with the seasonings this land has always given its people: olive oil, onions, herbs, greens and vegetables. These hands, steeped in the wisdom of the kitchen, continue a culinary tradition of long standing. They have no need for dates, manuscripts or written records, because their art is enshrined in the deepest levels of historical memory. The hallmark of this art is ultimate simplicity incorporated in an ancient, carefully thought-out code of existence inscribed both in the structuring of the Greek version of the Mediterranean diet and in tastes based on simple though wise combinations: the happy marriage of olive oil and aromatics (bay, thyme, oregano, rosemary, dill, onion and garlic) or its binding with vinegar or lemon; the supreme taste of rose-vinegar or of liasto (sun-dried) wine; the simple recipe of a porridge made of cracked wheat or barley or corn flour, whether the ancient Greek tragós of Hippocrates, the Byzantine tragós and traganós of the time of Constantine X Porphyrogennêtos, or simply grandmother's trachanós and trachanás.

Greece

Zsuzsanna Tátrai

Hungary

The komatál: symbol of friendship and affection

One of the most important rituals involving food in traditional Hungarian life was known as the komatál. The word komatál contains two ideas: koma means "godparent" and tál means "plate". Hungarian tradition recognised two types of komatál. One was related to a holiday custom confirming friendship. This komatál was usually presented on White Sunday, the first Sunday after Easter. The other provided for women who had just given birth.

The komatál confirming friendship

This type of komatál was usually exchanged by young girls wishing to cement their friendship, although in some parts of Hungary it was also exchanged between boys and girls. The presentation of the ritual plate was also an important way to choose one's future godparents, who played a large role in family life.

The komatál was presented either on White Sunday, Easter Monday, or at Whitsuntide. In southern Transdanubia the custom went as follows: a girl made her gift from foods typical for Easter. She placed a plaited brioche and other cakes, painted eggs, fruit, and a bottle of wine on a plate, then covered it all with a cloth. She usually sent a younger girl to take this plate to the girlfriend's house. The handing over of the present was a solemn occasion, during which the young girl recited a poem or sang a song, such as

I've brought a komatál
A gilded one,
It's a gift from a friend to a friend,
If she does not want it, she may give it back.

209

Stuffed cabbage Ormánság style

Even in the 1950s this practice was still alive in Somogy County. The specific customs and the kinds of food on the plate varied from village to village. In the early twentieth century the komatál was prepared on White Sunday afternoon. In the middle of the

plate stood a bottle of wine, with a doughnut ring on its neck, surrounded by some eight to ten Easter eggs, oranges and cakes. The plate was sent with a young girl to the selected house. If it was accepted, the girls exchanged some of the presents, tasted the

210

Hungary

©Hungarian National Tourist Office

wine, refilled the bottle and returned it to the original sender. In the mid-twentieth century in certain regions, girlfriends exchanged two apples, two Easter eggs and an orange, and then kissed each other. In other places the receiver substituted one of the foods on the plate – replacing a cake with an apple, for instance – after which the girls shook hands and vowed: "till we die, we shall remain friends." In some villages, five Easter eggs, three oranges, a big pack of Easter candies and a chocolate bar were put into a soup bowl decorated with rose patterns, and the bowl was covered with a beautiful woven cloth. In other places, such as in the Ormánság region, the girls went to see each other personally, and the plate consisted of Easter eggs, baked and boiled sweets and a bouquet of ribbons. A rhyme was hidden behind the bouquet:

Bride, bride, let's play bride
By tomorrow let's be komas,
Live or die
We'll remain komas.

Then the girl would enter the house and kiss her friend, who took the plate to return it the following year. As an expression of their mutual respect, from that time on the friends addressed each other more formally, calling one anther koma or mátka (godparent).

At the turn of the nineteenth and twentieth centuries young children swore to be friends forever by exchanging eggs. Although young boys called such a friendship egg a koma, they did not attach as much significance to it as the girls did. Hungarians in the Moldavian region cemented friendship by exchanging eggs. Girls or boys each held an egg in their hands and knocked them together, sharing the one that broke. From then on they considered themselves cousins (such kinship rites are practiced in almost every culture, a most ancient form being the drinking of one another's blood).

Sources from the town of Eger, famous for its wine, reveal that around the middle of the nineteenth century a komatál was sent at Whitsuntide. An 8-to-10 year old girl dressed in white, with a wreath on her head, presented a plate with a plaited loaf and a small bottle of wine, covered with a colourful cloth. Such a komatál could be presented by a young woman to a young man, or by a young man to a young woman. The little girl who carried the plate received some money for her services and was told where to carry the plate further. In the Palóc region the name of the sender was also mentioned along with the rhyme, "I've brought the komatál, please, accept it kindly!" If the present was indeed kindly accepted, the girl was invited to sit down and have some food. In some places the presents on the plate were exchanged immediately, in other regions only later.

We know of some regions in north-eastern Hungary where, in the late nineteenth century, the komatál contained eggs, popcorn, figs, apples, walnuts, a bouquet of lilacs and some wine. The plate was surrounded by sprigs of rosemary and adorned with acacia blossoms. The komatál did not just circulate within one village – it could involve the young people of neighbouring villages as well. In these regions it was customary to start a komatál around carnival time, and the plate – repeatedly renewed and its contents exchanged – eventually made its way back to the original sender.

Sometimes the presents were tied to a tree called a koma or mátka tree.

The komatál and the woman in childbed

Caring for a woman who had just given birth was largely the duty of her koma-sister or sisters. This duty was related to the childhood custom of confirming friendship by means of a komatál, since godparents were usually chosen from among childhood friends. Girl-koma or boy-koma was what friends belonging

At János Pál's wine cellar in Tarcal

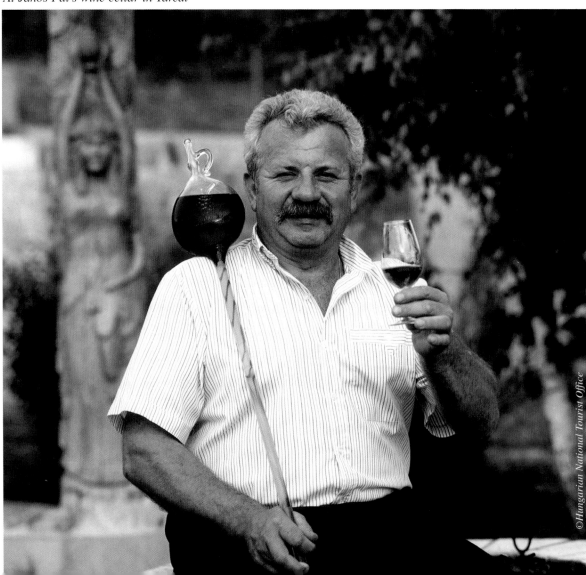

to the same social stratum were called. Godparents had a very special role in the family of their godchildren. They not only took part in the christening and cared for the mother after childbirth, but also helped out with work and were present at every family gathering. Roman Catholics usually chose one couple as godparents; Protestants often chose more. Around the town of Szeged in south-eastern Hungary the young mother was given chicken broth; in the Göcsej region of south-western Hungary the koma brought food for four days, then other female relatives took over for the next three days. With the Palóc people in the north-eastern part of the country, the woman in childbed was fed primarily by her mother and family until she was able to get up. In Kapuvár the new mother was brought food in a basket for three weeks. In Baranya County the poor carried their food in small baskets, while the well-to-do used a more voluminous basket that was carried on the head and covered with a decorated, handwoven cloth.

According to a mid-nineteenth century description from northern Hungary, "In the days following the paszita (christening feast) the woman in childbed got food and a large plaited loaf from her female relatives four or five times – the better-off even more often. Both the new mother and her koma would consider it a great offence not to prepare a chicken. It is the family's duty to offer a meal or especially some wine to the koma who brings the food." Another source from the same period states that "The woman in childbed is kept well for eleven to fourteen days by her koma and neighbours; the food brought, however, is mostly eaten by the young father."

Potato cake (Langos)

Ingredients:

3-4 medium potatoes, 1/2 envelope of dry yeast, 1/2 cup of warm milk for the yeast, 1/2 teaspoon sugar, 1.5 cups to 1.75 cups of flour, 1/2 teaspoon salt, lard for frying

Preparation :

Cook the potatoes in boiling salted water. Peel and mash them immediately, and allow to cool. (You should have about 1.5 cups.) Mix the lukewarm milk with the yeast and sugar. Let the starter sit for 5-10 minutes. Mix mashed potatoes with flour and salt, beginning with 1.5 cups of flour and adding more as necessary to make a pliable dough. Knead dough as long as it clings to your hand. It is ready when it no longer clings to the hand or to the bowl. Put dough in a clean bowl and cover. Let rise in a warm place until double in bulk (about 50-60 min.)

Roll out dough with a floured rolling pin on a floured board to approximately 1.5 cm thick. Cut into rectangles or squares. Prick with a knife to keep air bubbles from forming. Melt enough lard in a frying pan to come at least 2 cm up the sides of the pan. Fry the dough over medium heat watching closely, till browned. When ready, rub each langos with a cut clove of garlic and sprinkle with salt. Serve hot from the pan.

In this part of the country, even during the twentieth century the young mother was brought food for one week by her koma. The koma put on her best dress and covered the plate with an embroidered cloth. The lidded bowl or szilke contained a soup made of chicken, hen, duck or pigeon, with noodles or pasta. A festive kind of noodle was the so-called snake noodle prepared by means of a special tool. Rice cooked in milk, chicken with sour cream, dried apples, pears or plums were also offered, as were doughnuts. The food was distributed not only among family members but also to the midwife. The koma was then offered schnapps with honey. The food was carried in baskets, bowls, or on a plate, beautifully arranged and decorated, and covered with an ornamented cloth that had usually been made especially for this occasion.

As a rule, the foods offered were heavy and nutritious, to help strengthen the woman in childbed but also to provide ample food for the poorest relatives. On such occasions the whole family was well taken care of. The woman who brought the food was supposed to enter the house at noon when the church bells rang. In the Palóc region soup had to be part of the presentation. The more affluent brought chicken soup with a whole chicken cooked in it, or, less frequently, pork or beef soup. The broth contained noodles or pasta. On Fridays, that is fast days, egg soup or vegetable soup with grated noodles was common. The soup or broth had such special significance in koma meals that often several varieties were prepared.

Meat was offered as a second course only by the more well-to-do. It consisted of stuffed or roasted hen or pork in batter. Poorer people took the hen that had cooked in the soup and then stuffed it or roasted it with eggs. Scrambled eggs could replace meat; sometimes there was no second course at all.

Sweets, however, were a must, usually doughnuts or strudels filled with poppyseed or sweet cream

Butter cake (Pogacsa)

Ingredients:
3 cups flour, 1 cup butter, 4 egg yolks, 1 cup sugar, 1/2 teaspoon salt, 1 whole egg for wash

Preparation :
Mix flour and butter with a pastry blender until the mixture resembles coarse crumbs. Add egg yolks, sugar and salt and mix together. Turn onto a lightly floured surface and knead for a few minutes. Form into a large ball, cover with wrap and keep in a cool place overnight (or in the refrigerator).

Preheat the oven to hot. Roll out the dough between sheets of wax paper to a thickness of 2-3 cm. Cut into 5-6 cm rounds. Score a lattice-work design on each piece with a knife. Beat the whole egg and brush the tops of the pieces with egg wash. Bake 25-30 minutes, or until golden brown. Let cool before serving.

NB: this cake can be kept fresh for 2-3 weeks if kept in the refrigerator and warmed in a hot oven before serving.

Hungary

Still life with peppers and eggs

cheese. On Fridays when no meat was served, a plain plaited loaf or "empty bread" was given. In some communities the amount of food was defined: a rich farmer in a Palóc village brought six cheesecakes, six strudels, and twelve bodaks, whereas a poor one took only six brioches or bodaks. A wealthier koma was expected to bring one litre of wine, while the poorer ones had only to bring a few decilitres. The koma gave a nice, polished apple; some presented even orange. Schnapps was thought to help postpartum women gain strength.

Meals were traditionally carried in pottery dishes, but in the 1930s food boxes also appeared. Sweets and cakes were put on a plate or in a basket and covered with a nice cloth.

The women carried the food in both hands. The godmother usually went by herself, greeted the new mother, and then handed the food to another member of the family. She was then offered schnapps with honey. After the food was removed, the dishes or baskets were washed, and some sweets were packed in them in return. If the new mother was home alone, the godmother took the food into the kitchen, transferred it into dishes, and took her own dishes home unwashed. In wealthier families the godmother was invited to stay for lunch. Other female members of the family helped the godmother to feed the new

Harvester's goulash

mother, but this custom had no strict rules. In better-off families the practice of presenting a koma meal lasted for about a week, in poorer families only for a couple of days.

Although the koma meal traditionally consisted of some kind of meat soup or broth and baked sweets, in the twentieth century new types of food came into fashion, such as coffee with milk, Wiener schnitzel (meat in batter), minced meat, cake or candies. This centuries-long tradition of providing for women in childbed illustrates well the communal spirit and control so characteristic of Hungarian villages.

Örn D. Jónsson

Iceland

The creative fight for survival

My generation was brought up in the wake of Iceland's independence during the Second World War. As in other neo-independent nations, our upbringing was tainted by a heroic past. We had the sagas of the Vikings and the Althing, the first demo-cratic institution or government. We were told that Leif Eriksson, the hero of our textbooks, had discov-ered America. He was an Icelander, although, admit-tedly, a son of Norway.[1] The tales we were told in our youth did not quite fit in with the realities that emerged under closer scrutiny. By any standards, Icelanders were extremely poor, and had been ever since they first settled the island, and as we neared the twentieth century the country became even poor-er. But here is a tale of rags to riches, a story of a nation state that developed from extreme poverty into one of the most affluent societies in the world.[2] Even more important, in the context of this article, it all happened through the export of fish.[3]

In this essay I will first focus on the period between the tenth century (the time of settlement) up to the start of the twentieth century, the crucial period when

©Thorvaldur Árnason

Grímur, an old farmer, sits on his bed, where he also eats

Iceland

217

Icelandic food traditions were shaped. The second part will discuss "learning by interacting"[4] – how Icelanders slowly began to appreciate fish, the foodstuff that was the lever of their wealth, and that they had been exporting for several decades. I will end with a short look at Iceland's contemporary situation and the question of whether we are now entering an era of post-conspicuous consumption.[5]

Sin pas sal[6]

Fighting for survival was a way of life for nearly all Icelanders.[7] A specific characteristic of the Icelandic food culture or regional cuisine was the widespread shortage of salt.[8] The raw materials and utensils that exemplify most European food traditions and consumption patterns were painfully absent. In addition to a lack of salt, the cultivation of grain became increasingly difficult as the climate grew colder. Wood became scarce quite early on, and usable metals had to be imported. Icelanders were not even able to make cooking utensils out of clay,[9] so daily cook-ing or baking was difficult, sometimes even impossible. The houses, for the most part, were small huts (torfbæir) with no room for tables. People had to sit on their beds eating cold food from a lidded vessel that served as an all-in-one soup pot (askur). These vessels were often beautifully decorated.

Those who could afford it ate meat for the most part. As bread was scarce to non-existent, buttered dried fish was eaten instead. Vegetables were curiously absent until the end of the nineteenth century.[10] People knew about potatoes earlier, but their cultivation and consumption were not widespread until the end of the nine-teenth century.[11]

The lack of salt made the use of whey[12] from milk a widespread method of preservation. Meat and sausages were stored in whey, which kept them edible over the winter months. Another popular technique was drying, used for both fish and meat. Dried and lightly smoked leg of lamb, and skyr, a fresh cheese made from whey and

Askur, the traditional Icelandic covered bowl

©Ívar Brynjólfsson

originally cultured with enzymes from a calf's stomach, are still a part of the Icelandic diet today.[13]

In retrospect, the food choices of the population for survival were curiously healthy. Food preserved in whey is nutritious and full of proteins. The same can be said of dried fish. However, it must be admitted that life must have been harsh, and scurvy was quite common in the late winter months due to lack of vitamins.

The sugar-glazed path to modernity

When William Morris visited Iceland in the 1880s, he expected to meet the heroes of the Sagas which he had written so much about. Instead, he was terrified to meet so many poverty-stricken peasants living in what he could only describe as huts.[14] As soon as he returned to England he collected money in order to send basic clothes and foodstuffs to Iceland.[15] Such relentless poverty caused a large portion of the population to leave for America. Those who remained gradually became accustomed to a new way of life.

As part of Iceland's colonial relationship with Denmark, the modernisation of the Icelandic palate followed Danish customs. Traditional Icleandic meals were based on lamb, rather than pigs or poultry as in Denmark, and definitely not on grain.[16] Sea birds of all kinds were seasonally important food, especially their eggs. Since lamb is much leaner than pork, many traditional Danish dishes were transformed when prepared in Iceland; Icelanders also made all kinds of processed foods from the intestines. Nothing went to waste. Imported grain was used sparingly in thin breads or added to prepared foods such as sausages made from fat, blood or liver.

The modernisation of Icelandic eating came about through the introduction of sugar into the daily diet, and in a incredibly short time Icelanders became obsessive consumers of sugar. It is a well-known phenomenon from nearly all newly industrialised nations or so-called developing cultures, that excessive consumption of food or of certain foodstuffs can evolve into a marked characteristic of the national diet. Thus, for instance, we find Argentina's passionate meat eating; North America's obsession with big portions; and Greenland's heavy drinking. The Icelandic diet might have taken on each of these characteristics, but due to heavy taxation and import restrictions set by paternalistic politicians, the Icelandic path to modernity was glazed instead with sugar. One prominent Icelandic economist has termed this process the industrialisation of sin, arguing that this sugar-coated path resulted from stiff import taxes or, even more generally, import bans on processed products or foodstuffs. Icelanders had to make their own sinful indulgences,[17] and they

©Thorvaldur Árnason

Empire of sugar

added ample amounts of sugar to everything. Artificial ingredients symbolised modern times: one popular soda was even branded "Artificially" coloured with fake tasting sparkling sugar water.

Cultural encounters through fish

Now we shall turn to the Icelandic fisheries. One consequence of the shortage of quality timber and metal was the lack of good fishing vessels. The Viking ships that had brought the first settlers to Iceland had long ago deteriorated, leaving the Icelanders in isolation. But the abundant fishing grounds were a valuable source of nutrition, especially in the "dark" Middle Ages, between the thirteenth and late nineteenth centuries.[18]

Through the ages fishing had been a way for the farmers to survive the winter; it was seen as an evil necessity rather than a proper livelihood. So the modern fishing industry in our country got off to a slow start, developing only after the introduction of freezing technology in the late 1930s. This technological trajectory really took off after the Second World War. Still, the farmers' representatives in government, who were quite powerful politically, did not

220

believe that the Icelandic fisheries could be a healthy contribution to the economy because the fish markets were so unstable, and fishing was such a dangerous enterprise.[19]

Various European nations have a long tradition of fishing the North Atlantic waters. Brittany makes a salad made of herring and potatoes called "salade d'Islande". Cotaxas – salted cods chins – were a specialty of Basque cuisine, and Icelandic herring (Islands sild) was considered a necessary part of the Danish Christmas dinner (julefrukost). Nor can we forget cod as the basis of a hearty meal of fish and chips. In the heyday of the Icelandic salting and canning period industry of the 1920s and 1930s, our herring and cod liver travelled afar and became a major export to the Eastern bloc. But historically, it was salted and dried fish that supplied the necessary medium of exchange for Iceland's modest import of bare essentials.

Iceland is a late developer,[20] even a late, late developer. America's Great Depression came when Iceland was only just beginning to urbanise, and the civil war in Spain prolonged the economic crisis.[21] Numerous fishing villages had been established, mainly close to the herring grounds in the north and the east. But the herring was both unstable and seasonal. Only with the general use of freezing technology did the industry begin to modernise. But then came the Second World War.

The British soldiers, who were the first to arrive, were not nearly as well off as the Americans who came later, after NATO decided to locate a military base in Iceland. This development had a paradoxical twist. Icelanders, along with the British from the Faroe Islands, supplied the Allies with fish during the war and were repaid, for the most part, in a lump sum after the war. This money was invested in trawlers, and all of a sudden, Icelanders became active in fishing the rich waters surrounding the island. It was necessary to find new markets for all of the fish being processed. At first, the emphasis was on salt cod, which was exported as far away as South America. But in a relatively short time the focus shifted to blocks of frozen fish, and the most affluent buyers were in the emerging superpower, the USA.[22]

Why Ray Kroc was forced to offer fish burgers

McDonald's was established in 1954, just when Icelandic fish companies were beginning to gain ground in the USA. McDonald's was strictly a hamburger company, and making fish dinners was not part of its policy. But as the chain grew more successful, especially among the growing middle class, it felt increasing pressure in regions with large Catholic populations to serve fish meals, particularly on Fridays.[23] This demand coincided with Iceland's success in supplying breaded fish sticks or patties, a tradition that came from middle European cuisine via Canada.[24] In only few years, McDonald's became the largest buyer of fish in the USA, advertising "North Atlantic white fish."[25] From that time on, the Icelandic fish industry focussed on the American market, especially since the Europeans more or less caught their own fish. Given this American focus, and considering the continued presence of the American military in Iceland, it is surprising how long Danish and European influences on Icelandic eating habits lasted.[26] Icelanders were never "McDonaldised", or only indirectly so.[27]

It has become fashionable to bash the fast-food chains, blaming their spread for the destruction of regional, even national, culinary traditions. This is, of course, partly true, but it is also important to note why the franchising of food service was so overwhelmingly successful in the post-war period. Fast food was synonymous with hygienic, homogenous meals that the mums and dads of the world could trust and give to their kids.[28] Eating out may have been a daily practice in the Mediterranean and in other warm countries of Europe, but it was definitely not a given in the colder areas of Europe, where it was considered either a luxury or something done only for special occasions. This was certainly the case in Iceland. The strong demands that McDonald's made on their suppliers had a positive disciplinary effect on the Icelandic filleting factories, and strengthened the market position of the Icelandic-owned processing plants in the United States. Because of this

all-important market access, Iceland was able to declare a fishing war on the nations with a long history of fishing in North Atlantic waters. In the context of the story being told here, it is appropriate to emphasise the positive aspects of this development. The irony is that Icelanders, who had learned the art of hygiene and homogeneity from the McDonaldised Americans, were now ready to supply food for the cultures that had a long and refined tradition of fish consumption. Icelanders had to learn to respect the needs and traditions of countries where fish consumption had strong culinary resonance. The French and Italians, and later the Spanish, Portuguese and Greeks, began to buy fish from Iceland in increasing quantities as the diminishing supply from their own national fleets could not meet the demands of ever more affluent consumers. If the product could meet their high culinary requirements, cost was not the main issue, as it was with the fast-food chains or mass-production factories.[29]

It is now fitting to return to the development of Icelanders' eating habits. In a sense, food intake was not a big issue in the post-war period, until the beginning of the 1980s. This is not to say that food did not matter; rather, it was seen as a waste of time to sit too long at the table. Because of Iceland's late development, manual labour was still widespread, and was dominant throughout the country. Everyone ate salted cod on Fridays, lamb on Sundays (you could choose between saddle of lamb or leg, cut or uncut, so you had at least four variants).

©Helgi Arason

Icelandic fishermen

You had meat days, fish days and Sunday steaks. On special occasions, the grown-ups ate gargantuan cakes, if it was a family gathering, or drank endless amounts of alcohol while the kids indulged in sweets.

The export of fish provided a means of buying things from abroad. For such a small country, a formerly isolated colony, everything imported seemed very exciting, especially to the young. But even so, eating out was still seen as a luxury, and food was not that important. What people did with the fish frozen in the fillet factories was more a matter of curiosity than of genuine interest. It was only through an increase in tourism that the food culture in Iceland began to resemble something that could be termed a civilising process.[30]

Everyone knows that Icelandic water is the best in the world

Icelandic consumption preferences and eating habits changed for good with the advent of mass tourism. This process worked both ways; tourists, coming from near and far, created demand for more and more sophisticated restaurants. The French, Italians and later the Japanese often expressed astonishment at the way the locals handled the excellent raw materials in our country. Icelanders, on the other hand, were

Keldur

sceptical of foreign food. In the early years of tourism to the sandy beaches of the Mediterranean, they were careful not to be too adventurous when it came to dining, to the point of bringing their own "safe" food from home, even their own water. This phenomenon – to feel at home abroad – is well-known, but as sun-seeking tourists became more seasoned, they began to appreciate local gastronomy, indulging in it and eventually bringing it back to Iceland. Although the Japanese buyers of whale meat, herring or capelin were initally seen as oddballs when they ate meat or fish raw, now nothing is considered more healthy or elegant than a piece of sushi or sashimi.

The diffusion of culinary traditions has become one of the more dominant features of the modern condition or the so-called "glocalisation" process. Many modern classics are American inventions, such as Irish coffee or the California variant of sushi, the California roll. Chile con carne is Tex-Mex, and Icelandic youth are called the pizza generation. To fully enjoy the taste of your meal, each bite should be followed with a sip of San Pellegrino water.

To conclude...

We began our journey sitting in a damp hut in a cold winter's night, eating cold food from a bowl due to lack of utensils and wood to cook it. Our journey continued from the raw to the cooked and, curiously enough, came back to the raw again.[31] In my upbringing we were taught to finish the food on our plates, not only to show respect to the starving children of Biafra but also to our poverty-ridden and starving ancestors. Be that as it may, Icelandic food and its preparation and consumption had a curiously rational aura. It was a system, a mode of survival under harsh conditions. The Japanese commonly feel that their culture is a combination of the best aspects of numerous cultural encounters throughout history. In the case of Iceland this is only partly true, since our forbears were so often caught up in a struggle for their very survival. However, to paraphrase the Japanese experience, it has taken influences from all over the world to make us appreciate the riches surrounding us, and the endless possibilities for their preparation.

----

1. As former American President Bill Clinton so diplomatically put it in one of his millennium speeches.
2. According to OECD Iceland is rated among the five highest GNP nations in the world.
3. According to FAO surveys, fishing was a poverty-stricken occupation. Fishing usually has only marginal economic significance, although it is of high regional import in some nations.
4. Lundvall, B. *National systems of innovation : towards a theory of innovation and interactive learning*. Pinter Publishers, London, 1992.
5. Ironically, the Norwegian-American Torstein Veblen had a keen eye for the conspicuous consumption of the newly rich upper class in America (Veblen, T. *The theory of the leisure class: an economic study of institutions*. Unwin, London, 1970).
6. In Clinton Chenier's music the definition of absolute poverty is beans without salt, which has become an anthem of Louisiana's Zydeco music (Tisserand, M. *The Kingdom of Zydeco*. Arcade Books, NY, 1998).
7. Jónsson, Ö. 1994, "Nature as a demanding ally" Pesto Papers, Aalborg University.
8. In the next paragraphs much of my information is based on Hallgerður Gísladóttir's research on the history of Icelandic food culture. (Gísladóttir, H. *Íslensk Matarhefð*. Mál og Menning, Reykjavík, 1999).
9. Gísladóttir, H. *Íslensk Matarhefð*. Mál og Menning, Reykjavík, 1999.
10. Sigríður Toarensen
11. One of the advocates of the Enlightenment in Iceland, Eggert Ólafsson, wrote a pompous poem, *Búnaðabálkur*, to convince the farmers of the benefits of growing potatoes!
12. The watery liquid that separates from the milk solids when it turns sour or when enzymes are added in cheese making.
13. "Skyr" is similar to yoghurt or some of the lighter cultured variants of skimmed milk that have been transformed by fermentation with a culture, but its taste is a bit more sour and it has a thicker consistency.
14. But he hastened to add that these people were unbelievably well informed, even speaking several languages (Morris, W. *Icelandic Journals*. Mare's Nest, London, 1996).
15. William Morris also took a second trip, which must be interpreted as renewed interest in the land and its inhabitants.
16. Due to the lack of grain.
17. Björnsson, Ó. "Þróun Efnahagsmála 1945-1960" *Friðjónsson*, (ed.) Íslensk Haglýsing. Almenna Bókafélagið, Reykjavík, 1986.
18. Sverrisson, Á. "Small boats, large ships: social continuity and technical change in the Icelandic fisheries 1800-1960", *Technology and culture*, Vol. 37, No. 2, pp. 227-253, 2002.
19. Sigurðsson, J. Samvinnufélög í Norðurálfu, 1945.
20. Jónsson, Ö. "Fiskerinæringen i Island" *Fisknæringens hovedtrekk – landanalyser av Danmark, Færöerne, Grönland, Island og Norge*. Nord 30, 1992.
21. One of the most important importers of Icelandic fish and generators of foreign revenue before the Civil War.
22. Valdimarsson, V.U. and Bjarnason, H. *Saltfiskur í Sögu Þjóðar I og II*. Hið íslenska bókmenntafélag, Reykjavík, 1997.
23. Luxenberg, S. *Roadside empires: how the chains franchised America*. Viking, NY, 1985.
24. Saga.
25. Ray Kroc's dislike for cod, due to cod oil (Kroc, R. *Grinding it out*. Contemporary Books, Chicago, 1977).
26. This is due to the Icelandic government's paternalistic policy of an almost complete ban on the importing of processed foods/goods. Travel abroad was also a pure luxury for the chosen few.
27. Ritzer, G. *Mcdonaldisation of society*. Pine Forge Press, NY, 2000.
28. Langdon, P. *Orange roofs, golden archades. The architecture of American chain restaurants*. Michael Joseph, London, 1986.
29. This is a part of the rationalisation process of the fast-food chains, which is partly justifiable, as it made eating out a daily, affordable practice for the masses.
30. Elias, N. *The civilizing process*, Blackwell, Oxford, 1994.
31. Lévi-Strauss, C. *The raw and the cooked : introduction to a science of mythology*. Pimlico, London. The history of table manners as the movement from the raw to the cooked, 1994.

Regina Sexton

Ireland

Simplicity and integration, continuity and change

This all too prevalent attitude to the nature, range and function of Ireland's traditional dishes and food patterns reinforces the erroneous conclusion that Ireland's culinary evolution and identity are so frail as to warrant little if any attention.

An island lying at the furthermost fringes of northern Europe in the Atlantic, Ireland enjoys a moderate, wet climate, tempered by the North Atlantic stream, especially on her western shores. This climate provides the ideal environment for grazing by dairy herds, and traditionally the country has excelled in the production of dairy produce-milk, sour milk preparations, butter, buttermilk, and curds together with soft and hard cheeses. However, apart from natural resources and favourable climatic conditions, the Irish diet has also been influenced by a succession of settlers from abroad, by the growth of a strong market economy and trade in foodstuffs, and by the large growth in the commercialisation of the food industry from the second half of the nineteenth century. In short, the interaction of geographic location, geology, climate, historical developments and market forces gives Ireland one of the most interesting culinary traditions in western Europe. Far from being simple, the story of Irish food is layered with complexities and contradictions where the themes of rejection, continuation, fusion and integration sound a strong presence.

From archaeological excavation we know that the island was inhabited from c. 7000 BC onwards. These earliest Mesolithic communities hunted wild pig, and possibly hare, while the mixed coniferous and deciduous woodlands provided birds like thrush, woodpigeon, woodcock and capercaillie. In summer, migratory fish species, in particular salmon, trout and eels, provided additional protein and could be preserved by smoking for winter and spring consumption. Evidence suggests a strong reliance on plant foods in season, with particular emphasis on wild apples, wild raspberries and hazelnuts. In the

later Mesolithic diet (c. 5500 BC onwards) marine resources played an extremely important role. The Neolithic Period (c. 4000 BC-2000 BC) saw the introduction of agriculture and people with knowledge of crop cultivation and the management of farm animals introduced what in time would become the dietary staples. Domesticated cattle, sheep, goats and pigs were introduced along with two main cereal crops – a free-threshing species of barley and einkorn and emmer wheat. The transitional period between the introduction of agriculture, its gradual acceptance and the development of the requisite skills to make it effective saw a continued reliance on the resources of the wild as evidenced in the range of flint hunting equipment and the discovery of wild apples, possibly dried for winter use, on one Neolithic site.

The fish market – Galway

Harry Furniss

From The Illustrated London News, *21 Feb, 1880*

The Bronze Age (c. 1800 BC onwards) and the Iron Age (c. 800 BC onwards) are characterised by clear evidence of different social ranks, all of which have implications for the diet. Fulachta fiadh (cooking-pits), an outdoor system for boiling meat by means of using heated stones placed in a large water trough, become prevalent at this time. Similarly, the use of cauldrons for cooking first appears. These are associated with the wealthiest sites and suggest that boiled flesh, as opposed to spit-roasted meat, may have been considered superior. Indeed in the saga literature of early medieval Ireland, which purports to idealise a warrior-based society, roast and particularly boiled flesh is the stuff of elaborate aristocratic feasting. Diversification of the cereal economy may have been influenced by contact with Roman Britain in the pre-Christian period. It is believed that oats were introduced at this time, while there is also a greater emphasis on bread wheat. Domesticated fowl were probably also introduced from the Roman world.

The arrival of Christianity in Ireland in the fifth century not only effected change in the belief system but the monastic church encouraged the merits of learning and literacy. As a result, a wide range of early medieval texts offers a detailed picture of the dietary spectrum. Dairy produce and cereals were now the everyday staples. The former was consumed in the form of fresh milk, sour milk, thickened milk, colostrum, curds, flavoured curd mixtures, butter, and soft and hard cheeses. The existence of several varieties of named soft and hard cheeses in this period is of particular note. Cereals, most commonly oats and barley, a little rye together with more prestigious and high-ranking wheat, were used in the production of flat breads, and it is also likely that leavened wheat loaves were also prepared. Various wet preparations – porridge, gruel, meal pastes and pottages and cereal-milk-fruit-and-nut combinations were also consumed. Additional condiments included hen and goose eggs, honey, fish, butter, curds, seaweeds, apples and a root vegetable – possibly carrot – together with different types of onion, garlic and kale. A wide range of wild foods, notably watercress and wild garlic, brought additional relish.

The historical sources also detail the wider socio-economic functions of food items as they circulated in society in the form of rents and taxes. There is specific detail of the food provision and hospitality afforded the nobility and their retinues as they make their annual circuit. There are accounts of special diets for different groups: for example, children while on fosterage were fed soft fare including porridge, milk, curds and eggs. The establishment of Norse towns like Dublin, Wexford, Waterford, Cork and Limerick from the tenth century onwards not only developed the concept of a market economy and its effect upon food production, but these towns may also have looked more closely at the sea as a food resource. The fact that many boating terms and, more specifically, the Irish words for cod (trosc) and ling (langa) entered the Irish language from Old Norse suggests that a taste for sea fish, be it fresh or salted, was developed under Norse influence. It is interesting to speculate on the effects of the Norse settlers, with their emphasis on trade and fishing, upon the dietary patterns of the rest of the population.

The twelfth century Anglo-Norman invasion and the subsequent Norman settlements brought additional dietary changes and developments in certain social quarters, most particularly in the eastern regions of Norman influence. Both prior to and in tandem with the Anglo-Norman developments, the new monastic orders from the twelfth century onwards actively diversified the ingredient base, specifically by broadening the range and variety of kitchen garden and orchard cultivars. This emphasis upon the produce of the fields was facilitated by the Anglo-Norman innovations to arable agriculture. On the table, these advances were manifest in the increased use of wheaten loaves, which varied in quality from heavy wholemeal types to finer loaves of white bolted flour. The production of these loaves in quantity was made possible by the introduction of the built-up oven.

Certain varieties of animals, birds and fish were also introduced at this time, including the white-fleeced sheep, domesticated duck, mute swan and pike. The extensive estate lands were actively populated with rabbits, pheasants, pigeons and fallow deer. These new introductions were managed for the table, with game items like rabbit and pheasant and young pigeon squabs providing an important source of fresh meat throughout the year.

Changes in cooking styles, types of dishes and an alignment of the palate to the medieval European norm became prevalent in areas of direct Norman influence. Meat and fish pies and pasties were consumed, while both meat and fowl were distinctively flavoured with garlic and spices. Church, manorial and trade records testify to the importation and use of luxury goods like almonds, spices, honey and sugar, pepper, figs, verjuice and rice.

However, familiarity with and use of these new ingredients was limited to the wealthy in areas of Norman influence and settlement. The ingredients therefore became a mark of wealth, location and cultural outlook while ease of access to these exotic ingredients differentiated the urban and rural diets. The use of these expensive ingredients also characterized feast and fast days with spice used to celebrate special and festive days. Almonds were used to prepare almond milk as a substitute for dairy milk during Lent and days of abstinence and for use in dishes of white fish and stockfish. Rapid economic growth during the thirteenth century encouraged the growth of towns and trade, especially along the south and south-east coast. Here the elite merchant aristocracies had access to oven-baked wheaten bread together with imported spices and exotic fruits that could be used in dressing meat, fowl and fish dishes. Their secure economic standing set their tables apart and expressed their practical and aspirational links to England and continental Europe to set fashions.

Feeding into these trade developments was the emergence of a viable commercial fish industry in salted cod, ling, cured herring and pickled salmon. While much of this produce was destined for export markets, the prevalence of fish in the home diet grew accordingly. Indeed, salted white fish and herring were medieval staples dominating the diet during Lent and days of abstinence.

By the later medieval period, Ireland was home to a number of dietary systems, which differed in accordance with social rank, region and access to market. The older Gaelic diet based on dairy produce, salted meats and fat in addition to oats coexisted with the wheat-dominated, plant-rich, spicy meat, fish and fowl diet of the Norman regions. However, for most people the staple foods were cereals and dairy produce supplemented with salted meats and cured fish.

To the incoming Tudor and Stuart settlers, Gaelic foodways were seen as objectionable and at times unacceptable. It was not so much the choice of ingredient that offended them but rather the carelessness of the cooking and lack of attention to dressing; "ill-cooked and without sauce" is a phrase cited in condemnation of Irish cookery. The unconventional nature of Gaelic table manners also highlighted the waywardness of the "wild Irish." In line with the general colonial mindset of the rapidly expanding

English state, the Irish were identified and defined in terms of the peculiarity of their social mores. The food of the Gaelic Irish, its preparation and means of consumption were an easily targeted expression of difference, and with a divergent food culture that lay outside acceptable conventional practice the Gaelic Irish were seen as uncivilised and therefore deserving of colonial subjugation.

The perceived rudimentary nature of Gaelic foodways was drawn into even sharper focus by the co-existence of more elaborate, refined and acceptable food patterns. The English travel writer Fynes Moryson, for example, writing in the early seventeenth century, gives what might be interpreted as a

From The Illustrated London News, *25 Dec, 1880*

©Courtesy of Regina Sexton

hierarchical run-down of the island's cultural groups and their associated foodways:

"Touching the Irish diet, some lords and knights and gentlemen of the English-Irish, and all the English there abiding, having competent means, use the English diet, but some more, some less cleanly, few or none curiously… The English-Irish, after our manner, serve to the table joints of flesh cut after our fashion, with geese, pullets, pigs, and like roasted meats, but their ordinary food for the common sort is of white meats, and they eat cakes of oats for bread, and drink not English beer made of malt and hops, but ale. In cities they have such bread as ours, but of a sharp savour, and some mingled with anise-seeds and baked like cakes, and that only in the houses of the better sort."

On a domestic level, the seventeenth century English settlers, most especially at the upper levels of society, brought new cooking styles and taste preferences. As promoters of horticulture and to support a varied diet, landlords and their agents undertook the importation of seed and fruit trees to stock their gardens, especially in the period of relative peace and stability after 1660. Most famously the new settlers introduced the potato to Ireland, possibly in the late sixteenth century, as a New World exotic that was grown initially in the gardens of the wealthy for its novelty value. The treatment of these new ingredients, imported or homegrown, is dealt with in detail in manuscript recipe books from Irish country houses, which come on line in a steady stream throughout the eighteenth century. They reveal a food culture that follows closely English styles and fashions. Underpinning the rich and diverse tastes of the Anglo-Irish elite was the emergence and solidification of the estate system from the late 1720s onwards. The demesne lands were not only carefully land-scaped for their aesthetic appeal but they were also moulded with the concerns of the table in mind. On occasion estates were sited near bog or wetlands and subsequently maintained and well stocked to accom-modate the taste for game. Access to game and its consumption in winter months introduced a seasonal touch to the gentry diet, while the organisation of hunting parties and post-shoot celebratory dinners affirmed the shared tastes of those of similar cultural outlook and allowed for further social bonding.

For those located near developing and thriving urban centres what could not be produced domestically was available from the growing number of grocers' shops. Household accounts of the economically secure reveal the healthy business relationship between the customer and the growing number of confectioners, grocers, poulterers and bakers. In addition, sustained attention to the creation of a canal system and road network also allowed for the inland transportation of fresh fish as well as luxury import-ed goods like tea, sugar, sweetmeats, pepper, ginger, oranges and lemons to the homes of those who could afford them.

The eighteenth century was a period of sustained economic growth, and the demand for Irish cured beef and butter was maintained. Yet, as dairy herds became larger, cattle were drawn out of the households of poorer families, thus closing off an important food resource. Most significantly, the withdrawal of foods from the diet of the poorer sectors of Irish society left room for a substitute non-commercial crop to fill the gap.

The integration of the potato into the diet of the rural poor and labouring classes was encouraged by the merging of several factors. Ireland's heavy acidic soils and mild, wet, relatively frost free conditions proved ideal, while the potato was easily adapted to the prevailing ridge system of crop cultivation.

Initially the potato was adopted as a supplement to a grain-strong diet; it also proved an invaluable fall-back food in times of shortage or famine. As its cultivation spread throughout the first half of the eighteenth century, it was used increasingly as the winter food of the poor. From the 1760s onwards, cereal cultivation expanded in response to growing British markets, and the potato, as an excellent cleansing crop in rotation, assumed a high profile not only in facilitating the growth of arable agriculture but also in its increased presence at local markets where prices were competitive.

The potato also supported and encouraged the population boom of the late eighteenth century (from c. 2 million in 1750 to c. 4.4 million in 1790). Changing

An Irish lord feasting in the open air. From John Derrick, "The image of Ireland", 1581

demographics witnessed a frenzied subdivision of holdings together with a migration into previously unsettled areas of poor and marginal lands. The potato responded well to both movements. If well manured, the potato gave excellent returns, and it has been estimated that an acre of well-managed potatoes was sufficient to meet the yearly dietary demands of a family of six. Its merits as an invaluable reclamation crop brought settlement to hill, mountain, and bogland, and once established, the potato flourished in these seemingly unfavourable conditions. A mushrooming of small farm holdings was especially associated with the west and south-west coast of Ireland, where a particular regional dietary pattern developed amongst the small poorer farmers based on potatoes supplemented with shorefoods-periwinkles, limpets, whelks and seaweeds such as carrageen, dulse and sloke.

The second half of the eighteenth century was the high point for the potato in Ireland, with several varieties under cultivation. On the eve of the Great Famine, however, one variety, the Lumper, a prolific cropper, was almost the universal food of the poor whose numbers stood at c. 3 million. Their dangerous reliance not simply on one food, but on one variety of potato which was highly susceptible to potato blight, made inevitable the dire consequences of the arrival of the fungal disease Phytophthora infestans in 1845.

The impoverished diet of the poor in the years immediately preceding the Great Famine is exemplified by the simple manner of potato cookery. Lumpers, a thick, waxy, creamy potato variety, were simply boiled, drained and eaten communally from a basket, sack or cloth placed centrally and convenient to family members. Depending on the time of the year, two or three potato meals were taken each day, with daily individual consumption rates varying from 7 to 14lbs. Boiled potatoes were taken with a restricted variety of foods – herrings, seaweeds, shellfish, buttermilk or simply salted water. Salted pigmeat was an occasional indulgence and was taken as a relish or "kitchen" to the potato meal. Potatoes were also ember-roasted in the open fire with the soft cooked flesh squeezed free from the fire-blackened skin. In late summer this repetitive pattern of potato consumption was disrupted, as the poor, who had exhausted their stocks of old potatoes, awaited the arrival of the new season. For some oatmeal was the fallback but for others the waiting month of July, variously known as "hungry July" or "July of the cabbage", was a time of hardship and want.

For those of moderate means, potato breads and mashed potato dishes were popular. In particular, potatoes were mashed with kale or white cabbage, along with the occasional addition of turnips or parsnips to produce a dish of colcannon. From the early eighteenth century colcannon was the supper dish for Halloween Night, which as the vigil of All Saints' Day was reserved as a meatless feast day.

The potato continued to play an important part in the post-famine diet although it did not resume its former dominance in the life of the rural poor, except in the most impoverished areas of the west. And while the status of the potato had changed, it still remained an indispensable item in the meals of all classes, thereby giving a distinctive character to Irish foodways. It also gave rise to regional patterns of potato cookery. In the oatmeal zones of the north, for example, potato-oaten cakes were prepared, as were potato-apple cakes in the orchard-growing areas of County Armagh. Many northern counties developed a tradition of preparing potato puddings – a dish of mashed potato kneaded with flour, eggs, caraway seeds and sugar and left to slow cook for four to six hours over the open fire in a pot oven. Boxty, a type of potato bread or dumpling made with grated potatoes and optional extras of mashed potato, sugar and spice, found appeal in some northern, western and south-western counties. Indeed, boxty was not only regionally specific but its preparation in summertime with early new potatoes introduced a seasonal dimension to the diet in these counties.

The second half of the nineteenth century was a period of intense and rapid commercialisation, a process propelled and sustained by a general improvement in living standards, especially amongst the poor. Accordingly, dietary patterns at the lower end of the spectrum diversified with a notable increase in the consumption of shop-bought foods. The increased number of grocers' outlets offered an alternative to the familiar litany of foods born of self-sufficiency. The playing-off of the luxury commercial product

Colcannon

Traditionally the dish for Halloween night celebrations, colcannon was served in individual bowls topped with a knob of melting butter.

Ingredients:
2 1/2 to 3 lbs (c. 1.2-1.5 kg) of old floury potatoes
1 spring or Savoy cabbage
4- 5 large spring onions
6-8 fl.oz (175-250 ml) milk
Liberal quantities of butter

Preparation:
Boil the potatoes in their skins until tender.
While the potatoes are boiling wash the cabbage and cut it into quarters.
Remove the hard core and cut finely across the grain.

Cover the bottom of the pot with about 13 mm of salted water or bacon water if at hand and add the cabbage. Boil until soft and then drain. Add some butter and black pepper.
Once the potatoes are cooked and have been left to dry, remove their skins.
Chop the spring onions and sweat for a little while in some melted butter.
Put the milk in a saucepan and bring to the boil.
Mash the potatoes dry first and slowly add enough of the hot milk until the potatoes are soft and fluffy.
Combine with the cabbage and onions and mix thoroughly. In general the potato and cabbage should be in roughly equal proportions.
Serve in a large bowl and don't forget to serve with little "lakes of melted butter on top".

against the familiar homemade was dramatised in the appreciation and worth assigned to different bread types in the late nineteenth century. In this period white yeast-leavened baker's bread, traditionally the prerogative of the wealthy, became increasingly popular with the importation of cheaper American wheat. This development, coupled with further improvements in milling technology, directed quantities of refined flour to the baking trade. The white loaf was held in esteem above the homemade and was the choice for special occasions; it was the bread offered at wakes with sweet milky tea and it was bought for

©Bord Bia

Champ – one of Ireland's best-loved creamed potato dishes

the Christmas and Easter celebrations. It was also the choice symbol of hospitality extended to special guests, as is evident in the term "priest's bread".

Despite the advance of the baker's loaf, in a domestic context a wider variety of hearth-baked breads became prevalent from the late nineteenth century. The availability of gluten-rich American wheat in the period, together with increased use of chemical leavens, in particular bicarbonate of soda (bread soda), and the wider use of a bastible or pot-oven, made possible the successful production of a raised wheaten soda bread. The pot-oven, suspended over the fire and with embers placed on its lid, proved a multifunctional baking tool. Wheaten meal or flour, bread soda and buttermilk together with the pot-oven were the basic requirements for home baking; additional farm-produced ingredients – eggs, milk and butter – enriched special-occasion cakes. Luxury items – sugar, dried fruit, treacle, and spice – were also incorporated to produce different varieties of soda breads and cakes. Maize bread, made in a similar fashion to soda bread, also remained popular.

By the close of the nineteenth century, the food economy of the rural populace was balanced by a system which saw a percentage of home-produced goods hived-off to supply the market, with the sales subsidising further food purchases, rent, household necessities, stock and seed. The sale of a pig or two, butter, potatoes, eggs and fowl allowed for the purchase of wheat flour, white "shop" bread, yellow meal, tea,

sugar, salt fish and fatty American bacon. In a curious response to market forces, relatively high-quality home-produced bacon was sent to the market where it earned good returns, while cheaper, inferior-grade American bacon was purchased for home use. In the poorest households, notably those of the impoverished west coast, bacon was but an occasional indulgence and good use was made of every scrap. Fat was rendered and poured over cabbage or boiled up with milk and flour to season a white sauce for potatoes.

Throughout the first half of the twentieth century the rural diet, although increasingly susceptible to the influence of commercial forces, depended largely on home-produced goods and local produce. Potatoes, oatmeal, imported Indian meal, buttermilk, sour milk and butter were staples, along with home cured meats, and in particular pig meat remained standard. The diet followed seasonal changes with wild foods when accessible – berries, mushrooms, watercress and rabbits making an occasional presence, while the coastal diet leant towards fish and shellfish and, at times, seabirds and their eggs. Festive occasions called for fresh meat or fresh fowl, especially a goose, while on fast days salted fish (salted ling, cod, pollock or wrasse), was eaten with potatoes and a simple white sauce. The woman remained guardian of the hearth and controller of food preparation. Her work revolved around the open fire; utensils included the large boiling pot, the pot oven for roasting, stewing and baking and, in certain areas, the griddle for quick baking. Open hearth cooking remained a feature of a sizable percentage of rural households until the second half of the twentieth century.

In urban areas increased commercialisation and industrialisation of food production brought easier access to a wider variety of goods. In line with rural patterns, the urban poor became increasingly reliant

Roast goose with potato stuffing

Goose was brought to the table on three special occasions in Ireland, Michaelmas (29 September), St Martin's Eve (11 November) and Christmas Day. It was also served the day a "match" between a young couple had been settled. Although goose waned in popularity, it has made a comeback in recent years as the choice bird for Christmas.

Ingredients:

1/4 lb (120 g) streaky bacon, finely chopped
1 large onion, chopped,
2 lb (900 g) potatoes boiled in their skins,
3 oz. (90 g) melted butter,
Milk,
1 tablespoon freshly chopped sage,
1 tablespoon freshly chopped thyme,
Salt and pepper

Preparation:

Fry the bacon until crisp, remove with a perforated spoon and reserve.
Cook the onions in the bacon fat until soft but not browned, and reserve.
Peel the cooked potatoes and mash with the melted butter and enough milk to render then smooth and lump free.
Add the bacon, onion and chopped herbs, mixing well.
Season to taste.

Prepare the goose:

1 well-hung oven ready goose with giblets (preferably a bird of not more than 10lbs/4.5 kg, lighter ones roast best), salt, a little lemon juice

Prepare the bird by washing thoroughly both inside and out, pulling away any fat from inside the cavity. Dry well.
Stuff and truss the bird, binding the legs and wings to maintain shape while cooking.
Rub salt into the skin and prick all over with a sharp fork to allow the free flow of excess fat.
Sit the goose breast side down on a wire rack in a roasting pan.
Cook the goose in a preheated hot oven (200°C/400F/mark 6) for the first 30 minutes, then reduce the heat to 160°C/325F/mark 3 and roast for three to four hours depending on the weight of the bird. Geese from 8-10 lbs (3.6-4.5 kg) need 3 to 3.5 hours; geese from 10-12 lb (4.5-5.4 kg) from 3.5 to 4 hours.
Check the bird from time to time, periodically pouring off the fat collected in the roasting tin. (Reserve this fat, which is ideal for future roasting of potatoes).
Half way through the cooking turn the bird breast side up.
Once cooked place the goose on a serving dish and return to a low oven while making the gravy.

To make the gravy:

Pour off most of the fat, retaining a little to very thinly coat the base of the pan.
Blend in 2-3 tablespoons of flour to make a paste.
Add a pint of the giblet stock and bring to the boil, stirring constantly, thereby loosening the crispy meat bits adhering to the pan base.
If the gravy is too thick add a little more stock.
Season to taste.
Strain and pour into a gravy boat for serving.

on refined white bread, spread or fried with lard or taken with cheap factory-made jams. In time bread and tea became a constant for all meals amongst the mass of the urban poor. The growth of the commercial bacon curing industry throughout the nineteenth century increased the availability of pig offal and inferior meat cuts in the cities strongly engaged in the bacon trade. Shops specialising in the sale of fresh and salted products like pigs' heads, feet (crubeens), ribs, tails, backbones and kidneys allowed the poor greater access to cheap meat items. At home these were simply boiled or stewed with potatoes and available root vegetables.

Even for those of better means in urban settings cooking styles and taste preferences remained largely conservative and highly repetitive. However, the second half of the twentieth century was a period of dietary change in Ireland. Increased economic prosperity during the 1960s fuelled consumer demand for a greater variety of foodstuffs and for kitchen equipment. In addition, increased foreign travel during the 1950s and 1960s together with the liberating effects of television from the 1960s onwards encouraged dietary experimentation. Central to these developments was the rise of the supermarket. In the social sphere, Indian and Chinese restaurants became increasingly popular thanks to their highly spiced and flavoursome dishes, which contrasted with the bland Irish plate. Food cooked in the French style was considered the epitome of fine dining.

The mid 1970s saw the beginnings of a movement that would redirect attention back to home-produced quality foods. In 1976, on a small holding in west Cork, Veronica Steele began producing cheese with her surplus milk stocks, thus heralding the emergence of the hugely successful farmhouse cheese industry. In a near contemporary development, Myrtle Allen, proprietor and chef at Ballymaloe House in East Cork, began a very persuasive campaign to promote the merits of quality Irish foods. In time, carefully handcrafted foods found a following, especially amongst those who considered the production of cheap industrial-style foods objectionable.

The unprecedented economic boom of the 1990s provided another impetus for further dietary diversification. For the economically buoyant, appreciation of food and an adherence to a regular pattern of restaurant dining became a lifestyle choice, if not a hobby. In the home, lifestyle changes also encouraged a more fluid and non-conventional approach to eating and meal-time rituals, while at the same time the link between good diet and sound health encouraged many to adopt specialised dietary regimes.

In more recent times, the movement of non-European food products into a global market has heightened the issues of traceability and the demand for effective and honest labelling. On the one hand, a high price is now commanded for organic, locally produced foods in season that have been ethically produced with attention to animal welfare. On the other hand, however, a thriving multi-national food industry finds a ready market amongst those whose food purchases are dictated by price alone. In addition, a fast food industry is providing a steady stream of high fat, high sugar, salty, low fibre food to an insatiable youth population. Older dietary survivals are detectable in the continued taste for butter, pig meats, potatoes and, to a lesser extent, oatmeal. But the arrival of various ethnic groups in Ireland provides the potential for even further dietary expansion in the twenty-first century.

Viviana Lapertosa

Italy

Food in Italian cinema

It is always difficult to describe the relationship between Italians and their food. As for any other people, it is necessary to focus on many disciplines, including anthropology, sociology, history, economy, food studies, folklore and, last but not least, gastronomy. Each approach helps to explain the apparently simple and immediate connection between men and what they eat, and we need all of them to reach a satisfactory analysis. For the purposes of this essay we have recourse to yet another approach: the analysis of Italian films. This approach might appear less scientific and objective than others, but it is surely useful for new insights into the Italian way of eating and being.

Un americano a Roma (An American in Rome), *Steno, 1954. This scene has become so popular in the Italian imagination that it practically symbolizes the Italian way of eating.*

Cinema has been particularly important in our country. It mirrors our history, it observes and registers our habits and our vices. More than other media, films have succeeded in capturing the essence of Italy, particularly when it comes to showing how Italians consider their food. There is no better light to guide us through the different phases of Italian history over the last fifty years, years that marked a clear transition from penury to plenty, from a poor and hungry rural world to a rich and bountiful society, but a society that nevertheless reveals many dangers and contradictions.

Through Italian films we will see how the way we eat, our habits and preferences have changed. We will also analyse the visceral connection between Italians and their food, the reasons for such a strong tie, for such total identification between a people and what they eat. We will also examine the table and sites dedicated to eating – kitchens, restaurants and canteens – as well as professions, language and idioms, and the frequent references to the body and to physical image.

Since many aspects of Italian customs and society – perhaps even of society itself – are extremely connected with food, it is not surprising that references to food, both explicit and allusive, are so common on the silver screen. In movies, food talks; it posits itself as a distinctive sign that individuates time, places and people. Seeing even a single item of food, a dish, or a table set for a meal in a film sequence is enough to recognise epochs, nationalities, historical events,

and social conditions. For instance, if in a single scene we spot a dish of spaghetti, we immediately think about Italian-style comedies, a quite popular movie genre. But we also refer to a specific point in time, to specific habits, to real society, not only to its depiction in the movie.

This identification works even better abroad, allowing audiences all over the world to know the charms and the vices of the average Italian, creating an immutable image that is recognised everywhere. If it is true that the stereotype of the eating, and often uncouth, Italian is born with films, then this is not entirely a disadvantage. That same image has made Italians known everywhere, and once you get beneath the surface, the stereotype turns out not to be so negative after all. It is enough to consider the actor Alberto Sordi in his famous role of the "American in Rome" (*Un Americano a Roma*, directed by Steno, 1954). His face could very well be printed on the Italian flag. We all remember the scene where Sordi plays a young Roman guy, Nando Moriconi, in blue jeans and baseball cap, who lunches on a dish of provocative but also victimised macaroni after assigning American-style foods to others: milk for the cat, yoghurt for the mouse, mustard for the roaches… This scene has entered so powerfully into the collective imagination that it quite possibly symbolises the Italian way of eating.

Nevertheless, this character, a pasta vigilante, is not your average guy: he embodies an extreme

Totò Peppino e la malafemmina (Totò Peppino and the Hussy), *Camillo Mastrocinque, 1956. Immigration from the south to the north is a growing phenomenon, with enormous implications for Italy's culinary traditions. Food differences become symbols for a cultural clash.*

exaggeration of gastronomic passion. On the other hand, his pro-American attitude was average at the time when the movie was made. In the 1950s Italy had just come out of the Second World War and was rebuilding itself with the US-sponsored Marshall plan. The whole country lived in the shadow of "Yankee" culture, importing habits and behaviour models from America. Food, clothes, furniture, films, shows and idioms from across the ocean deeply modified the image of a country that was still weak and exposed to foreign influences. The result was that young guys like Nando Moriconi, the main character of *An American in Rome*, wanted to speak the language from "Kansas City" and be fed popcorn, chewing gum and steaks. It is interesting to note that Nando uses the generic term "macaroni" for the pasta he's eating, "macaroni" being an expression widely employed at the time for anything coming from Italy,

including people. We know very well that in Italy pasta has myriad of highly specific names.

These characters have a hard battle to fight. They are actually fighting against themselves, against that part of their culture that is unabashedly Italian that sticks to the most Italian symbol. They have to oppose their own nature when they attempt to give up that dish of pasta to adopt milk, yoghurt and mustard. It is no use trying. The "stuff" Americans eat, although "healthy and nutritious", does not taste right to Nando ("This is junk!" he says) and above all cannot compete with an inviting dish of pasta. It feels like a defeat, but he has to accept his Italian nature. He throws himself on the bucatini pasta and forks it up.

In this sense we can speak of something that is "average Italian": a visceral attachment to pasta that expresses itself in forms that defeat time and space. The filmic exaggeration confirms unconscious, almost innate connections where such hyperbolic acts feel both extreme and liberating. The actor Sordi is not only Nando, the wannabe Yankee from the 1950s: he is the average Italian who rediscovers his food and indulges in it, creating a symbiotic relationship with it and identifying with what he eats. Cinema has made this image strong and immutable. Nevertheless, the image goes beyond a mere exaggeration aimed at comic effect; it responds to the need to affirm an Italian identity, both on the strictly cinematographic level (Italian-style comedy versus American movies) and in a more generic social sense (Italian taste versus foreign influences). The gastronomic rite performed by Nando Moriconi speaks to a wider Italian way of eating, thinking, and being.

If Alberto Sordi showed the nature of Italian taste by juxtaposing two opposite and incompatible alimentary regimes, actor Antonio de Curtis, better known as Totò, created an unforgettable mask of hunger through his myriad facial expressions. Here we are speaking of a deeper hunger, a universal and philosophical one shared by all mankind. But before we discuss it, let us review a fundamental concept: Italian films seem to talk about food and the relationship between Italians and the table essentially through two main lenses, hunger and conviviality. Nevertheless, we cannot limit ourselves to enjoying only those few famous scenes while remaining anchored to prejudices. First of all, we have to

understand the choice of these two lenses by so many Italian filmmakers who limited themselves to some aspects of our national life while neglecting or even censuring others. Secondly, the better-known movies can help draw attention to other, less famous works where viewers can discover different foods and a different Italy.

We cannot deny that hunger actually dominated, or at the very least underlined, most of Italian film production beginning in the first years after the Second World War. The reasons for this phenomenon lie in all that the war meant, in all the irreparable damage it provoked. Yet the roots for such an important and original relationship lie far back in time. One need only read Piero Camporesi's description of seventeenth-century Italy in *The Land of Hunger*[1] to enter a living hell on earth populated by beggars, parasites, monsters, and human garbage – dejected, hungry, and desperate characters. Hunger was a constant element in Italian history and provides a universal key to comprehending it. How many of these same characters do we find in history, art, literature and, of course, cinema?

Hunger dominates history and projects itself onto culture. For this reason we cannot neglect its influence on the development of the culinary traditions of the common people that are vastly different from the better known gastronomic arts of the courts and the noble banquets. In another book, *The Magic Harvest*, Camporesi provides us with fundamental information about Italian culinary liturgies, agrarian rites, and

Italy

244

...otograph of the actor Totò
...Naples alley with two tins in his hand.
...h his impish looks and sly smile,
...ò comes to symbolise universal hunger.

Miseria e nobiltà (Misery and nobility), *Mario Mattòli, 1954. With his body, face and attitude, actor Totò (Antonio de Curtis) declares his solidarity with the hungry poor and proclaims the victory of creativity over bad luck.*

peasant tables.[2] By explaining the use of fats, milk, corn meals, breads and flours, he reveals the existence of an immense regional and natural cultural heritage.

Other food historians have explained the nature of the relationship between Italians and their food precisely through the evolution of taste, by acknowledging a typically Italian pathology in the renunciation of certain foods, in unsatisfied appetites, in the deprivations of peasant society and, more recently, in fasts in the name of thinness. Foods such as pasta and pizza have been identified as the most significant

symbols of Italian national unity, more important than any flag. In his introduction to a reprint of Pellegrino Artusi's 1897 *Science in the kitchen and the art of eating well*, one of the first national cookbooks after the unification of Italy, Piero Camporesi states: "It is necessary to acknowledge that *Science in the kitchen* has done more for the national unification than the Promessi Sposi."[3] Thus it is evident that the relationship between Italians and their food is far from being merely utilitarian. It is, rather, visceral, passionate and not easy to interpret.

It may be a fault of Italian cinema that, being unable to transmit the Italian rural tradition, it has neglected the relevance of peasant culture. In many ways, films acted just like the society that generated them, trying to turn its back on the world of the peasants and deny its own origins, but ending up by rediscovering the flavours of a lost world. Post-Second World War society refused to admit and consider pain, poverty, and the culture of hunger. Not many films succeeded in looking into the past to understand the deep roots of modern imbalances. As a result, Italian cinema reveals two different approaches when dealing with food: a popular one; and a more cultivated, deeper one.

To back up my argument I will analyse two famous tables: the one in the 1954 movie by Mario Mattòli, *Miseria and nobiltà*, and the one in *Il Gattopardo* (*The Leopard*), the 1963 internationally acclaimed hit by Luchino Visconti. The meals that constitute an important focus in both movies symbolise, respectively, the foodways of the common people and those of power.

In *Miseria and nobiltà*, the main character, played by the Neapolitan actor Totò, grabs a dish of vermicelli with tomato sauce and eats it with his hands. A popular and simple dish thus becomes the object of a desire aimed at satisfying an all-consuming hunger. This meal scene clearly epitomises the art of survival by taking advantage of all kinds of situations. Binging becomes a way of exorcising the fear of future hunger, of enjoying the food that is here today but not necessarily tomorrow. This attitude has a long history in Italian culture, dating back to the masks of the Commedia dell'Arte, a theatrical comic genre where the same stereotypical characters, all embodying different elements from popular society, created

different plots in each play. It is not by chance that the script of *Miseria and nobiltà* derives from a theatre play by Eduardo Scarpetta.

Il Gattopardo, on the other hand, focuses on the table and the parties of a Sicilian nobleman at the time when the Italian armies – rather, the armies sent by the Savoy king – were trying to invade the island, which was still under the control of the local Bourbon dynasty. Here, the food that embodies this whole dying world is a timballo di maccheroni, a complex, rich, and sophisticated pasta dish that reveals its aristocratic origins. Visconti makes the audience relive the table of the princes, the courtly culinary traditions, and the aristocratic relationship with food. Lights, colours, and a certain order are all expressions of a refined culture. Just as the elegance

Dramma della gelosia – tutti i particolari in cronaca (The drama of jealousy), *Ettore Scola, 1970.*
Italians desire more substantial food; the film responds by offering protein and the first luxury items.

and refinement of the table of the Prince of Salina descend from a regal tradition, the script for the movie comes from literature, from a novel by Giuseppe Tomasi di Lampedusa.

These films represent two different traditions, and not only in terms of their subject matter: hunger and the lower classes on one hand; wealth and elitist food on the other. The main difference is in the way they represent the visceral relationship with food: popular versus intellectual. Even when he describes the hunger of the Velastro family in *La terra trema* (*The earth trembles*, from the novel *I Malavoglia* by the realist author Giovanni Verga), Luchino Visconti shows the cultural side of food. This is not to imply that the eternal hunger shown by the actor Totò is not culture: we will shortly consider the philosophical attitude behind his greedy attitude. But the filmmaker, in this case Mattòli, does not emphasise this aspect; he concentrates instead on the comic effect. All of the movies that convey a low image of Italians bingeing and vulgarly overindulging on food take the same approach. We cannot condemn this image in itself, since it reveals certain realities, but it does not sufficiently transmit the complexity of the enormous Italian cultural and culinary heritage.

With these preliminary considerations in mind, we can now survey the last fifty years of Italy's social history through its culinary habits as represented in films. In the films produced right after the Second World War that belong to the so-called neorealist style of cinema, filmmakers focus on the everyday food of the poor, revealing a totally new approach to the subject matter. In fact, during the fascist era, it was almost impossible to find sequences representing lower-class food; movies limited themselves to bourgeois tables, always very neat and tidy, or to fashionable restaurants where patrons consume cases of sciampagna (at the time, it was absolutely forbidden to call champagne by its French name, for political reasons). War negated all that, bringing Italy back to the level of the most basic needs. The only imperative was to find enough bread to survive. Every film after the war showed the desperate search for and avid consumption of food, or the total lack of it. Cinema and history coincided in focusing on hunger. Many filmmakers felt the obligation to deal with misery, seconding the historians in an attempt to come to terms with the current situation. It so happened that cinematic food was always more dramatic than reality. Through the eyes of the filmmakers, a soup, a loaf of bread, or a handful of rice became symbolic of wider and deeper themes. Food thus transcends its value as nourishment to become poetry, memory, aesthetics, ideology, or comedy.

In its cinematic depiction of lower-class eating habits, Luchino Visconti's 1943 film, *Ossessione*, marks a transition. After many years of divas and glossy dishes audiences were finally exposed to real kitchens, dirty tablecloths, and the real, wild and instinctive appetites of common people. Visconti used food to illustrate the history and geography of

Rocco e i suoi fratelli (Rocco and his brothers), *Luchino Visconti, 1960.*
When the sons refuse her bread, the family falls apart and the values it represents disintegrate.

Italy, aiming to grasp things in their authenticity while creating powerful metaphors. He always paid great attention to details concerning food, from the banks of the Po river in the 1940s (*Ossessione*), to the coast of Sicily after the war (*La terra trema*), where he showed stale bread made of whole meal flour and soups made of discarded fish cooked in an earthen pot. In that film the "authentic" soup eaten by Sicilian fishermen is not simply a Sicilian soup; it becomes symbolic, representing not only the hunger of every fisherman in the world, but also hunger itself. In *Il Gattopardo*, another movie with a Sicilian theme, the recipe for the timballo served in the dinner sequence is exactly the same as the one Lampedusa described in his novel, and the poured wines are real. Here, too, food represents something else, namely the aristocratic customs doomed to disappear with the unification of Italy. In *Bellissima*, which takes place in Rome during the reconstruction, the modest but neat kitchen of the main character, Maddalena Cecconi, is described with great care. In *Rocco e i suoi fratelli (Rocco and his brothers),* on the other hand, Visconti focuses on food to express the drama of the new immigrants moving to Milan from the south.

Other neorealist movies, such as Ladri di Biciclette and *Roma Città Aperta (Open city)*, looked without pity at the hard conditions of the poor, even as they explored their deepest desires and their humanity. Bread and movies reveal different aspects of the same necessity, and it is hard to say which is more urgent. Real bread and cinematic bread are difficult to distinguish, as if audiences went to the movies to contemplate their own greater hunger; but precisely for that reason cinematic hunger is more remote, more unreal, and less dangerous. Paradoxically, the food visible on the screen is scarce and limited, even as it is mentioned and desired. In this way the absent, invisible, and imaginary food becomes greater than actual food. Compared to everyday life, the scarce elements on the neorealist table acquire a deeper, more universal value. On the silver screen, brown bread, sacks of flour, or pasta in blue paper bags become the symbols of a whole historical period, able to convey a credible sensation of hunger and need. Memories are thus stored for the new generations who did not live in that period and rarely have heard the tales of those who did.

Movies from 1950s show clear changes in Italian food customs. People are finally living and eating again. Filmmakers paid new attention to dialects and regional diversity while acknowledging the growing difference between those families who still struggled to get enough food and those who were already exploring new culinary horizons. The American model triumphed both on the silver screen and in the kitchen, but local taste still hinged on spaghetti and fettuccine. After the domination of brown bread during the immediate post-war years of sad black and white films, 1950s films are full of colours and pasta. The success of pasta is a consequence of the desire to identify with good food that reflects the positive sides of Italy.

We have already discussed *Un americano a Roma*. The same approach to food emerges in *I soliti Ignoti (Big deal on Madonna Street)* from 1958, where pasta soup with chickpeas plays a pivotal role (the recent American remake *Welcome to Collinwood* misses most of the cultural subtext). Let us go back to the 1954 *Miseria e nobiltà*, to the famous sequence where the actor Totò is busy bingeing on pasta by grabbing it with his hands. As we have already noted, this stereotype refers to the picturesque image of the Neapolitan "mangiamaccheroni", even as it simultaneously symbolises hunger. Totò, with his impish look and sly smile, becomes its mask.

In the 1960s the Roman film industry, centred around Cinecittà, determined the success of chicken and lamb dishes from the local cuisine. At the same time a new style was emerging, and *La Dolce Vita* was mirrored on the table, too. With the beginning of the economic boom Italians wanted more substantial food, and films responded to these changing needs with more protein and luxury items. At the same time, immigration from the south to northern industrial cities became more intense, causing an encounter of very different culinary traditions that were often used as symbols for the larger cultural clash. Like the culture they embody, traditional foods are threatened by modernity. In the film *Rocco e i suoi fratelli*, the simple bread cut by the immigrant mother symbolises the ties that keep her family together in a new environment. When that bread is

La ciociara (Two women), *Vittorio De Sica, 1960.*
The scarce food on the neorealist table becomes more significant than its real-life counterparts.

deemed insufficient, when her sons refuse it, the family disintegrates along with its values.

During the 1970s the political violence that erupted in social turmoil and terrorism in Italy was translated onto the silver screen as voracity. Filmmakers created violent and voracious movies that focused on the worst aspects of society. This era saw the end of the light-hearted, merry atmosphere of the previous decade. Ettore Scola highlighted the bitter taste of comedy, Federico Fellini preferred its sweet and sour manifestations. Pierpaolo Pasolini did not avoid obscenity, while Marco Ferreri depicted obsessions.

In Ferreri's masterpiece, *La grande bouffe*, food is not food any longer: in wealthy societies the desire to exorcise ancient and terrible fears becomes overindulgence, to the extreme of self-destruction. Through a hyperbolic representation of food and sex, Ferreri explores all that is hidden in human nature, with its most disturbing and obscene traits.

Movies from the 1980s reflect Italy's growing wealth, which found its best expression in the yuppie culture. In its desire to become profit-making like the rest of society, the film industry concentrated on commercial products that sought to please audiences looking for an easy and pleasant lifestyle. Excessive abundance provoked nausea and refusal: in the minimalist 1990s, films ended up focusing on pathological relations with food, such as intolerance and obsession, rather than on taste and passion. The last decade of the twentieth century was full of complications and confusion. On the one hand, food became less and less relevant, and excesses were strongly frowned upon. On the other, the body was exposed, almost to the point of becoming the object of symbolic cannibalism. On the silver screen a minimalist regime did not admit the presence of any edible matter but allowed more and more bodies, more and more flesh to be admired.

Thus the circle is closed, from hunger due to lack of food to a self-imposed fast, to a new meaning of hunger rooted in modern man's growing fear of eating. The fear of eating is as excruciating as the fear of hunger: man and food keep on tormenting each other. And the cinema bears witness.

Recipes

Here is the shopping list that the actor Totò, in the role of Felice Sciosciammocca, who has been hungry for days, "orders" from his friend to create a tasty menu that will satisfy his whole family. Unfortunately, the shopkeeper refuses to give him any more credit, so his only chance to eat anything is to pawn his frayed overcoat. The list of these foods is a triumph of fantasy, the sublimation of a meal through narration. It is enough to simply name some of these ingredients to start salivating: "Violin strings" or bucatini (a thick kind of spaghetti, hollow inside), tomato sauce (two big cans at least), and sausage gravy ("it has to be fresh, otherwise I'll pass", says Totò). For the entrée, a couple dozen eggs (even if the party is made up of five people) with mozzarella from Aversa ("only it it's still trickling milk, or I'll pass"). Then some dried fruit and sparkling red wine from Gragnano, to wash the meal down. And to finish it off, two nice cigars!!

The recipes follow the directions given in the film as well as culinary traditions from Naples.

"I would like to thank the author of the text, Viviana La Pertosa, and Giovanni Gifuni, who carried out the iconographic research, for their voluntary contributions to this work."

Roberta Alberotanza, Chair of the Steering Committee for Culture of the Council of Europe

1. Camporesi, Piero. *The land of hunger*. Cambridge, UK: Polity Press, 1996
2. Camporesi, Piero. *The magic harvest: food, folklore, and society*. Cambridge, UK: Polity Press, 1999
3. *I promessi Sposi*, by Alessandro Manzoni, was one of the first novels to actually use the national language in the modern way. Artusi Pellegrino. *La scienza in cucina e l'arte di mangier bene*. Torino: Einaudi, 1970. For an English translation of Artusi's book, see *Science in the kitchen and the art of eating well*. New York: Marsilio, 1998 (1897).

Eggs and mozzarella in the pan

Ingredients for ten people
4 tablespoons extra virgin olive oil, 1 teaspoon butter, 10 anchovies in olive oil, 20 eggs, 400 g buffalo mozzarella, freshly ground black pepper

Preparation
In a pan, sauté 5 anchovies in the oil and butter on low heat until they break down and form a paste. Break the mozzarella with your hands and place it in the pan without mixing. Crack the eggs into a dish, making sure not to break the yolks. Slide the eggs on top of the mozzarella in the pan, spreading the whites to cover the bottom of the pan. Raise the heat and cook for a few minutes. The mozzarella does not need to melt entirely, but it must blend with the egg whites. The dish is ready when a thin crust begins to appear at the edges. Remove from the heat, add pepper and salt (just a little, as the anchovies are already salty), and decorate with the remaining 5 anchovies.

"Violin strings" with sausage gravy

Ingredients for four to six people

400 g "violin strings" or bucatini,

400 g fresh sausage (ground),

1 onion (chopped),

4 tablespoons extra virgin olive oil,

half a glass red wine from Gragnano,

2 cans (400 g) peeled San Marzano tomatoes (diced), freshly ground black pepper.

Preparation
In a pot, sauté the chopped onion in two tablespoons of olive oil. Add the sausage and let it brown for a few minutes. Add the red wine, let it evaporate, then add the tomatoes and season with salt and pepper. Meanwhile, fill a big pot with water, bring it to a boil and cook the pasta "al dente". Drain and season it in a big bowl with the gravy and two spoonfuls of olive oil. Grind some fresh pepper on top.

References

Piero Camporesi, *Il paese della fame*, Bologna, Il Mulino, 1978, pp. 5-19
Piero Camporesi, *La terra e la luna.*
Dai riti agrari ai fast food un viaggio nel ventre dell'Italia, Milano, Garzanti nuova ed. accresciuta, 1995, (prima ed. Milano, Il saggiatore, 1989)
Piero Camporesi, introduzione a Pellegrino Artusi, *La scienza in cucina e l'arte di mangiar bene*, Torino, Einaudi, 1970

Films cited

Un americano a Roma by Steno, 1954
Miseria e nobiltà by Mario Mattòli, 1954
Il gattopardo (The leopard) by Luchino Visconti, 1963
La terra trema (The earth trembles) by Luchino Visconti, 1948
Ossessione by Luchino Visconti 1942
Bellissima by Luchino Visconti, 1951
Rocco e i suoi fratelli (Rocco and his brothers) by Luchino Visconti, 1960
I soliti ignoti (Big deal on Madonna Street) by Mario Monicelli, 1958
Ladri di biciclette by Vittorio De Sica, 1948
Roma città aperta (Open city) by Roberto Rossellini, 1945
La grande abbuffata (La grande bouffe) by Marco Ferreri, 1973

Italy

Ieva Pīgozne-Brinkmane

Latvia

Old customs and contemporary habits

Latvia is located in a temperate climatic zone with fairly long, cold winters and warm, short summers. Due to their harsh climate and relatively poor soil, Latvians have always worked hard to provide food for themselves and their families, and thus food has always been greatly valued by Latvians. Bread has a special place in the Latvian consciousness, and respect for it is encouraged from early childhood.

Although Latvian cuisine has traditionally been based on agricultural produce, meat also features prominently in the diet. People living along the 500 km of Latvian coastline have always been involved in fishing, so fish is an integral part of their diet. Fish is also caught inland, but these freshwater species are considered more of a delicacy, just as crayfish are.

Food preparation

Women were the cooks in traditional Latvian homes, the ones responsible for feeding the household three times a day. Longer days in summer meant that people worked longer, and thus ate four meals a day. At first, food was prepared in clay pots which were placed in the fire or on the open hearth.

Over time, cauldrons hung above the hearth, and ovens for baking leavened bread became popular.

Latvian foods are characteristically bland, without strong spices but with a reasonably high fat content. Because Latvian territory was ruled for seven centuries by the German aristocracy, Latvian

Rye bread

peasants learned to use new ingredients and to prepare food in different ways. For example, one of the most popular Latvian foods today – sautéed sauerkraut – is a tradition inherited from the Germans.

Ancient cooking traditions

If we look back over 1 000 years, we find that the Baltic and Finno-Ugric tribes inhabiting the territory of Latvia subsisted mainly on grains – rye, wheat, barley, oats, millet and hemp. Porridges, patties and leavened bread were made from these grains. People also ate peas, beans, turnips, black radishes, linseed and its oil, wild carrots and garlic. Livestock farming developed alongside agriculture, so fowl, beef, horsemeat and pork also came into the Latvian diet. Game – beaver, deer, wild boar, duck, goose – and over twenty-five different species of fish were also eaten. As there are no sources of salt in Latvia, it was obtained through trade or barter and was used sparingly. Food was made more flavoursome through the use of caraway seeds, onions, garlic and white mustard. It is probable that if we tasted these ancient foods today, they would seem to us lacking in salt and other spices. The only sweetener used was honey, but the most popular desserts were probably wild berries and hazelnuts.

Cooking 100 years ago

The most detailed information about the traditional Latvian diet stems from the nineteenth century. At this time a plant from North America was spreading quickly – the potato. Thanks to potato farming, Latvian peasants no longer had food shortages in winter and spring when stores of grain had been depleted. It is believed that the most common meal for Latvian coastal fishing families in the nineteenth century was boiled potatoes with cottage cheese and herring or pilchards. Today, potatoes prepared in different ways are still a very popular component of the Latvian diet.

In autumn, the cellar of each farm was used to store dried sausages and pork, and barrels of salted cabbage, cucumbers, mushrooms, meat and herring, all of which were used throughout the winter. In summer, when there was a lot of outdoor work to be done further away from home, people would eat a moderate breakfast, for example, milk porridge. Lunch consisted of food brought from home, such as rye bread, cottage cheese, rūgušpiens (curdled milk), and sometimes also fried meat or patties. After lunch, people would usually have a nap before beginning work again. On returning home in the afternoon, soup or porridge was eaten with a drink of rūgušpiens. On Sundays stewed meat, white bread, pīrāgi (bacon rolls), pancakes, sweetened cottage cheese or berry jelly with milk were served.

Beans and bacon

Latvian eating customs

Similar eating customs were widely spread in rural areas up until the Second World War. After the war, more and more country dwellers came to live in cities, and Latvians began to structure their eating schedules around work, as is the case in many other industrialised countries. Today, people often do not prepare meals at home. However, many ancient eating customs are still practised, and traditional foods are still eaten by Latvians both daily and on special occasions.

Latvians have always been great fans of dairy products. Milk, rūgušpiens, cottage cheese, cream, cheese and butter used to be eaten in every house at almost every meal, and this tradition has continued. Latvians have always been able to find many delicious edible foods in the wild, foods that do not need to be cultivated, only gathered. For centuries Latvians have picked berries in the summer – wild strawberries, bilberries, raspberries, loganberries – and cranberries, mushrooms and nuts in the autumn. Many Latvians like to eat honey, and bee-keeping traditions have developed over the centuries. Today, Latvian farms often have their own beehives, and many farms produce honey. Coastal families still smoke fish at home, and in many areas people eat smoked eel-pout, flounder, eel, lamprey and cod.

257

Food at traditional Latvian celebrations

The most typical ancient foods eaten by Latvians are still found today at traditional Latvian celebrations. These celebrations are related to annual seasonal events, and to the rhythm of farming in the northern hemisphere, which is dependent on the solar year. This is why Latvian foods and drinks at traditional celebrations are those which are the most convenient to prepare at any given time of year. Food and drink were also traditionally assigned mythological significance, although few Latvians would be able to explain this significance today.

The harvest festival

In autumn, when the harvest had been brought in and food was abundant, farms would usually celebrate the harvest festival. Because of this, weddings were usually held in autumn. After the harvest, a piglet or ram was often slaughtered and a feast organised. The new season's sauerkraut was eaten, and bread was baked from the newly harvested grains. Bread baked from the flour of the first harvest was assigned particular powers: when eating this bread, a wish was made, which would be fulfilled. Whenever a domestic animal was slaughtered, the meat which could not be eaten straight away was salted and dried, or made into sausages. Blood and pearl barley were used to make special blood sausage, and brawn was made by boiling meat scraps.

Pīrāgi filled with diced fatty bacon and onion are still baked today for almost all Latvian celebrations. Various sweet breads are also baked, which are topped with rhubarb, apples, or berries in summer and sweetened cottage cheese or dried apples in autumn.

Debessmanna
(Whipped cranberry dessert with milk)

Ingredients:
75 g (2.65 oz) cranberries (or other berries), 200 g (7 oz) water, 50 g (1.75 oz) sugar, 30 g (1.05 oz) semolina

Preparation :
Rinse cranberries. Crush and squeeze out juice. Place cranberry solids in a saucepan, cover with water, boil for five minutes and strain. Add sugar. Gradually add semolina, stirring constantly. Heat until semolina thickens, then add cranberry juice. Pour mixture into a bowl and cool rapidly. Whip mixture until it becomes light and airy and has doubled or tripled in volume. Serve in deep dessert dishes with cold milk.

Latvia

Christmas dinner

Special foods were eaten at the winter solstice, a celebration to mark the lengthening of the days. Many of these foods can still be found on contemporary Latvian Christmas tables. A popular dish used to be a boiled pig's head with boiled pearl barley, although today the most popular traditional Christmas dish is boiled grey peas with pieces of fried meat and fatty bacon, usually eaten accompanied by a drink of rūgušpiens or kefīrs (cultured milk). This dish can be found in many restaurants and cafés in Riga all year round. All of the peas boiled at Christmas must be eaten by the morning, otherwise there will be a lot of tears shed in the new year. Another special Christmas food is the once-popular blood sausage with pearl barley, because its rounded shape is reminiscent of a circle, symbolising the solar year. In western Latvia a traditional Christmas snack is sklandu rauši (tarts filled with

Sklandu rausi (vegetable tarts)

mashed potato and carrot). In the last 100 years baking gingerbread at Christmas has also become popular, another tradition inherited from the Germans. Today, one of the most popular Christmas meals is roast pork with sautéed sauerkraut. A modern festive table also often includes carp, and fish scales are placed in pockets and purses to ensure that the new year will bring a lot of money. According to Latvian tradition you should eat nine meals at Christmas so that the coming year will be rich, although today this ritual is only rarely performed.

Easter eggs

At the spring solstice, or Easter, food supplies were usually running low, so eggs were saved for some time before Easter. Boiled eggs, coloured with brown onion skins and decorated with scratched-on designs, have been the main Easter food for centuries. Many families still boil and eat their own home-coloured eggs at Easter. Another once-popular Easter food – sprouted grain – today no longer appears on the table as a festive delicacy, but is used as décor instead.

Celebrating the summer solstice

Today the most popular celebration in Latvia is Jāņi, or the summer solstice. This marks the shortest night of the year, when throughout Latvia special Jāņi folk songs are sung, floral wreaths are made, and countless bonfires burn until morning. The main Jāņi foods are fresh caraway cheese and beer, which is found on every Jāņi festive table.

Usually the table will also be laden with pīrāgi, sweet breads, various meats and many other modern foods, which suit contemporary Latvian celebrations. Because it is an outdoor celebration, an increasing array of modern picnic foods is being eaten at Jāņi, for example, fried sausages, barbecued meat and various salads.

At the Latvian wedding table

Another Latvian celebration that should be mentioned is the wedding, which since ancient times has been associated with an abundance of food. Even today food is an important component of a Latvian wedding.

It is hard to imagine one without the ancient festive dishes – pīrāgi, sweet breads and beer. There are also usually at least five types of salad on the table, various meat-based snacks and a lot of fruit. It is

A set table

L a t v i a

Jāņi (summer solstice) cheese

Version 1 :

1 kg (2lb., 3oz) whole milk dry cottage cheese, 50 g (1.75 oz) milk, 50-75 g (1.75 – 2.625 oz) sour cream, 2 eggs, 50-70 g (1.75-2.625 oz) butter, salt, caraway seeds

Version 2 :

1 kg skim milk dry cottage cheese, 5 l milk, 100 g (3.5 oz) sour cream, 2 eggs, 100 g (3.5 oz) butter, salt, caraway seeds

Preparation :

Heat milk, stirring occasionally, until the temperature reaches 90-95°C (194-203 F). Grind or process cottage cheese and add to milk. If the cottage cheese is sweet, mix with rūgušpiens (curdled milk) for the whey to separate more easily. Continue to heat at 85-90°C (185-194 F) for 10-15 minutes. When a clear whey separates, remove from heat, and allow cheese to sit. Pour off liquid. Place cheese into a dampened linen cloth. Holding corners of the cloth together, roll cheese back and forth to allow any extra liquid to separate out before the cheese cools down. Put cheese in a bowl. Mix sour cream with eggs, salt and caraway seeds and gradually add to cheese, mixing with a wooden spoon. Add the mixture to a saucepan with melted butter, and stir continuously over a low flame for 10-15 minutes, until cheese is smooth and shiny, and has a temperature of 75-80°C (167-176 F). (The lower the temperature and shorter the heating time, the softer and more crumbly the cheese will be. A higher temperature and a longer heating time will make the cheese harder). Place cheese in a dampened linen cloth. Gather corners of the cloth together and tie, smooth out any folds, and place under a weight in the refrigerator. When cheese is cool, remove from cloth, place on a shallow dish and slice. Jāņi cheese is served with butter or honey or as a snack with beer. If you wish to store the cheese for a longer period, rub with salt, wrap in paper or plastic wrap and store in a cool, dry place. The cheese can also be spread with butter and baked in a hot oven until brown.

traditional to eat ground meat pīrāgi together with broth or meatball soup as a first course. This is followed by the main course, which at a Latvian wedding and birthdays can be sautéed pork ribs, pork chops, schnitzel, roast, steak, rolled veal or rissoles with boiled potatoes and sautéed sauerkraut. These are served with a sauce made with a milk or cream base. Dessert is usually made of berries or a milk jelly with a sweet sauce. After midnight the guests are offered the "new wife's torte", which is served with coffee.

If you find yourself at a large Latvian party, then assume that you will have to do a lot of eating, drinking and singing. In many homes you will have the opportunity to drink herbal tea (made from a range of herbs, not just peppermint or chamomile), which will possibly have been gathered by your hosts during the summer.

The contemporary Latvian menu

On an average day Latvians usually eat a moderate breakfast before going to work. People drink a morning coffee or tea and eat sandwiches with cheese, sausage, tomatoes or cucumber. For many Latvians the day is unimaginable without milk, which is usually drunk at breakfast. A boiled egg or omelette is also a popular breakfast dish for many.

Lunch in Latvia is eaten between midday and three: this is dependent on what time the day has begun. People usually eat a hot lunch consisting of a type of fried meat (pork chops, rissoles, sautéed fillet, steak, chicken) or fish (salmon, trout, cod, pilchard), potatoes (boiled, fried, or mashed), boiled rice or buckwheat, and a fresh salad. Sour cream, or a sauce using cream as a base, is usually eaten as an accompaniment. Some people also eat soup as an entrée, which in Latvia is usually made with pork (it can also be made with a fish stock), onions and carrots. Meat soups may also contain potatoes, beets, sauerkraut, beans, peas, sorrel or fresh nettles. Many different kind of desserts are eaten. These usually are made of dairy products and fruit, with gelatine or potato starch added. At lunchtime Latvians drink fruit juices, kefīrs, milk, tea or coffee.

On arriving home from work, a second lunch, or supper, is made. This is eaten around 6 p.m. or 7 p.m. At this time there is great diversity in the Latvian home – supper can consist of soup and various salads, or it can be a hot meal (similar to lunch), or a more traditional food, for example, a milk-based soup. However, many people who do not wish to spend a lot of time preparing food after work buy ready-made or frozen foods, or eat a number of sandwiches or buns together with a cup of tea. Latvians also enjoy eating pastries and other bakery products, and pizza has become a popular and easy meal to prepare.

Sorrel soup

The dark green sorrel leaf resembles spinach in look and taste. However, sorrel has a lovely tart flavour that can't be replaced in this recipe.

Ingredients:
250 g (8.75 oz) pork, 800 g (28 oz) water;
300 g (10.5 oz) sorrel, 30 g (1.05 oz) carrot,
20 g (0.7 oz) onion, 10 g (0.35 oz) parsley,
20 g (0.7 oz) fat, 20 g (0.7 oz) pearl barley,
salt, sour cream, dill and parsley

Preparation :
Soak pearl barley for 6-8 hours in cold water. Dice pork. Put pork and drained barley in a saucepan, add water to cover and cook until the meat is almost tender. Chop sorrel, onions and carrots and sauté in butter. Add sautéed vegetables, parsley and salt to the saucepan, and continue cooking until meat is tender.

Before serving, sprinkle with chopped dill or parsley and add sour cream. You may substitute 200 g (7 oz) of diced potato for the pearl barley. Boil potatoes with the meat. Steam sorrel separately and add it to the soup when the meat and potatoes are tender.

Drink

Many Latvians drink innumerable cups of tea or coffee during the day, usually without milk. Fruit juices or spring water are also drunk. Spring water has now become so popular that it can be found in almost every office. Over the last ten years more and more families have not purchased spring water from shops, but instead collected water for the whole week from natural springs. Two of the most popular traditional Latvian drinks today are rūgušpiens and kefīrs. Other popular traditional drinks include kvass (a non-alcoholic drink made from yeast), and fresh or fermented birch juice and beer.

Beer is a traditional Latvian beverage – it is impossible to imagine ancient or contemporary Latvian celebrations without it. Beer is the most commonly mentioned drink in Latvian folklore, and innumerable folksongs are dedicated to it. In Latvia beer was traditionally brewed from barley and hops. Honey was also often added during the brewing process, in which case the product was called medalus (honey beer). Juniper berries or wormwood were also added to flavour the beer. Today many types of beer are brewed throughout Latvia. The most popular are Aldaris, Cēsu, Piebalgas, Tērvetes, and Lāčplēša beers. Beer is the most popular alcoholic beverage drunk when friends meet in a tavern in the evening, or when they celebrate a wedding or the summer solstice.

Caraway Seed Tea

5 g (0.175 oz) caraway seeds (Carum carvi L.),
15 g (0.525 oz) sugar, 250 g (8.75 oz) water

*Add caraway seeds to boiling water.
Boil gently for five minutes, allow to steep for
10-15 minutes. Caraway seed tea can be served
with milk or cream.*

Vitamin Tea

1 tablespoon drogas (three parts dried nettle
leaves (Urtica dioica L.), 3 parts dried carrot,
3 parts dried rosehips, 1 part dried blackcurrants),
300 ml (10.5 oz) water

*Add drogas to cold water, boil for 10 minutes,
allow to steep for 2-4 hours in a well sealed container in a cool place. Strain. Drink 1 glass 2-3
times per day.*

Latvia

Another special strong alcoholic beverage made in Latvia is Rēga Black Balsam, first made in the eighteenth century and based on an ancient recipe used by Rigan pharmacists. The ingredients include various herbs, making the liqueur dark and fragrant, with a thick consistency. It is considered medicinal.

Beliefs associated with eating

There are many beliefs and customs associated with food and eating in Latvia. One of the most important features of Latvian "eating etiquette" is to offer food to others if you yourself are eating.

Latvians are enthusiastic bread eaters, and in many homes, when cutting the first slice from a loaf, the end is called a "farmer's son". Young women compete to eat this slice, so that they might marry a "farmer's son" – someone who has their own home and farm. Another belief is that a loaf of bread should be sliced from the fatter end, in order for the eldest daughter to be the first to marry. Today, people still hold a number of beliefs about salt. Each Latvian knows that if a food has too much salt added, the cook is in love. If salt is spilled on the table or on the floor, then there will be a quarrel in the house.

Sitting down to a meal is serious business, which requires that people be calm and act with decorum, to demonstrate respect for the food and for those who have worked to put it on the table – the ploughman and the cook. The place of honour is at the head of the table, where the head of the household usually sits. Those who sit at the corner of the table should not be afraid of being cursed – that they will not be married for seven years. And everyone knows that if a spoon or fork falls to the ground, a female visitor will arrive, whereas if a knife falls, the visitor will be a male.

You are welcome at our table. We wish you Labu apetīti!

Sautéed sauerkraut

Ingredients
400 g (14 oz) sauerkraut,
water, 50 g (1.75 oz) carrot,
30 g (1.05 oz) onion,
50 g (1.75 oz) butter,
salt, sugar

Method
Melt butter in a large saucepan. Chop onion and sauté it in butter until light brown. Chop sauerkraut into smaller pieces and add to the saucepan. If you want the sautéed sauerkraut to be light in colour, cover sautéing onions with boiling water, cover the saucepan immediately and cook over a low flame. If you want the sauerkraut to be darker, sauté onions in an uncovered pan, adding water only after some time. Cook sauerkraut for 2-3 hours. In the last 20 minutes, add grated carrots. When sauerkraut is tender, add salt and sugar to taste. (If the sauerkraut is not as dark as you would like, add caramelised sugar to the pan). Serve with roast pork, chops and other fatty meat dishes.

Birutė Imbrasienė

Lithuania

Rituals and feasts

Lithuanians appreciate good, tasty and filling foods. "Eat until you burst at the seams, and work until your eyes pop out" reads the wisdom of ancestors, as "only he who eats well, works well". This wisdom still holds true today in our modern life, although in many cases changes in the way we live and the pace of life have brought about changes in our eating habits.

We hope to introduce you not only to traditional Lithuanian cuisine but also to let you feel the Lithuanian spirit, which finds expression in our food culture. Because ritual and traditional dishes are usually related to the main transitional moments in nature, human life or the religious calendar, this is what our story will be about. We will also talk about the influence of our neighbours and about the common traditions of hospitality that we share.

Lithuania contains five ethnic regions. Since olden times Lithuanians have cultivated cereal and vegetable crops and engaged in animal husbandry, fishing, apiculture, gardening. They also have gathered mushrooms, berries, wild fruit and nuts in the forest.

But the eating habits of the various ethnic groups reveal some differences. Samogitians (žemaičiai), who live in the north-west, are particularly fond of porridge and gruel. There is not a Samogitian who would not enjoy šiupinys, a stew of peas, beans, potatoes and meat, or kastinis, a dish made of butter and sour cream. Various pancakes and dishes made of cottage cheese are the favourite dishes of the Aukštaičiai, who live in the central and north-east regions of Lithuania. Dzūkai, the inhabitants of the south-east, cook countless dishes and bake delicious cakes (called babkos) from buckwheat, which they have always cultivated in their sandy soil. Living in woodlands, dzūkai are unsurpassed mushroom and berry-pickers and are very inventive in using. The suvalkiečiai, who dwell in the south-west, favour smoked meat dishes and fatty pork; they even stew fat "to make the meal more filling". Traditionally, along the sea coast fish ranks first among food products.

As dictated by custom, cooking was done by the mother of the family, who passed her skills on to her daughters so that as that people would say "they are equally clever at cooking and entertaining". Even today women often rely on cooking secrets they learned from their mothers and grandmothers, though now their creativity is no longer restricted to seasonal products since fresh fruit, vegetables, and various spices and herbs are available year-round.

Lithuanians go for simple, tasty and wholesome foods. They do not eat much, but they like their meals to be nourishing. They also have a natural feeling for what should be used. There is a traditional understanding that no dish should have more than three different products in it.

Since early times Lithuanians have used honey in their cuisine. For many centuries it took the place of sugar. Even though sugar is now consumed daily, it has not replaced honey, a natural and healthy product, in Lithuanian diet. In fact, honey is often offered to guests straight from the jar, with cheese or milk. The Lithuanian word bičiulis (friend or pal), derived from the word bitė (bee), was formerly used to refer

The Kūčia (Christmas Eve) table

to fellow beekeepers who kept bees as common property and had relationships that were almost as close as blood relationships.

Today, as in earlier times, we use imported spices for seasoning when preparing something special for a festive occasion. To flavour everyday or ritual foods, Lithuanians always give preference to herbs grown in their own kitchen gardens or gathered in the fields or at the edge of the forest. Used sparingly and creatively, they add a pleasant savour, and quite a few of them have curative properties.

Times of change

Traditional Lithuanian food culture took centuries to shape. Despite certain influences from neighbouring countries, the Lithuanian national cuisine does not contain many foreign foods. This feature might be explained by the fact that Lithuanians are known for a certain conservatism of character; they are cautious and distrustful of new things and ideas and take time to get used to them. However, once they recognise something as suitable and adapt it to their taste, they consider it their own and never let go. This is true of bulvių plokštainis (potato cake), which came to Lithuania from German cuisine and is now thought of as a traditional dish. It ranks as one of the most popular meals in Lithuania.

Many new foods came to Lithuania at the beginning of the twentieth century, including all kinds of tortai (elaborate rich cakes) and šakotis (the well-known German Baumkuchen), which has now become almost a must on special occasions. People have been travelling more and they see what others eat. Of course, changes in everyday diet take longer to become evident; it is on festive occasions when the influence of foreign cuisines becomes most obvious. The Lithuanian people do not traditionally have a sweet tooth. Cakes, pastries, and sweets are not part of their daily diet, and if they feel like indulging, dessert is usually commercially made. Yet homemade cakes and pies are commonly regarded as better-tasting, so each homemaker devotes a great deal of effort to create her own "house cake" to proudly treat her guests and please her family.

During the fifty years of Soviet occupation – from the middle to the end of last century – Lithuanian food culture experienced destructive transformations. The lack of meat, cereals, vegetables and other natural and wholesome foods made people look for substitutes. Potatoes became the main product to replace meat and cereals and were consumed every day of the year. Lithuanians can prepare a variety of dishes from potatoes to make a square meal. Especially filling are dishes prepared from grated potatoes; those from boiled potatoes are not so heavy. To make them more tasty, various sauces and fillings are used.

Lithuanian forests have always abounded in a great variety of mushrooms. Mushrooms and berries gathered in the forest were important staples of the Soviet-era diet. People ate them both fresh and preserved. Even today Lithuanian women use traditional methods of keeping them (drying, pickling, and brining) as well as more modern ones (marinating, bottling, and freezing). When the autumn mushroom season is at its peak, whole families pour into the forests to gather them.

Food and ritual

Lithuanians can pride themselves on having maintained a number of traditional dishes even though most of the time-honoured rituals they are associated with have already faded away. Ritual dishes accompany certain rites, whether to celebrate calendar or family holidays. Even though most rites have not survived in their entirety, neither have they been fully forgotten. For instance, the tasting of the first food of the harvest is now accompanied merely by tapping a spoon against the taster's forehead.

The Lithuanian custom of remembering their ancestors, which people faithfully observed, played an important role in preserving ritual. People believed that during family and calendar holidays the dead arose from the grave and returned to visit their homes. In an effort to gain their favour and protection, the living sought to please the souls by carefully preparing a warm welcome for them and treating them to the foods they had inherited, according to hallowed tradition. These practices can be clearly seen in Christmas, Shrovetide and Easter customs.

Holiday dishes

Traditionally, Christmas Eve, Kūčios, has been a very important day for Lithuanians. It continues to be observed as a day of family reunion with a ritual evening meal, the main dish of which is kūčia . This is a word of ancient origin, common to many European languages. Kūčia stems from the old Greek word kukkia and was borrowed from Slavic with some modification of meaning in the twelfth century. Kūčia is a porridge of cooked barley, rye, oats, peas and beans mixed with miešimas (water sweetened with honey). A sacrificial meal, it was meant, in the first place, for the souls of ancestors invited to the feast and was eaten in honour of the dead. The evening meal and Christmas Eve day have taken on the name of the dish.

The central role in Kūčios traditions is given to the table, around which, just once during the year, the whole family, both the living and the dead, gathers. Until recent times it was customary to leave food on the table throughout the night for the refreshment of the souls of the deceased. This old custom of remembrance symbolises a union of the living and the dead.

Kūčios is a day for peace and harmony in the family. Any discord, anger, or conflicts are to be resolved and peace made. All debts were to be paid off before Kūčios so that one could cross the threshold of the new year with a clear conscience.

For the evening meal the table is covered with a white linen cloth, with a handful of hay spread under it, in the memory of the birth of Christ in the manger and in the belief that the souls of the deceased are resting on it. The first dish to be placed in the centre of the table is the consecrated "God's cake" – semi-transparent wafers brought home from the church – called kalėdaičiai in Lithuanian. Bread is placed next to it, followed by all the other dishes, the number of which, traditionally, should be seven, nine or twelve. Usually, twelve dishes are served, one for each month in hope of a generous and plentiful year.

Traditionally, meat and milk are excluded from the Kūčios feast. Among the dishes are the kūčia , barley porridge with sweetened water, beetroot soup with mushrooms, fish (especially pike), herring and various mushroom dishes. Christmas Eve biscuits are only served once a year. They are baked from wheaten unleavened dough and eaten with poppyseed milk. Thin oat pudding (kisielius), served with sweetened water, is another ancient and popular dish. Apples and nuts can also be placed on the table. The traditional drinks and semi-liquid dishes of the Kūčios feast are cranberry jelly and dried fruit compote cooked with starch for thickening.

After all the dishes have been placed on the table, candles are lit. Family members take their usual places at table, leaving a special place for those who died during the year. Some families invite lonely or poor neighbours to join them for the meal, or they share some Kūčios food with them. Inviting the poor is a time-honoured tradition. It is said that happy will be the home in which a beggar has his Kūčios meal.

The evening meal begins with the breaking of wafers. You are also supposed to eat a bite of bread handed to you by the head of the family. He breaks the wafer and shares it with the others, at the same time extending his Christmas greetings and good wishes. Then everyone wishes one another good health, happiness, success, peace and love in the family, and wishes that work will be rewarding and the harvest rich. Family members who are far from home are remembered too.

There are no hard and fast rules as to which dishes should be eaten first. It is a matter of choice. There is one basic rule, however: for the coming year to be plentiful you must have at least one morsel of each dish.

On Christmas Eve day and night people used spells and charms to foretell future events, especially death, marriage and the harvest. Young people today like to remember these charms but they do not take them seriously. For example, during the meal or right after it a straw is pulled out from under the tablecloth. This must be done only once, with your right hand and with your eyes closed or averted. A long straw means a happy and long life; a broken, crushed, thin or bent straw augurs a hard and needy life; and a thick and split straw promises wealth.

Christmas is an ancient holiday, celebrated in pre-Christian Europe as the return of the sun. Christianity replaced the solstice celebration with the Feast of the Nativity of Our Lord. The Lithuanian name Kalėdos can be found in historical sources beginning in the sixteenth century. Christmas morning starts with clearing up from Kūčios evening. If there are animals in the household, the hay and the leftovers are fed to them so that they will be healthy and strong. The table is cleaned and covered with a new white linen cloth. Since the Kūčios feast broke the fast, the table is now laden with meat dishes. Thus starts a period of eating richly, often, and to satiety (mėsiedas, "meat eating"), which lasts till Shrovetide (Užgavėnės in Lithuanian). Traditional Christmas dishes are prepared from pork: stewed pig's head decorated with greenery, baked ham, sausages, roasted piglet, šiupinys with a pig's tail protruding from the middle of the bowl (in Samogitia). There are also all kinds of cakes, homemade barley beer and gira, a fermented drink made from bread, sugar and yeast).

Shrovetide (Užgavėnės) is a noisy and fun-filled holiday, which is celebrated between 5 February and 6 March, depending on what day Easter falls. The true Shrovetide day is always a Tuesday. Traditionally, however, the celebration starts on a Sunday and lasts for three days.

The Shrovetide feast is a transition from the waning winter to the coming spring. Therefore, no matter how early Shrovetide is celebrated, it is considered the beginning of spring. Some merrymaking customs of Shrovetide are still observed. Shrove Tuesday is the last day of post-Christmas meat-eating (mėsiedas). On that day one eats richly, and often – up to twelve times during the day.

Traditional Shrovetide dishes are various pancakes, fatty pork, and šiupinys. The mother of the family lays the table for the whole day, loading it with food "to make the stomach harder than the forehead" and to have enough to treat any masqueraders who might drop by.

Masqueraders symbolise the souls of ancestors. They sneak around the house trying to steal pancakes from the frying pan or a chunk of meat from a boiling pot. If treated well, they wish the family good health and rich harvest. Inhospitable housewifes may find their kitchen utensils stolen, hidden on the roof, or heaped

Feasting on pancakes at Shrovetide

©*Henrikas Sakalauskas*

up on the chimney. Unwilling to be seen as tight-fisted, all housewives treat the masqueraders the best they can. No one refuses the treat, since "he who eats to satiety on Shrovetide, eats to satiety the whole year through".

Easter (Velykos) is the first great spring holiday. From ancient times it has been celebrated as the rebirth of nature, and for many centuries now it has been observed as the major Christian religious festival of the death and resurrection of Christ. The most important symbol of the festival is the coloured Easter egg that is lovingly called by Lithuanian people margutis, a diminutive from marginti, that is, to variegate. Like many other peoples throughout the world, Lithuanians look upon the egg as a symbol of life, prosperity and fertility, and also a magical remedy to evoke the vital forces. The custom of variegating, or colouring, eggs in their shells during spring festivals can be traced back to olden times. Lithuanians have preserved this custom at Easter, when people break and eat the eggs, exchange them, or give them as gifts. They also play popular games of rolling Easter eggs. Families try to decorate the eggs as skilfully as they can, with the whole household engaged in the activity.

The decoration is accomplished in one of two ways: either the eggs are plunged into the coloured liquid and the design is then engraved with a sharp tool (a

271

knife or a piece of glass), or the patterns are designed by application of hot wax and the egg is afterwards soaked in colour. The most intricate and ornate way is to apply hot wax. The sharpened end of a match or a pinhead is dipped into hot wax and then used to paint elaborate patterns in short strokes on the eggshell. The decorated eggs are carefully submerged into a bowl of deeply coloured cold liquid (if warm, the liquid would melt the wax and blur the patterns). Before long the colour penetrates the wax-free surfaces, leaving the area under the wax design white. The wax is then scrubbed off to reveal the pattern.

The easiest and the most popular way to colour eggs is with onion skins. The moistened egg is covered with onion peels, wrapped in a piece of cloth, tied tightly with thread, and boiled in blue, green or red liquid. The result can be quite unexpected, as no two eggs turn out exactly alike. A colourful Easter egg is essential to the festive Easter table and is its main decorative element.

The Easter table is covered with a white linen tablecloth. The first thing placed on it is a bowl or a basket of coloured eggs, usually decorated with sprigs of rue, red bilberry or wolf's-claw. The eggs may also be arranged among the green shoots of oats or rye specially sprouted for that purpose in a bowl or a plate. Another traditional decoration is a "tree" of Easter eggs (kiaušinynas). This is a branch or stick with nine or twelve twigs with wire rings for holding Easter eggs. The kiaušinynas is decorated with greenery and strips of multicoloured paper; it may also be adorned with branches of birch and white or pussy willow that have been forced to blossom. Little birds made of pastry or egg shells are perched on the branches. Only the most ornate and colourful Easter eggs go onto this "tree", which symbolises the tree of life.

The ceremonial Easter table abounds in traditional foods prepared from pork, veal, poultry and dairy products, including a roast pig, a pig's head, a veal ham, sausage, cheese and butter. The table and the

Easter eggs decorated by applying hot wax

©Antanas Ališauskas

food are decorated with greenery. The table is also spread with various baked goods, including a special Easter cake (Velykinės bobos) and cookies. Beverages include beer and kvass, and also maple and birch sap.

Once the members of the house have taken their seats, the Easter ritual of breaking the fast begins. First the eggs are struck against each other to determine which is the sturdiest: one person holds an egg in his hand and the other breaks it with his own egg. The sturdiest egg usually remains uneaten.

The first day of Easter is usually devoted to the family, and people do not go visiting until noon. In the afternoon, however, children are permitted to run to their neighbours' or godparents' homes to exchange eggs or roll Easter eggs.

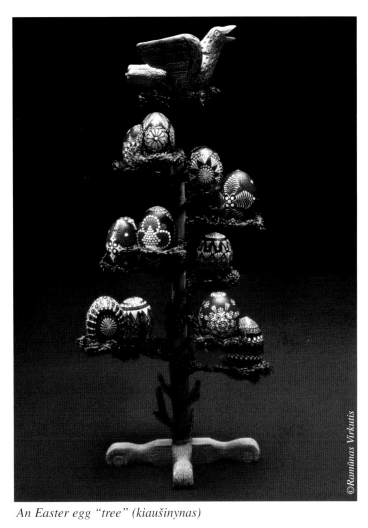

©Ramūnas Virkutis

An Easter egg "tree" (kiaušinynas)

The ritual foods of family gatherings

Birth, marriage and death represent the most significant transitions in the human life cycle. Thus they are accompanied by various rituals, including the christening ceremony (to mark birth), the wedding ceremony (to mark marriage) and the funeral ceremony (to mourn the dead). These are occasions for the entire family, relatives and neighbours to gather

and be entertained. The major ritual element of those gatherings consists of eating and drinking together, which is regarded as sacramental.

The essential ritual symbol of family gatherings is bread. Black rye bread is the basic element of our daily food. Each human being is symbolically associated with bread from the moment he or she is born. Bread is also believed to have a protective function. A newborn baby was usually laid on the table next to a loaf of bread, which was believed to guarantee the safety and well-being of the entire family. As a result, bread was regarded as holy, and people strictly followed all bread-related rituals, beliefs and prohibitions. Responsibility for bread was generally placed on the mistress of the house, who passed it on to her daughters. The initiation rites of young girls also involved bread, culminating in the granting of permission for her to bake bread. The baking of bread was usually accompanied by spectacular rituals performed in the presence of the entire family and representatives of the local community who, after tasting the newly baked bread, would decide whether the girl were ready to become the mistress of her own house, that is, to get married.

The wedding feast stands out from all other feasts because of its exceptional abundance and variety of foods. People begin preparing for the festivities well in advance: villagers kill pigs, calves and other animals and make home-brewed beer. Sometimes a special brewer is invited to make beer, and a talented cook found to prepare the food. The cook is helped by women from the neighbourhood who prepare all the food for the feast, including a ham and other meat dishes, a roast pig and chicken, different kinds of fish and all sorts of cakes and cookies. The skilfulness of the cook and her helpers determines not only the taste of the food but also the way it is arranged on the table and served, which is of great importance at traditional wedding feasts. The wedding feast tables, if laid by a really smart housewife, can become transposed models of the real world, showing wildlife images, including herds of animals, flocks of birds and shoals of fish in "flowing rivers".

Among present-day wedding customs involving ritual dishes we can mention the moment when the parents greet the newlyweds after the wedding ceremony by offering them bread, salt and drink; and the cutting of the special ceremonial svočia's (Lithuanian for "matron of honour") cake, known as karvojus.

Even today, following long-standing tradition, guests bring cakes and alcoholic drinks to wedding celebrations. In olden times, most of the food for traditional wedding celebrations was prepared and brought by the bride's svočia, the most important item being the karvojus. There could be two kinds of karvojus: a loaf of black rye bread imprinted with circles; or a decorated cake made of wheat flour. The first would be placed on tables in the homes of both the bride and the groom. The cakes were usually baked for the wedding by the bride's mother and the matrons of honour on both sides. The most ornate cake (karvojus) was the one made by the bride's svočia. It was decorated with various patterns along with flowers, fruit and pastry figures of birds and

Karvojus, the ritual wedding cake of "Svočia"

animals. Karvojus is a symbol of the newlyweds' fertility and well-being. The ritual of placing karvojus on the table and serving it to the guests was once accompanied by various rituals and songs. Before the departure of the guests, the remaining karvojus was usually cut into pieces and distributed among them.

The tradition of karvojus is an old one. Only at the end of the nineteenth century was this ritual wedding cake displaced in Lithuania's south-western region, Suvalkija, by a new cake that arrived from western Europe. Initially called bankukas (cf. German Baumkuchen), it is now known as šakotis or raguolis. In other parts of the country karvojus was replaced by tortai, big, luscious and intricately decorated cakes. These new styles of cake continue to be called karvojus and are even decorated as such: šakotis is often sugar-coated, with miniature birds, animals or human images, stars and candies; tortai have openings for bottles of drink and are decorated with birds, squirrels, hedgehogs, swans and hunters.

The oldest written information about the funeral repast in Lithuania is found in old sourcebooks and travellers' accounts, where they are described as events to commemorate and feed the soul of the deceased. Those meals apparently often went beyond moderation. Mourners would pay their last respects and drink to the deceased, wishing the soul a safe journey to a different world.

Despite the fact that the Church forbade the consumption of such funeral meals, Lithuanians always considered it necessary to give a proper funeral repast to those who came to mourn the deceased. Funeral ceremonies became the most important family gathering and often lasted for several days. Of those who did not take the time to bury the dead, people might say: "the deceased had hardly stayed overnight before being rushed out" or "the poor soul could not even enjoy the stay".

The Lithuanian custom of holding funeral repasts is undoubtedly very old. Even though the ceremonial "feeding of the soul" of the deceased is no longer practiced at present-day funerals, everyone looks upon the funeral repast as the fulfilment of the last will of the deceased and also a fitting ritual to bid final farewell to the dead. That is the reason why relatives and neighbours are treated to food and drink when they come to pay their respects.

Across Lithuania there still remains an ancient custom of inviting the relatives and neighbours of the deceased from the graveside back to the home of the buried man or woman (or, in towns, more often to restaurants or cafés) for dinner. This is known as the mourning burial dinner. The idea behind it is to feed once again the soul of both the deceased and other dead people within that family, who are believed to have come from on high to lament the deceased and escort him or her to a peaceful eternal life. It is also intended to entreat the souls to leave that home and safeguard it from any harm. The popular belief is that only a grateful and properly fed soul will leave with its entire entourage to meet its maker.

Another custom that is still alive offers proof that the burial dinner is intended to feed the soul of the deceased and other souls of the dead in the family: if the mistress or master of the house offers something to the departing mourners (which, on other occasions, is common practice), the mourners refuse the gift, believing that if they take anything home, someone may soon die in their house. Accepting food meant for the souls can bring death into one's own home.

Lithuanian hospitality and alcohol

The Lithuanian people have always been famous for their hospitality, which often goes beyond moderation: "without loving others you will never be loved yourself". Before the arrival of guests, they cook, roast and bake so much of everything that the dinner table, heavily laden with food, can hardly bear the weight. There is no shortage of drinks, either. No efforts are spared to please and hear their guests comment that "There was enough of everything; the only thing missing was pigeon's milk".

Foreigners have noted this lavish hospitality as a distinctive feature of Lithuanian culture. In historical and travel accounts they marvel at the hospitality Lithuanians show every individual, including guests from foreign lands, by welcoming and treating them to the best food and drink available. Peter von Dusburgh was one of the first to describe Lithuanian hospitality in his fourteenth-century *Chronicle*, writing that "They share all the food with their guests… They believe that unless they drink their guests under the table, they may not have afforded them enough hospitality".

Guests do not start eating or drinking without first being asked to by the host or hostess. The host's continuous urging of his guests to help themselves is considered a sure sign of hospitality and is part of the ritual. When speaking of a well-prepared feast at which, however, the host did not urge his guests to eat and drink, it is said that "there was enough of everything, except for urging", the idea being that the guest may have returned home without enough hospitality having been shown. In this respect, today's situation has not changed much. Taking time to raise the glass and drink, urging (by the host) and excuses for delaying the act (by the guests) are only a few features of the Lithuanian hospitality ritual which visitors from foreign lands noted as far back as the early nineteenth century. One traveller's description notes that "Lithuanians are happy and sober, take their time while drinking in order to prolong their communication and table-talk and often sending the same glass round the table".

An example of such communication as an expression of an exceptionally warm welcome is the survival of the ancient custom of "drinking all round", that is, sending the glass with the bottle around the table. Before having a drink, the person raises his glass and salutes his or her neighbour, and the neighbour says something in response. The most popular toasts and responses are: "To your health!" and "Thank you" ("Būk sveikas" – "Ačiū"); "Your health!" and "Bottoms up" ("Į sveikatą" – "Pilk į savo žyvatą"); "Chin-chin" and "Chin-chin" ("Kinku kinku" – "Strazdu-brazdu"); and "Cheers" and "Thanks a lot" ("Sveikas būk" – "Dėkui, cibuk"). After emptying the glass, the person refills it and passes it on, and thus the glass goes round the table, mostly from the left to the right "in much the same way as barley and rye are sown". To bypass and fail to salute anyone in the round would be considered terribly rude. Women cannot be bypassed, though they are welcome to drink only as much as they like in a gesture of appreciation of the hospitality offered. The host keeps urging the guests to help themselves to drink, and the guests urge one another on, too.

The atmosphere around the festive table is always cosy and friendly. The table is kept entertained and guests can experience real joy in communicating with one another. They can sit ("pasėdėti") and talk ("pakalbėti") or just relax in silence ("parymoti")

among their close neighbours ("kaimynėlis") or their family ("giminėlė").

Historical accounts of the traditional Lithuanian drinking-related customs show drinking as an act that marks the most significant events in people's lives. It manifests community solidarity; consolidates the start and finish of communal work, or of coming to mutual aid; it seals the resolution of conflicts and confirms deals. Quite a few of these ritual moments are still marked by drinking today, especially in the countryside.

Historical evidence shows that in the ninth to seventeenth centuries the only alcoholic drinks in Lithuania were beer and mead. Mead is the oldest and noblest drink. As far back as the ninth century, the Anglo-Saxon traveller Wulfstan mentioned the mead that Lithuanians and Prussians made from honey. Other travellers and chroniclers confirmed its merit. Nineteenth-century authors often mention vodka and krupnik as popular drinks offered by Lithuanians to their guests. Treating guests to honey or krupnik, an alcoholic drink made by boiling vodka and honey, is regarded as the most lavish gesture of hospitality. Krupnik is reserved for special occasions, whereas mead and home-brew are preferred for daily use. Beer is drunk on all occasions, including at weddings and funerals. Lithuanian folklore, in particular accounts of wedding customs and traditions, indicates that in the late nineteenth and early twentieth centuries sweetened vodka was usually intended for women. Today, in addition to beer and mead, Lithuanian people like to have stronger alcoholic drinks.

Lithuanians are fond of singing at the festive table. Their drinking songs often contain diminutives for beer, mead, hops and barleycorn. In these songs Lithuanians thank the host and hostess for their warm welcome and hospitality, and praise the masters of the house.

Each guest must remember the saying "Come expected, and leave loved".

Before seeing guests off after a wedding, christening or other feast, the host and the hostess must give them something, known as "rabbit's cake", to take home. The host and the hostess usually walk their well-loved guests as far as the front door or gate, where they stop for a final drink, to wish their guests "Have a good journey home" or "May the road rise to meet you". Then they say good-bye.

It is worth noting that in the past the entire family took their meals together. However, due to recent changes in the pace of life, today family members eat separately. This is also the reason why typically good Lithuanian food is being replaced by fast food. One can only hope that despite all the differences, the decisive factor in choosing one or another cuisine will continue to be the quality of the food.

Georges Hausemer

Luxembourg

A gastronomic expedition

For centuries, Luxembourg has been a border region and crossover point for an extremely wide variety of European cultures. First settled by Celts, Romans, Teutons and Franks, it has in the more recent past seen the arrival of Burgundians, Spaniards, Austrians, Netherlanders and Germans. Although they all at some stage departed, each has left traces of their presence behind in the Luxembourg cooking-pots. As a result of the numerous waves of migration occurring in Europe in the twentieth century, Italian and

Portuguese influences, too, can now be perceived in Luxembourg dishes.

All over the world, indigenous culinary cultures are influenced by the geographic and climatic conditions in which people live, and that of Luxembourg is no exception. Thus, a great many recipes are inextricably linked to the rhythm of life of the rustic world that characterised large sections of Luxembourg society until well into the twentieth century. The

The food of Great Sunday

©Patrick Galbats

most important ingredient in this simple, traditional cuisine was the potato. For decades, along with milk and bread, potatoes – the "simple man's truffle", which arrived from South America in the sixteenth century – remained the staple food. Potatoes are robust and unassuming, adapt to the poorest soils and the harshest climate, produce a high yield, are easy to store and have multiple uses. When cooked, they can be transformed into a nourishing main meal without flashy effect; or, as is more often the case, they can be eaten as a side dish of tasty simplicity or sophisticated originality. Thus, even today, for many Luxembourgers the supreme culinary maxim is still: "It's not a proper meal without potatoes!"

Nowadays, of course, the gastronomy of the Grand Duchy has become incomparably more varied. Yet there is one common characteristic that has been

Bouneschlupp (thick bean hotpot)

Thick bean hotpots rank amongst the classic dishes of Luxembourg, having all the delicious characteristics to be found in good thick soups. For decades, pulses, and especially beans, have occupied a special place in the simple, rustic cuisine of Luxembourg. As a starter, "Bouneschlupp" is almost too filling, unless it is served as an elegant little soup, thereby tantalising the taste buds.

Ingredients (for six persons) :
1 kg green beans (fresh or frozen),
150 g celeriac (peeled), 3 potatoes, 2 onions,
1 leek, 1 teaspoon salt, 2 tablespoons flour,
50 g butter, Freshly ground pepper,
4 tablespoons chopped parsley,150 g sour cream

Preparation :
Clean, wash and cut the beans into pieces 1 cm in length. (Allow frozen beans to thaw and likewise cut them into pieces.) Chop the celeriac into 5 cm cubes. Peel, wash and finely cube the potatoes. Peel and finely chop the onions. Wash the leek, removing the thick green outer leaves, and finely chop the white and light green interior. Place the vegetables, without the potato cubes, in a saucepan containing two litres of salted water. Boil the vegetables for about 20 minutes, then

©Patrick Galbats

add the pieces of potato – but not before, or they will disintegrate. Make a roux with the flour and butter. Strain the water used to cook the vegetables through a sieve and mix in little by little to create a creamy sauce. This should then be sieved and added to the vegetables. Let it all boil for a further five to ten minutes. Taste, add parsley and serve with sour cream. Instead of sour cream, you can also use whipped cream with a little vinegar stirred into it.

retained by all authentic Luxembourg dishes: they are, without exception, simple, unpretentious and substantial. At the same time, they provide no grounds for exaggerated patriotism: there is not a single indigenous dish which can in all conscience be described as typically and exclusively Luxembourgish. Take the frequently cited example of "Kuddelfleck". Although this is defined in the official dictionary as "a Luxembourg national dish made from well-boiled tripe or cows' stomachs which are then covered with bread crumbs and fried in fat or oil", variants on the same theme are highly prized by the Italians, the English and the Scots. Or take "Kachkéis", which is no less frequently described as a Luxembourg speciality. In all probability, this dish derives from the "concojota" imported into Luxembourg by Spanish troops in the seventeenth century.

There were times when traditional culinary dishes which now delight the palates of discerning gourmets enjoyed as bad a reputation as the peasant customs from which they originated. Nowadays, however, ideas have changed, even in the kitchens of the more exalted restaurants. Thus, modern menus increasingly feature traditional Luxembourg dishes such as "Judd mat Gardebounen" (smoked collar of pork with broad beans), "Träipen" (fried black pudding) with apple purée and crayfish à la luxembourgeoise. Even more lavish creations, such as pigeons in honey sauce, are sought after by certain gourmets. And one increasingly finds typical side dishes and accompaniments reappearing like flashbacks to earlier bills of fare: a morsel of "Tiirteg" (leftovers of cooked sauerkraut and mashed potato) with duck breast, or a miniature "Gromperekichelchen" with a steak; occasionally, as an entrée, nettle soup or, with fried trout, a "Kniddel" (flour dumpling) seasoned with smoked bacon.

These dishes are best accompanied by one of Luxembourg's wines or beers, which for many years now have been increasingly acknowledged as masterpieces by connoisseurs throughout the world.

The wines of Luxembourg

The future belongs to Luxembourg wine – on this, all wine producers and wine lovers agree. Nevertheless, it is worth indulging in a brief look back into the past to remind us of the long history, so rich in tradition, of Luxembourg viticulture.

The River Moselle has had close links with wine production for over 2 000 years. As early as AD 357, the Roman poet Magnus Ausonius, in his *Mosella* epic, spoke of "hills and cliffs green with vines". At the start of the twentieth century, the first steps were taken to organise the national wine-growing industry on a more uniform and quality-oriented basis.

The year 1935 represents a milestone in the history of Luxembourg wine. That year saw the enactment of a Grand-Ducal regulation creating the "marque nationale" – a quality label awarded to Luxembourg wines following chemical and organoleptic analyses. A further high point in more recent years was without doubt the introduction in 1991 of the designation "Crémant de Luxembourg".

The wine-growing area of the Luxembourg Moselle extends over 42 kilometres from Schengen – famous for the Schengen Agreement signed in 1985 – to Wasserbillig. The total growing area amounts to some 1 300 hectares. Luxembourg is one of the most northerly regions of Europe in which quality wines are produced – a phenomenon made possible by the special climate and the excellent soil in the Moselle valley.

One of the strengths of Luxembourg wine is the wide range of grape varieties. Whilst it is almost exclusively white wine that is produced, there are a great many varieties:

Riesling: the king of wines – a fragrant, elegant wine of distinctive quality;

Pinot Gris: an unmistakeable, full wine, rich in various extracts which make up its opulence;

Pinot Blanc: pleasantly fresh, yet very smooth;

Auxerrois: fruity and elegant, full-bodied, with a distinctive bouquet;

Pinot Noir: capable of being made into white, rosé or red wine, very fruity, with an elegant bouquet;

Gewürztraminer: unmistakeable aroma, spicy bouquet, extremely elegant;

Luxembourg vineyards

Chardonnay: a fruity, full-bodied wine;

Rivaner: pleasantly mild, with a fragrance all its own;

Elbling: a light, acidic wine, very refreshing.

The best Luxembourg wines excellently complement the mouth-watering national cuisine, which, like those wines, has won international renown in recent years. The fruity bouquet and lingering taste of Riesling, for example, make it an ideal accompaniment to "Riesling trout", "Schinken in Teig" (ham in a pastry casing) or "Krebsen nach Luxemburger Art" (Luxembourg-style crayfish). Pinot Gris goes best with poultry or red meat. The fruity Pinot Noir is extremely good with substantial meat dishes. Auxerrois, by contrast, is the perfect match for dishes

Lammrücken im Kartoffelmantel
(saddle of lamb in a potato casing)

In 1989 this recipe won Léa Linster the "Bocuse d'Or" prize – the most prestigious award conferred in France for a single dish. It definitively catapulted her to the highest ranks of practitioners of contemporary gastronomy and provides the best expression of the creativity that makes Léa Linster's culinary art so special.

Ingredients (for four persons):
400-500 g saddle of lamb, boned and trimmed, salt, ground pepper, 50 g bread crumbs, 800 g firm potatoes, cooking oil, 2-3 tablespoons smooth parsley, coarsely chopped
For the sauce:
1/2 litre lamb stock, 1 sprig of rosemary, 50 g cold pieces of butter, fine sea salt

Preparation :
Cut the lamb fillet into two pieces of similar size, 20 cm long, dry them with kitchen towel, add salt and pepper and coat them in bread crumbs. Remove any excess bread crumbs.
Peel and wash the potatoes, then slice them thinly, pressing the moisture out and leaving them to dry between two layers of kitchen towel. Heat a large non-stick frying pan, add 3 tablespoons of oil and place one half of the potatoes loosely in the pan, so as to create a potato cake 0.5 cm thin and 24 cm in diameter. Fry the potato cake on one side, without turning, until it is golden brown, making sure that none of the oil gets onto the upper surface. Slide the potato cake, cooked side down, onto a piece of kitchen towel, and sprinkle half of the parsley on top. Repeat with the remainder of the potatoes to make a second potato cake.
Place one piece of lamb onto the lower third of one of the potato cakes and, using a kitchen towel, roll it up. The potato should stick to the meat and to itself at the lateral ends. Place the pieces of lamb next to each other, but a little distance apart, on a griddle with tinfoil underneath, and roast in a pre-heated 220°C oven for 15 minutes, until pink.

For the sauce: reduce the lamb stock with the sprig of rosemary in it by half, then remove the rosemary. Shortly before serving, cut the butter into small pieces and add it to the sauce, stirring until it melts and the sauce thickens slightly. Season with salt.

To serve, remove the lamb from the oven and cut each piece immediately into four pieces. Serve two pieces per person on pre-heated plates, pour the sauce around – et voilà!

made with mushrooms or cheese. Pinot Blanc provides an excellent accompaniment to fish or white meat. Gewürztraminer is at its most delicious when drunk with goose liver, cheese or a dessert. Elbling is a popular favourite with fried fish, whilst Rivaner may be enjoyed as an aperitif.

Villeroy & Boch: from ceramics manufacturer to lifestyle purveyor

Villeroy & Boch, known throughout the world as a manufacturer of fine ceramics and purveyor of a distinct lifestyle, celebrated its 250th jubilee in 1998. Its history is very closely linked with Luxembourg. In 1767 the first production plant was opened on the outskirts of the capital. Today, it runs a modern factory in Rollingergrund, a suburb just to the north of the City of Luxembourg.

The origins of Villeroy & Boch go back to a small pottery founded in 1748 by François Boch and his three sons in the village of Audun-le-Tiche in Lorraine, very close to the border between France and Luxembourg. Two decades later, the first Luxembourg works were set up under the patronage of the then Regent of Luxembourg, the Austrian Empress Maria Theresa. In 1836 the firm merged with the earthenware enterprise founded in 1791 by Nicolas Villeroy in Wallerfangen on the River Saar.

Today, Villeroy & Boch, which has operated as a public limited company since 1987 and has been listed on the stock exchange since 1990, is one of the world's most successful industrial companies. The head office of the group is located in Mettlach on the River Saar, in the triangular region comprising Germany, Luxembourg and France. Last year the company, which is made up of the "bathroom, kitchen and tiles", "wellness", "tableware" and "project business" divisions, achieved a turnover figure of nearly 1 billion euros. In twenty-one locations throughout the world, approximately 11 000 employees manufacture and market an extensive range of high-quality, beautifully designed ceramic products, as well as numerous articles made from modern, reliable materials such as acrylics, quaryl, glass, plastic, wood and metal, meeting every need in the creation of a stylish and individual home.

At Villeroy & Boch

The reputation of Villeroy & Boch's hotel division as one of the world's most highly renowned suppliers of first-class hotel and restaurant tableware is due not only to its comprehensive range of products but also to its excellent customer orientation.

The company, which today operates in 125 countries, has always been known for its special expertise in the design field. In the production of its tableware, for example, it has collaborated time and again with designers of international repute such as Paloma Picasso and Matteo Thun. These partnerships have resulted in exceptional creations which strikingly demonstrate the inventiveness and innovation of Villeroy & Boch – for whilst remaining firmly wedded to the old traditions, the company also ranks as a real trend-setter in its field, both nationally and internationally.

A traditional Luxembourg menu

This menu has been created by Léa Linster (born 1955), without doubt the most renowned of Luxembourg's cooks – both in her native country and internationally. In 1989 she was the first – and, indeed, she remains the only – woman ever to win the prestigious "Bocuse d'Or" prize. Since 2001 this

Apfelkuchen mit Eierguss
(apple pie with egg frosting)

Another typical Luxembourg treat, formerly served up only on feast days and holidays. It was often unthinkable that a wedding, for example, should take place without several days of feasting, and fruit pies always featured amongst the desserts on the multi-course menus. This much-loved apple pie produced by Léa Linster is best served warm and eaten fresh.

Ingredients (for twelve persons):
400 g yeast dough,
700 g apples (Cox's orange pippins),
2 medium-sized eggs, 2-3 heaped
tablespoons of sugar, 100 g cream,
100 ml milk,
Icing sugar or granulated sugar

Preparation :
Roll out the yeast dough till thin and place carefully in a greased mould 28 cm in diametre. Pare and core the apples, cut them into eight segments and lay them out on the dough base so that they overlap. For the frosting, whisk the eggs, sugar, cream and milk together and pour over the apple slices.
Place the apple pie in a pre-heated oven (180° C) and bake it for about 50 minutes. The apples should be soft, the egg frosting should be solid and the dough should be an appetising light brown colour. The pie should then be placed on a wire rack to cool slightly. It tastes best when warm and sprinkled with icing sugar or granulated sugar. Semi-whipped cream, sweetened with a little sugar, may be added or, for a really sophisticated touch, a little maple syrup.

grande dame of Luxembourg cuisine has also been food and drink columnist for the well-known German magazine *Brigitte*. In addition, she has recently made a name for herself as an author. Her first work, *Einfach und genial*, was nominated best German chef's cookery book in 2002, and her latest publication, *Best of Léa Linster, Cuisinièr*e, has received rave reviews. However, Léa Linster's most significant success has been achieved since 1982, as proprietor of her renowned restaurant in the small Luxembourg village of Frisingen, which best expresses the personal touch characterising her sophisticated, elegant and classic cuisine. Since June 1991 she has also been running the somewhat simpler "Kaschthaus" in the neighbouring village of Hellingen, which serves exclusively Luxembourg specialities.

"Bouneschlupp"
(thick bean hotpot)
"Kniddelen"
(flour dumplings)
"Lammrücken im Kartoffelmantel"
(saddle of lamb in a potato casing)
"Apfelkuchen mit Eierguss"
(apple pie with egg frosting)

Luxembourg – A culinary map

Special products
1. Wine and "crémants" from the Moselle-river
2. Tea, meat, herbs, spelt etc. from nature park "Upper-Sûre-Lake"
3. Cheese from Hupperdange
4. Nuts from Vianden

Regional Menus

"Éisleker Ham" / Öslinger Schinken
Smoked ham, nowadays available in the whole country, but originally a farmhouse specialty in the north of Luxembourg.

"Fischfritüre"
Little deep fried fishes from the river Mosel, baked so crisply that you can bring them to your mouth with your fingers and eat every bit of them.

"Türteg"
Leftovers from cooked sauerkraut and potato mash, originally mainly made by wine growers at the Mosel. Eaten with "Träipen" and "Mettwürste".

"Kuddelfleck"
Tripe, boiled, then breaded and baked in fat or oil.

"Judd mat Gardebounen"
Smoked pork neck with broad beans – Luxembourg's national dish.

"Träipen"
Baked black pudding, consisting of pork meat that cannot be used for a stew, including a lot of variety meats, many vegetables.. and of course fresh blood.

"Gehäck"
Offal casserole in the Luxembourg way, can be served as soup or as a whole meal. A typical winter dish.

K n i d d e l e n (f l o u r   d u m p l i n g s)

Patrick Galbats

Léa Linster includes her "Kniddelen" amongst those favourite dishes that transport you, in the twinkling of an eye, back to your childhood. And sometimes, as she says, they can serve as a sort of "comfort food" to which you can treat yourself in difficult moments.

Ingredients (for four to six persons):
500 g flour, 6 eggs, 200 ml milk, salt, 20 g butter, 2 slices of white bread, crusts removed (optional), 100 ml milk (optional), 1 tablespoon of sour cream (optional)

Preparation :
Mix the flour together with the eggs, milk, a little salt and the melted butter, stirring them into a semi-firm dough. If desired, when mixing this dough you may also add in the white bread, previously soaked in the 100 ml of milk, and the tablespoon of sour cream.

Scoop out the dumplings with a tablespoon and boil them for a short time in plenty of salted water, but only until they float to the top. Then let them stand for two to three minutes in the saucepan.

By using a teaspoon to scoop them out, you can make little dumplings which are truly appetising – and they taste wonderful as an accompaniment to roast veal or beef. Leftover dumplings can be refried in butter the following day.

Kenneth Gambin

Malta

Continuity in change

Nourishment is fundamental. Food provides the basic source of nutrients that the human body converts into energy to grow and maintain itself. It is both the substance of life and that which makes life materially possible. Reduced to essentials, the story of human history revolves around the basic needs for survival. Any civilisation which managed to establish itself and to survive had a huge appetite; it

was thrust forward by the grumblings of the stomach, that basic impulse which organised entire cultures and societies. Yet food represents much more than that. It is the basis of any type of economy as well as of the political strategies of families, communities and nations. Food, moreover, is an incredible, fascinating storehouse of condensed social meanings and symbols, a repository of cultural

A colourful display of vegetables

heritage, a system of communication, a body of images, and a protocol of practices and behaviour in particular situations. Food techniques comprise a nation's entire experience, the accumulated wisdom of our ancestors and a reflection of their vicissitudes. Food is, therefore, a tool in the hands of the cultural historian through which to examine and interpret a society, its culture and institutions, religious beliefs, social classes, personal and collective attitudes and identities.

As aptly indicated by the title of this essay, food is also one of the most effective means to document change, be it quick or slow, and a most powerful instrument for expressing and shaping interactions among humans. This observation is especially true for the tumultuous 7 000 years of Maltese history. Malta may be considered as representative of all of the Mediterranean islands, in that the history of our culinary culture is a history of continuous change and transition from one phase and ruler to another in constant succession. We find a process of modification and adjustment, conversion and re-adjustment, which has nonetheless retained the basic characteristics of the Mediterranean context.

In order to understand and therefore better assess the present situation, it is necessary first of all to embark on a rapid culinary tour along the ups and downs of Maltese history, with particular emphasis on the introduction of new products, influences from abroad, and slow or long-term changes.

From Prehistory to the Middle Ages

The first colonisation of Malta, around 5000 BC, followed relatively quickly a momentous change in the history of humankind: the agricultural revolution. Man learned how to cultivate plants and rear animals instead of depending exclusively on what nature provided. Indeed, Malta, with its minute territory, could not have been occupied prior to this period because the island did not have enough resources to support a hunter-gatherer society. Most probably the first settlers hailed from Sicily, and they brought with them the Neolithic knowledge of the agricultural revolution. The cultivation of cereals and the rearing of animals were fundamental to this first community. The remains of mortars and of carbonised grains of wheat, barley and lentils, together with the various bone fragments and representations of animals including goats, sheep, pigs and cattle, bear witness to this agricultural activity. Other activities such as hunting and fishing were also practised, although on a limited scale. Most likely the structure of this first community was egalitarian, with all of its elements concentrated on the food supply. It was only later, with the construction of such complex prehistoric megalithic temples as Hagar Qim and Mnajdra, considered to be the oldest freestanding structures in the world, that the food supply probably

Maltese vines

became steadier and safer, to the extent that some members of the society could become "artists" and dedicate themselves exclusively to temple building. In fact, it appears that even the religious beliefs of this early society rotated around the cult of fertility. This preoccupation with the provisioning of food may account for the end of this isolated and exclusive Maltese culture. It appears that around 2 500 BC this culture came to an abrupt end, possibly because of over-extensive use of the resources of the island, which could not support its community any more.

Just as food had made colonisation possible and social and economic advancement achievable, the lack of a reliable food supply led to the end of a magnificent culture. Alimentary resources, or the lack thereof, led to drastic economic and social change. The Bronze Age (c. 2 500-725 BC) ushered

in a new Maltese society, when a subsequent wave of settlers arrived, once again bringing the same plants and animals that the previous civilisation had.

The Bronze Age came to an end in the eighth century BC with the arrival of the Phoenicians, who gradually took over and absorbed the previous prehistoric community. The Phoenicians, mostly known as a people of sailors and traders, were also great agriculturalists; they specialised in the cultivation of cereals as well as vines and olives. They were also harbingers of change in the local context: in fertile inland areas they built the first countryside villas fully equipped for agricultural activity. These structures indicate a healthy agrarian economy. The Phoenicians are believed to have introduced the cultivation of vines and olives for the production of wine and oil, two products which would characterise and influence Maltese culinary culture for centuries to come.

The Maltese islands came under Roman rule in 218 BC. The continuation of agricultural activity is evinced by thirty country villas fully equipped for the production of oil, which was possibly exported. It appears that under Roman rule Malta was prosperous for long periods of time. The island was certainly considered part of the civilised world since it produced and consumed vegetables, honey and, most importantly, the trinity of bread, wine and oil – as opposed to the Barbarians, who relied on raw, unprocessed products and hunting. Bread, wine and oil were also the most important symbols of Christianity, which represented a momentous societal change.

In the sixth century (AD) the Byzantines succeeded the Romans as rulers of the island. We find a basic continuity with the preceding period, with the main feature probably being the documented coexistence of Christians, pagans and Jews, with all their food rituals, preferences and prohibitions. They lived side by side and presumably influenced each other. There were also good commercial contacts and economic activity abroad.

Change and counter-change

After the arrival of the Arabs in the late ninth century an upheaval in political, cultural and social terms, and therefore even culinary, occurred. This new civilisation, not entirely Mediterranean, reinterpreted the classical authors and amalgamated their knowledge with Persian culinary culture. The new

Maltese bread

rulers excluded pork and wine from their diet and probably introduced sugar and citrus fruits to Europe. Moreover, upon their arrival in 870 the Arabs devastated Malta, leaving the island so depopulated that it fell back into a state of a natural economy. When they reclaimed Malta around the late tenth century, the "Arabisation" of the island appears to have included all cultural aspects. The Arabs lent great importance to the rearing of animals, especially goats and sheep. They relied heavily on dairy products and developed the industries of beekeeping and fishing. Although they continued to produce olive oil, this industry was already in decline. There is evidence of a clear-cut difference between the diets of the urban and the rural classes, with the former reflecting the strong influence of broader Arabic cooking methods and preferences, while the latter utilised mainly local products and customs.

Even though direct Muslim rule came to an end in the twelfth century, Islamic culture had permeated the island so deeply that Malta continued to be considered Muslim long after the official handover to Norman rule in 1127. It was only then that Malta was reintroduced once more to the Catholic Latin European cultural tradition. In political, social and economic terms Malta became part of Sicily. This included the importation of Sicilian products such as grain and wine. Frequent bad harvests led to disasters, and from the second half of the fourteenth century onwards Malta became completely dependent on imported wheat for its survival.

Bread was at the centre of the culinary system. Social status was marked by the type of bread one consumed. White bread meant power and status, while brown bread made from barley was widely consumed by the lower classes. Wine was also considered essential and was consumed in great amounts, even though it was mainly imported. Meat and spices were consumed mainly by the upper classes as symbols of strength and power. Fish was relatively unimportant since it was considered a penitential food for fast days due to the strictures of the Catholic Church. Culinary restrictions were, in fact, clear markers of identity: it was obvious if one was a Catholic or a Muslim from what one ate and when.

Transition to modernity: The Knights of St John

Malta changed completely following the arrival of the Knights of St John in the sixteenth century. The harbour area was transformed into a heterogeneous urban zone boasting people from all corners of Europe, beginning with the knights themselves, who hailed from the best aristocratic families of Europe, down to the thousands of "Turkish" slaves from all over the Mediterranean region and beyond. This was a period of reform ushered in by the Protestant reformation, which made religious belief into even more of an identity marker. Diet was regulated not only by the seasons but also by the ecclesiastical calendar, which dictated when people had to eat lean or fat, in a constant struggle between monotony and abundance as exemplified by Lent and Carnival.

The early modern period was also a time of great culinary discoveries from the new world, including the tomato, the potato, and chocolate. These new products, along with innovative culinary ideas, were spread far and wide by another innovation: printing. However, as we shall see, in some instances centuries passed before these foods made a real impact on local culinary traditions; often they were accepted only following severe crises. Such was the case with rice, which was popular at first only as an emergency substitute for wheat.

The rift between rich and poor grew increasingly large. While the latter feared dying of hunger, the former worried about not being able to spend as much

as their status demanded. Table manners were a further means of distinction between urban and rural, rich and poor. Meat became scarcer and therefore more important as a status symbol for the upper classes.

Malta became ever more dependent on imports from abroad, especially wheat. Bread, the fulcrum of life, was accompanied by vegetables and cheese. Pasta also became very popular, and wine remained as important as ever. From the eighteenth century on vines were no longer cultivated due to a shift in favour of cultivating cotton. Fish was still considered a penitential food. Huge quantities of salted fish were imported from are north, especially during Lent. One important innovation was the introduction of coffee. Malta appears to have been among the very first European countries to taste this new drink, which was probably brought by Muslim slaves. Chocolate was mainly consumed by the upper classes, while tea was practically unknown.

Colonial influence: the British

The nineteenth century was basically a continuation of the eighteenth, with the exception of one great innovation that would change the Maltese culinary scene forever. New solutions had to be found to feed the rapidly growing population. One solution was the forced introduction of the potato by the British. Similarly, the tomato encountered a lot of resistance, even though it had been imported into Europe in the

sixteenth century. Tomatoes only found their way to the Mediterranean in the nineteenth century but they changed the nature of Mediterranean food once and for all. Other innovations following the new colonial rulers included beer and tea, which had been practically unknown in Malta; even so, until the twentieth century the majority of the Maltese rejected them. Under British influence the consumption of alcoholic

Local agriculture

drinks and of sugar also increased considerably. The importance of wine, on the other hand, diminished slightly as a result of the increased popularity of coffee and tea.

Although technological advances led to greater production and cheaper prices, there was no industrial revolution in Malta. The general diet did not improve; it just became more constant and less subject to crises. Bread retained its central importance, followed by vegetables, pasta and salted fish. Meat remained scarce, as in the rest of southern Europe. A particularly humiliating innovation popular in the

harbour area was gaxin – the leftovers of British military forces sold to the Maltese poor. Malta fared better in times of war, when the harbour area became a beehive of activity, with economic spin-offs for most of the population. However, the economy stagnated again for long periods once there was peace.

The upper classes of the harbour area, who potentially had easy access to industrialised foods, were still mainly entrenched in home-style Italian cooking, and their receptiveness to foreign imports was limited. The inland rural classes, largely cut off from British influence, continued to eat conservatively and rather simply, relying on what was accessible locally. However, their meals were never static. They took every opportunity to absorb and copy the dietary patterns of the higher classes. The urban lower classes, due to their proximity with the British, were certainly the most innovative and ready to experiment with new ideas and products. A characteristic which cut more or less through all social classes was the submission of the diet to seasonal and religious culinary rhythms which dictated what to eat, how to eat it, and when. Everyday monotony was interrupted by a series of special occasions, some of which were regular while others occurred at random. The former included the village feast, Christmas, Carnival, Easter and other popular festivals such as L-Imnarja on 29 June. The latter were mostly wedding and baptism ceremonies or funeral rituals.

Revolution

A complete transformation of Maltese culinary rhythms took place after the Second World War. This great conflict permanently and violently transformed Maltese society to its core. After the war many Maltese, seeking better prospects abroad, chose to emigrate for a few years, generally to English-speaking countries. They returned, richer, bringing a multitude of new ideas and influences. As the standard of living slowly began to increase, many more people were tempted, and had the means, to try new products. The great majority of pre-war traditions were discarded as people sought to forget the hardship of war and turn over a fresh page. This renewal applied to all aspects of life, not least to food. Scarcity turned into abundance. However, not only the quantity but also the quality of the food changed. Many now sought to imitate the British rulers and began to consume quantities of foreign and industrialised "northern" food. To eat like an Englishman became a status symbol demonstrating an open and modern mentality. By imitating the British one was, after all, following a victorious model.

Many farmers abandoned the fields and gathered in the harbour towns. Those who still practised farming now sought to produce according to the demand of the market rather than aiming to be self-sufficient as before. Women slowly started going out to work, and fresh food was no longer considered a priority. Meat, for centuries reserved for special occasions, became

Capers, cheeses and other Maltese products

everyday food, and bread lost its centrality. The road was wide open for the inevitable invasion of the fast food industry. As the rhythm of life became different, so did the rhythm of food. Seasonality was no longer a problem, and religious culinary concerns were slowly put aside following the secularisation of society. The dichotomy between the harbour and rural areas began to erode through the process of international standardisation.

It was only during the 1980s that a slow counter-reform began to take place in the culinary mentality of the Maltese. With increasing awareness of the health aspects of food, the focus slowly began to shift from quantity and extravagance to quality and

discretion. Today, the focus is again shifting toward more natural and Mediterranean products. This re-evaluation includes the tentative resurrection of old recipes and traditions.

Unfortunately, most of the latter are nothing more than recent inventions which more than anything else serve to project our ideal of the past, which we are happy to present for the demands of the tourist industry. More recently, this movement toward the past received a further impetus with Malta's progress towards joining the European Union. Threatened by the overarching power of greater Europe, the Maltese are going back to their roots to try and discover what really makes them what they are.

Works in progress

Thus Maltese society is yet again undergoing a transition phase in its food history. As we have seen, it is necessary to delve into the past, sometimes the distant past, in order to understand the culinary culture of the present. Malta's food culture is an amalgam of old and new, an eclectic choice from various rulers, trends and influences; it is the result of centuries of experimentation, trial and error, of amalgamations and introductions from abroad. Its roots are firmly planted in the southern European tradition, but it does not disdain a sprinkling of North African and northern British influence as well. One must bear in mind that traditions are not fixed in time whenever they were created. Traditions are formed and defined

through a long and traumatic evolutionary process in which cultures and ideas meet and clash and consequently influence each other reciprocally. Every culture is contaminated by other cultures. Each tradition is the result of history, and history is never static. Geography, economy, technology, politics and religion influence changes in diet. Identity, especially as it affects culinary traditions, is formed anew and confirmed in continuous, never-ending experience. Cooking is the art of amalgamation more than invention; its processes involve variation rather than pure creation. Different traditions meet and combine – courtly cooking with popular cooking, urban with rural – just as the cooking of one country is absorbed by another through the reciprocal movement of objects, ideas and persons, often in an imperceptible manner.

The cultural history of food is the story of conflicts between old and new models, between emergent ideas and others in decline; a history of mentalities regarding preferences or rejections. Change is inevitable. Present and future generations bear the burden of having to strike the right balance between past, present and future, tradition and change. If we manage to find the correct balance between conservatism and innovation we will enrich our culinary heritage.

Varvara Buzilă and Teodorina Bâzgu

Moldova

Ritual breads through the seasons

The foods that define Moldovan cuisine are simple and nourishing. Moldova's most important contribution to European cuisine is its expressive tradition of ritual breads. More then 200 forms of ritual bread exist in our culinary culture; they are formed into various shapes that look like sculptures after baking. Our assortment of homemade pies is also remarkable. They are made with cherries, apples, plums and cream cheese. Fresh vegetables and dishes made from them are prized during the hot summers; in the late autumn the produce is preserved for wintertime use. The meat of fowl is the most preferred, followed by pork and, in the south, lamb. Cottage cheese and sheep's- and goat's-milk cheese are served plain as appetizers or mixed with cream or cornmeal. Wines are produced in great variety and are served regularly at table.

Easter Sunday food

©Eugen Bâzgu

Moldova

Funeral offerings

on the bread, near a table laden with similar breads. They kiss the bread, which is later distributed to the wedding guests. In southern villages, the blessing takes place a week after the wedding ceremony when the newlyweds return to the girl's parents' house with "bread and salt". They bring two knot-shaped breads as a symbol of their union and to symbolically ask forgiveness for past mistakes.

All major life events such as birth, marriage and death are accompanied by important feasts. After a christening, the participants are invited to dine at a table laden with food. The godparents are each given two knot-shaped breads to honour their important role in protecting the child. At weddings, the ceremony lasts for one or two days and serves to unite the families of the bridegroom, the bride, the godfather and godmother. The ceremonial meal is lavish, with plenty of food and drink, mirth and toasts, and gifts for the young couple. Several ritual meals mark various important stages of the ritual: the separation of the bride from her parents; her entrance into the groom's house; and her transformation into a young married woman. To sanctify the new relationships the bride's parents present ritual breads of different shapes to the most important wedding guests. Before the bride leaves her parental home to go to the bridegroom, the couple is blessed by their parents. In the northern and central regions of Moldova, the young people kneel before their parents with their foreheads

The greatest number of meals for guests is associated with death. Funeral meals are not as luxurious as wedding feasts, but they respect the culinary traditions and tastes of the deceased. The women from the

The tree of life in rites of remembrance

302

family of the deceased are forbidden to bake bread or prepare any of the ritual foods, in order to avoid contaminating the guests with death. Relatives, neighbours, and sometimes the whole community join the family to accompany the dead in procession to the graveyard. Women from outside the immediate family bake many ritual breads whose shapes symbolise the passing from one life to another such as ladders, bridges and birds. These breads are distributed to the funeral guests. Food is prepared in large quantities to ensure that there will be enough for all those who take part in the procession.

When the coffin is removed from the house in preparation for burial, many objects are left in the yard as gifts representing things necessary for daily existence, such as a bed or bedclothes, chairs, or a table arranged with plates of hot and cold food. Many jugs of water are also left, as are ritual breads and sweets, and tree branches decorated with fruits. The main food served at the funeral meal is porridge made from boiled wheat grains mixed with pounded nuts and honey. In accordance with tradition, everyone present must taste this funeral porridge. After burying the dead, the guests return to the house of the deceased, where

Ritual bread forms

they are seated at a table to partake of the foods that the dead person liked. First the priest blesses the

meal, then everyone tastes the funeral porridge again before eating the other dishes. Tradition calls for only wine to be offered, three times, but no hard liquor is served.

Funeral meals are organised on the third, ninth and fortieth days after the funeral, then again six months later, one year later, and then annually for seven years. Only then is the deceased considered to have definitely entered the world of the dead. These ritual meals unite the living and serve to recall the dead in the collective memory of those still alive. Everyone who helped at the funeral, the relatives and the neighbours are invited to these meals. As they eat, they reminisce about the deceased. Each guest receives as a gift one knot-shaped bread, along with a candle.

Foods used in the rituals of the traditional calendar are linked to the cosmic rhythms of the sun and nature. Thus, the ritual meals served at Christmas and on New Year's Eve must contain nine or twelve kinds of foods prepared from field produce (cereals, beans, vegetables, fruits). These foods are handed out to the guests who come singing carols, bringing messages of well-being and happiness to the hosts; they are also symbolically presented to the dead. The ritual breads for these holidays are fashioned into different shapes, each with a distinct purpose and

Men enjoying a drink

significance depending on occasion as well as on the social standing and age of the recipient. For instance, the symbolic Christmas and New Year's bread is shaped into a figure 8, because it is circular and represents infinity. On Christmas Eve, an intense exchange of foods takes place. Children bring their relatives two lipii (cakes) over planed, like two plates made from bread, on which is placed a small amount of food. The relatives replace the top cake with food from their own table. This ritual exchange between visitors and hosts takes place throughout the community, so that everyone takes part.

Easter commemorates the resurrection of Jesus Christ and the rebirth of nature. On Easter Eve special foods are blessed at church: eggs dyed or painted red; pasca (a round Easter cheese cake with a cross in the centre), lamb, cheese and salt. For three days after Easter families eat these foods for breakfast. One week after Easter, so-called "soft-hearted" Easter, or the Easter of the Dead, is celebrated. This is the day when the living and the dead are reunited at the graveyard. Relatives arrange different foods typical for the Easter holidays on the graves: pasca, eggs, sweets, fruits jugs of wine or water. They also leave new clothes. All of the food is blessed by the priest before being distributed to the poor.

On Great Sunday, which is celebrated fifty days after Easter, the houses are decorated with walnut and lime branches. Jugs of boiled milk and tocmagi (a kind of homemade spaghetti) are served, and all sorts of pies and sweet cherries are given to the poor.

Festive meals are organised and offerings of food are made for all of the transitional rituals in Moldovan culture. As a rule, the food is intended for the poor, for children and for the elderly, to involve them in the common celebration. The goal of these festive meals is to unite family members, relatives, and the entire community during times of crisis, conflict, and other significant social change.

Françoise Gamerdinger and René Novella

Monaco

A rich culinary heritage

The Monegasques' particular attachment to their land undoubtedly stems from memory of a time when the principality was cut off from the outside world and needed to be self-sufficient. They have existed as a people for more than 700 years, and used to depend for their survival on their olive, lemon and orange groves. A love of the sea and fishing has also been handed down through the generations, while Monegasques have continued – despite difficulties at different periods of their history – to observe religious festivals and their own customs.

The principality's culinary heritage is therefore closely linked to the religious traditions that punctuate the changing seasons.

Pissaladière (a pizza-like onion tart)

Candlemas

On St Blaise's Day (3 February, the day after Candlemas) it was customary for the faithful to attend church for the blessing of the throat – the part of the body believed to enjoy the saint's protection. Believers also brought the new season's seed to be blessed, as well as a small package of dried figs which they would then use to make an infusion, adding cloves, slices of apple and cinnamon. This drink was believed to be a miraculous cure for throat ailments.

Ash Wednesday and Lent

The traditional midday meal on Ash Wednesday consisted of chickpea soup flavoured with aromatic herbs such as sage and bay leaves, as well as garlic.

S o c c a

Socca is a speciality thin as a pancake, made with a batter of chickpea flour and olive oil

Ingredients
250 g chickpea flour - 2-3 soupspoons virgin olive oil - 1 teaspoon table salt - freshly ground pepper - 1/2 litre water

Method
Preheat the oven to maximum temperature.
Pour the chickpea flour into a large mixing bowl.
Make a well in the centre and pour in the olive oil. Whisk continuously while adding 1/2 litre of cold water.
Mix well. Strain the mixture to remove any lumps.
Add the salt.
Oil a baking tray and coat it with the batter to a depth of 2-3 mm.
Cook in a very hot oven with the grill lit.
Burst any blisters that form in the batter.
Sprinkle with pepper, cut into small squares and serve immediately.

The Monegasques were strict in their observance of Lent, and one of the dishes traditionally prepared at this time of the year is known as barbagiuans, which are a sort of large deep-fried ravioli filled with a mixture of rice, marrow, and egg. Barbagiuans have now come to be eaten all year round.

Easter

Easter Day, after church, is a time when people gather for a family meal, the traditional centrepieces of which are roast kid and a chard pie known as pasqualina. In times gone by, the table would have been decorated with colourfully painted eggs, which were used for a game that involved trying to crack the tip of one's neighbour's egg without breaking one's own. At this time of year, street vendors offered light Easter pastries called canestreli: these were decorated with red-painted hard-boiled eggs held in place by a pastry lattice which gave them the appearance of little baskets. On Easter Monday and on fine days in spring and summer the inhabitants of Monaco liked

Fougasse Monégasque

This traditional though hard-to-find recipe varies from family to family. It is jealously guarded by each and handed down through the generations.

Ingredients :

550 g flour – 20 g fresh yeast mixed with 1/2 glass of lukewarm water – 200 g sugar – 200 g butter or margarine – 1 soupspoon rum – 1 soupspoon curaçao – 1 soupspoon anisette – 1/2 glass orange flower water – 2 soupspoons olive oil – grated zest of one lemon – 2 pinches of red and white aniseed (fenuyëti) – sugared almonds – almonds – hazelnuts icing sugar

Preparation :

Put a little of the flour in a mixing bowl. Make a well in the centre and pour in the yeast and water mixture, mixing to make a leaven. Leave to rise for around fifteen minutes.

Add the rum and liqueurs, orange flower water, olive oil, aniseed, lemon zest and sugar with the remainder of the flour. Stir in the flour gradually and incorporate the butter in small pieces.

Keep mixing until the dough is smooth and pliable.

Leave to rest for at least four hours.

Spread the dough into moulds pre-greased with butter. Ensure that the fougasses remain quite thin.

Cover with sugared almonds, almonds, hazelnuts and fenuyëti (red and white aniseed).

Cook in a hot oven for approximately twenty minutes (thermostat 5/6).

On removing from the oven, sprinkle with orange flower water and dust with a little icing sugar.

Fougasse (pastries flavoured with orange-flower water)

to get outdoors and picnic in the surrounding countryside or by the sea. The picnic, traditionally carried in a cavagnetu (a wicker basket), would consist of cold dishes cooked the previous evening. Typically the basket would contain the familiar barbagiuans, a savoury tart, an omelette made with fresh green leaves, and sardiná – a savoury dish of soft flour-and-olive-oil pastry topped with anchovies, machetu (anchovy mousse), olives and garlic. Families would meet up with one another at these picnics to share a cundiún, a summer salad of tomatoes, peppers and tuna. Nowadays the picnic tradition is carried on by the municipality, which organises an open-air meal at the end of June, giving Monegasques a chance to get together amid the olive trees of Princess Antoinette park. At the end of July and the beginning of August the Saint Roman Festival Committee also organises two open-air meals in the Saint Martin gardens.

The Monegasque Christmas

Christmas has always been a big family festival in Christian countries, and in Monaco people would traditionally meet in the parental home on Christmas Eve to share a special evening meal. Before they took their places at the table, the youngest member of the family, clutching a small olive branch that had been dipped in old wine, would go over to the fireplace and make the sign of the cross by the log fire, saying the words: Parmura auriva, u ma se ne vā e u ben arriva ("By the grace of the olive tree, let evil be gone and

Monegasque stockfish

Ingredients (for six people) :
2 halves of dried cod, pre-soaked – 6 pieces of dried cod innards, pre-soaked – 1 red pepper 1 green pepper – 3 large onions, chopped 3 good-sized leeks – 1/2 head of celery, thinly sliced – 1 kg tomatoes (or a tin of chopped tomatoes) - garlic and parsley – mixed herbs 1 teaspoon good curry powder – olive oil – some small black olives – 6 medium–sized potatoes

Preparation :
Carefully skin and trim the cod and cut it into large pieces. Cut the innards into thin strips.
Fry the onions, leeks and celery in 10 cl of olive oil in a casserole until soft but not browned.
Cut the peppers into large pieces and fry lightly in a separate pan with a little olive oil, then add to the vegetables in the casserole.

Add the large pieces of cod and curry powder and simmer for a few minutes in the covered casserole.
Roughly chop the tomato and lightly fry it on its own with olive oil and herbs, then add to the casserole.
In a small pan, gently heat 5 cl of olive oil, toss in the garlic and parsley to soften them without browning, then add to the casserole.
Lastly add the innards with a little salt and pepper, and some water if there is not enough liquid in the casserole.
Mix gently with a wooden spoon, then simmer for at least an hour.
Add the potatoes, diced, and continue simmering until they are cooked.
Adjust the seasoning and add the black olives just before serving.

Barbajuan (rice and pumpkin pastries)

good prevail for ever"). He would then drink a little of the wine before passing the goblet to the rest of the family – starting with the eldest – gathered round the fire. After that it was time to eat. A white cloth would be on the table, and a range of special dishes would be served: the delicious brandaminciún, a salt cod dish; cardu (cardoon or artichoke thistle) in a white sauce; apple friscioei (fritters); and fougasse, the traditional

Some Monegasque proverbs

E megliu ün pulastru anchoei che üna galina deman
A chick today is better than a hen tomorrow.

Grussiè cuma ün pan d'oerdi
As coarse as barley bread

Natale ün famiglia cun'na tora ben garnia e na dinda ben rustia
A family Christmas means a well filled table and a well cooked turkey.

Cü ā denti nun ā pan, Cü ā pan nun ā denti
The person with teeth has no bread and the person with bread has no teeth.

Dui pai che sortu d'u meme turelu nun se semigliu
Two loaves might be kneaded on the one board, but that does not make them the same.

Galina veglia fa bon brodu
An old hen makes good stock.

Cun de pan e de vin, se po envitā u vijin
If you have bread and wine you can invite your neighbour in.

Ün pastu forte e l'autru mezan mategne l'omu san
One big meal and one smaller one keep a person healthy.

Ventre zazün nun scuta nüsciün
An empty belly is deaf.

Fo büve u vin vegliu e l'eri nevu.
Choose old wine, but new oil.

Ciacün sa seche buglie ent'a so pignata
We all know what's cooking in our own pot.

cake with its scattering of fenuyëti (red and white aniseed). Pride of place in the centre of the table went to u pan de Natale, the Christmas loaf. U pan de Natale is a circular loaf decorated with four walnuts in the shape of a cross. In the centre of the bread are placed sprigs from an olive and an orange tree. After the fireplace blessing, the loaf is ceremonially carried to the centre of the table, where it remains – along with thirteen traditional desserts – until Epiphany. Between meal times the four corners of the cloth are folded over to protect the dishes. The old belief was that performing this ritual would ensure an abundant harvest and prosperity for the household. The dishes containing the thirteen desserts – green or black grapes, three types of ground nuts (walnuts, almonds and hazelnuts), three kinds of dried fruit (figs, raisins and prunes), two citrus fruits (oranges and mandarins), two deep-fried desserts (apple fritters and the twists of dough known as ganses), and seasonal pears and apples – were kept filled until Epiphany.

It was also customary to bake mariote e gali for the children.

Mariote were little cakes made at Christmas with dough left over from the fougasse. In the shape of dolls, they resembled the gingerbread men on sale at fairgrounds. The mariota was the traditional Christmas gift for girls, while boys received a cockerel – u galu – made with the same dough. Sugared almonds were used for the eyes and mouth, and the body was scattered with aniseed.

On Fridays all year round, the traditional Monegasque dernā (lunch) consisted of u stocafi, or stockfish, a dish of dried cod, tomatoes and peppers. Other traditional foods eaten as snacks were machetu, a type of anchovy paste spread on bread, and the fariná, a thin pancake made with chickpea flour which is known in present-day Nice by the name of socca.

Of course, some of these recipes are also used outside Monaco, in Provence or Italy, where they provide evidence of a common heritage that has been adapted to specific traditions and the skills of the different cooks.

Bibliography

Quelques notes sur les traditions de Monaco
Louis Notari, Imprimerie nationale de Monaco
S.A., 1960

Notre passé
Louis Canis, Comité national des traditions monégasques, 1963

Le Comité national des traditions monégasques
Musée du Vieux Monaco, Monaco City

Saveurs de Monaco:
Les recettes authentiques
Paul Mullot, Epi éditions, 2003

Cuisine monégasque, Cüjina de Munégu:
100 recettes
Jean et Danièle Lorenzi

En parcourant la Côte d'Azur
Gabriel Ollivier, Editions Les flots bleus, Monte-Carlo

Bert Natter

Netherlands

Twenty-two minutes at the table

It may be that the national cuisine of a country is best described by someone not born there, since the culinary achievements can otherwise be overcoloured.

Johannes Vermeer (1632-1675), "The Kitchen Maid"

Fortunately there is little such risk when describing the Dutch kitchen. Plenty of people may like their pea soup, hotchpotch and gently braised meat, but it

©Rijksmuseum, Amsterdam

is another thing again to take pride in those dishes or to derive one's national identity from sprouts. No – the Dutch are proud of what a small country can be big in: the battle against water, our painters, our footballers and our indestructible gezelligheid.

The Dutch like being what they call gezellig. In fact, they are so proud of being gezellig that they cannot think of any other language with a word having quite the same connotations. It's about people getting together agreeably but has nothing to do with hospitality. The Dutch have a word for those moments when they are not doing anything but are just being.

Everything has its appointed time in the Dutch household: breakfast, coffee, lunch, tea and dinner. These are the breaks between working and sleeping, the moments when we are gathered together, and which must be gezellig. This kind of gezelligheid is reserved for one's family. Relatives, friends, immediate neighbours and close colleagues may share in the fun, provided it has been announced in advance. Even popping in for a cup of coffee is generally

Jan Steen (1626-1679), "The Merry Family"

Floris van Dijck (1575-1651), "Still Life with Cheeses"

arranged by appointment. For however gezellig the Dutch might like to be, there are few things you can do to aggravate them more than turn up unannounced on the doorstep just as they are sitting down to a meal. With luck you'll be allowed inside and then be frozen out, but more likely you will be told before you can even get a foot in the door that, "Sorry, but we are just about to have our meal."

The Dutch traditional kitchen does not lend itself well to unexpected guests: everything has to be ready at the same time, but potatoes take a long time to prepare whereas boiled vegetables quickly turn to pulp and you can hardly offer a guest half a meatball. But tuck into a succession of small hot and cold snacks all evening, like they do in the south? That's not what the Dutch call a meal, they're just titbits.

Holland may not be known for its exquisite cuisine, but curiously enough a meal played an important bit part in the history of the nation. The royal house goes back to the ancestors of William of Orange, who is still revered as the "father of the fatherland". The chefs in his employ were famed throughout Europe. The most important leader of the revolt against the Spanish occupiers was murdered in Delft on 10 July 1584. One witness declares that the murder took place after the meal was over, when the prince had finished his wine. William was also said to have been so well away ("raoust") that he would have been totally incapable of uttering his famous last words, "Mon Dieu, ayez pitié de moi et de mon pauvre peuple."

The Dutch rose up against the Spanish from 1568 onwards, a period that later became known as the Eighty Years War and which came to an end in 1648 with the Treaty of Westphalia. In one of his historical works the French writer Voltaire relates an appetising anecdote about how the Twelve Years' Truce between the warring parties came into being in 1609. When the Spanish ambassador Spinola and the diplomat Richardot went to The Hague in 1608 in order to negotiate an armistice with the Dutch, they saw eight to ten people get out of a little boat somewhere along the way. They simply sat down on the grass and each produced his own bread, cheese and beer. The Spanish ambassador took in the scene and asked a farmer just who those gentlemen were. "They are the members of the States-General, our sovereign lords and masters", replied the farmer. In response the Spanish ambassador said to his entourage: "You can't defeat this lot. The best thing to do is to make peace with them."

But when the truce came to an end in 1621 the struggle was resumed. Despite the war Holland entered its Golden Age. The republic dominated world trade for 150 years. It remains a mystery how the sole contribution to world culinary heritage made by a country with a virtual monopoly over the trade in spices should have been the Dutch doughnut or "oil ball".

Since there was no absolute monarchy, the country lacked a flourishing court culture. Those setting the trend in cultural life were wealthy citizens – sober merchants who earned their fortune in the colonies. Despite the reports of sumptuous banquets, the luxuriance displayed in showpiece still lifes and the opulent recipes to be found in the cookbooks of the time, it is difficult to imagine that the Dutch were prepared to spend a lot of money on things that would not last long, let alone something to be enjoyed by letting it slip down into the intestines.

The wealthy citizens inhabiting the splendid canal-side houses were certainly not averse to flaunting their extravagant still lifes. These paintings teach us something about the eating culture of that time, for example that it was the custom to present animals on the table as intact as possible, preferably with head and all attached. These days we do all we can to make food appear as though it has come from the factory rather than from nature. Even at the butcher's we do not like seeing recognisable pieces of an animal. Before it reaches the refrigerated display units of the supermarket meat it is sealed into plastic trays so that a couple of chicken fillets look like a supermodel's rear cleavage. Vegetables are popped into a plastic bag all clean and pre-cut so that nobody will notice that they have been pulled out of the ground. Everything that is dead must look as though it has never lived. People have become so accustomed to being surrounded by manufactured items that they no longer appear to know what to do with things that have grown naturally.

The history of our food is the story of how the inedible has been made tasty. Take the innumerable ways of making coffee: what a long road those unsightly berries have had to travel in order to become the "gezellige" fuel of each Dutch household. And that in the case of a beverage described as "bitter and characterless" by the psychologist Robert C. Bolles

Daniel Vertangen (1598-1681), "Portrait of Dima Lems, wife of Jan Valckenburgh"

(1928-1994), who notes that the first time you taste coffee, it tastes awful. But after a few thousand cups you can't do without it. Children don't like it, adults unfamiliar with it don't like it, rats don't like it: nobody likes coffee, he says, except people who have already downed a considerable quantity of the stuff.

People appear to think that our ancestors were continually on the lookout for new, even more delicious tastes, but the opposite is in fact true. However odd it may sound, cheese is essentially no more than a way of preserving milk. All sorts of food treatments that we regard as tasty were intended to conserve products before the advent of the refrigerator: salting, pickling, sweetening, smoking and marinating.

Many of these techniques are to be found in the cookbooks from the Golden Age. The writers would frequently lift recipes from other cookbooks, but new techniques were certainly also introduced by immigrants making their way to the republic from all over Europe in the Golden Age.

During this era Amsterdam was the second-biggest city in Europe and the most important trading centre in the world. At least a third of the population was of foreign origin. It is estimated that no fewer than 1 million immigrants moved to Holland between 1600 and 1800, three quarters of them for economic reasons.

Whether this mass influx of foreign peoples has left its traces on the Dutch kitchen is hard to establish. Ironically, the most clearly discernible influence is that of the Spanish occupation. After the siege of Leyden the Spaniards are said to have left behind a pan of hotchpotch on 3 October 1574 – although the dish did not contain the two main ingredients of the present-day version, carrots and potatoes, but spicy meat with onions and parsnip.

Similarly, the migratory movements of the second half of the twentieth century have left barely any traces behind in the Dutch kitchen. When the former Dutch colony of Surinam was granted independence in the 1970s, no fewer than 300 000 people – half the Surinamese population – decided to move to the Netherlands. Anyone in search of Surinamese products in a well-stocked supermarket, however, will return home empty-handed and with an empty stomach. The Surinamese buy their wares in the market in the big cities, in which you may find the odd Surinamese restaurant, but that's where it ends.

Traces are, however, to be found of another colony, Indonesia, such as the rice table or rijsttafel, an amalgam of small dishes from all over Indonesia that is not a traditional dish but an invention of the Dutch colonists, which they took back with them to the fatherland after Indonesia gained independence in the late 1940s.

Large groups of Spaniards and later also Turks and Moroccans came to Holland as guest-workers in the 1970s, but don't imagine that the Dutch cook paella, couscous or pilaf once a week. At most we buy ready to eat appetisers, snacks and fast-food from those countries, but cooking techniques and dishes have hardly found their way into our kitchens.

The Dutch kitchen is a sensible kitchen. In *Allerhande*, the free magazine issued by the Albert Heijn supermarket chain, the recipes accordingly do not just show the ingredients but also the preparation time, the cost per serving and the number of kilocalories, along with the fat, protein and carbohydrate content.

In 2003 Albert Heijn published a survey entitled "How do the Dutch eat?" To quote: "A hot meal is shared at a laid table with fixed places at a set time between 5.30 p.m. and 6.30 p.m. And that in a record time of twenty-two minutes (including dessert!). All in all the average cooking time for a hot meal during the week is around thirty-two minutes. Stir-frying and woks have now become a firmly established part of the scene. And among the ten most popular kitchen appliances, the frying pan has been the big loser in favour of the microwave and wok. Health comes first when choosing the menu, followed at some distance by cost. Potatoes, vegetables and meat are increasingly losing ground on the menu to pasta and rice. Pizza, lasagne and shwarma are the favourite foreign dishes."

Demolishing a meal, including dessert, takes the average Dutch person twenty-two minutes on weekdays. I think that most Dutch people would consider that quite long enough if they were to reflect on all the useful things they might otherwise be doing in that time. On the other hand, such a figure makes one curious as to how long people spend eating in other countries.

In preparing a meal, the Dutch therefore increasingly look beyond the border. It's as though we are in search of surprises and tastes other than the traditional evening meal consisting of boiled potatoes, a piece of meat and cooked vegetables (in spring and summer) or the traditional mashed potatoes and cabbage known as stamppot (in autumn and winter). But what precisely are these foreign dishes? Pizza, shwarma and stir-fries. What these dishes have in common is that they are easy to prepare and create little washing-up.

The Dutch multicultural kitchen is not the consequence of changing tastes or wider horizons but involves something else. Now that our food has become so denatured one would be inclined to think that evolutionary or unconscious processes no longer play a role when we buy and cook our food, but the beast in us will not lie down. Our meal is not based around what is healthy, cheap or nice-tasting but what we do not have. Throughout history the unavailability of certain ingredients or techniques has been the decisive factor. Our cuisine is determined by the time that we are able or prepared to

Aert van der Neer (1603-1677), "River view by moonlight"

devote to it. Looking for, finding and trying out other products is intimately bound up with the fact that people are unwilling or unable to spend much time in the kitchen during the week.

We do of course sometimes set aside time for a meal, for example going out to enjoy ourselves. Our restaurants are the object of growing international acclaim. At home too the Dutch will sometimes make a special effort in the kitchen. Once guests ("eaters") have been announced the lord of the manor will go in search of exotic purchases for that one meal before standing

guard over his exorbitantly expensive cooker like a beleaguered knight in order to conjure up the most challenging dishes from the best-selling cookbooks.

But these are fair-weather cooks. No, the true Dutch cook – a species threatened with extinction – is a woman, an earth-mother. She keeps a sack of potatoes in the cellar, has a garden full of cabbage and root vegetables and in the shed she keeps a pan with solidified gravy and braising cuts or home-made meatballs. She is not waiting for visitors, for that would be, well, the very opposite of gezellig.

Rembrandt van Rijn (1606-1669), "Dead Peacocks"

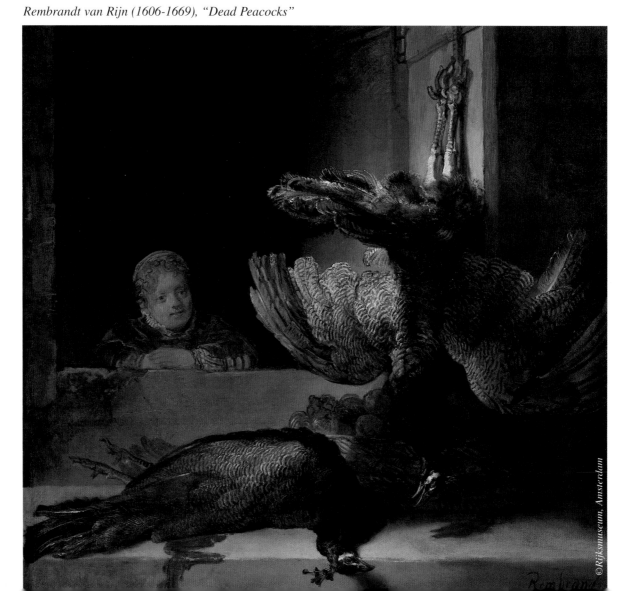

©Rijksmuseum, Amsterdam

Henry Notaker

Norway

Between innovation and tradition

No fewer than three Norwegian chefs have won the prestigious "Bocuse d'Or" gold medal in Paul Bocuse's culinary competition in Lyon, France. In some ways this recognition might help to rectify the culinary reputation the Norwegian kitchen has had for over 1 000 years. A story from the year 1247 exemplifies the expectations foreign visitors from the more fertile parts of southern Europe had when arriving in the far north. That year the papal delegate Cardinal William of Sabina arrived to participate in the coronation ceremony of King Haakon Haakonsson. The Cardinal informed his hosts that before he left for Norway he had been warned that the quality of the food would be poor, and that the only beverage he would be offered was blanda, a sour mixture of water and whey. As it turns out, he was pleasantly surprised by the quality of the food and drink he was served – a result of the fact that by then the Viking Age had ended, and Norway had entered into a more refined era. Unfortunately, the cardinal's positive experience did not quell the malicious rumours, despite the praise lavished on Norwegian raw materials such as salmon, reindeer and strawberries by many foreign visitors over the next centuries.

One of the reasons why Norway's professional culinary art was poorly developed is probably because after the Middle Ages, Norway, unlike most of the larger European countries, had virtually no nobility and therefore no court traditions. The members of the elite were limited to a few families of higher officials, land-owners and wealthy merchants. Nor was there any large, urban, upper-middle class to lay the foundations of a modern restaurant culture. Norwegian restaurant culture as such has emerged only in the past few decades; it is during this period that the new celebrity chefs have entered the field.

The food served to Cardinal William in Bergen was in all likelihood equivalent to the fare he was accustomed to receiving at more southern latitudes.

The elite of the various European countries had good contact with each other, and fashions spread quickly. But the food of the upper echelons differed greatly from the food of the commoners. Norse literature makes this abundantly evident.

The medieval poem *Rigstula*, recorded in Iceland in the thirteenth century, tells the story of the wanderings of the Norse god Rig. During his travels he visited three homes, each representing a different rung on the social ladder. In each home Rig slept with the mistress of the house, which resulted in the birth of three children. It is easy to see that the poem describes and possibly explains medieval class society. The first son was dark of skin and ugly of countenance, with a stooped back and wrinkled skin. He was named Træl[1] and became a slave. The second was a clear-eyed, red-cheeked boy. He was named Karl[2] and became a farmer. The third son had blond hair and golden skin. He was named Jarl[3] and became a knight and a warrior. To make the story credible to its readers (listeners), the poem must depict the three homes in a manner they can recognise. Thus, a description is given of the furnishings, the women's clothing and the food that is served. In the first house Rig is given a simple soup with a lumpy piece of bread full of chaff and husks. In the next he is served veal stew. But in the last house, where the table is set with silver and linen, he is served wheat bread, wine and roast fowl:

On the table she placed
platters of silver, juicy meat
and roasted birds.

Wine served in beakers,
goblets adorned
They drank and chattered
throughout the day.

The Poetic Edda

(Translation by Lee M. Hollander, Austin, 1986).

White bread and wine were, of course, imported goods. In the Icelandic *Egil's Saga* a merchant is described as travelling to England to sell stockfish and buy wheat, honey and wine for Harald Hårfagre, king of Norway in the late ninth century. Such trade was not, however, viewed with unequivocal enthusiasm. A later king, Sverre Sigurdsson, criticised the German merchants for buying up too much stockfish and butter and in return supplying Norway with vast amounts of cheap wine – which led to increased drunkenness.

Sverre's tirade had little effect. Norwegian contact with foreign countries continued, partly due to the economic impact of the country's seafaring activities, and partly due to immigration. Bergen emerged as an important centre for merchants from the mighty North German Hansa League. Citizens and craftsmen from the countries around the North Sea settled in smaller towns along the coast, bringing their trade as well as new foods and traditions. Moreover, in the late Middle Ages Norway lost its independence and came instead to be ruled from Copenhagen. As a result, all the government officials employed in the districts from the south to the far north came from Denmark, or at least had a Danish education and cultural background.

A selection of historic Norwegian cheeses. In the foreground on the left, gammalaost; brunos is on the right. In the background is a soft, sharp cheese called pultost, which was not as prized as gammalaost and was eaten on bread by servants and other commoners.

©Tine BA

The country these outsiders ruled was, until the end of the nineteenth century, a peasant society. The bulk of the population lived in rural areas and worked either in farming or fishing. It was therefore natural that this society's food traditions revolved around regional and local products, often prepared on the farm or at home.

Nevertheless, Norwegian and foreign food customs did not occupy two completely separate spheres. Norwegian culinary traditions have always been influenced by the meeting between the indigenous peasant culture on one hand, and the partly urban, partly aristocratic European culinary traditions on the other.

Traditional peasant fare

Traditional Norwegian cooking is influenced by a very short growing season and a very long and cold winter. Most traditional courses are prepared using ingredients that have been preserved in one way or another, either through curing, drying or some kind of fermentation. Spices are used only sparingly, as they were

rare and therefore expensive. Most traditional dishes still emphasise the natural qualities of the raw materials, using only nature's own flavours as seasoning.

The Norwegian mainland stretches from 58° to 71° N and has a growing season of a mere 190 days in the

Oatmeal porridge

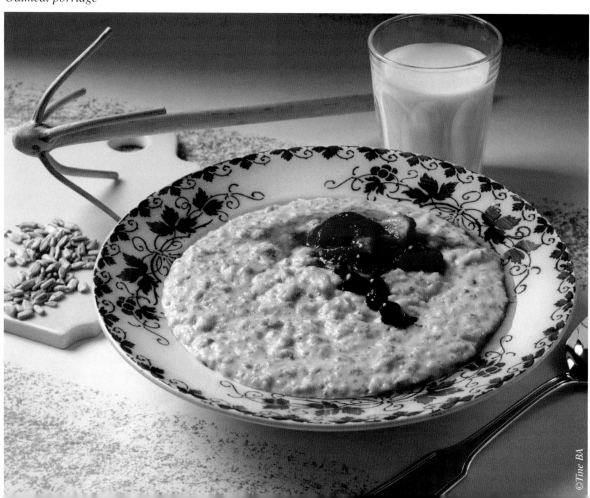

south and 100 days in the north and in the mountains. It is only thanks to the warm currents of the gulf stream that Norway has a viable agricultural sector at all. As far as vegetables are concerned, Norway seeks to be self-sufficient in varieties that tolerate storage, such as potatoes, carrots, onions, cabbage and swedes (rutabaga), also known as "Nordic oranges". Moreover, the cold climate has certain advantages. Slow ripening during long Nordic summer days produces vegetables, berries and fruit that are aromatic and sweet. As a result of Norway's northern latitude, proximity to the sea, scattered farms, and high standards of food production, there are no serious animal or plant diseases in the country.

Historically, diets in Norway varied from region to region depending on local resources. For example, fresh fish formed a much greater part of the diet in the coastal parts of Norway than in the inland parts, while the diet in inland Norway consisted of agricultural products, such as dairy products, meat and grains. On the other hand, there was very little daily use of meat and fish. Most people lived mainly on porridge and crispbread, cheese and curdled milk. The finest meat products and the best parts of the slaughtered livestock were sold, while the farmers themselves used the entrails and blood. Along the coast some of the less valuable types of fish were eaten, while cod catches were usually dried and exported. While other European countries enforced strict hunting laws and privileges, Norway permitted commoners to hunt in the forests. However, the game seldom went to the hunter's household; it was sold to higher officials and others who, like their peers in many European countries, viewed game as somewhat of a status symbol.

The Norwegian poet and writer Jens Bjørneboe pays homage to the culinary traditions of various countries in his long poem *About places on Earth and food I like*. He has the following to say about a few of the more distinctive Norwegian products:

**Moreover I have eaten,
in old, rainy Norway,
the two things
that have elevated
the country
to a cultural nation:
fermented trout and
"old cheese".
Food for dukes and freeholders!**

Dairy products: a central part of the everyday fare

Gammelost ("old cheese") is one of the traditional products that was extremely popular for a long time, but that lost its status when new types of cheese were introduced to the Norwegian market. Today gammelost is a bit of a rarity, completely marginalised both in everyday and holiday fare. Many other kinds of cheese and several types of milk-based dishes, both sweet and soured, represent an essential component of what is considered to be traditional Norwegian food. One festive dish that was often prepared for special occasions and seasonal celebrations was sour-cream porridge, made from sour cream and flour. This porridge was also one of the most common "gifts" brought to mark childbirths and weddings.

The Norwegian custom of utilising whey is probably one of the most unique Norwegian uses of milk, and is a tradition shared only by Iceland and the northern parts of Sweden. Whey is the sugary liquid that is left over after making cheese. It was mixed with water and used as a drink, making the blanda that Cardinal William was warned about. It was also used as soup, or made into prim – a soft whey cheese – or mysost – a hard whey cheese moulded into the shape of a brick.

The sweet cheese was the most popular, and therefore the most expensive, while cheese made from sour whey was given to the servants and spread on bread instead of butter. This type of whey cheese gradually disappeared when, in the last part of the nineteenth century, a "mutation", the modern brunost ("brown cheese"), was developed.

Ever popular, brunost is one of the foodstuffs Norwegians miss the most when they are abroad. It has almost assumed the role of national dish. This hard, brown cheese is produced only in Norway, and there are those who claim that its caramel-like taste can be appreciated only by Norwegians. Brunost is normally made from cow's milk with a little goat's milk mixed in. The version that is made from goat's milk alone is called ekte geitost (genuine goat's cheese) and has a stronger, less sweet taste. In Norway these cheeses are typically eaten in thin slices on top of brown bread for breakfast or lunch.

Fermented fish

Half- or wholly-fermented fish is the result of a distinctive way of storing fish that was especially common in sub-Arctic regions. Until the nineteenth century, fermented herring was a common dish among the poorer parts of the coastal population, as it needed little salt. It was referred to as bondegods (peasant provisions) and was kept out of the normal channels of sale. Correspondingly, the finer herring, amply and properly salted with expensive, imported salt, was called kjøpmannsgods (merchant provisions). In the nineteenth century, the use of fermented herring gradually declined, largely due to an intense campaign from doctors who believed this "rotten" fish to be unhealthy and dangerous.

However, fermented freshwater fish, especially fermented trout, has remained a tradition up to the present, although it no longer comprises a major

Stockfish drying on racks in Lofoten

©Scanpix

component of the Norwegian diet. In fact, consumption of fermented trout, especially in connection with holidays such as Christmas, has been revitalised, with renewed attention being paid to local roots and ways of production.

In some parts of inland eastern Norway, fermented trout was eaten together with the aforementioned sour-cream porridge, a combination that proved difficult for the Danish officials of bygone days to digest.

The potato revolutionises the Norwegian diet

Until relatively recently, it was unthinkable that a Norwegian dinner – the warm meal often eaten late in the afternoon – would not include boiled potatoes. Potatoes were not merely something one chose, they were absolutely necessary to the meal. The potato became an important staple in Norway during the

Napoleonic wars, approximately around the year 1800. It became a part of the Norwegian diet in the same way as in many other countries: as a substitute for grain in times of need. Norway's severe lack of grain gave the potato a strong foothold, and it gradually replaced flour as part of the everyday fare. The customary

Norwegian flour was made from barley or wheat and was usually used for three different dishes – porridge, ball (dumplings), and bread.

Porridge has accompanied the Norwegian people for over 1 000 years, representing an important staple throughout the nineteenth century. Descriptions of the country diet in the beginning of the 1900s indicate that porridge and milk was still a common supper in many regions.

Norway's many forms of ball comprise one of its distinctive uses of flour. The names of this traditional dumpling are many – kompe, komle, raspeball, raspekake, krumme, klubb, klot, kams. Similar types of dumplings are found in other European countries, but none are quite like the ones served in Norway.

The traditional Norwegian bread is flatbrød (crispbread). Up until approximately 1900, when the word "bread" was used in rural parts of the country it always referred to flatbrød. Foreigners were somewhat less enthusiastic about this bread, finding it hard and dry. However, a soft variety of flatbrød did exist, known as lefse. This type of bread was buttered and later also sprinkled with sugar, and was served on more festive occasions. Since around the year 1900, leavened bread, baked in ovens, has taken over as the common type of bread, and until a few years ago a matpakke (packed lunch) consisting of several slices of bread topped with different types of meat or cheese in thin slices formed the customary lunch for most Norwegians.

When the potato arrived, it also became an ingredient in ball, and today no one can imagine these dumplings without the potato. The potetlefse or lompe, in some places called stomp, replaced the flatbrød and lefse. The lompe has become a classic alternative wrapping for hot dogs, and in some parts of the country it is also buttered and sugared and served as a light snack for afternoon coffee. At dinner, the potato assumed the role of flatbrød as accompaniment to a main course of fish or meat. As a matter of fact, the potato gained such dominance during the nineteenth century that the 1920 Norwegian Nobel laureate in literature, Knut Hamsun, described the the potato with these words in *Growth of the soil* (Markens Grøde):

"What was that about potatoes? Were they just a thing from foreign parts, like coffee; a luxury, an extra? Oh, the potato is a lordly fruit; drought or downpour, it grows and grows all the same. It laughs at the weather and will stand anything; only deal kindly with it, and it yields fifteen-fold again. Not the blood of a grape, but the flesh of a chestnut, to be boiled or roasted, used in every way. A man may lack grain to make bread, but give him potatoes and he will not starve. Roast them in embers, and there is supper; boil them in water and there's a breakfast ready. As for meat, there is little needed beside. Potatoes can be served with what you please; a dish of milk, a herring, is enough. The rich eat them with butter; poor folk manage with a tiny pinch of salt. Isak could make a feast of them on Sundays, with a mess of cream from Goldenhorn's milk. Poor despised potato – a blessed thing!"

Three classic ingredients for the autumn dish fårikål: cabbage, mutton and black peppercorns

A dietary transformation

The potato was only one of the newcomers that transformed Norwegian dietary traditions from the nineteenth to the twentieth century and established the cuisine that has been the norm up to the present. This was a period of industrialisation, urbanisation and increased democratisation. During this time the "old" peasant fare (dairy-based dishes, flatbrød, porridges, boiled and cured meats and fish) were gradually replaced by dishes that could be prepared using new equipment such as stoves and meat grinders (cutlets, rissoles, roasts, oven breads and cakes).

The farm-based production of traditional cheeses was gradually discontinued during the late 1800s, and the milk was sent instead to dairies that produced cheese based on Swiss and Dutch models. The names of these cheeses tell us of their origin – Swiss, Gouda, Edam and nøkkelost. The latter, Dutch clove cheese, was named after the key in the shield of the city of Leiden. Together with brunost, these yellow cheeses became regular fixtures in the Norwegian diet, and it was in light of these traditions that Norwegian specialists developed a new type of cheese, Jarlsberg, in the late 1950s. Jarlsberg cheese has been tremendously successful on the international market, especially in the United States.

The end of the twentieth century has witnessed the emergence of a new culinary tradition. Potatoes are gradually being replaced by pasta and pizza, and minced meat is used in dishes such as tacos and lasagne that originate in places far away. Given the variety of new foods available in the rising number of "immigrant stores", combined with the influence of the fast-food culture, Norwegian cuisine is growing more and more similar to the cuisines of other countries. Still, food traditions are being kept alive, partly due to the use of traditional foods at holiday celebrations. Each part of the year also has speciality dishes based on seasonally available raw materials.

Autumn dishes

Many dishes that Norwegians consider "national" can be said to exemplify the transitions between the seasons, and even today there are certain dishes that are served only at particular times of the year, even though it is possible to obtain the raw materials year round. This is typical of fårikål (Norwegian lamb and cabbage stew), a dish that is served in the autumn, starting in September, to mark the end of summer and the beginning of fall. Norwegian lamb is given great acclaim by Norwegian chefs as the best in the world. This is because the meat comes from animals that have spent a long summer grazing on juicy grass and herbs in Norway's vast highlands. Although lamb or mutton stews are found in many European countries, what makes this dish typical of Norwegian cooking is the way in which it is made – a simple dish, seasoned only with salt and peppercorns and accompanied by boiled potatoes and nothing else. Traditionally, fårikål is made using mutton, although it has recently become more common to use newly slaughtered lamb instead. Although many stores now only sell fårikål meat of lamb, some traditionalists claim that for a satisfactorily rich taste the meat should come from an adult animal, preferably one at least 7 years old. Judging from the name of the dish, it is most historically correct to make it with mutton – "får-i-kål" literally means "mutton in cabbage".

As autumn rolls on, game frequently appears on the menu. It is not uncommon for Norwegians, men and women alike, to spend an autumn week or two in the mountains hunting big game such as elk and, more seldom, deer. It is also common to hunt smaller game, especially various types of grouse. Still, game is considered a delicacy and is not something that appears on the everyday menu.

Christmas

Lutefisk (lye-soaked dried fish), rakfisk (fermented fish), pinnekjøtt (roast ribs of mutton) and ribbe (pork ribs) are all typical Christmas dishes in Norway, although restaurants may start serving them in the beginning of November, and restaurants serving traditional Norwegian food serve them all year round. During Christmas most of the food is fatty and hearty. The Christmas meal is always served on Christmas

Eve, followed by the opening of presents. There is a large degree of regional variation in Norwegian Christmas dinners. In the eastern part of Norway a typical Christmas dinner consists of roast rib of pork. Many families kept a pig that was heavily fed until close to Christmas, when it was slaughtered and could therefore be consumed without requiring any form of conservation. Pork rib is served with pork sausage patties and Christmas sausages, accompanied by cabbage à la Norvegienne – a type of pickled cabbage similar to sauerkraut – made from both white and red cabbage. Many people serve wild cranberry jam with the pork. This has been done since the 1700s, probably a remnant of traditional medieval cooking that often mixed sweet and sour. Serving wild cranberry jam alongside meat is not only a Christmas tradition, but is common throughout the year with many types of roasted meat.

In the south the typical Christmas meal consists either of poached cod with cod liver or of halibut, while in the north, tables are frequently graced by lutefisk. Today, lutefisk (dried cod soaked in lye and softened in water) is eaten only by Swedes and Norwegians and Norwegian and Swedish ethnic groups in the USA. They all consider it a traditional national dish. The main ingredient comes from the northern coast of Norway, where a large type of cod, called skrei, swims towards the coast in large shoals during February and March. The harvested fish are hung on large wooden frames, where the cold, arid climate allows them to dry slowly without rotting. In the early part of summer most of the moisture has evaporated from the fish, and the small, light pieces of fish can be packed and exported. This is a tradition that dates all the way back to the Viking Age. Throughout the Middle Ages, Norway supplied Europe with stockfish, as it was usually called. Stockfish was an important commodity due to the many fast days on the Catholic Church calendar. However, at the end of the 1700s stockfish lost ground to the salted and dried fish called klippfisk by professionals. Thus, exports sank, and the fish became more available for use in Norway. The most common use of the stockfish was to flatten it with a hammer and soak it in water. The use of lye or soda in the water has been documented in Sweden, Germany and the Netherlands as far back as the 1500s. This

Lamb and cabbage stew

Ingredients
1 kg lamb – 1 kg cabbage (approximately one head of cabbage) – salt black peppercorns – 30 g wheat flour

Method
Slice shoulder, breast, back or loin of lamb into portions and layer the pieces in a casserole alternating with layers of cabbage. Sprinkle salt and peppercorns between the layers of meat and cabbage. Add boiling water. Bring to the boil and simmer until the meat is tender (2-3 hours). Make sure that the pot does not boil dry. Flavour with salt and pepper. Stir the flour into a little cold water and then add this carefully to the stock to thicken it. Bring to the boil. Serve with boiled potatoes.

tradition emerged in Norway sometime in the 1700s, when lutefisk was used at wedding feasts. After a while its popularity declined and it was for a time viewed as simple, common food. It has regained a following in recent decades and now enjoys status as a costly festive delicacy.

The speciality of the west is pinnekjøtt (stick meat), dried, salted and sometimes smoked ribs of lamb, soaked in water overnight and steamed for several hours. In the traditional preparation, the long ribs rest on a grid of sticks, usually birchwood, during the steaming process. This dish is usually accompanied by mashed swedes (rutabaga).The only common denominator shared by these meals is the accompanying boiled potatoes. Even the type of potato is traditionally the same – almond potatoes. The beverages of choice are usually beer and aquavit, although wine has become more and more common.

Often, rice porridge is served earlier in the day, while the other preparations are in full swing, or as starter. Usually the pot of porridge is served with a single almond hidden in it. The person who finds the almond

Typical Norwegian desserts. In the front, from left to right, an almond wreath cake, cloudberries, caramel pudding and cream puffs. In the back is an assortment of different cakes, fruit salad and rice cream with red fruit sauce.

also gets a prize, usually a marzipan pig. For dessert many families serve rice cream with red fruit sauce or cloudberry cream.

After dinner, cakes and cookies are served along with coffee. For many people Christmas still means making gingersnaps, doughnuts, cones and several other types of cakes and cookies. Traditionally a good housewife should be able to serve at least seven types of Christmas cakes or cookies – a custom that is still upheld in many homes.

Springtime and summer

Spring and summer are the seasons for sowing and growth, and the traditional foods of these seasons reflect this fact in that they have usually been preserved in some way or another. The means of preservation are usually salting, drying, curing, pickling, fermenting or brine-curing (especially salmon). Rømmegrøt og spekemat (sour-cream porridge with cured meats) is traditional summer fare, still served on festive occasions. Although there is a much richer tradition of curing meats in the southern parts of Europe – Norwegians still have a lot to learn about how to cure the perfect ham – the way the cured meat is served, together with sour-cream porridge, is typical of Norwegian farm life. Fenalår (cured mutton) is also a very Norwegian dish, which was traditionally brought along when travelling.

Cakes

Many of the cakes served in Norway are similar to those found all over the rest of the world. Both cream cakes and chocolate cakes are common and popular. One cake that is very Norwegian, and which is probably the only Norwegian dish reminiscent of the food pyramids once found in the courts of Europe, is the kransekake (almond wreath cake).

This "pyramid cake" consists of different-size rings made from almond-based dough, placed on top of each other and decorated with thin strips of icing, Norwegian flags and bonbons. It is typically served at christening parties, confirmation parties, weddings and on Norwegian Constitution day, 17 May.

International influences

The Norwegian kitchen has been and continues to be greatly influenced from abroad. Fish has always been an important part of the Norwegian diet, and Norwegians still consume a relatively large amount of both fresh fish and a lot of fish-based products, such as fish sticks and fish au gratin. Nevertheless, many foreign dishes have now been adopted into the everyday diet. Frozen pizza and pasta-based dishes have become more and more common. This trend is also seen on more festive occasions. Although baked salmon remains a popular banquet dish, the traditional Sunday roast has roots in continental Europe, and a wide variety of party dishes have been inspired by European cuisines, especially those of France, Italy, Spain and Greece, as well as by non-European culinary traditions.

---

1. The word træl means "thrall" or slave.
2. The name Karl is a typical commoner's name, and means "man".
3. The name Jarl means "earl" and is a Viking title.

Kazimierz Krzysztofek

Poland

Cuisine, culture and variety on the Wisla river

Cuisine is more than anthropologically defined culture – it is an art, because it creates artefacts, artificial beings. In nature, eggs and bacon, coffee and milk, tea and lemon would never have met, yet they are wonderful artefacts that please our taste. Taste may be the least known of all the senses, since we do not yet know the secrets of taste buds. And tastes vary. As we say in Poland: "The hay smells different to a lover and to a horse". This diversity can lead to lively discussion. The French scientist Jean-Anthelme Brillant-Savarin, patron of many gastronomical associations, noted in his *Physiologie de gout ou meditation de gastronomie transcendente* (1826) that people may be bored with each other, but they never are bored at the table – at least for the first hour. Although the author had the French in mind, his observation is universal.

Cuisine is power, as is evident from Abraham Maslow's famous hierarchy: at the table we can satisfy nearly all of the needs, he notes. First, the physiological needs of hunger and thirst; then, affiliation and association with others; and then, at times, status, in the form of recognition and prestige. It may happen that we satisfy our need for self-fulfilment or for exploring the world through its tastes, images and aromas. Surprisingly, people use many spices with interesting and exotic names without having any idea of the world. Yet cuisine has played and continues to play a more significant role in cross-cultural communication than we realise. Sometimes it has even served as a code of communication: in the old days in Poland, serving a suitor black broth was a sign that he had been rejected.

Thanks to our varied tastes we have an energising pluralism that enriches life: *varietas ludet et delectat*. Why did God or, as some prefer, nature give people taste? We can see in this a functional value, but also a value within itself. In the case of animals, the functional value is evident: taste enables them to

333

distinguish the edible from the unhealthy and poisonous. The problem is more complicated with humans, because a human being is not only a product of biological evolution, but also of cultural evolution. And culture changes tastes: not all that is tasty must necessarily be healthy. As one writer has said, all that is good is, unfortunately, sinful, fat and sweet. Thus taste in our culture is rather a value in itself, a source of sensations and experience, which are becoming more and more important in our society: the whole art of influencing people (advertising) is based on an invitation to consume.

Culinary nostalgia

Poland is not a culinary superpower, like some nations recognised for their cuisine. But Polish cuisine is certainly recognisable in the world. Polish specialities can be easily named: king bigos (sauerkraut and meat dish), żurek (rye soup), flaczki (tripe), pierogi, various soups and broths. We can also mention Polish sausage (popularised in America by Polish immigrants, although there it hardly resembles the original). As far as sweets are concerned, the oldest known recipe is for gingerbread cakes from Toruń. According to an old saying, "vodka from Gdańsk, gingerbread from Toruń, a maiden from Kraków and shoes from Warsaw are the best things in Poland". It is interesting to note the order in which they are listed!

Easter table

©Jerzy Mańkowski

Bigos

Among all the specialities considered typically Polish, bigos still occupies an honorary place. In old Poland, no hunt could take place without it. Bigos is not only a complex mixture, it also has many variants. Warmed up in a cauldron over the fire, this stew was prepared with sour cabbage or sweet cabbage on beetroot leaves, or with a mixture of ingredients prepared separately and then added to the pot. Meats of different kinds and sausage were boiled together with the cabbage, but roast venison, and especially hare, were added only at the end of the cooking.

It is notable that according to our gastronomes, the actual ranking of Polish delicacies differs from popular conceptions of them. An analysis of forty-eight Warsaw restaurant menus published in the December 2003 edition of *Sztuciec Warszawski*, a supplement to *Gazeta Wyborcza*, shows the following results:

Dish	Frequency on menu
1. Duck prepared the old Polish way, with fruits, sweet	21
2. Home-made pierogi	18
3. Golonka (pork knuckle) the Polish way	8
4. Żur (rye soup) with white sausage and egg	7
5. Fillet in mushroom sauce	4
6. Mushroom soup in bread	4
7. Buckwheat flour dumplings with herring and apple in cream	3
8. Pike-perch the Polish way	3
9. Pork steak with cabbage, mushrooms and potatoes	3
10. Collop in black bread	3

Duck is a popular domestic bird in Poland, but until recently it never really found its way onto restaurant menus. Yet here we find it as the king of dishes. The presence of dumplings is also surprising, because they are usually associated with Russian cuisine. The most surprising finding is that this top-ten list does not include bigos (which was available in only one restaurant). Perhaps bigos is considered plebeian, even though plebeian foods are once again becoming popular? At grand receptions, such as film premieres, "peasant food" is served – farm bread with lard, pickled cucumbers, bigos and other dishes.

Although Polish cuisine has always been as culturally and ethnically diverse as the Polish state throughout its history, it has never lost its identity. The pluralism of the state ensured the pluralism of the cuisine. The process also worked the other way around: the diversity and richness of the cuisine upheld the diversity of successive Polish states. In Europe, Poland was no exception. We took flavours and aromas from everywhere, but we also gave them to others. We can see certain influences from the west (from France we took baked beans à la bretonne, surprisingly not known in today's Brittany), and many from Germany (which we will consider later), but we took mainly from the east – both from the Slavic countries and Turkey. We can still trace these influences in the names of dishes: Ruthenian pierogi, Lithuanian meatballs, Ukrainian borsch – these are the most democratic courses served at home and in restaurants.

These names bring back memories of Poland's eastern borderlands. The term "borderlands" – the Polish Kresy – fins de territoire, the multi-ethnic lands in the east of the Polish Republic which now belong to Lithuania, Belarus and Ukraine – has been fixed in the memory of Poles partly due to the diversified cuisine, the "joint supper" consumed by many different ethnic groups. Old Polish borderland cuisine was neither exclusively plebeian, nor the exquisite cuisine of the nobility, parochial gentry or bourgeois from Lvov and Vilna. It contained elements of all of these groups, and at times the food was the same on all tables. This was a mutual relationship of culinary cultures, a multiplication of inventiveness that blossoms when people of different cultures live together. Without borderland cuisine, many specialities would be absent from our menu: knysz, kutia (a sweet dish of poppy seed, honey and nuts), stuffed cabbage leaves, sękacz (pyramid cake), kołacz (a kind of cake), the above-mentioned meatballs, ravioli, cold borsch, potato pancakes, pickled food, "zeppelins", and salted bread rolls. Most likely we would never have heard of "kurdesz", the old name for a table companion and the subject of many songs and toasts. If at times guests had no appetite, it was not because the food was not tasty, but because there was no proper prinuka (encouragement). It would be regrettable if in the future the Schengen Treaty were to prevent this mutual enrichment of flavours.

Although old Polish menus sound tasty, today we would not be able to touch some of the courses, such as sparrows or starlings. Let us read the menu of the lunch given on the occasion of the "Hygienic Congress" in Lublin on 28 September 1908: Vodkas and sandwiches, borsch, bouillon and pastry, fillet with Madera sauce, hot salmon with Dutch sauce, fowl and turkey, rye and mushroom soup, liver and kidneys, stewed sparrows and starlings with asparagus, cauliflower and peas. For dessert: ice cream, ginger coffee and tea, French wines and slivovitz from the Vetter shop.

During the entire nineteenth century and the beginning of the twentieth century, five generations of Poles lived under Prussian, Austrian and Russian occupation. Although we did not have an independent country of our own, we had our culture as a sign of our identity. We usually do not say much about cuisine in this context, but food also played a role in the preservation of this identity. Polish cuisine did not erode; on the contrary, it absorbed new elements and participated in cross-cultural communication. In Kraków we can still have a taste of Vienna as we consume Wiener Frühstück in old-fashioned cafés. This gives a sense of continuity, something that the city enjoys. In the north, in Wielkopolska, Toruń or the Kujawy region, one can taste "false hare" (falscher Hasenbraten) roasted in a bratrura (a polonised name for the German oven). From today's perspective we can say that Polish food was not dietetic (it was hardly fat-free), but it was certainly specific.

Polish cuisine was significantly enriched by two diasporas represented for centuries on Polish territory: the

Mushroom stew in bread

Jews and – to a lesser degree – the Roma/Gypsies. Certain names have remained to this day, such as cutlets prepared in "the Gypsy way". This may sound very strange to Roma/Gypsies, but I believe that despite political correctness we should not forego this culinary continuity. Until recent times, the names of Jewish dishes sounded exotic to the majority of Poles born after the Second World War, in a country which became a Jewish cemetery. Perhaps only carp the Jewish way was familiar. Today, however, we are witnessing a resurgence of interest in the culture and cuisine of the Polish Jews. In many places in the Kazimierz quarter in Kraków, in the Menora restaurant in Warsaw or in Tykocin in the Podlasie region (which was the best-preserved shtetl), we can taste goose rumps, beef with chick peas, stuffed cabbage leaves, gefilte fish, and other long-forgotten dishes.

These traditions are mentioned in every edition of the vast cookbook *Polish cuisine*. We do not have enough space here to say any more about old Polish cuisine beyond one other thing. Whether the food was rich in prosperous households or modest among the poor, it was always offered from the heart: "We welcome you and wish to share with you all the wealth of this hut". "When a guest enters the house, God comes with him". (Only when the visit lasted too long, did the host think to himself: "When a guest enters the house, God only knows when… he is going to leave").

Poverty, especially in the period leading up to the harvest (przednowek), forced people to eat whatever they could find. The greatest variety was found among products that could be preserved well for the winter: cabbage, turnip-rooted cabbage, turnip, kohlrabi, porridge and peas all provided the necessary protein. Cabbage dominated the diet of the Polish peasant, as it did throughout central Europe, from Poland to Alsace. The smell of fried cabbage and beer marked the cultural borders of Mitteleuropa.

Preserved foods provided a system of life support to millions of poor people. When a society has been able to survive so many generations, its traditions for nourishment have obviously adapted to the environment. Local knowledge, accumulated throughout generations, is important cultural capital, indispensable to the process of self-sustainable development.

Cuisine in crisis

There was a time, not so long ago, when we could not enjoy culinary delicacies. In the epoch of anti-free-market experiments in Poland and other countries under the same system, the gastronomic tradition was violated, and low-quality industrial cuisine prevailed.

Socialism liberated people from before-the-harvest hunger, but at the same time it oppressed the art of cuisine. This was not always connected with the fact that certain products were not available on the market. The reason was different – it was a certain philosophy.

Eating itself was not regarded as something worth celebrating and cultivating. A functional approach triumphed: eat to the fill and build socialism. A stereotyped picture of a Pole "na delegacji" (on a business trip) shows a nylon raincoat, the indispensable beret, a briefcase, and pork steak with cabbage. Neither did restaurant signboards attract the eye – they were, rather, "eating-houses for the masses".

Very few people cared about the preservation of regional and local identity. Of course, the times had something to do with this: the massive migration of peoples and the displacement of Poland from east to west, when millions of people were separated from their roots. The immigrants did not feel anchored in their new dwelling places, because they found themselves in regions in the west and the north where Polish tradition was absent.

Sękacz (pyramid cake)

P o l a n d

Nevertheless, Polish culture survived in the people themselves, as did Polish cuisine. It survived in households, reviving like grass that springs back to life after being trampled. The Christmas tradition, especially the Christmas table, was important in this revival. Without the wonderful Polish Christmas supper with its obligatory twelve courses served when the first star appears in the sky, many special dishes would likely have been lost. The Christmas tradition is probably Poland's strongest Kulturträger, which transmits culture across the generations. The strictures of Lent, when meat is excluded, meant a certain convenience for the poor (it was also convenient under socialism when meat was in short supply), but these limitations also spurred creativity. A true master can be recognised by the way in which he handles shortages and restrictions.

One lesson emerges from the recent past. Under authoritarian rule, tradition is usually enforced; it is used for political purposes to compensate the people for lost privileges. But cuisine usually loses in this process, since it is not seen as an important element of collective memory. It would be difficult to treat bigos, the flagship of Polish cuisine, as an inherited remembrance.

The renaissance of regional cuisines

The *annus mirabilis* of 1989 liberated forces which had significant influence on many domains of life, cuisine among them. Initially no one noticed the food, since everyone was preoccupied with far more important issues like democracy, economic reform, and the creation of new state institutions.

The free economy introduced fast food to Poland: pizza, the Big Mac and chips (Coca-Cola had arrived in Poland somewhat earlier). As in many other countries, McDonald's invaded the Polish landscape, entering the centres of historical cities, as in the case of the old-town district in Kraków, where the restaurant was built on the most frequented promenade on Floriańska Str. This expansion was unavoidable for two reasons. First, after decades of forced austerity and renunciation, Polish society allowed the introduction of a broad stream of western culture, a symbol of opening up to the world. This new openness appealed especially to the youth – the forbidden fruit syndrome. Secondly, Poland did not have a history of particularly high-quality popular restaurants. On the one hand we had expensive restaurants, a salon culture, with high-level cuisine; on the other we had the "saloon", unattractive pubs or canteens. In between was a gap, which fast food filled. Fast food is still popular, but after their initial enchantment, many people longed for familiar food. McDonald's quickly responded by offering a "glocal" (simultaneously global and local) hamburger called a "wieśmac" ("village-Mac"), which implies that it is a product from the Polish village, made of healthy local meat. The hamburger tasted the same, but it had a Polish flavour and, more importantly, referenced our own symbols.

Foreign products and standards are often not immediately accepted; they must first undergo a hybridisation, or, to use anthropological terminology, indigenisation. This process offers guarantees and domesticates foreign influences. The rush to McDonald's may be seen as modern variant of the old Polish winter tradition of kulig, when people amused themselves with sleigh rides, often in cavalcade, stopping to refresh themselves with food and drink at the homes of the local nobility.

Jesting aside, cuisine and its celebration are serious matters, as is well understood by the rulers and inhabitants of various regions of Poland. It is on the local level that the pluralism of cuisine is having a renaissance in an unprecedented flourishing of local and regional cultures. Every town or commune has something of their own to offer to emphasise their identity. Everyone wants to show their originality, their flavours and smells.

A single word can explain this phenomenon: the market. Although to a certain degree the market can spoil tradition (as has happened in Poland, as elsewhere), it cannot spoil the cuisine; on the contrary, it regenerates and pluralizes it. The market creates diversity, which sells well. At the same time it serves to promote the city, the region, the commune. (Sometimes this promotion can be carried too far: I heard of a traditional cooking competition, where only new dishes from the traditional repertoire were accepted!) The courses listed on a menu comprise a history of local flavours, legends and myths, a poetry of aromas. This wealth can bring about dizziness even without alcohol – but that is another story. The trend itself is worth praising: everyone wants to regain power over their own symbols, to portray themselves by means of their own cuisine. It is especially important in today's model of consumption, where culture, broadly understood, is beginning to play a significant role. Cuisine is not just a culinary matter, it is also – perhaps first and foremost – culture.

It is important that people who have lost contact with the past return to their roots "through their stomachs", to the sources and standards of their own culture. This can be achieved by translating these traditions into "tourist tastes". The sale of provincialism and naturalness (milk "straight from the cow", eggs "directly from the henhouse") is an invitation to agro-tourism, which provides jobs and income as well as the satisfaction of being able to offer something to the world. It is predominantly through consumption that new generations acquaint themselves with the richness of cultures.

To the European Union with Polish cuisine

One of the consequences of the EU enlargement by ten countries is its new cultural face. Cross-cultural communication becomes an increasing challenge. Each culture has its own idioms, which constitute its richness. The problem is to translate these idioms into discourse – ideas easily understandable by others – in order to solve Europe's problems together. Similarly, national, ethnic and regional cuisines have their own idioms, but their wonderful characteristic is that they are easily assimilable, simple because they are tasty.

Obviously, it is not only a problem of communication, but also of economy. Nations that offer attractive flavours and aromas can earn a good deal of money and protect their culinary ownership rights, much as they do their intellectual property rights. This culinary ownership does not belong to individuals, but to territorial communities.

Regional dishes nourish. It does not matter that often they are offered for visitors and not for residents. In Poland, the lower classes, in particular, did not cultivate the celebration of eating on an everyday basis – they concentrated on holidays (this may explain the popularity of fast food). Today's reality does not help. The poor eat the cheapest food, which certainly is not regional. Only in regions with a strong feeling of cultural identity (like the Podhale region) has local cuisine survived, not only because of the necessity of promotion, but also due to the needs of everyday life. Until now we did not attach much importance to the meaning of "appellation controllée", because there was no need. Today, however, because of accession to the European Union, we are more conscious of the fact that culture has an economic dimension, that there is a trend towards something we can call the "culturalisation of the

Pierogi from the oven

This recipe (by Magdalena Wenzel) reflects an old method of making wheat and whole-meal pierogi

Dough
200 g wheat flour, 50 g rye flour,
30 g yeast, 3 spoons olive oil,
1/2 spoon marjoram, sugar and salt,
1 egg to brush the pierogi

Stuffing
200 g black pudding, 4 chicken livers,
2 onions (150 g), 1 sour apple (200 g),
1 spoon olive oil, 1 spoon freshly ground pepper,
1/2 spoon of salt and marjoram

Prepare the dough
Mix the two kinds of flour, add the crumbled yeast and the rest of ingredients, mixing well. Add enough lukewarm water to make a pliable dough and knead until elastic. Dust the dough with flour, place it in a bowl, cover with a napkin and set aside in a warm place to rise.

Prepare the stuffing
Remove the casing from the black pudding and crumble it with a fork. Fry the livers in hot oil and cut into cubes. Chop the onion and sauté it in the oil used for the livers. Core the apple and cut it into large cubes. Mix together the sausage, livers, onion and apple, then add the marjoram, salt and pepper.
When the dough has doubled in volume, dust it with flour and roll it out on a table to 3 cm thick. Cut out disks 15 cm in diameter. Place the stuffing on the disks, slightly moisten the edges and pinch the dough together to form a decorative edge. Prick the pierogi with a fork, brush with the lightly beaten egg and bake in the oven at 200 C°. until golden (20 min.). Serve hot with beer or red semi-dry wine, or with sour cabbage salad and a cup of strong tea.
Serves four.

economy", connected with the expansion of the cultural industry.

Thus we have begun to catalogue the treasures of our regional cuisines. The Polish newspaper *Gazeta Wyborcza* has undertaken the task of making Poles sensitive to this issue. This campaign represents a certain novum among the Polish battles for awareness: Polish history was for ages dominated by great issues such as independence, democracy, restoration of the economy, and moral issues like abortion. Today this battle is being fought for the preservation of the regional symbol. This is not a romantic or ideological cause, like the ones mentioned above, but one can see in it a sign of normality, of mental adaptation to Europe, of understanding the demands of integration.

Although it is impossible here to name and describe all of the treasures of Polish cuisine, some of them are definitely worth mentioning.

Cheeses manufactured from sheep's milk. Passed on from generation to generation, the art of making oscypek (smoked sheep's milk cheese) and the customs of shepherds, along with the music, dress and dialect of the inhabitants of Podhale, should be included in the heritage of highlander culture. Cheese from the Polish mountains has found great public favour in the largest regional products trade fairs around the world.

The production of mead. This is a custom that we can proudly introduce to Europe, a real "slow food".

The tradition of producing mead, which is among the oldest alcoholic drinks, has not died out in Poland, as it has in most other European countries.

Narew cucumbers. These cucumbers, which grow close to the Narew River, near Białystok, in a specific microclimate, are pickled. They are packed tightly in barrels, submerged in river water with salt and spices, and then sealed to ferment for two weeks.

Sękacz (Polish pyramid cake). This cake originated in Lithuania, where it was called gałęziak, or branch cake. It is indispensable at wedding receptions and holidays throughout eastern Poland, from Suwałki to Lublin. It is also known in Germany, where it is considered the king of cakes.

Plum jam (powidła). This jam comes from the area of the Wisła river. Women clean, stone and boil the plums in a cauldron while men add wood to the fire. All of the farms in Strzelce Dolne are engaged in the process of making plum jam. There, nearly 8 500 jars will be filled with jam.

Borowiacki bread. This traditional Polish bread is prepared according to a recipe that dates back to the First World War. It is called "borowiacki" because it is made in the middle of the Tuchola Forest, in the village of Krzywogoniec (bor means "old forest" in Polish). Unlike other bread, whey is used instead of water to prepare the leaven. This is a rye-wheat bread, with rye flour, the main ingredient.

Poland

Cuisine and life

So what is it like, this reborn Polish cuisine? What important events in the life of a Pole does it celebrate?

Our contemporary cuisine is one of the few areas of life that integrates tradition and modernity; it helps reveal the transformation of social culture. The petty gentry and magnates in Poland and elsewhere traditionally organised sumptuous receptions and banquets based on the principle of "go bankrupt, but prepare a feast". You might be poor, but when guests arrived you had to serve an abundance of dishes and alcohol. This practice, common in both the cities and the provinces for such important events as births, first communion receptions, weddings and funeral banquets, was dictated by the need to display one's status as well as to escape bleak reality. Socialism preserved this old custom. Rich people visiting from abroad were surprised: how is it possible to have such an abundance of dishes on the table when the grocery store shelves are empty? Even on more casual occasions, such as name-day celebrations, dance parties and drinking sessions (prywatki), food was abundant: these gatherings helped to maintain ties among people and social networks through the informal sharing of support, knowledge or information. The parties prevented atomisation; at the same time they upheld the culinary art. Every housewife had to demonstrate her culinary skills and mastery, since catering was not available in those days.

"These culinary displays were a popular form of cultural entertainment". People created a culture for themselves at the table. The table encouraged expression – the discussion of life and work experiences, flirtations, emotions, reminiscences, fears. All of this was created for the diners' use, thanks to flavour. To use a term popularised by Alvin Toffler, here was a kind of prosumption – production and consumption in one. This community of diners, this commensality, created an interpersonal network that facilitated the flow of ideas, celebrated creativity, and represented a special form of collective intelligence. This was a culture of banquet and conversation, careless and devoid of standards; an escape from tiring institutions into the sphere of social action and unforced communication.

The table generated positive energy, allowing for the solution of problems. Meetings at the table solved many local issues, encouraged genuine sincerity, had a therapeutic effect, and helped in the settlement of disputes and conflicts. Unfortunately, sometimes the table also created disputes, when dishes were accompanied by alcohol (as we say in Poland: "the herring likes to swim"). Alcohol encouraged frankness and direct expression of opinions, but it also made country celebrations unpredictable.

The mention of herring leads us to an interesting story. Fish have never been an important part of

Christmas table

Polish cuisine. The renaissance writer Mikołaj Rej distanced himself from our neighbours across the Baltic Sea by saying: "I can not say much about the Swede and the Dane; I have never been to the sea and I do not wish to fish for herring". In fact, however, the herring (apart from the carp, which during Christmas shares the fate of the American turkey on Thanksgiving Day) is the only fish that conquered Poland. When there was a shortage, herring was imported from the Soviet Union – the so-called iwasi, which in Polish means "and your". When we refused to eat this "mud herring", the Russians said: "our people" can eat it, "and your" people can eat it too. This linguistic pun offered a certain consolation.

Much can be said about the alliance of table and humour. At the table there is less restraint, less self-censorship, and more invitation to humour. The oldest known "biotechnology" – fermentation, to which we owe the richness of alcoholic drinks – encouraged this behaviour. But the richness and diversity of household culture disappears with unavoidable modernisation, which began with the introduction of television. A miraculous invention: by looking at the screen people avoid looking at each other. By providing us with humour and laughter, professional entertainment producers and distributors deprive us of initiative.

At present the tradition of "going bankrupt, but preparing a feast" is evidently in decline. Poland is undergoing a process of modernisation, and such lavish displays of food characterise the past. Yet modernity and post-modernity do not destroy culinary culture – they simply transform it. The tradition of spending time at the table loses its self-regulatory function and becomes just another narrative of consumption, in which norms and rules are suspended – a carnival interlude in everyday life, like the Bavarian Oktoberfest, which represents a living tradition of drunkenness in Europe.

Let us now return to the Christmas supper, probably the most important religious, culinary and popular cultural institution in Poland. In 2003, shortly before Christmas Eve, Poles were surprised to learn from the Catholic Church superiors that meat was allowed to be eaten on that day. Nevertheless, the people, on the strength of their own tradition, refused to consume meat on this occasion. It would be interesting to know how great the power of tradition is, and how many families will continue to follow it. Christmas supper is one of only a few unchanged cultural patterns in Poland. Perhaps this new church decree will open the way to having Christmas supper at McDonald's?

I would not be surprised if in the years to come after the church prayer reform, we begin to proclaim the following: Lord, grant us our daily pizza.

Ana Pessoa e Costa

P o r t u g a l

A dialogue of cultures

More than five centuries ago the people of Portugal set out on a great adventure: to open up new worlds to the world. The caravels set sail from Lisbon, taming the seas and bridging gaps between civilisations. The Age of Discoveries was born. This extraordinary seafaring adventure led to the discovery of new places and new peoples. Portuguese culture mixed with other cultures in a wide variety of fields, from art and science to religion and language. Ever since then, the adoption, development and exportation of everyday habits, inspirations and aesthetic values, scientific knowledge and technical experience have left a permanent mark on Portuguese cultural identity. The "Portuguese soul" sung by the poets and laid bare in so many "Fados" carries in it all the things that characterised this Age of Discovery: races, religions, songs, flavours and cultures.

Portugal has contributed both to the introduction of a wonderful exoticism into Europe and to the spread of the European cultural identity to far-off continents, changing the course of history. These discoveries were essential to Portugal's development, giving it access to the immense variety of products that made it a successful trading nation. Their influence on Portuguese "tastes" and cuisine is also undeniable. The well-known "bacalhau", the salt cod so prized in other culinary cultures (after de-salting), is a part of this adventure-filled past that can still be found on Portuguese tables today. What other people would take a product that did not even exist on its territory or along its coasts and turn it into a culinary tradition? Cod is fished in northern climes, then salted, a tradition dating back to the first expeditions to Newfoundland in the fifteenth century. Seafarers took stocks of it along with them on their voyages, pickled in brine to preserve it during the long months they spent on the high seas.

Although salt cod is also found in other countries' culinary traditions, in Basque and French cuisine, for example, few are those who, like the Portuguese, call it their "faithful friend". The Portuguese take pride in the fact they have as many recipes for salt cod as there are days in the year.

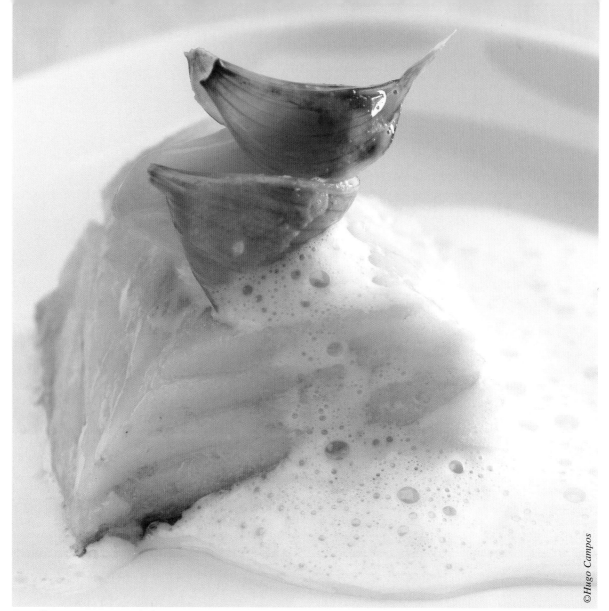

©*Hugo Campos*

Bacalhau com espuma de leite (cod with milk sauce)

The spice route: exoticism comes to Europe

The spice route brought exotic spices from India to Europe: pepper, cinnamon, ginger, and nutmeg. It was one of Portugal's most important trading routes in the transition from the Middle Ages to the modern era. Despite the country's small size, in those days Portugal's influence reached as far as the distant continents of Africa, Asia, South America and Oceania. The adoption of sugar and other products such as potatoes, maize, tomatoes, rice, tea and cocoa beans revolutionised economies and eating habits in Portugal and in Europe. There is no denying that they influenced artistic development, too, by fostering exchanges of products, for example through the Portuguese trading posts in Flanders.

At the same time the Portuguese developed exchanges of flora and foodstuffs between the continents, introducing manioc, pawpaw and pineapples from Brazil into Africa, for example, and coconuts, bananas and mangoes from the east into Latin America and Africa. In those days Europe marvelled at and delighted in these new products and flavours that brought originality and exoticism to their eating habits. Some people even credited the new foods with medicinal powers. In Portugal these new products inspired some inventive dishes which continue to delight the taste buds to this day.

A touch of Mediterranean influence

Although essentially Mediterranean, with its origins in the Roman and Arab presence on the Iberian Peninsula, Portuguese cooking has been constantly enhanced over the years, acquiring a personality of its own thanks to the country's grand and colourful history. The discovery and colonisation of the new world brought a variety of new products to Portuguese tables: "malaguetas" (little red peppers used to make very hot chilli sauce), tomatoes, avocados, sweet potatoes, courgettes and even turkey. In the Alentejo and Algarve regions of southern Portugal there are undeniable Moorish influences, visible in the use of almonds, honey and orange blossom in various desserts, for example. In Madeira, too, the use of couscous semolina is another clear sign of contacts with Africa.

The memoirs of William Beckford, set out in his log books and travel journals, give an example of the wealth of influences present at a Portuguese table when he describes a banquet given at the monastery in Alcobaça in the eighteenth century: "The banquet itself consisted of not only the most excellent, usual fare, but rarities and delicacies of past seasons and distant countries; exquisite sausages, potted lampreys, strange messes from the Brazils, and others still stranger from China. (…) Confectionery and fruits were out of the question here; they awaited us in an adjoining still more spacious and sumptuous apartment, to which we retired from the effluvia of viands and sauces. (…) Cassolettes of Goa filigree, steaming with a fragrant vapour of Calambac, the finest quality of wood of aloes."

Over the years soups – "canja" (consommé with rice), "caldo verde" (green soup made with cabbage and chorizo), vegetable soup with meat or fish at the beginning of each large meal – meat and fish dishes with vegetables, different varieties of cabbages and beans, salads and desserts, all became part of European eating habits, local products, to which we added seasoning based on recipes and spices brought back on Portuguese caravels from long voyages to Africa, India and Brazil.

Bread, made of corn, rye or maize, is an essential addition to any meal. It was brought to Japan by the Portuguese, the first westerners to arrive in those islands in 1543. It is also the main ingredient in such dishes as "açordas" (a herb, olive oil and garlic broth to which slices of bread are added), or "migas" (breadcrumbs fried with bacon), and is used to give consistency to regional soups seasoned with aromatic herbs. Tasty as they were, however, the exotic spices from the east never fully eclipsed the local aromatic plants – parsley, coriander, pennyroyal and rosemary.

Portuguese cuisine uses olive oil, a local product of the highest quality. Onions, garlic and tomato fried together in olive oil bring out the Mediterranean flavour of Portuguese cooking. Although it was Portugal that exported the famous "tempura" to Japan in the sixteenth century, however, there are not many fried dishes in refined Portuguese cuisine.

Salt cod, as we saw earlier, is a staple ingredient in many Portuguese dishes, in plain or refined forms, but it is only one of many fish varieties present in Portuguese cooking. Others include gilthead bream, whiting, turbot, rock, bass, red mullet and many more, not to mention the ever-present sardine. The shellfish and seafood stewed in the traditional "caldeirada" also figure among Portugal's greatest culinary treasures.

Kid, lamb, veal, pork, small game and sausage meats are the main meat products, which may be served roasted, grilled or stewed with vegetables, as in the famous "cozido à portuguesa". In Portugal sauces are not prepared separately but are based on the juice in which the ingredients cook.

Meals are usually washed down with wine and sometimes even planned around the wine, although wine is rarely drunk outside mealtimes, as in other countries. Wine is also an ingredient in various dishes, for example when the food is marinated in a mixture of wine, vinegar, salt and spices. Purists recommend using the same quality of wine for preparing the food as for drinking with it. "Carne em vinha d'alhos" (marinated meat) is one example of this tradition of cooking with wine which is so widespread in inland Portugal. The fact that Portugal, Goa and north-east Brazil all lay claim as part of their cultural heritage to the dish called "sarapatel" (the liver and heart of pigs or sheep that is mixed with fresh blood, then cooked with tomatoes, peppers and onions) is a curious illustration of the bridges Portugal has built between cultures.

Many people find traditional Portuguese entremets too rich in sugar. In fact, many desserts, cakes and pastries illustrate the Arabian influence on Portuguese cooking, being rich both in fruit (grapes, figs, bananas from Madeira, pineapple from the Azores) and in eggs, sugar and almonds. The traditional "conventuais" cakes (made in convents) are made mainly of eggs and sugar (syrup heated to various temperatures). They were a source of income for the convents, and often had rather strange names: "papos-de-anjo" (angel puffs), "gargantas de freira"

Entrecosto com migas (spareribs with bread crumbs)

(nuns' waddles), "barrigas de freira" (nuns' bellies), "toucinho do céu" (bacon from heaven), "fatias da china" (bits of China). These are all traditional Portuguese pastries that have come down through the centuries, much to the delight of the new generations.

In the olden days nuns had to find ways of using up the surplus egg yolks generated by their religious activities. The whites were used to make the communion wafer and starch their habits. What better to do with egg yolks than invent a thousand delightful recipes! "Arroz doce" (rice pudding), "leite-crème" (a sort of 'crème brûlée'), "pudim de amêndoa" (almond pudding), "trouxas-de-ovos" (egg rolls), "nozes de ovos" (egg walnuts), "pão-de-ló" (egg and sugar sponge cake) and "fios de ovos" (sweet egg yolk strands) – for which recipes still exist in Thailand and Japan, are so many excellent ways of concluding a meal, when they are not served as tea-time treats (the habit of drinking afternoon tea was introduced to Great Britain by Queen Catarina de Bragança following her marriage to King Charles II) or with coffee (from Mozambique, Angola, Saõ Tomé or Timor).

Portuguese cuisine today is the result of all that and more. Portugal has always been open to other cultures and influences, and this has helped it to adapt to new social and cultural realities without ever losing sight of its Mediterranean heritage. Anyone who travels round Portugal will be surprised by the "genuine dialogue" that has developed between traditional Portuguese recipes and dishes of African, Asian or east European origin. Even before the term "fusion cuisine" was coined, it had already long been a reality in Portugal.

Mainland Portugal and the Portuguese islands are very varied in terms of their geology and climate.

Pastéis de Nata

Pastry to line the moulds
500 g flour, 300 g water, 10 g salt
400 g margarine appropriate for pastries

Preparation
Mix together the flour, water and salt. Form the dough into a ball, then cut a cross in the centre and pull the four sides outward to form a four-point star. Place the margarine in the centre of the dough and pull the points upward to cover the margarine. With a rolling pin roll out the dough to 40 x 15 cm. Make a simple fold (in thirds). Let the dough sit for 10 minutes, then fold it again, this time in quarters (book fold). Let sit for another 10 minutes.
Roll out the dough to roughly 4 mm thick and sprinkle it all over with water. Beginning from a wide end roll it into a cylinder with a diameter of 4 cm. Slice it into rounds 1 cm thick and place them in the moulds. Let rest 10 minutes. Wet your thumb with water and press into the centre of the round to push the mixture to the top edges of the mould. (The moulds should be the same size as the custard tarts we buy in pastry shops.)

Custard cream
0,5 l skim milk, 70 g flour (without leavening)
5 g corn flour (Maïzena), 0,5 l light sugar syrup
5 egg yolks, 1 whole egg, lightly beaten, Vanilla (just a bit) or a little lemon zest

Preparation
Prepare the sugar syrup by mixing 1 kg sugar with 0.5 l boiling water. Boil until the sugar melts and a light syrup is formed, about 3 minutes.
Dissolve the flour and the corn flour in approx. 1 dl of the milk. Boil the remaining milk, pour it over the flour mixture and beat until smooth.
Add the sugar syrup gradually, stirring constantly, then stir in the yolks and the whole egg. Cook over low heat until thickened, stirring constantly. Carefully spoon the warm pastry cream into the prepared moulds. Bake at 350° for just 8 minutes, no longer.

Variation
Easy custard cream
0.5 l skim milk, 275 g sugar, 35 g flour (without leavening), a pinch of salt, 1 tablespoon of margarine, 5 egg yolks, 1 whole egg, vanilla, or zest of one lemon

Preparation
Heat the milk with the margarine. In a bowl mix the flour with the sugar and salt. When the milk starts to boil add the flour mixture, beating well, then remove it from the heat and let it cool slightly. Stir in the yolks and the egg and mix in a little vanilla and the zest of one lemon. Cook as above over low heat, stirring constantly, until thickened. Fill the prepared pastry moulds with the warm custard and bake as above.

Almond and egg desserts

©Nuno Calvet

It is this variety of soils and climates and the products they yield that makes for so much variety in Portuguese gastronomy. In the north the food tends to be heavier, perhaps, more consistent, unpretentious yet tasty and aromatic. Green wine, Douro wine and port wine are very present in the north. "Caldo verde" (green soup) and "tripas à moda do Porto" (Porto-style tripe) are examples of this region's culinary tradition.

In central Portugal, the food is perhaps lighter, made of the generous natural ingredients the country abounds in, including fish. Some of the best among Portugal's numerous cheeses are made in the central region, including the renowned "queijo da serra" made in the Beira Baixa region, so appreciated by food lovers the world over. "Leitão à Bairrada" (Bairrada-style suckling pig), rock lobster or fish "caldeirada" (stew) and "frango na púcara" (chicken in red wine

Sopa de caldo verde (potato soup with kale and chorizo sausage)

prepared in an earthenware pot) are specialities of this central region that can be served with the excellent local wines, still or sparkling. Further inland, the Trás-os-Montes region has numerous specialities. "Alheira de Mirandela" (chicken sausage) and "presunto de Chaves" (cured ham), for example, are staples of Portuguese gastronomy.

Lisbon and its region offer a wide variety of fish and meat dishes, such as "cozido à portuguesa" (a stew made of pork, beef, sausages and vegetables) or "iscas à portuguesa" (liver marinated with garlic and bay leaves), which may be served with wines from Colares du Ribatejo or Moscatel from Setúbal. Further south, in addition to its magnificent plains, the "Alentejo" region offers the visitor a wealth of soups and "açordas". Cork production is one of the region's major economic activities, and there are those who claim that the meat from black pigs raised among the cork

oaks has a special flavour. One of the region's most typical dishes, popular throughout the country, is "carne de porco à alentejana" (a stew made with pork and soft-shell clams, flavoured with fresh coriander). And the rice so present in Portuguese cuisine is grown along the coast here. "Arroz de Marisco" (rice with seafood) and "Arroz de Cabidela" (rice cooked in poultry blood) are two popular ways in which rice is prepared.

In the Algarve, the sunny southern region so popular with tourists which gets its name from the Arabic "Al-gharb", the cuisine uses local products grown in the mild climate that reigns there all year round: vegetables, lemons, oranges, almonds, cane sugar and so on, as well as a wide variety of fish prepared in the "cataplana" copper cooking pot, grilled or boiled, with no need for added flavouring. "Arroz de lingueirão" (rice with razor clams), "robalo ao sal" (bass in a salt crust), "caldeirada à Fragateiro" (fish stew) and marzipan cakes made with eggs are all specialities of the Algarve region that go well with the local wines.

In the islands, the excellent quality of the meat and fish and the wide variety of tropical fruits have given rise to a highly creative and flavoursome culinary tradition. In the Azores, the cinnamon used in the traditional "alcatra" and in various desserts made with pineapple, for example, yields some particularly felicitous associations of tastes. In Madeira, too, the quality of the local cuisine is a pleasant surprise. It includes such delicacies as swordfish with banana, meat on

Traditional dishes

laurel-wood skewers and the famous honey cake and passion fruit pudding. And, of course, Madeira wine is a well-appreciated aperitif all over the world.

Portugal has always produced excellent cheeses, which are well worth mentioning here, even if they are produced in such small quantities that they are seldom exported. Made with ewe's, goat's or cow's milk, they are surprisingly little known, but whether they come from the mountain regions, the Azores, Serra Azeitão, Serpa or Rabaçal, they are well worth tasting with a glass of good port. Cheese is also used to make the famous "Queijadas", cakes that are found in many variations throughout the country.

A word, too, about what is no doubt the most international of Portuguese pastries: a custard tart called "pastel de nata", made with egg custard in puff pastry, that delights sweet-toothed palates from London to Beijing, from Tokyo to New York and from Rio de Janeiro to Goa. Very few people know the secret of the original recipe, which is stored away like a precious treasure under lock and key in the coffers of the famous "Pastéis de Belém" patisserie facing the Tagus. Even its production is shrouded in mystery. The "pastel de nata", flavoured to taste with cinnamon and icing sugar, is an icon of Portuguese gastronomy. Starting a day with an espresso coffee and a "pastel de nata" is a delicious Portuguese custom – don't you want to try it?

House of Guides and
Ministry of Culture and Religious Affairs

R o m a n i a

Discoveries and delights

Traditional Romanian cookery can be divided into five periods: Dacian cuisine (sixth century BC second century AD); Roman influence (second century AD third century AD); the age of migration (third century AD eighth century AD); eastern influences (eighth century AD to 1821); and western influences (1821-1918). Modern Romanian cuisine, in turn, can be categorised by four distinct periods: the cuisine of all provinces (1918-1950); Communism (1950-1980); "rational" eating (1980-1989); and restoration (1990 to the present).

Dacian cuisine *(sixth century BC to second century AD)*

Archeological findings over the last fifty years offer clear proof of the formation of the Latinate Dacogetic culture at the end of the second century AD. The Dacians cultivated grain, raised cattle, fished and hunted; and their use of iron tools and pottery enabled them to process and preserve food. When the Roman ambassador Mauricius Flavius Tiberius visited Dacia in the sixth century, he was served grilled veal, roast wild pigeons, meat on a spit, honey, aromatic muscadelle wines, juicy pears preserved in hay, white, pink and black grapes, and red and golden apples. Even so, the Romans considered us barbarians because of our eating habits.

The Dacians used vegetables (cabbage, spinach, mustard), but the only dishes they prepared were

> **"If I were to speak about this extraordinary 'tchiorba' and this dreamy 'tourta' I would say not only that the world doesn't know anything about Romania, but also that you as Romanians don't know your miracles. Speaking of cuisine, you are very, very rich in your so-called poorness."**
>
> **Jacques Yves Cousteau**

357

millet soup, boiled buckwheat groats, and the famous boiled wheat eaten at funerals, which became our well-known coliva.

In caves and earthen dwellings, our ancestors preserved their produce by smoking, salting and brining. Although they raised animals and drank milk from both cows and sheep, the Dacians did not excel in cheese products, knowing neither butter nor cream.

It was in this early period that the polarisation of Romanian cuisine began, when the diverse, rich and sometimes sophisticated foods of the rulers started to diverge from the simple, poor food of the peasants. Sadly, this discrepancy between the daily meals of the peasants and the wealthy still exists today.

The Roman influence (second century AD to third century AD)

Many historians believe that the Dacian eating habits prevailed over those of the conquering Romans, especially since the legions brought their simple campaign recipes rather than the opulent feasts of the rulers. But the Romans did introduce pie to Dacia (they had learned to make it from the Greeks). These early pies consisted of dough filled with various kinds of forcemeat. A series of sauces were also introduced, some quite similar to today's sour soups (although sour soups are a much later Slavic influence from the south).

Archeological finds have uncovered Roman containers – lidded earthenware pots like a type of early pressure cooker – which allowed for both baking and boiling and thus diversified methods of food preparation. Bread, and use of preserved olive oil, also date to the period of Roman domination.

The age of migration (third century AD to eighth century AD)

For centuries our ancestors ate on the run to escape various hordes of invaders. This period left us with many place names reflecting the different invaders, as well as a memory of eating wild edibles and meat stored under saddles. Because this nomadic life isolated the Dacians, ancient eating habits were

preserved for nearly 1 000 years. Even today, some communities in Hateg, Apuseni and Maramures eat at the sheepfold, as they did in Dacian times. Despite the population's isolation, southern Slavs from the Danube region introduced vegetable and meat borsch. Also at this time the two-pronged fork, brought by Venetian Black Sea merchants, appeared in the homes of local rulers.

Eastern influences (eighth century AD to 1821)

The Orient's contribution to Romanian cuisine is very diverse, with Byzantine, Turkish, Greek, Arab, and Armenian influences. Over the years these culinary cultures intermingled to create an eastern flavour that is consistent in Romanian food, even any one influence is hard to identify. The eastern influence, based largely on customs in the Ottoman Empire, also changed local eating habits. This is the era when pilaf, stew with white sauce (and goulash!), tuslama (tripe), stewed aubergine, shish kebab and syrupy sweets like baklava entered the country. Southern influences brought aubergine, tomato, onion, pepper, okra, quince and watermelon to the Romanian principalities. Coffee and tobacco

arrived, too, as did corn (maize), called gran turco ("Turkish grain") because it was intro-duced from Turkey.

The Romanians had to pay tribute to the Ottoman Empire in the form of wheat. In protest, they began to

grow maize instead, for which the Turks had no use. In this way for almost a millennium we became a people of mamaligari (polenta eaters). In further protest Romanians began to raise pigs, since the Turks, as Muslims, wanted beef. Thus the so-called "pigs alms" came into being – food that the Empire did not tax.

The influence of the church also began to be felt in this period. Fast days were instituted, especially in the countryside, where most of the monasteries were located, and where many rulers from the Fanar district of Constantinople lived. Fast days could be observed in style with such delicious non-meat dishes as walnut sarmale (meat-stuffed cabbage rolls), baked celery with olives, vegetable "caviar", brined fish with garlic, nettles with garlic sauce and mamaliga, monastery goulash with mushrooms, aubergine meatballs, and caviar.

Western influences (1821-1918)

During this era, Romanian society opened up to the world and to modernity, namely to the west. The revolutionary generation of 1848 – the children of noblemen who had studied in Vienna, Paris or Berlin – returned home with a burning desire to get the Romanian principalities into the European orbit. At the same time they felt a patriotic desire to reclaim the national past, and thus the atmosphere was ripe for the appearance of the first Romanian cookery books, including the famous *200 tested recipes, cakes and other home activities*, published in 1841 by M. Kogalniceanu and C. Negruzzi, two pioneers in the history of modern Romanian cuisine.

Kogalniceanu and Negruzzi belonged to the new generation, and their book reflects a turning point in Romania's larger history, as well as in the history of its cuisine. While visiting Paris, Kogalniceanu asked his sister for jam recipes, complaining about how bad the meals were in the German poorhouses. When he returned home, he was determined to upgrade the national cuisine, because, in his opinion, Romanians

Meatball ciorba

ate coarsely, with no dainty dishes. Kogalniceanu's and Negruzzi's snobbishness was in tune with the times. These two westernisers ignored borsch and sour soups in favour of trendier recipes. They developed Romanian cuisine as a high art, which included both local, medieval dishes (especially those prepared at the courts of noblemen and rulers) and French specialties in a sweet, spicy and delicious gastronomic bonanza.

The cuisine of all provinces (1918-1950)

In Bucharest and other major cities luxurious as well as popular restaurants appeared at the end of the nineteenth century, in which renowned French and German chefs cooked. Here local chefs were gradually trained. Romanian cuisine was developed between the 1877 War of Independence and the First World War, a mixture of native traditions (of the rulers, noblemen, and regular citizenry), together with eastern and more recent western influences.

The cultural, political and business elite prized not only imported dishes but also native, homespun ones like sarmale, grilled meats, and various types of sour soup. Some of the most ancient Romanian recipes were recreated, and the meagre cuisine of the Romanian peasant was esteemed right alongside the luxurious dishes of high society. Thus Romanian cuisine is Parisian in its cookies and culinary language, Viennese in its Indianer Krapfen (doughnuts) and apple strudel, Russian in its hearty hot meat pies, Greek in its jams, and Turkish in its baklavas and sherbets.

Casa Capsa, the famous confectionery shop, restaurant and hotel established by Grigore Capsa in 1874, had much to do with Bucharest's fame as "Little Paris". Capsa brought hundreds of recipes to Romania – not merely humble imitations of Parisian creations, but outstanding and creative confections in their own right. He traveled frequently to Paris, Vienna, London, Leipzig, St Petersburg and Pest for supplies as well as for new ideas. At Casa Capsa, foods from Byzantium and Russia were paired with Swiss or Dutch cheeses and French wines in a triumph of Romanian national cuisine. One confection still beloved today is the Joffre cake, originally made at a banquet held in Bucharest in honour of the French Marshal Joffre. Even in the 1930s Paul Morand wrote that Bucharest's confectionery shops offer a "sweet pit stop", with the city itself a gastronomic heaven reflecting a broad palette of flavors and influences.

In 1918 the principalities of Romania were united, and many different regional recipes came together to form a truly national and modern cuisine.

Communism (1950-1980)

The communist period did not help the evolution of the national cuisine; on the contrary, the culinary arts reached a low point as traditional rural food and very basic recipes came to predominate. A large segment of the population was forced to return to a domestic survival economy, re-enacting ancient, pre-modern ways of preparing and preserving vegetables and meat. The Communist period of proletarian dictatorship impoverished the country's natural resources and introduced mandatory recipes. Steak with French fries became the workingman's (and woman's) delight. Working-class dives appeared; the Diplomats' Club became the Comrades' Club (it hasn't fully recovered even today). Water made its presence felt in wine, especially in the case of the notorious wine merchant Stefanescu, who made a fortune by adulterating wine. He was eventually condemned to death. Only at the seashore and in Poiana Brasov did the regime allow tastier recipes to be prepared for foreign tourists. Like everything else at the time, food service had an export section, with finer foods that were unavailable to those living inside the country's borders.

"Rational eating" (1980-1989)

This era was characterised by export madness, as decreed by Ceausescu. Because so many food products were sent out of the country, Romanians did not have enough to eat, and everyone felt anxious about food. When good products were found, they were eaten at home. It wasn't just hunger; it was a national psychosis. The restaurants that still served food belonged to the "blue-eyed boys" (a euphemism for the secret service). Romania became a police state.

This was the darkest era for Romanian cuisine: links with tradition were destroyed, the urban population turned boorish, and the Romanian peasant eating habits and taste became an absolute mess.

Restoration (1990-the present)

Since 1990 we have found ourselves, gastronomically speaking, in full recovery: in economically difficult times we are reforging broken links and re-establishing lost contacts, trying to recreate the gastronomic paradise that existed before the Second World War. Romanian cuisine is once again back on its course of internationalisation, absorbing new ideas and global trends, thanks especially to the large hotel restaurants where traditional foods are prepared along with the most refined, cosmopolitan

Traditional beef ciorba

Ciorba is a Slavic dish, prepared throughout the country.

Ingredients
600 g boneless beef – 100 g carrot
100 g parsnip and parsley root – 1 celery root
2 onions – 350 g potatoes — 1 bell pepper
3 tomatoes – 20 g tomato paste – 30 g oil
1 l borsch – 150 g peas and canned green
beans, lovage, salt

Method
The beef is chopped into small cubes and boiled in salted water, together with chopped onions. The carrots, the parsnip and parsley roots, the celery root, the bell pepper are cleaned and chopped into small cubes, and then fried in oil and a little water. After they have been fried, the vegetables are added to the pot in which the beef is being boiled. The cubed potatoes are also added. They are all left to boil together for approximately 20 minutes. The borsch is boiled separately, its foam is skimmed, and is then added to the ciorba pot together with peas, green beans, tomato paste, salt and quarters of peeled tomatoes. They are all left to boil for another 5 minutes. The ciorba is taken off the stove and finely cut lovage is added. The soup is served hot, garnished with lovage sprinkled over and chilli pepper. The ciorba can be accompanied by a small glass of tzuica.

dishes. Fast-food chains are connecting Romanian tastes with those of others on our planet and carrying on the workingman's tradition of light meals. Today, in a single meal, we can enjoy the gastronomical art of over 2 000 years of tradition and influences – some imposed, others chosen freely. From this perspective, at least, the Romanian should have something to smile about: he is a winner.

Romanian cuisine represents a triumph of history. Through the foods that we eat, our ancestors, from the humble peasant to the rich nobleman, speak to us, perhaps more clearly than in any other domain.

The meaning of mamaliga

Before villagers got bread from workers who had travelled to the city, they lived with a kettle and stirring stick, feeding on the cornmeal mush called mamaliga by the Romanians and polenta by the Italians. Until recent times, mamaliga was the Romanian peasant's and poor man's food. The word was also a metaphor for sloth, and most of all helplessness; it even entered phrases like "the mamaliga does not explode", which meant that, just as mamaliga will never explode, no matter how long it's cooked, the Romanian people would never revolt (of course, the uprising of December 1989 proved this statement false). The truth is that Romania is the best representative of the culture of cornmeal mush, and we shouldn't be ashamed of it.

Simply put, mamaliga is an amazing dish, better than Spanish paella or Italian pizza or other famous dishes of the poor. There are over a hundred variations in the Romanian kitchen, including Oas mamaliga in paturi, Ardeal sheepherders' bulz, Bucovina balmus, the potato mamaliga of Dolj, and Moldavian

Smoked ham

mamaliga with onions. Cold fried mamaliga is served with plum jam from Bucovina and Banat as a dessert or breakfast dish. Mamaliga can be served with eggs and scrijele (scrambled eggs), with cow's-milk cheese and cream, even cold with hot milk.

Italian stonecutters and millers in Banat invented polenita, a sort of pizza made with mamaliga as the base. Although mamaliga didn't always give us strength, this low-calorie food will soon conquer the city, where energy for haymaking and hoeing is no longer needed.

The healthy burn

Romanians have eaten onions and garlic for ages. The Romanian word for onion, "ceapa", comes from the Latin "cepa", but garlic's nickname of "usturoi" comes from the word for burning pain, usturime. As vegetables, seasonings, medicine and mythology, onion and garlic beat all other ingredients in Romanian cooking. Throughout the ages the onion has remained a faithful companion to sheep's cheese. Green onions or chives, new onions, mild or red onions, are everywhere: fried or cut up in sour soups, in stewed aubergine, mixed with brined fish, in pies or salads, used with cheese fillings, walnuts, olives and mushrooms. Rice and onions is a delight, as is veal goulash with onions. If someone is considered good for nothing, then he's "not worth as much as a frozen onion". A variety of sweeter onions called leeks can be found in Oltenia. These gentler cousins account for the fact that Oltenians are presented in Romanian folklore as either dumb or slick. Although the Romanian cries frequently, out of hypocrisy, when peeling an onion, the burn is healthy, and it helps him prepare some wonderful dishes.

Garlic

Garlic has its own mythology. It also has a smell that knocks you out. But garlic can protect you from cancer, bad luck and other misfortunes. A rope of garlic heads or cloves is placed near icons, on towels and plates. Mujdei is a Romanian garlic sauce that was brought to the Delta region by Ukrainian Cossack soldiers. Garlic, either fresh green or minced, is added to fried fish, bread, mashed beans, meat and even cheese. In Ardeal and Bucovina all grilled meat is studded with garlic. Magically, garlic gets rid of warts and skin spots and fortifies your eyes.

Salt

"Life tastes good", proclaims a recent Coca-Cola advertisement. Perfectly true. But there is nothing truer than the fact that salt makes life even tastier – just try eating without it. Romania boasts Europe's largest salt deposits, and many landscapes, villages, cities and people are called Slanic, Slatioara or Sararu – all words that relate to salt. So it's not surprising that salt is so important to the Romanian diet. Other nations may preserve vegetables, meat and cheese artificially, but Romanians still use salt.

Pastrami is made with salt; fish is salted and preserved in barrels. A popular dish is fish or chicken cooked in hot salt brine, and all real pickles are made using salt. Pickled cabbage and cucumbers are best when they are seasoned with dill, peppers, lovage, parsley, carrots, and celery, then salted and sunk in barrels underwater, to ferment anaerobically. Pickle brine is

enough to wake the dead. It cures ulcers and goes wonderfully with grilled sausage and tzuica (plum brandy) boiled with sugar, especially in the snow in wintertime.

Of the world's cheeses, cottage cheese is the best of all because it's made with salt! Just add an onion, fresh tomato, and bread, and your mood suddenly changes. Salt is who we are. We add salt to food because it's the way of our land, of our soil, and our subsoil.

There is no smoke without fire

This saying refers to gossip, but it applies to cooking as well. When the embers of the fire had died down, peasants discovered another way to prepare food, one that was slower but longer lasting, a way to preserve meats without further cooking. This was smoking. The Romans considered smoking barbaric, but the method spread quickly.

At first foods were smoked in the caves used as shelter in the wintertime. The inhabitants of Ardeal moved the smoking space to the attics of their houses, and even today, attic smoking rooms are still being built. In the mid eighteenth century urban residents built their own smokehouses in their backyards for use especially at Christmas time, when pigs were ritually slaughtered. Ham, sausages and lard are the tastiest Romanian smoked dishes. They are eaten with bread, onions, and garlic and accompanied by 50% proof palinca (plum brandy) from Ardeal,

40% proof tuica (a plum brandy) from Pitesti, or sometimes a cold glass of dry wine.

In the highlands, the sheepherders smoke cheese both in skins and plain, making caciocavallo and fresh sheep's cheese. Near the Danube, the fishermen

Charcuterie

smoke fresh fish or fish dried in the sun. In the city, merchants have again begun to smoke chicken, following an old custom.

Of all of the European methods for smoking foods, ours is the most varied, since we use all types of wood, from pine to willow.

Truth is in wine – In vino veritas

The Dacian King Burebista has gone down in history for having created a united Dacian state, but also for having ordered that vineyards be destroyed. However, archeological sources reveal that not all the vineyards were ruined, and shortly after his proclamation, Burebista was dethroned – no doubt because he tried to separate the Dacians from their vineyards. Closer

to our own day, even phylloxera did not succeed in doing this.

Today, Romania is eighth in the world in terms of area planted in vines, and also eighth in wine production; it is seventeenth in its volume of wine exports, after Moldova, Hungary, Bulgaria and Australia. Romania

Cabbage à la Cluj

Cabbage has been known and eaten since the Dacian era. Under eastern influence it was later combined with minced meat. This dish is prepared especially in Ardeal.

Ingredients
400 g pork – 25 g rice – 1 kg sauerkraut
100 g onions – 30 g smoked bacon
15 g tomato sauce – 80 g pork fat
80 g cream, pepper powder, salt, freshly ground pepper

Method
Peeled and sliced onions are fried in a pan of hot pork fat. The pork is chopped and mixed together with the fried onion. After it has boiled and cooled, the rice is added to the minced pork. All is mixed until a homogenous paste is obtained,

which is then salted and peppered. The sauerkraut is washed and squeezed, then cut into thin strips. The tomato sauce is fried in pork fat together with pepper powder, and then the sauerkraut juice is added. When it comes to a boil, the sauerkraut is added. After it has boiled, the sauerkraut is removed from the pot and layered in another pot alternately with minced meat, ending with a layer of sauerkraut on the top. The sauce left after the tomato paste was fried is added, and the pot is put into the oven, where it is left to simmer for 2 hours. The dish is served hot with cornmeal mush, cream and chilli pepper. It can be accompanied by a glass of palinka, white or rosé, dry or semi-dry wine.

has indigenous grape varietals which produce such unique wines as Creata, Banat Riesling, Galbena de Odobesti, Iordana, Grasa de Cotnari, Feteasca Alba, Feteasca Regala, Banateana, Tamaioasa Romaneasca, Babeasca Neagra, Busuioaca de Bohotin, and Feteasca Neagra.

The Romanian always has a jug of wine on his table. The noblemen of Moldavia and Ardeal in particular were known for their wine cellars; they produced famous wines that foreign travellers tasted and praised. Today, Romanians are expert in sensing the colour, taste and aroma of wine because they have such a fine selection to choose from.

Romanian wines

Strength is in tzuica

During the long, harsh winters of his Black Sea exile, the Roman poet Ovid must have understood what gave the "savages" strength. If he had entered the interior of the country, especially the mountainous areas, he would literally have discovered the Romanians "strength", as their tzuica (plum brandy) is called. He would have discovered that wild fruit-bearing trees, like the wax cherry tree, or noble trees like the plum, produce a strong, aromatic drink called tzuica in Muntenia, horinca in Ardeal, and vinars in Maramures. It is homemade from natural ingredients, resulting in a 100 % ecological product.

Romanian tzuica is an appetizer as well as a digestive aid. It is good before eating, as in Ardeal with

onions and lard; or as in the Delta with little fish and onions; or with pastrami, as they do in Dobrogea. It can also be drunk after the meal, with papanasi (jam-filled doughnuts with cream), pancakes, pie or gingerbread. But tzuica works best with fresh air, far from the big cities. After drinking two or three ciocane (small tzuica glasses) or toiuri (long-necked tzuica glasses), you fall into a pleasant sleep, with no dreams or headache on awakening, and fully in the mood for work, travel or love. Tzuica is an anti-stress drink, a medicine and a blessing.

And it has one more quality: if you "burn" it in a two to three hour walk outdoors in the fresh air, through the woods or the hills, it doesn't make you fat.

Tzuica is born of the hills; if you enjoy nature, it will evaporate into the air. Today's Romanian tzuica was the strength of the Dacians; it is kept for those who desire to know their past. Tzuica is always accompanied by bread and salt and a very warm "Welcome"!

Bulz (Cornmeal mush and cheese balls)

Bulz is the descendent of the Dacian boiled dishes made of millet and buckwheat groats, to which pieces of meat or cheese were added. After maize entered the Romanian principalities, maize flour replaced millet (also because the Ottomans levied taxes on grain). Bulz is prepared throughout the country, but especially in the highlands.

Ingredients
400 g maize flour – 1.6 l milk
300 g cheese – 200 g butter – salt
100 g cream

Method
The milk is set to boil and salt is added. When the milk comes to a boil, corn flour is added, and the paste is stirred over a low flame for another 10 minutes. The mixture is then scraped out onto a wooden board and cut into cubes, which are filled with cheese mixed with 100 g of butter. The solidified cornmeal mush cubes are shaped into balls, buttered, then put into a greased tray, which is set in the oven. The dish is served hot, covered with cream. It can be accompanied by tzuica or white wine.

Baked apples with whipped cream

This is an ancient, indigenous dish (the Dacians used to bake the fruits on embers). The recipe has been influenced by the eastern custom of eating fruits with jam.

Ingredients
8 average-sized apples
120 g sugar or jam
30 g butter
cinnamon
vanilla
50 g raisins
20 ml rum

Method
The apples are washed, then dried with a clean piece of cloth. Their cores are carefully removed so that the apples do not crack. The holes are filled with a little butter, sugar or jam, cinnamon and raisins, then the apples are laid in a tray and baked in a moderate oven. When they are ready, they are sprayed with rum and returned to the oven for a few more minutes. The tray is then removed from the oven, the apples are placed on a plate and sprinkled with the juice in the tray. They can be served warm or cold, with whipped cream or filled with jam.

Alexandra Grigorieva

Russian Federation

Rediscovering classics, enjoying diversity

Over the past 100 years Russia has experienced so many shattering changes – some her very own, others along with the rest of Europe – that it is no wonder the private life of her citizens has also undergone some powerful mutations. The basic implement of Russian cuisine up to the twentieth century – the so-called "russkaya pech", a mighty stove which took up half of the house and also served as a warm sleeping place – can now be found only in remote villages. This stove determined the way that traditional Russian dishes were prepared: cooking begins at the extremely high heat of a well-stoked oven, then the temperature gently drops as the logs burn down

(most of the cooking was done overnight). Hence the profusion of soups, gruels and breads in Russian cuisine. These dishes have now been adapted for modern gas and electric stoves. With the arrival of new products some traditional ones, like turnips and barley, have fallen into disfavour, and culinary habits and tastes have also changed. Thus certain new patterns of food behaviour, especially in the big cities of Moscow, St Petersburg, Nizhniy Novgorod, and Yekaterinburg are beginning to emerge. To better understand these gastronomic developments, we must place them in historical context by first going back a century in time.

Russia before the 1917 Revolution

"A clean teapot, some fragrant tea
Boiling water
My love is slicing a fresh lemon…
I will never forget this sweet moment!"[1]

Idyllic scenes at teahouses where endless pots of tea could be had for quite a moderate price were customary at the turn of the nineteenth century. By that time, especially in the towns, tea drinking had become popular among all classes of Russian society, from the poorest workers to the wealthiest members of the aristocracy. An aristocrat's day often began with a cup of tea, since a substantial breakfast of two courses was not served until noon. In the country, kvas (a mildly alcoholic drink made from fermented rye bread) was still the typical drink for every occasion; the "tea invasion" spread much more slowly, and not without some funny "casualties" on the way: not knowing what to do with the new product, some peasants tried boiling tea for hours with carrots and onions, trying to make a tolerable soup.

Soup was indeed basic fare for most of the Russian population in the nineteenth century. Some soups had been made in Russia for many centuries, such as cabbage soups (shchi) or soups made with salt-cured cucumbers and their brine (solianka, kalya); others, such as Ukrainian beetroot soup (borsch) or Tatar clear soup with pasta (lapsha), had been borrowed from neighbouring nations. There also existed a variety of cold summer soups, most of them based on kvas (okroshka, botvinya) and the soup of the most destitute members of society – stale bread crumbled into water (tiuria) or sometimes milk. The latter is, perhaps, close to another staple of Russian cuisine, kasha (groats, porridge or gruel, depending on its thickness, though thick kasha was most common). In the country kasha was made mainly with buckwheat, barley, oats or millet; more prosperous and cultured families in town used semolina or rice.

Even more important for national self-identification than soup or kasha was bread. Heavy, black Russian sour rye bread made with yeast was much appreciated by the Russians, but those unaccustomed to this bread were unable to stomach it. Ever since the sixteenth century western visitors to Moscow had complained about its indigestibility, and Caucasian prisoners of war used to their flatbreads sometimes fell ill and died because of the prevalence of rye bread in the prison diet. On the other hand, the Russian aristocracy commonly returned from trips to Paris quite put out, since one could not get "normal bread" there at all.

Russian bakers were also proficient in making other, less formidable kinds of breads, as well as pirogi (various filled pies, sometimes with different fillings combined in a single pie) and kulebiaki (fish pies). Street vendors wandered about town hawking individual pasties (pirozhki), some baked, some fried. The bakeries were full of luxury breads and buns, and many towns had their specialties. For instance, Moscow kalachi, made of fine wheat flour in the shape of a lock with

Shrovetide means plenty of bliny (pancakes), sturgeon and salmon caviar, and sour cream

Traditional festive foods include yeast breads and pastries

370

a plump, purse-like body and a slender handle, were sent to the court of the Emperor in St Petersburg by special train every morning. Some of the loaves were frozen unbaked and dispatched to Siberia to be baked on the spot.

At the same time, most people of means enjoyed a highly international menu every day. Although there were many Russian dishes, for the most part the food was distinctly French (cream soups, meat, fowl and fish with exquisite sauces). English dishes such as beefsteaks and roast beef were also quite indispensable. German mince, herrings and potatoes (which eventually superceded the traditional Russian turnip) and Italian macaroni with parmesan were very popular and often served even in the simplest households. Some culinary influence from the east was also present: aubergines and pilafs were no longer regarded as exotic, and Georgian kebab stalls had already appeared in Moscow by the turn of the nineteenth century. Once they had been adopted into the cuisine, all new dishes were fitted into the standard pattern of fasting and non-fasting required by the Russian Orthodox Church.

Church regulations stipulated over two-thirds of the year as fast days. There were two fast days a week, Wednesday and Friday, and three special fasting periods in addition to Lent. Although not all people of means continued to fast in the nineteenth century (preferring to fast seriously only during the week before Easter), most of Russia's population observed the regulations, obtaining much-needed protein from wild mushrooms – "our forest beef", as the peasants lovingly called them. During the seven-week Lenten fast, even fish was allowed to be eaten only once before Easter, on 25 March, the Day of the Annunciation. Lent was preceded by Maslenitsa (Shrovetide), a week of pagan merrymaking in true carnival spirit, when everyone baked various bliny (pancakes of buckwheat, wheat, or semolina) and devoured scores of them with butter, sour cream, eggs, caviar, smoked and salt-cured fish (everything but meat was permitted). After much skating, sleigh rides, snowball fights, flirting, dancing, hard drinking and overeating, a female effigy of Maslenitsa was burned at the stake in a symbolic farewell to winter. On Forgiveness Sunday everyone asked for forgiveness; the next day, on Pure Monday, the populace plunged into forty days of abstemious repentance until Easter.

Easter was and still is the most important holiday of the Orthodox Church, much as Christmas is for western Christianity. On Sunday after midnight mass people celebrated and broke the long Lenten fast (a literal breakfast). There are three main protagonists on the Easter table. Painted eggs are often dyed in onion skins to yield a rich, warm, golden-brown colour. Kulich (Easter cake) is a tall, glazed dome not unlike Italian panettone. A sweet yeast dough, ideally made only with egg yolks, is enriched with lots of butter, studded with raisins and sometimes almonds, coloured with saffron and spiced with mace. Paskha (which means "Easter") consists of thick curds that are creamed with sugar, heavy or soured cream, butter and egg yolks, with blanched almonds, candied orange peel and sometimes raisins added. The mixture is then packed into a special pyramid mould to set overnight. Kulich, paskha and painted eggs are all eaten together. Beside them on the Easter table there was usually a lamb made of butter, plenty of roast game and whole hams, and many other dishes according to the hostess's whim.

Christmas was celebrated on a less grand scale. A special Christmas vigil table (sometimes laid with the tablecloth spread on a layer of hay) contained only dishes suitable for fasting, since the feast took place on Christmas Eve. Various gruels, mushroom pasties and jam fritters were served; sometimes a carp cooked with honey, almonds, raisins and saffron was offered (which is somewhat ironic, as this dish originated in the eastern European Jewish settlements). The fun began the next day when freshly slaughtered pork and sausages were eaten. This meal was followed by days of merrymaking, including fortune-telling, singing for treats (koliadki) and masquerades that went on until the Epiphany.

The Soviet era

**I can't wait for communism to happen,
a time of limitless possibilities,
I could have a helicopter then
and my relatives could always phone me
if for example butter is on sale
in Rostov or some other USSR town
with my helicopter I'd just fly there from
Moscow and be on the spot in a jiffy, first in
the queue for butter'.[2]**

After the mishaps of the revolution and the five-year Civil War that followed, the Russian land lay in ruins, the past only a distant memory. Bread, flour, even grain of any kind was scarce. Meat was nonexistent. Tea was made of dried carrots; soup of anything one could find, including old tea leaves. One result of these shortages was the 1922 famine in the Povolzhye (Volga) region of Russia (whose stores had been depleted to supply the army). This famine claimed the lives of over 6 million people, twice as many as had died in the Civil War. Then the Soviet Government introduced the so-called NEP (New Economy Policy), a touch of capitalism to boost the frail position of the new state and build up the economy. Within two or three years people began to make money, products appeared on the market, and things finally began to work. But shortly afterwards Stalin and his government decided that NEP had fulfilled its purpose. The state began to suppress NEP and send anyone who was too eager a capitalist to prison or labour camp.

The collectivisation of villages and the industrialisation of towns followed. People in towns who had jobs dreamed of communism and the time of plenty to come. They ate whatever they could get (the state had, at least, set up canteens) and never thought much about cooking, allegedly one of the vices of bourgeois society. Besides, living as most of them did, four or five families to a communal apartment, cooking was no easy feat to perform. But people in villages had their property confiscated by the state, and thus lost nearly all means for survival. They began to starve. A new famine, this one imposed by the state, occurred in 1933-1934, killing over 5 million people in Ukraine, the Northern Caucasus and the Volga region.

Even though there had been famines in the nineteenth century (for which Russian revolutionaries blamed the tsar and his inefficient government), never had they occurred on such a scale before, when not thousands but millions of lives were lost. Collectivisation and industrialisation were followed by further political repressions. On the surface, the USSR was enthusiastically building the future by working round the clock (which is not surprising when one considers that being even twenty minutes late for work could land you in a labour camp for several years of hard labour among murderers and thieves, not to mention ever-growing numbers of political prisoners). Good-quality food was still scarce in the shops. Every little success, such as obtaining 200 grams of ham for a holiday dinner, or buying an ice-cream waffle stamped with one's name (such ice-cream had become history by the early 1950s) brought a feeling of happy achievement, which was, however, somewhat marred by the constant underlying current of fear and the anticipation of unwelcome footsteps at the door as one's friends, neighbours and relatives kept disappearing one by one.

Such was the life of society when the Soviet culinary manifesto, *The book of tasty and healthy food*, first appeared in 1939, quoting in the preface a little bit of Lenin and much more of Stalin – the USSR's two greatest "authorities" on everything, including food. The main body of the book consisted of the same recipes that had appeared in Russian cookbooks before the revolution (such as those by Molokhovets, Avdeeva, and Radetsky), although they were greatly simplified, and all the fancy touches like foreign names and expensive ingredients had been removed. Recipes for national dishes of some of the Soviet republics were included, from Georgian cuisine above all. There were no recipes for bread (only for making sandwiches), and it was proudly noted that industrial breadmaking had completely obviated the

Sterlet (the daintiest fish in the sturgeon family) on colourful aspic, one of the classics of Russian cuisine

Easter: domed kulich of various sizes, creamy paskha and brightly painted eggs

Roast suckling pig for Christmas

need for home baking. As a later edition of the same book stated:[3] "The population must acquire the habit and taste for semi-processed products, dry break-fasts,[4] concentrates, tinned products and all the rich and varied assortment of ready-to-eat and conven-ience factory foods".

However, the Second World War interrupted the food industry's rapid development. During the Leningrad blockade people ate everything they could[5] simply in order to survive on the tiny rations allotted (125 grams of bread a day per person). Still they died of starvation by the thousands. By comparison, life in wartime Moscow was ultra-prosperous; the rations were much higher, and with connections one could sometimes get such luxuries as a 25 kilo sack of pota-toes. The first years after the war were still very lean. Supper after a hard day's work often included nothing more than a couple of stone-cold bluish potatoes and perhaps a boiled carrot or onion. Famine again rav-aged Ukraine and other regions of the USSR in 1946-1947. But by the early 1950s products of every kind again appeared in the shops, and despite the cost it was possible to buy 25 grams of caviar for a child recovering from a fainting spell or suffering from asthma. Nevertheless, most of the time people could afford only the cheapest food.

To keep people in good spirits after the war the gov-ernment instituted many colourful festivities and even reintroduced the Christmas tree that had been prohib-ited in the 1930s. Now it was a New Year's tree, and New Year's celebrations were encouraged to distract people's attention from Christmas (which, according to the Russian Orthodox Church's Julian calendar, was celebrated on the 7 January). Believers had to observe this holiday quietly to avoid getting into serious trou-ble. Maslenitsa (Shrovetide) and Easter were likewise celebrated very quietly within close family circles. But whereas for Christmas people simply baked a modern festive cake, they still made bliny during Maslenitsa and, for Easter, painted eggs (making it difficult to get eggs before Easter). They made paskha and baked kulichi as best they could without good ovens, proper moulds or even some of the traditional ingredients (one of my friends knew a very sophisticated woman who used to put a drop of Chanel No 5 perfume into her kulich dough to make up for the missing spices; it apparently worked wonders).

Eating outside the home remained difficult. Going out to canteens, cafés and even restaurants usually turned out to be a grim experience. The preparation of every dish was codified by the state, and the cook had no right to add anything or alter an approved recipe, much less invent something of his own. There were also serious problems of theft. The best ingredients never seemed to reach the simple consumer, the one from the street who didn't have any important con-nections. The result was that the food served was very rarely tasty; mostly it was bland and unappetising and sometimes downright inedible. Canteens had an espe-cially bad reputation: thin, burnt kasha; soups of grubby beetroot and other vegetables sporting black spots, with bits of unidentifiable stringy meat floating in them; the omnipresent minced meat kotlety that seemed to consist almost entirely of bread (from the French cotelette, which once meant "chops" in Russian, but in Soviet times came to mean meat patties). The slogan "Bread is the head of everything" hung in many canteens. Since bread was free and often wasted, it is no wonder that when making kotlety the canteen staff preferred to set much of the valuable meat aside for themselves and use up lots of stale bread instead. In cafés and restaurants the food was better, but the service was agonisingly slow, and the waiters were usually smug, rude and inattentive.

The problem of food quality was due to the period of deficit (from early 1960s to the end of the 1980s) that followed the improvement of the Soviet population's financial status. As more and more people were able to afford various foodstuffs, the comparative abundance of the 1950s began to disappear. This new era was partly triggered by the extremely bad harvest of 1962; by 1963 the entire country was standing in long queues to get bread. After that year it was difficult to name even a single foodstuff that at some point failed to vanish from the Soviet shops. The deficits came in waves: months without sugar, months without butter, months without meat, months without rice, and so on. Some products, such as expensive caviar or cheap buckwheat – traditional Russian staples – disappeared for years. The capital, Moscow was much better off than the rest of the country. Its shops were better supplied, so people from other towns came by special

buses or by train to buy food, making the queues in the shops even longer. They bought kilos of sausages to bring back to their families, giving rise to such riddles as "What is green and long and smells of sausage?" – "A train from Moscow". Or: "What slithers along, with burning eyes?" – "A queue for some deficit product". And so on. Even if some foodstuffs were available, they were of very poor quality. For instance, we never saw the better cuts of meat[6] in the shops: all the best went to the special communist shops (where deficits never occurred) that were open only to the members of the communist elite. The good products went to the friends and relatives of the butcher.

The constant shortage of fruit and vegetables (collective farms were not working too well) led the government in the 1960s and 1970s to enforce their dacha (country house) programme: city people got a 600-square-metre plot of land where they could build their country house and grow their own fruit and vegetables to make preserves in their spare time. Sometimes this plot could be as far as 100 kilometres from their home, so they would have to spend four or five hours to get there (by train, then by bus, then on foot – cars were also a deficit item in those days). They had to bring their own food along and stock up on as much as they could, since virtually nothing was available locally in the nearby villages except for some very bad bread, gray macaroni, matches and bars of coarse soap. In season the nearby woods could provide some berries and mushrooms, but not for long, since the undergrowth got trampled and polluted by the hordes of eager "professional" mushroom gatherers who came at dawn with big baskets or pails on trains specially scheduled for this purpose.

As a result, at the end of the Soviet era many Russians found themselves well stocked against every eventuality, with homemade preserves, canned food, various grains and legumes, salt and sugar. These stores helped a lot during perestroika, especially in 1991 when there was almost nothing in the shops. After this the government had to abolish price controls, and the store shelves throughout Russia grew fuller than they had been since the Revolution.

The Russian Federation in the twenty-first century – what next ?

At the beginning of perestroika[7] the ruling slogan was: perestroika, uskorenie, gospriemka (rebuilding, speeding-up, acceptance by the state). The following anecdote was very popular:

Somebody asks the man selling bubliki (a bagel-like roll): "Why are your bubliki underdone? – That's speeding up! Why does every single bublik have a piece bitten off? – That's because the state accepted them! Why are your bubliki square instead of round? – Why, that's perestroika! "

In fact, everything did speed up and change amazingly fast in just a few years. Incidentally, true bubliki have disappeared, along with the famous kalachi, saiki, sitniki, krendeli and many other unique breads and buns that were so popular in Russia before the Revolution and were inherited by the industrial bakeries of the Soviet Union. As for the basic Russian bread, wheat bread has generally become lighter and fluffier but has retained its characteristic touch of sweetness, while rye bread has lost much of its previous sourness. In Moscow, due to mass immigration from the former Soviet republics, various Caucasian and Asian flatbreads (from Armenia, Georgia, Uzbekistan and so on, all those breads that the Russians of the nineteenth century looked down upon) are steadily becoming more popular, as is pita bread. These breads lie on the supermarket shelves next to German-style multigrain bread, French-style croissants[8] and baguettes, Italian-style ciabatta and English-style toasting bread.

On other shelves one can find plenty of canned and instant Russian soups and kashas, along with Italian pasta, both dry and fresh. In the delicatessen department spicy Korean salads coexist with Russian meat in aspic and pirozhki, Caucasian dolma (stuffed vine leaves much like the Greek dolmades) and even Japanese sushi. Meat, fish, sausages, cheeses – everything is available as long as you are prepared to pay the price. You can also find Easter specialties[9] and plenty of bliny, but for the most part classic Russian Christmas dishes did not survive the Revolution, and only certain families still make the traditional sochivo, a special Chistmas dish after which Christmas Eve, Sochelnik, is named: wheat[10] cooked with honey and bits of fresh and dried fruit, which is eaten after the twenty-four hour fast when the first stars appear on Christmas Eve.

Today, all sorts of vegetables and fruit, even the most exotic, are available year round, and bananas have almost become a modern staple. To think that less than twenty years ago people stood in long queues eager to get green ones! No more than 2 kilos per person was allowed. These green bananas had to be wrapped in newspaper and stored in a closet. Sometimes they ripened and turned yellow and were enjoyed as a great luxury – perhaps once every two years, depending on the shopper's luck. More often they just remained green and had to be thrown away.

Fast food in Moscow and other big Russian cities is no less diverse. Before perestroika only pasties and ice cream and sometimes, much more rarely, kebabs could be eaten on the street. In summer, if one was lucky, one could find a cistern of kvas or diluted Russian beer and have a drink after standing in a long queue. There were also machines that produced soda water, with and without syrup. Now, ever since the arrival of McDonald's[11] in 1990 as well as other western fast-food shops, all kinds of ready-to-eat street foods are available from the chain stalls that

have cropped up like mushrooms around metro stations. The most typical are those selling shaurma (or shaverma, as it is called in St Petersburg – actually it's döner kebab, usually made of chicken), grilled chicken (the luxury of the Soviet 1980s), bliny with sweet and savoury fillings (some traditional Russian, some quite innovative, like baked pork and horseradish, but the batter is definitely more French than Russian as it is prepared without yeast), stuffed baked potatoes, Danish hotdogs (even more ubiquitous are the anonymous hotdogs and hamburgers sold at smaller stands), Chinese stir-fries and lots of freshly baked pirozhki and pasties made with puff pastry (yeast dough is becoming less and less frequent). Soft drinks, tea and coffee and sometimes beer are usually sold at the same stalls, hard drinks at drink and cigarette stalls nearby. If one takes a walk around the corner from the Moscow McDonald's to Pushkin Square, one of the city's hubs, one finds no less than seven different fast-food stalls crowded together, plus a great profusion of restaurants.

Now Russia is actually experiencing a restaurant boom. This is especially true for Moscow, where hundreds of new restaurants and cafés have been opening every year. Even though the material analysed is far from complete, a quick look at the statistics on www.afisha.ru (a kind of sophisticated *Time Out* which appears in both magazine and web form) reveals interesting information about the popularity of various national cuisines in Moscow. 150 restaurants consider themselves "Russian". Mainstream

Booths selling Chinese stir-fry, Russian pastries and Danish hotdogs stand across from McDonald's in central Moscow.

Alexandra Grigorieva

"European" (usually including some popular Russian dishes) number 260 (not to mention 90 restaurants serving "international cuisine", which in practice would hardly differ from the European). Chinese (168) restaurants are slightly more numerous than Russian, Italian (146) and Japanese (138) slightly less. 94 Caucasian restaurants should be tallied with the 52 Georgian, since Georgian cuisine is the most widespread among them. French cuisine is openly proclaimed by a respectable 52 restaurants. There are also beer restaurants[12] (90) that have mainly adopted some basics of German cuisine, and lots of pubs (106) that generally work along American food lines. The revival[13] of cafés (more than 300, mostly fake Wiener Café cum Konditorei style, and many of them chain establishments) is even more impressive. In present-day Moscow one can also find lots of restaurant "minorities" from the far east to the far west, from Tibetian to Brazilian, from Jewish to Siberian.

Although most of the Russian restaurants are content with the classic dishes of Russian cuisine as they were cooked in Soviet times, some chefs are interested in rediscovering the wealth of recipes from before the revolution. One of the most dedicated is Alexander Filin at the restaurant "Red Square, 1" in the State History Museum, who is bringing to light some of the museum archive's menus and recreating dishes from nineteenth-century Russian cookbooks. Despite its peasant origins, by the mid-nineteenth century Russian cuisine had a fine repertoire of culinary masterpieces that disappeared after the revolution due to the simplistic Soviet culinary policy. But now one can again taste the famous buckwheat club kasha with fried onions, hard-boiled eggs, brains, mushrooms and toasted walnuts; or Guriev kasha, a sumptuous semolina soufflé with fresh fruit and nuts. Botvinya, a cold summer soup made with kvas, greens and slices of fine fish (salt-curdd sturgeon, etc.) has again come into its own, as has the wonderful kurnik, a festive pie consisting of bliny with three kinds of fillings, one necessarily chicken, encased in a sour-cream crust. There are so many more breads, soups, kashas to be saved from oblivion… Alexander Filin acknowledges that the process of choosing forgotten recipes is rather tricky. Some seemingly strange things like rye bread sorbet become an instant success, while others, like kvas jelly, are better left on the pages of the old cookbooks. Still, there is always some past to look forward to, to modify and change into a fabulous new gastronomic reality.

Canned Russian soups, precut light Russian bread, instant kasha, deep-frozen processed foods and ready-made salads – that is probably what most Russians are finally settling for now, since authentic Russian cuisine is both too time-consuming and too rich for modern life. It would not be very possible to "eat Russian" were it not for the restaurants and for some families (fewer and fewer) who strive to keep up tradition. Eating Russian every day has become somewhat of a luxury. If in the Soviet era making traditional food was problematic due to a lack of products, now it is a lack of time that causes people to come home after a long day at work and boil some deep-frozen pelmeni (Siberian meat dumplings) – or even, perhaps, make some simple Italian pasta instead of working painstakingly from scratch on a magnificent Russian soup.

---

1. A "chastushka" (folk song) improvisation sung by factory girls at the end of the nineteenth century.
2. A Soviet anecdote from the 1970s, a great era for listening to jokes, since one usually wasn't sent to jail for telling them as had happened under Stalin.
3. Preface to the 1952 edition.
4. Cornflakes etc.
5. My father, then a teenager, had eaten about nineteen cats before he was finally evacuated in the final stage of emaciation.
6. I remember shortly after 1985 when the rules first began to change and state control began to slip going with my mother into a small kebab shop (there were a lot of them at the time). We ordered two pork kebabs. They were so unusually tender and not at all difficult to chew that we glanced at each other in dawning horror, both sharing the same thought: "It must be human flesh we are eating!" We fairly flew out of the establishment, abandoning our meal, although now I think it was probably just good pork.
7. "Rebuilding": the official name for the reforms undertaken by Mikhail Gorbachev in 1985.
8. These are mostly disastrous. I hope no true croissant-lover ever tries them.
9. These have actually been in the shops since the 1980s, kulich euphemistically masquerading as "spring cake" and paskha as "special curd paste".
10. Although now when wheat berries are no longer sold in the shops people make do with other grains, even pearl barley.
11. McDonald's fascinated thousands with its spotless WCs and smiling personnel, both previously very hard to find in Soviet establishments.
12. There is also a sprinkling of wine restaurants, which usually stick to creative French or Italian menus.
13. There were some pale versions of these in Soviet times, for instance Moscow's two "Shokoladnitsa" (chocolatière) cafés, almost the only two where something with whipped cream was served in the 1980s. Needless to say, one had to stand in long queues to get served.

Vesna Bizić-Omčikus

Serbia and Montenegro
A culinary quilt

Although the saying "Tell me what you eat and I'll tell who you are and where you come from" may still hold true for Serbia and Montenegro, today it is becoming increasingly less applicable. Serbs remain in the majority, but the country is home to over twenty ethnic communities whose names differ, but who are really very much alike.

Serbia and Montenegro lies in south-east Europe, on the Balkan peninsula. It has four distinct cultural and geographical regions: Pannonia, Central Balkan, Dinaric and the Adriatic coast. Existing as it does at a crossroads, Serbia and Montenegro has hosted many a nation over the centuries. Some peoples just passed through, or stopped for only a little while; others stayed and settled. Invaders, passers-by, settlers and neighbours all left their mark. Other cultural influences, including culinary ones, were brought by intellectuals returning from their studies abroad. Today the national cuisine consists of the native old Balkan and Slavic heritage combined with oriental, central European and Roman-Mediterranean influences.

In the Pannonia region, the administrative district of Vojvodina, Hungarians and Germans have had the greatest impact. The German influence may be seen in the use of dairy products, particularly sour cream and the white cottage cheese called "švapski sir" ("German cheese"). Under German influence, people in Serbia learned to make pastries, various cakes, and especially strudels. Various vegetable casseroles (Zuspeise) were also introduced. German culture is further reflected in the typical three meals a day (breakfast, dinner and supper).

A typical holiday dinner in Vojvodina

Poultry soup with wheat-berry balls or noodles
Meat and vegetables in broth with tomato sauce
Stuffed goose
Mashed potatoes
Lettuce with cracklings
Poppy seed or walnut strudel

381

Under Hungarian influence all sorts of spices were introduced, red pepper in particular. The local population began to prepare goulash and hot meat or vegetable casseroles, sometimes with pork or poultry.

Cured meat products – ham, black pudding, various haggis-like products (kavurma, svargla, and džigernjača), sausages, and cracklings – are a Vojvodina specialty.

The Central Balkan region, in Sumadija and the Morava valley, reflects a strong Turkish influence, as the Turks ruled there for several centuries. Foods were also introduced into this region by various merchants and craftsmen who travelled from the east. Here we find all kinds of pies: cheese (the Serbian version is called gibanica), potato, leek, cabbage, apple, sour cherry, and meat (burek); stuffed sauerkraut, cabbage, sorrel or vine leaves; moussaka; rice and vegetable casseroles; stuffed peppers, courgettes and tomatoes; and grilled meats, the most famous of which are ćevapčići (grilled minced meat rolls), hamburger and kebabs.

This region is noted for farming and animal husbandry, which define the diet even today. Local recipes have traditionally passed from generation to generation, and each household has its own way of making such typical Serbian dishes as kajmak (clotted cream), ajvar (grilled and chopped red peppers in spices), proja (cornbread) and various plum products.

When times were hard, cornbread was made from cornmeal mixed only with water. In better times, this simple proja became projara by adding rich ingredients like eggs, cottage cheese, milk, and cracklings.

Kajmak is a dairy product common to the Dinaric and Central Balkan regions up to the Sava and Danube rivers; on the other side of these rivers sour cream is more often used. Clotted cream, made by skimming freshly boiled milk and then layering it in wooden vessels, is another specialty.

Ajvar a red pepper relish, is served as a salad or a spread for bread. Although it takes some time to prepare, the recipe is quite simple. Red peppers are grilled on the stovetop, then peeled and cleaned of seeds and stems. Then they are finely chopped and mixed with sunflower seed oil, vinegar and chopped garlic. Ajvar may be eaten immediately or left in the larder for a winter preserve.

Sumadija holiday meal

Gibanica (cheese pie)
White stuff (clotted cream, cottage cheese)
Meat jelly
Stuffed sauerkraut leaves
Roast suckling pig
Potato salad, pickled beetroot with horseradish
Apple, cherry or pumpkin pie

Although cornbread, clotted cream and ajvar can constitute a whole meal, they are often served in

Serbian restaurants as an appetiser. For the main course you might be offered beans cooked almost as a soup, with or without meat, mostly dried or smoked.

A meal usually starts or ends with some plum products. As an aperitif plum brandy (šljivovica) is served. For dessert there are prunes or fresh plums or a cake made with prunes. Children in Serbia often get a piece of bread with plum jam as a midday snack, and in many homes guests are welcomed with plum slatko (sweet preserve) and a glass of fresh water. In addition to plum preserve, Serbian housewives also make preserves of cherries (white, pink or red), sour cherries, strawberries, apricots, currants, blackberries, raspberries, rose petals, grapes, green walnuts, and watermelons.

Plum trees began to be cultivated in the second half of the nineteenth century, when phylloxera destroyed all the vineyards and wine and brandy production plummeted. A plum native to Serbia is called the early ripe red. The plum and its products are of great importance to Serbs and part of numerous customs. On Family Saint's Days (Slava) and at weddings toasts are made with plum brandy; on Christmas Eve or during fasting periods prunes are always served. It is believed that the best place to build a house is where a plum tree grows best. Until the Second World War Serbia derived substantial income from the export of plums.

In eastern Serbia, the Wallachian population has left its mark on the local diet, contributing milk and dairy products as well as wild edibles like sorrel, nettle, mushrooms, wild garlic, forest strawberries and blueberries. An eastern Serbian saying describes the local food as being "for both the fold and the court".

Drying peppers and garlic

The food prepared in the villages beneath the Stara Planina is still generally old-fashioned. Food is mostly preserved by drying it under the house eaves. The best known shepherd dish is belmuz, made of melted day-old cottage cheese into which white cornmeal is poured and cooked. Characteristic dishes of the region are mamaljuga (Wallachian polenta with cheese or kajmak), bean aspic, sauerkraut with crushed walnuts, tripe, prune and mushroom soup, and dried fruits (sušenice).

The Dinaric region covers the mountainous countryside of western Serbia and continental Montenegro. The local diet consists mainly of red meat (mostly lamb and dry-cured mutton or beef), dairy products, and high-calorie but bland food. The most popular product in Serbia is dry-cured beef (known as prosciutto); in Montenegro it is dry-cured ham. Dairy products are mainly sheep's and cow's milk, clotted cream (kajmak in Serbia, skorup in Montenegro), cheese and yogurt. Dishes made of flour and dairy products are cicvara (cooked cornmeal with clotted cream), polenta (kacamak in Serbia, pura in Montenegro), bread pudding (popara or masanica) and fritters (uštipci or priganice). Polenta may be prepared from various meals, including barley, corn, wheat or buckwheat, and served with cheese and kajmak. It is traditionally stirred with a wooden spoon until everything is melted and well mixed. Common meat and vegetable dishes include cabbage and sauerkraut, beans, stuffed leaves, and various thick and clear soups. One Montenegrin speciality is cooked mutton (kastradina) with various types of thick-leafed cabbage.

A Dinara region holiday meal

Meze – a first course
(cheese, kajmak and prosciutto)
Lamb liver in sausage casing
Roast lamb or lamb cooked in milk

In the Mediterranean region (the Montenegrin coast) people most often prepare all sorts of fish – fried, grilled, boiled or simply dried – and combine it with other kinds of seafood and various vegetables, such as potato, tomato, large-leaf spinach, and different varieties of wild sorrel. All of these foods are seasoned with garlic, olive oil and lemon juice.

Traditional sweets in this region are shortbread (cake made from eggs and wheat flour), rostula and priganica (various fritters served with jam or honey) and rozata (cooked cream from eggs, milk and caramel). The Perast cake is an unusual specialty, with a story that dates back to the mid seventeenth century: When a new commander was chosen to oversee the city of Perast's army and administration, the inauguration celebration concluded with the presentation of a staff – a symbol of authority – and a Perast cake made of almonds by the city's most prominent ladies. The cake was given to the commander by the city's most beautiful girl, dressed in white, along with a bunch of wildflowers that had been picked by the region's most beautiful girls.

No discussion of Serbian and Montenegrin food would be complete without mentioning the cuisines of the minorities whose members have always shared both good and bad fortune with the indigenous population. Of particular note is Balkan Jewish cuisine. It is difficult to identify precisely the Jewish contribution to Balkan cuisine, since the cuisine itself is a mixture of so many different influences. Still, some contributions are quite obvious, like patišpanj (or patišma, as it is pronounced in some regions). This is a corrupted form of "pan di Spagno", or Spanish bread, a kind of a sponge cake that was a traditional dessert of the Spanish Jews, the Sephardim.

A second interesting influence is recognisable in the serving of slatko (literally, "sweet"), a kind of fruit preserve that is offered to guests and eaten on special occasions. The influence, however, may work both ways, as this custom exists among Jews and Christians alike, not only in the territory of the former Yugoslavia, but also in Bulgaria, Romania, Greece and Turkey. Common desserts include rice pudding, milk pie, čaldikus, tišpišti, patišpanj, baklava, and roskitas di alšahu.

The regions to the south of the Sava and Danube rivers were populated by the Sephardim, whose dishes were a combination of Mediterranean and oriental cuisines. Since the eighteenth century Ashkenazim have also lived in Serbia, in the north. They share a common cuisine with the Jews of the Austro-Hungarian Empire, which traditionally included goose, beans and noodles. Until the Second World War, the most common spices in Ashkenazi recipes were cinnamon and ginger. Since ginger is not locally available, it was dropped from all post-war recipes

A seaside holiday meal

Prosciutto, oil-preserved cheese, olives
Beef soup
Cooked prosciutto with white sorrel
Roast lamb and potato baked in embers
Lettuce

A seaside holiday seafood meal

Salted sardines, pickled gherkins, olives
Squid soup
Dried cod with potatoes
Fish soup
Fried squid or fish
Salad

and replaced by "vegeta," a new commercial spice mixture made of ground dried vegetables and salt.

Roma/Gypsy dietary customs

Like other aspects of Roma culture, Roma cuisine has been influenced by their nomadic way of life. Their diet seems rather scanty when compared to that of others, but it is not that the Roma are not interested in food. Rather, for them food is meant primarily to meet a physiological need. Making simple meals and eating only what is at hand are part of the culture. Today the majority of the Roma population lives in cities, where they improvise meals in their settlements and modest homes. Although a bare hearth, sometimes with an open fire, was once their whole kitchen, today it is a cooker.

The Roma have never engaged in serious farming or produced any food, although they often help others to work the land, or grow some vegetables themselves. Yet they have always been adept at gathering and preparing edible plants. Cooked nettle, sorrel, and mushrooms are made into simple soup-like dishes; eaten with cornbread, this may be the only meal of the day. Meat used to be rare, except on special occasions or holidays, when a feast was served on a table laid outdoors. However, such feasts never led to unexpected culinary combinations.

However limited the Roma diet may seem, they nevertheless eat differently than their forefathers did. The Roma have adopted much from other cultures in the region, adapting new foods to their taste. When preparing a non-Roma recipe, they never stick to the original but always play around with it. This open-mindedness to the foods of others represents acceptance and

Muslim dietary customs

One Roma group (the Askali) belongs to an Islamic community which follows the Koran's injunctions concerning food. Other Islamic communities include the Goranci, Albanians, Turks and Sandjakli (from Raska).

Unlike Serbian practice, Muslim dishes are made without roux, and with little water, so that the meat and vegetables boil in their own juices; few other spices are added. The diet consists mainly of vegetables such as spinach, aubergine, courgettes, tomato, peppers, legumes (chickpeas), and rice; it is also rich in dairy products (clotted and sour cream, milk and yogurt). Dishes often contain onion, legumes, butter and cooked tomatoes. Broths containing one or more types

A Roma holiday meal

Gibanica
Romani zuni – poultry and vegetable soup
(onion, garlic, tomato, peppers, celery, chickpeas)
Romani khanyi – Gypsy chicken
(meat cooked in a soup, then coated in flour and eggs and fried, served with a mushroom and lemon sauce)
Bread
(used to be unleavened cornbread; today it is wheat bread from a bakery)
Salad

understanding, as well as a recognition of the pleasure that can be derived from different cultures.

of vegetables along with legumes or grains, meat and parsley are characteristic, and they may constitute an entire meal. Meat is roasted and usually stuffed with vegetables or grilled. There are also pies, both sweet and savory. Because it is felt that all dishes should be juicy and tender, milk, butter or sour cream is poured

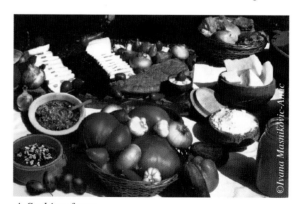

A Serbian feast

over them. One special group of foods are the meze served with drinks at evening gatherings (aksamluk), most often during Ramadan. These may consist of some simple raw foods, soups, or complicated cooked dishes and meatballs. In Muslim communities the most frequently served dish is halva, made of stir-fried flour over which sherbet (caramelised sugar with water) is poured. Oriental sweets such as baklava, tulumba, urmašica, kadaif, and tufahija are quite common throughout Serbia and Montenegro.

Drinks

Drinks are always served with meals, and in the countryside they are almost always homemade. The national drinks are plum brandy and grappa, served as aperitifs. With the main course various sorts of domestic wines (white, red, rosé) are served, often with fresh or sparkling water; in recent years beer has gained favour too. Wine and brandy production are quite widespread throughout Serbia and Montenegro. The majority of traditional Jewish families make homemade raisin wine for Passover. Throughout the country it is customary to serve black coffee at the end of each meal.

Roma wedding feast

Fasting

Some religious communities abstain from certain foods, or from food in general, at certain times of the year. Orthodox Christians refrain from eating all foods of animal origin on special dates in the church calendar. The Serbian Orthodox Church observes one-day fasts on Wednesdays and Fridays as well as lengthier fasts, of which the longest are the Great Fast (seven weeks preceding Easter) and the Christmas Fast (six weeks preceding Christmas).

The Orthodox believe that food also has a spiritual side, and fasting is a means of creating bodily and spiritual balance, both within oneself and with one's environment. Eating is considered a sort of service to God, in the same way that we eat during a service, a communion. The bodily aspect of fasting means a change in eating habits and abstinence from certain foods: milk and dairy products, eggs, meats and meat products (fish is allowed).

387

Forbidden foods for Muslims are pork and any meat originating from a cloven-hoofed animal, as well as any game. The consumption of alcoholic beverages is also forbidden. During Ramadan, Muslims honour takvim, a fasting period between prayers at dawn and sunset (from sehur – breakfast, to iftar – dinner, or better yet, from sabah – dawn, to aksam – sunset). As the Serbian Muslims often say "You sehur at sabah" – you have breakfast at dawn.

City life

Urban life has historically differed from that of the countryside. Not only did various cultures intermingle, but people in the cities spread European ideas. Parallel to its early nineteenth century political struggle for independence from Turkey, Serbia was also striving culturally to become part of Europe. Thus, new dishes were introduced in the cities, and food was accorded more prestige. Mealtimes and meal etiquette changed, as well. In the country, for instance, the meals were dictated by farm work. Breakfast (bread, cheese or cheese pie, or corn-bread) was at 10 a.m. or 11 a.m. After the field work was done, a hot meal was offered at 5 p.m. or 6 p.m. By contrast, the urban workday dictated mealtimes in the city. Breakfast (bread or some pastry with butter and jam and coffee with milk) was earlier in the morning. A hot lunch of soup, meat, and vegetables was served around 2 p.m., and dinner was at around 7 p.m.. It consisted of cold dishes like salads with mayonnaise, meat in aspic, cheese, cured meat products, and sandwiches. In the country, everyone ate from one common dish or large plate, each with his or her own spoon. In cities people had their own plates for each separate course. On special occasions

---

A Slava Day menu in the city

Wheat
(boiled wheat berries ground with walnuts and sugar)
Savoury scones and pastries
Various sorts of cakes (at least ten)

A Slava Day menu in the country

Wheat (boiled but not ground, with little sugar)
Broth
Stuffed leaves
A roast
Pickles (vegetables preserved in vinegar)
Gurabije (baked cakes made of lard, flour and sugar)

the dinner service consisted of numerous plates and saucers for all of the courses, and specialised pieces of cutlery were used for different kinds of food. The most luxurious meal was made for the Slava (Family Saint's Day) lunch, which only family members would automatically attend. Others, such as close friends and neighbours, had to wait for a formal invitation before they could come to pay their respects. Once these people had been invited, however, they could automatically come to the feast in the future. In the country Slava was also a very important day, but neighbours and relatives only came if invited.

Significant changes in Serbian eating habits occurred after the Second World War. People from Banija, Lika and Kordun (in Croatia), from Bosnia and Herzegovina, Montenegro and Kosovo and Metohija colonised the territory of Vojvodina and also moved to Belgrade in great numbers. Each group brought its own ways, which had a substantial impact on city life.

Over the past ten years the way food is treated has changed a great deal. The fast pace of modern life has decreased the number of traditional housewives who only take care of their families and make meals and winter preserves the way their grandmothers used to. Fresh produce can still be purchased in the country and at greenmarkets, but an increasing number of supermarkets sell all sorts of fresh fruits, vegetables, meats and spices from all over the world. European working hours are becoming the norm, and women, most of whom work outside the home, do not have enough time to make regular meals for their families. There is also an increasing number of fast-

Paprikač from Vojvodina

food restaurants where you can find hamburgers that are slowly replacing homemade meat patties and ćevapčići. At bakeries you may still find burek, but more often you'll find Danish pastry; there are more pizza places than shops selling ćevapčići, and recently shops selling Greek kebabs have opened. The Serbian countryside still has old-fashioned inns, but in Belgrade, only an odd inn here and there – tourist attractions, really – reminds you of the olden days. Now there are new Italian, Chinese, Thai, Indian, Mexican, and Libyan restaurants, as well as sushi bars, whose owners are not foreign. This atmosphere lends Belgrade cosmopolitan glamour.

However, now there are societies to protect traditional domestic cuisine in Serbia; the most active are the Svehran World Food Festival, Sveohran, Sveti Hrana, and Zlatne Ruke. Although local traditions are slowly fading, new ones continue to emerge. One thing is certain: no guest has ever left Serbia and Montenegro hungry.

Rastislava Stoličná

Slovak Republic

The character of Slovak cuisine

The central European country of Slovakia is made up of diverse regions that differ in both climate and terrain. The southern regions, which form approximately one-third of the country's territory, lie on fertile plains and adjacent uplands. Most of Slovakia is filled by the arc of the Carpathian mountains, which begin to rise in the south-west around the capital city, Bratislava, and culminate in the north in the High Tatras mountain chain, which then passes into Ukraine in the east and on into the Balkans.

The country's geographic and climatic conditions have significantly influenced the nature of traditional Slovak cookery. Up until the first half of the twentieth century Slovakia was largely agrarian. Most foods were produced on peasant farms, which supplied the surrounding market in addition to their own needs. For a long time, therefore, food retained a local and regional character. Nevertheless, Slovak cuisine was not isolated. Over the centuries various ethnic, social and religious influences came together to make it distinct.

Sheep

©Norbert Grosz.

In the fertile, warm Slovakian lowland, flour-based foods were a staple, in particular a wide range of pastas, pastries and cakes. Especially characteristic was a large, tall white bread made from wheat flour or a mixture of wheat and rye. The diet also included vegetables and fruits. Grapes were successfully grown for the production of wine. Among meat and animal products, pork and lard, cow's milk, butter and curds predominated. Poultry and eggs were plentiful.

The situation was quite different in the mountainous, colder regions of central and northern Slovakia, where peasants could grow only undemanding crops and therefore concentrated on raising livestock. Typical dishes of the mountainous zone were made from flour and potato dough, from which pastas, pancakes and breads were prepared. Bread was dark, usually made from rye and barley, with a high proportion of boiled potatoes in the dough. When flour was scarce, bread was often replaced by pancakes made from flour mixed with diced cabbage, beetroot or potatoes. A common meal for people living in the mountainous zone consisted of boiled or baked potatoes with a milk drink, boiled pulses, pearl barley and pickled cabbage. Meat was eaten mainly at various feasts and on Sundays. For the mountain areas of Slovakia lamb was typical, and sheep and beef fat were used. Sheep's milk products, in particular sheep's cheese and fresh curd cheese, brought variety to the diet. The preferred alcoholic drinks were spirits produced from fruit, such as slivovitz (plum brandy), pear brandy, or gin produced from the fruits of the juniper bush.

In the decades following the Second World War the Slovak diet began to change as the food industry industrialised and supermarket networks developed. Gradually the qualitative differences in the diets of the lowland and upland populations were erased, as were the differences resulting from people's social status. Certain tastes and preferences in the preparation of food have, however, remained, and some regions of Slovakia are still known for their own culinary specialities.

Wines of the Small Carpathians

As evidenced by archaeological findings from the seventh and eighth centuries, as well as by later written sources, viticulture and the production of wine as a specialised branch of agriculture have existed in Slovakia for roughly a millennium. The region of the Small Carpathians in the south-west of the country, centred on Bratislava, Svätý Jur, Pezinok and Modra, has a particular form of viniculture, which intensified in the thirteenth century thanks to the German colonists who arrived at the invitation of the monarchs. In contrast to other vine-growing regions in Slovakia, viniculture in the Small Carpathians gradually became the main focus of people's work, and they produced and stored wine right in their homes. Vintners soon became a privileged segment of society. They expanded their vineyards and exported wine to neighbouring European countries. Vintners became so rich that in the sixteenth century they could pay for the upgrading of their most important centres to free royal towns.

The vine-growing Small Carpathians region is the largest in Slovakia, producing quality varieties of white wine such as Grüner Veltliner, Silvaner, Wallachian and Rhine Riesling, Müller-Thurgau, Tramín, Dievčie Hrozno, as well as the red varieties Portuguese Blue and Frankovka.

For the people of this region, wine is not simply a source of income, but also the main alcoholic drink, which cannot be missed at any important gatherings in the field, vineyards, forest, or home. Help from neighbours is paid off in wine; successful deals are toasted with wine. Family celebrations, especially christenings and weddings, provide an occasion for copious wine consumption, as do feast-day and vintage celebrations. For important occasions wine is also imported into other parts of Slovakia. Like bread, wine has always been prized and used with great respect.

The specific work of vintners, the superior form of the grape, and the drink itself have influenced folk literature and the creative expression of the local people. Numerous adages, proverbs and sayings reflect the folk wisdom accumulated over the centuries based on the relationship of the weather to the expected grape harvest. Many Slovak folk songs also have do with wine. A bunch of grapes with mature vines and grape leaves have become the motifs of numerous utilitarian and decorative objects and have influenced other cultural spheres.

Over the past decade the traditional viticultural centres of the Small Carpathians have been revitalised, and old, medieval vineyard buildings restored. They can now be visited along the Small Carpathians wine route, where wines and local fare are offered. The traditional autumn vintage festivals are a special favourite.

Bozik (Bacchus)

©Municipal Museum Bratislava

Slovak Republic

393

Radostník: a wedding cake

Weddings have long been among the most important family celebrations. A wedding means the founding of a new family – the basic unit of society. According to traditional belief, a good beginning will influence the entire life that follows; therefore weddings are held as a sign of abundance and merrymaking. Various ritual objects and practices were traditionally used to ensure future prosperity and offspring. One of these was the wedding cake, a symbol of the wedding and the dominant feature of the wedding table. In Slovakia the wedding cake is baked for the bride by her godmother or confirmation mother. Traditional cakes are made from sweetened bread. They can be round, with or without an opening in the middle, oblong, or in the shape of a horseshoe. Bringing the wedding cake into the bride's home was a ritual of almost theatrical proportion. The woman who prepared the cake carried it through the village, accompanied by the groom's best men, so that everyone could see the gift she was bringing to the bride.

In the Hont area in south-central Slovakia the cake was baked in a special oblong form. This cake was called a radostník, a "joy-bringer," a name which also connotes the positive emotions connected with a wedding. The radostník was large and richly decorated on top, as local tradition required, with male and female ducks made from dough, symbolising the expected fertility of the wedding couple. It was also decorated lavishly with colourful paper cutouts,

dominated by a rose symbolising love. The bride's confirmation mother, dressed in wedding finery, carried the cake on her back in a large basket filled with other wedding pastries. At the end of the wedding reception it was the duty of the bride to cut the cake and give it to the wedding guests; people related to the bride and groom through christening and confirmation received priority. Accepting a piece of

Wedding cakes were embellished with decorations made of paste or paper. In fertile areas of Slovakia a large cake was made, which the bride cut at the end of the feast and distributed as a gift to the wedding guests.

the cake was a sign that the wedding had been successfully performed and duly celebrated. Once home, wedding guests displayed the piece of cake in their window to symbolise their relationship to the newlyweds.

The preparation of radostník lasted longest in the village of Sebechleby, where it was still being prepared in the 1980s. However, because this cake is so costly and labour-intensive, it is gradually being replaced by tiered wedding cakes. The traditional radostník is now baked only for local folklore feasts, where it functions as an attractive, theatrical prop. For the locals, however, it is still an important regional symbol that distinguishes them from northern regions, where such large cakes are not baked.

Bryndza

The European Union has recognized bryndza as a Slovak culinary speciality. In the foothills and mountains of the Slovak Carpathians sheep were traditionally reared in common stables to produce sheep's cheese. Fresh sheep's milk was cultured with rennet in the wooden shepherds' houses – sheepfolds – of the lush grasslands, and heated to make a fresh curd cheese. Most of the cheese was made in summer, then sold to special bryndza factories, where the curds were left to mature, then dried, pulverised, salted and ground in special mills. The resulting bryndza was pressed into wooden barrels and shipped to shops in Slovakia, as well as to Budapest, Prague and Vienna.

©Bryndziareň - Peter Makovický

Cheese labels

The first bryndza cheese factory was founded in 1787 in the small central Slovakian town of Detva. By the end of the eighteenth century several other bryndza

S h e e p   c h e e s e   d u m p l i n g s

These dumplings were once a part of ceremonial and wedding meals in Central Slovakia.

Ingredients
500 g wholemeal flour, 2 eggs, 2 boiled potatoes, 100-200 g sheep cheese, 150 g smoked bacon, dill.

Filling
Peel the boiled potatoes, then mash them and mix with an equal amount of sheep cheese, adding chopped dill to taste.
Make a stiff dough from the flour, eggs and a little water. Roll it out to a thickness of about 3 mm and cut it up into squares of around 5 x 5 cm. Fill the squares with the filling and fold them into triangles, pinching the edges to stick. Boil the dumplings in salted water for about 15 minutes. Drain, then top with cubed and lightly fried smoked bacon. Sprinkle the dumplings with chopped dill and sheep cheese. Serve hot.

©Bryndziareň - Peter Makovický

Sheep's milk cheese maker

bryndza has a high calcium content and contains many milk bacteria that contribute to the intestinal microflora. The cheese is said to help prevent both cancer and osteoporosis. It can also help in the fight against eczema, asthma, diabetes and sclerosis.

The original bryndza was hard and could be cut only with a knife. Only in the last decades of the nineteenth century did its consistency gradually change to the soft and spreadable cheese we know today. This change was achieved by adding a special salt solution and by grinding the bryndza in mechanical mills. Smaller wooden containers, so-called geletky, provided improved packaging.

production plants had started up, especially in regions where it was possible to buy quality sheep's cheese. Slovak Carpathian bryndza was already considered especially tasty, and even a miraculous medicine. Today's latest scientific research confirmss that

Good bryndza should be soft and easily spreadable, with the smell of sour milk, and with a refreshing taste and pale green colour. Bryndza is an important part of the Slovak national dish, bryndzové halušky – boiled flour and potato gnocchi with a bryndza sauce and sizzling smoked bacon.

Cabbage soup with pearl barley and mushrooms

Cabbage soup remains one of Slovakia's favourite meals, and there are many variations. It can be prepared with smoked meat or sausages or just with potatoes, thick home made pasta, dried plums, etc. Almost every family has its own recipe for cabbage soup and serves it at least once a year, as a part of Christmas dinner

Ingredients
*1.5 l sauerkraut with its juice,
300 g smoked meat, 5 g dried mushrooms,*
100 g pearl barley, 1 spoon lard, 200 ml sour cream, salt, cumin.

Method
Boil the smoked meat and dried mushrooms together with the sauerkraut. Cook the pearl barley separately. When the meat is soft, remove it and thicken the soup with a light roux made from lard mixed with flour and cream. Add the barley and the sliced smoked meat and bring to the boil. Season with salt and ground cumin to taste.

Janez Bogataj

Slovenia

The festive table

Diversity and contemporaneity

The special features of Slovenian cuisine and its rituals can be attributed to Slovenia's position at the cultural meeting point of the Alpine, Mediterranean and Pannonian environments, which through centuries of social and historic development have created the unique conditions that inspire the country's cultural forms and life styles.

Rituals with family and friends

Many of the traditional rituals surrounding the birth of a child, particularly in regard to the festive table, have been lost. However, even today, the birth of a child is celebrated with convivial eating and drinking (especially of wine) either at the family's home or at the father's workplace.

Until the Second World War, and for some time after, a festive table was extremely important to the christening ceremony. The child's godparent or godparents (in the past there could be more than one) presented gifts to the child, its mother and relatives. In Slovenia, these gifts had a number of different names. Most often they were called botrina, which was also the name of the feast held after the christening. The main christening gift was a krstna pogača or "christening loaf" – white bread shaped into an oval or braid. In Štajerska this loaf, called bosman, exemplifies the art of craftsmanship in dough. It has recently become popular again for godparents to present christening loaves at a child's birth. Thus this ancient ritual is being revitalised and taking on new meanings in acontemporary urban environment. To this very day, both a child's birth and christening are celebrated not only at home, but also at local inns and "tourist farms".

The wedding is another important family transition, in which friends and the local community also participate. Pre-nuptial and wedding rituals were highly

397

developed in Slovenia and were, at a very symbolic level, connected with specific foods, such as the wedding bread, which signified wealth. In modern Slovenia, these rituals are mainly expressed in the pre-nuptial stag party for men and hen party for women, at which festive tables are laid. Another rite of passage is the šranga, a "barricade" erected by young men from the bride's hometown or village in order to force the groom to "buy" his future wife. This custom has a clear economic basis, as the money and gifts obtained are used for the stag party at which everyone eats and drinks in the newlyweds' honour.

In the past, stag and hen parties, particularly in rural areas and smaller market towns, provided an opportunity for the unmarried young men and women in the community to gather. Nowadays these gatherings include unmarried as well as married men and women who are the bride's and groom's peers. At the parties, the betrothed, usually in locations rather distant from one another, undergo numerous trials, some of which are quite demanding and strenuous. These trials have to do with relations between the sexes, ironic portrayals of the future marriage, the testing of sexual maturity, and so on. These trials often involved making men perform typically female tasks. The food, drink and entertainment accompanying these often Bacchic gatherings increase the ritual nature of the event itself.

Wedding feasts have even greater culinary significance. Celebration feasts and parties take place after the ceremony has been performed at the registry office and/or church. In the north-east of Slovenia, it is still customary to bring a bottle of the finest wine to church, which the priest blesses during the ceremony. After the couple is married, the priest pours three glasses and toasts the bride and groom. In the modern wedding ritual, the festivities are compressed into a single day.

The ritual dish at traditional Slovene weddings is wedding bread (ženitovanjski kruh or ženitovanjska pogača). Its significance was so great in the past that all the guests were given a piece to take home. There is a great variety of such wedding breads in Slovenia. Today, in addition to all the cakes and other culinary masterpieces typical of modern weddings, wedding bread is being re-introduced, for example, in the shape of a braided heart.

The midnight wedding cake has great symbolic meaning in the modern wedding ritual. Both newlyweds must hold the knife when cutting the cake at midnight. The protocol of cutting the cake – the highlight of the wedding festivities – is often seen to by a specially trained person, either an employee of the catering establishment or one of the wedding guests. A slice of the wedding cake represents a piece of magic in our (post) industrial society. It is something special, with an exceptional taste, and in every regard it stands out from all the other foods served at the feast. Thus it is considered a great honour for guests to take a piece of cake home with

New Year's party for the staff of a Slovene company in Ljubljana

them as a gift from the newlyweds, particularly since television programmes have played an important role in propagating the cult of the modern wedding cake.

Contemporary Slovenia is also the site of wedding rituals for the other nationalities who live here, mainly immigrants from the Balkans. The degree of pomp in these weddings is always connected to the social, professional and economic positions of those taking part. The Serbian weddings are the liveliest, with loud motorcades playing Serbian music. Other than that, these ethnic weddings have been largely assimilated into local practice, another example of the way in which foreign cultures have been integrated into the Slovene way of life.

The third most important transitional ritual in Slovenian life is linked to death. The old belief in the ghosts of our dead ancestors has left its traces in the present. Most funerals still end in a social gathering of the relatives, friends and neighbours of the deceased at his or her home or, even more frequently, at a catering establishment. People often ask: "where did you go after the funeral?" or: "where was the wake?" rather than "how did you take your leave of the deceased?" These post-funeral gatherings, which have a decidedly social and culinary character, are called pogrebščine ("wake"). Also widely used is the word sedmina (seventh), which illustrates modern ignorance of the original meaning of this term. Sedmina signifies a festivity which used to take place on the seventh day after the funeral. In the days when the deceased was laid out at home until the funeral, relatives, neighbours and friends would come to splash the body with holy water; the family provided them with food and drink. People used to stay up with the body all night, during which time drinks (wine, spirits or cider) and food (cold cuts of meat, bread, pastries) were offered. Often during such wakes, feelings of sadness intermingled with feelings of fun and conviviality, even to the extreme.

All of these acts, accompanied by food and drink, ended when the practice of laying the dead out at home ended and was transferred to funeral parlours, which are now found throughout Slovenia. Yet the architecture of funeral parlours and other related premises shows an interesting link with the practices described above. In numerous cases, funeral parlours are built in such a way that next to the room for paying one's respects to the deceased there are also rooms where people can gather. A kitchen is often handy, which enables the preparation of certain foods and the serving of drinks. These facilities represent part of what might be called a funeral industry, which still preserves the social element surrounding death. Needless to say, the deceased's home is nowadays almost completely excluded from the funereal rituals, as everything that takes place before the funeral has been transferred to the funeral facilities, and the events following the funeral are often held at catering establishments. The festivities at the table, where those present reminisce about the deceased after his or her funeral, are only rarely organised at the home of the deceased. Catering establishments have developed a wide range of options for funeralgoers, which can be divided into three basic types: modest snacks with drinks; a choice of one hot dish (for example, sausage with bread, or blood sausage with sauerkraut) and drinks;

and more extensive menus in the form of an early morning meal or lunch, including, of course, a drink.

Various other celebrations take place within the circles of family and friends. Among these are birthday celebrations that mark the transition from one age to another. Celebrating the 50th birthday has been espeically popular since the Second World War. In Slovenia, these celebrations are called abrahamovanja or abrahamovine – to "meet Abraham" means to turn 50 years old. The phrase derives from the Gospel of St John, where the Jews say to Jesus: "you are not yet fifty years old and you have seen Abraham?" Abrahamovanja are organised for relatives and friends by the people celebrating their 50th birthday, and often special celebrations are organised for colleagues from work. The guests prepare the entertainment and present the birthday person with gifts. The actual ritual of transition is usually carried out at midnight with the cutting of the cake. The food at the abrahamovanja is not particularly distinct from that at other celebrations, the common thread being a plentiful and varied supply. Often special witty menus are printed, which the guests take home as a memento of the evening and a reminder of the food and drink consumed. Celebrations of wedding anniversaries, retirement parties and other events follow a similar model.

The ritual of Sunday lunches and leisure or holiday outings are other distinct forms of family-oriented celebration, in which it is, however, difficult to

S l o v e n i a

White bread, for years the hard-to-attain symbol of plenty, had ritual meaning as both a symbol and an object. In north-east Slovenia a bride received this symbolic "bosman" – plaited white bread – at her wedding, or sometimes it was presented by the godfather at the birth of a child. Ptuj, 1982.

discern transitional dimensions. All of these celebrations are very common in present-day Slovenia. Sunday lunches, particularly outside the home, have a considerable history, reaching back to the middle-class environment of the nineteenth century. The typical menu for these lunches has remained constant to this day: beef soup with noodles, sautéed potatoes, boiled beef with horseradish or a roast, salad and apple strudel. These foods were, and often still are, also the main components of the Sunday lunches that are prepared at home. During the autumn and winter Sunday lunch is often supplemented with koline (pork and sausages); in the summer, fish, chicken fried in breadcrumbs, or another type of meat (steak or a roast) is served.

Of the annual holidays in which food has always played an important role, the most important are Christmas, New Year's and Easter. These holidays represent transitions when people move from a phase of expectation to a state of new knowledge and experience. They are, of course, tied to the religious belief system of every individual and family. Most often these annual celebrations take place within the home. The exception is New Year's – the transition from one year to another – which is of the most recent origin and which often includes the company of friends or an even wider circle of acquaintances. Boisterous New Year's Eve celebrations have only been known since the first decades of the twentieth century. Christmas and Easter are very different from New Year's, both for Catholics

and for those belonging to the Orthodox Church. It is difficult to place these holidays within the traditional system of transitional rituals as outlined by Arnold van Gennep in *The rites of passage*. However, these holidays do have the three typical phases that Gennep identifies. First, there is preparation or creation, when actions connected with the preparation of food take place (for Christmas this includes Christmas bread, pastries and potica; for Easter, foods such as painted eggs, bread, ham, potica and horseradish). Preparation is followed by performance: at Christmas, the blessing of the house; at Easter, the blessing of the food. Finally, there is completion, represented by the festivities at the table or the experience of the holiday "through" food. This is the peak of the celebration, and in the case of believers, it is a deep, and highly personal, experience.

In the changed social conditions of post-Second World War ideology, the public celebration of both Christmas and Easter was prohibited, so people withdrew into the more intimate circles of family or friends. The liberalisation process prior to Slovenia's independence in 1991 returned both holidays to the framework of official state holidays, and thus they acquired certain dimensions even among non-believers, particularly thanks to their rich culinary heritage. The central symbolic food for both Christmas and Easter, which to Slovenes means something similar to America's Thanksgiving turkey, is potica, a rolled bread with various fillings. The most common potica is made with walnuts;

Croatian "kotlovina" reveals the Balkan influence on foods offered at winter sports events in Planica. Žvirče, 1998

other fillings include honey, poppy seeds, raisins, almonds, chocolate, carob, ocvirki (cracklings), and, at Easter, tarragon. In recent years, even though potica is readily available in shops, bakeries and catering establishments, there has been a growing tendency, particularly among young families, to bake it at home, in order to heighten the festive atmosphere. In fact, nowadays the table is at the very centre of Slovenian rituals.

The foods served at Easter have the greatest ritual significance, and socialising at table is connected to the iconographic meaning of the various dishes. For example, potica is a symbol of Jesus' crown; horseradish is supposed to represent the nails used to nail Jesus to the cross; and so on. Eggs are the central feature, either coloured or decorated in some other way. They are an old Indo-European symbol and the most perfect image of fertility, which was given new meaning by Christianity. Like other foods, decorated eggs differ according to the different regions of Slovenia, as reflected in their names: pisanice, pisanke, pirhi, remenke, remenice. In recent years, various old-fashioned social games involving eggs have been revived to accompany Easter foods at the festive table.

By definition, New Year's Eve celebrations are also transitional. From a developmental point of view they are relatively new, with hardly any links to the past, but their variety is rather incredible. In present-day Slovenia there are three basic models of celebration: celebrations within the family, which can take place either at home or at a weekend cottage or mountain lodge; festivities within a wider circle of family and/or friends; and various forms of public festivities. With regard to the first and the second type, the festivities are most often linked to a large range of culinary items, which have a representative as well as a presentational character. For instance, everyone might agree to prepare only traditional dishes for the New Year's Eve dinner, or to prepare a special dish which is not part of the everyday menu. In this way a certain dish becomes associated with the New Year's Eve ritual. It need not be the main dish of the meal, or even the most festive one; it is simply the one that appears annually and comes to be known as the dish "served after midnight" or the one "served in the morning". Sour soup from štajersko region, goulash and stew are among the popular dishes of this kind. The transition from the old year to the new is not achieved not only through a gradual increase in culinary pleasure, but also by means of social games like bingo and raffles.

Few other annual customs can be described as transitional. In modern society, such customs have retained only their external, obvious or even tourist character: they are orchestrated, play-acted, theatrical re-creations of history. Their heritage, however, demonstrates the links between man and his natural and cultural environments, and the special foods that are prepared confirm this. The transition from winter to spring is marked by St Valentine's Day (14 February) and St Gregory's Day (12 March). Because of changes to the calendar in past centuries, both of these holidays are considered the start of the mating season of birds, and thus are harbingers of spring. The mating or "marriage" of birds is connected with the preparation of decorative birds from the finest bread dough; in the past these "birds" were baked and stuck on bushes and trees in people's gardens and on estates. When young people came to wish for a good crop, they collected the bread birds. The children from poorer families were able to collect enough bread to dry and use as a basic breakfast food (by soaking the birds in warm milk) right up until the next harvest and threshing. Nowadays, this lovely custom is known only in some parts of north-eastern Slovenia; otherwise, for Valentine's Day we have adopted all the characteristics of the Anglo-American celebration, including all the marketing dimensions of this lovers' day. On St Gregory's Day, another form of celebration took place which did not involve food. Small model vessels, lit up with candles or fire, were released into rivers and streams in old handicraft centres around Slovenia, particularly in Gorenjska. The event had symbolic meaning, as people used to believe that on St Gregory's Day the days began to grow longer, and from this day on it was no longer necessary to work in the dark. Today, this tradition

Slovenia's most widely celebrated festival is still "koline". Beyond the slaughter of the pig and the processing of the meat, it is a family holiday. Sharing fresh pork sausage at the table creates a bond among the participants and strengthens family and local ties. Žvirče, 1998.

appears in the form of theatre. In numerous places, young people still release lit-up vessels along rivers, even in places where in the past this ritual was unknown, such as in Ljubljana.

Another festivity involving food is Shrovetide, which in modern times has been concentrated into just a few days: the Thursday before Shrovetide, also known as "Fat Thursday", the following Saturday and Sunday, Shrove Tuesday and Ash Wednesday. Linked to all these days are Shrovetide dishes, involving mainly meat and various sweet fried foods. The consumption of these dishes once introduced the long Lenten fast preceding the Easter holidays. In modern Slovenia, people are trying to rediscover the most typical Shrovetide foods, even though these endeavours often lead to the adoption of stereotypes.

However, central to Shrovetide cuisine are cakes made from fried dough, such as krofi (doughnuts), bobi and flancati. All of these have, from technological and terminological points of view, their own regional forms, which serve as a further proof of Slovenia's culinary diversity. Of course, the transition from winter to spring, which is supposedly at the very core of the Shrovetide festivities, occurs not only within families and among friends, but also in a wider context. One important element of the festivities is koline or furež (sausages and other pork products), the preparation of which represents the biggest family holiday in Slovenia today, as it did in the past. The slaughter of that "great family friend", the pig, signifies a peculiar drama within family life, which until the Second World War enabled the survival of whole settlements. By visiting the family which had just killed their pig, the whole village was able to feed itself. These koline used to, and in some places still do, provide substance and order to the system of neighbourly or village reciprocity. In regard to koline we must speak not only of production but also of exchange. For farmers, the pronounced rituality of both the material and social aspects of this event is really a means and a framework for expressing their identity. The last koline of the winter, particularly in wealthier families, takes place in the period leading up to Shrovetide. Prior to this, koline are held just before St Martin's Day and before Christmas and New Year's. The communal consumption of food (blood sausages, sausages, roast or cooked meat, sour soup, pig's tail with horseradish, pig's head and numerous other regional variants) during koline signified the forming of a bond within the family community and strengthened the links between the individual and the community. Thus, koline, which are one of the most typical Slovene transitional rituals, can also be listed among the most typical community rituals, particularly in rural areas, but also today even in urban areas, even though the actual slaughtering takes place in the countryside.

Community rituals

Our description of transitions connected with annual customs continues with the celebration among family and friends of St George's Day (23 April), which represents a typical spring festivity that was in the past connected with the life of shepherds and herders. Today this holiday marking the transition from spring to summer is in some places still closely associated with the preparation of jurjevo cvrtje (St George's scramble). This egg dish is eaten together by all the inhabitants of a village. Interestingly, even today this dish is consumed in the early morning hours, a custom that lingers from the past. It still happens that a bus stopping to pick up workers will stop for a while in one of the villages en route so that the passengers can sit down with the locals to eat the scramble together.

Based on old rituals involving young men and shepherds, some celebrations of St Florian's Day (4 May) are still re-enacted for tourists, although they do not include any typical culinary elements. The same is true of the festival days of late spring and summer that are linked to various religious holidays, such as St Urban's Day, the Feast of Corpus Christi, St John's Eve and St John's Day, the Assumption and the Nativity of Our Lady. These festivities centre around the family; meals are shared either at home or in a restaurant or some other catering establishment. Since the weather is usually nice at this time of year, the consumption of food on these holidays often takes place outdoors, on excursions and picnics.

On All Saint's Day (1 November) children, in some places, still go from house to house to collect buns called vahči or vahtiči, sometimes also prešce. This practice is a modern interpretation of an earlier ritual, in which children, particularly from poorer families, collected a great number of such buns, which served as their main food for the ensuing winter. In wealthier families, more than 200 such buns were baked to be given away. A blending of old and new also takes place on St Martin's Day (11 November), when martinčki or vahtiči, buns given to children and beggars, are baked. St Martin's Day has a distinct culinary image in Slovenia – it is the day when grape must turns into wine, the day which our ancestors marked as thanksgiving for all of their efforts throughout the year. The traditional dish was St Martin's goose (also duck or turkey), which is linked to the famous legend of St Martin, who was supposed to have hidden among a flock of geese before accepting the bishopric. With respect to the consumption of food and drink, St Martin's Day is one of the biggest holidays in Slovenia; it can be compared to the culinary festivities at Christmas and Easter. St Martin's Day celebrations are community-centred, particularly in the wine-growing regions.

Another custom representing a community transition is the so-called marriage to God or new mass, which marks the first mass said by a newly ordained priest. This celebration ends in a magnificent feast that has all the characteristics of a traditional wedding feast. Although the food at new masses is now organised

A feast of Slovene dishes at the popular winter sports events in Planica. People get to know one another over traditional Slovene foods. Žvirče, 1998

by caterers, the meal still preserves some of the basic characteristics of traditional feasts, such as noodle soup, different types of roasted and cooked meats, sautéed potatoes and other side dishes, followed by desserts. Numerous regional specialities are also served.

Tepežnica or "pametiva" (the Holy Innocents – 28 December) also takes many forms as a community ritual. In Strane, a village located below Nanos mountain, even today young men "thrash" young women, in contrast to other places in Slovenia, where children usually thrash adults (this thrashing is carried out with a rod and is not meant to injure the participants). On the first Sunday after Twelfth Day young men thrash young women, saying, "Why didn't you marry on time? Oh, girls, you'll get a bit of a thrashing now!" In this way an important transition in the life cycle is promoted by means of charmed thrashings with a symbolic magic "wand", which is supposed to make weddings occur. Young men are rewarded with sausages, dried meat, eggs and money. The thrashing culminates in a communal dinner, where in addition to dancing there is also an auction of small, decorated loaves of honey-enriched dough, which have been baked by the young women of the village.

There are other modern ritual events in present-day Slovenia that have a transitional character. Of course, often these are just fictive transitions lacking any "logical" background, such as moving to a higher rank in society or simply "moving up" and acquiring social status and importance. For instance, in the years surrounding independence in 1991, receptions, banquets, feasts and gatherings proliferated. Many individuals now go to great lengths to take part in state celebrations, since their presence at such events is documented by the mass media. These celebrations always end with a reception, usually in the country's main cultural centre, Cankarjev dom, and they always have a suitable culinary content, which usually takes the form of a hot and cold buffet. In both a social and a "psychological" sense, these transitions are innovative, especially in the ways they involve food.

For instance, one special type of culinary event is the annual employee gathering or party. The roots of these company gatherings can be found in the socialist period, when workers would gather and, through sports, conversation and food, reaffirm their sense of belonging to their employer and, in a larger sense, to the current ideology. Even today such gatherings demonstrate culinary excess: hundreds of grilled chickens, enormous quantities of goulash, and so on. Students from Dolenjsko developed their own form of promotion involving masses of people when they started organising thematic outdoor gatherings called Cvičkarija after the main wine of the region, cviček. The cvičkarija is like a fair. Where it once took place only at stands in the Dolenjsko region, it has now spread to other parts of Slovenia and serves to promote cviček. Specific dishes (sausages, dried smoked meat, goulash) and entertainment are linked to the

The grape harvest means both work and celebration. Each of Slovenia's wine regions offers the labourers a wide variety of dishes after their work is done. Avber on the Karst, 2000.

celebration, which also marks a kind of transition for students in late spring.

Joining an organisation can also be seen as a transitional moment involving food. This occasion is often referred to as a "christening". There are hunting, fishing, camping and many other "christenings" or rituals to mark new membership in a particular society or organisation. The celebration is always capped off with a feast.

Rituals associated with the completion of gimnazija (academic secondary school) or the matura (baccalaureate examination) are yet another modern transition. There are valete (celebratory feasts) and balls, which have a rich heritage going back to the medieval period. These feasts and balls have undergone a complete transformation, which was partly brought about by the temporary abolition of this type of schooling during the socialist period. University students have their own ritual, brucovanje (freshmen's party), to welcome first-year students into the university community. Brucovanje goes back to the associations of Slovene students at Austrian universities in the nineteenth century. For today's celebration the students simply gather at discos or engage in various other activities that have no connection to the rich university tradition (except at the University of Ljubljana's Department of Mining and Metallurgy, where the older rituals are still enacted). The main emphasis at such meetings is, of course, on drink, with food playing only an incidental role. Finally, this survey of people united at a festive table can be rounded off by numerous tourist events, which have no truly transitional elements.

In traditional societies food was simply one part of many-layered celebratory rituals, which had different meanings and functions. Today, for many holidays, food is the centrepiece of the ritual, whether at the level of family, friends or community. Individual dishes, groups of dishes, and even entire meals form communicative links among people; they become the subject of conversation, the bases for beliefs and views, and the guidelines for the formulation of norms and values.

Diego Valverde Villena

Spain

Agape and conviviality at the table

Although the words of the great writer and connoisseur Álvaro Cunqueiro may sound excessive nowadays, they could have been written by the latest batch of Spanish master chefs who are so close to alchemists in their discoveries. All Spaniards agree on the great importance of eating in their lives, and Spain is one of the world's most gastronomically diverse countries.

Spain also boasts an extremely large number of restaurants per capita. Any occasion will do for people to gather round a table: meeting up with friends, signing a deal, celebrating a birthday, gathering monthly with colleagues, and, especially, revelling in Pantagruelian feasts at traditional Spanish weddings. Fast food may be fighting to get a foot in the door, serving up daily rations to tourists fearful of an exotic touch, but the family restaurant with its traditional dishes and its tapas still rules supreme in Spain. And in cases of need or urgency, people will more often opt for the timeless bocadillo sandwich filled with potato omelette or cured ham than for that outsider, the hamburger. When it comes to imports, Italian pasta has made the greatest inroads. Chinese and Japanese cooking and the kebab remain on the threshold of exoticism, while hamburger joints depend to a large extent on teenage or younger groups who are more concerned with fashion and games than with cuisine.

The strategic location of the Iberian Peninsula has meant that Spain, along with her sister, Portugal, has

> **"Cooking is a matter for the soul and a supreme art, an investigation into the innermost secret of nature".**
>
> **Álvaro Cunqueiro,**
>
> *Viaje por los montes y chimeneas de Galicia*
> *(Travels among the hills and hearths of Galicia).*

been visited by countless peoples and cultures, who brought their own foods and cooking styles along with other customs. Until the imperial age of the Hapsburgs the Tartessians, Iberians and Celts were joined by Phoenicians, Greeks, Romans, Carthaginians, several tribes of Goths, various contingents of Muslims, Jews and pilgrims who followed the Santiago de Compostela pilgrim route.

Spain has great geographical diversity and wealth, containing the largest number of animal species in Europe. The country's many mountains and plains create microclimates that yield excellent crops and special ways of preparing food, such as the stuffed pork sausages or embutidos typical of the very dry areas. Meanwhile, Spain's maritime heritage has made fish a regular part of everyone's diet. Each region boasts its own dishes, traditions and local produce as well as imported products that have taken root. From Persia the Arabs brought us the oranges Valencia is now famous for, just as they brought apricots and other fruits that remind us of their origin by their very names (the Spanish words for capers, peaches, artichokes, and saffron all begin with the Arabic article "al"). Other culinary contributions from the Arabs include sugar, syrup, and almond pastries. From the opposite direction – from an America discovered by ships bearing the flag of the Catholic sovereigns – came other foodstuffs that have become mainstays of our cuisine, such as the tomato and the potato, which were dispersed from Spain throughout Europe. All of these factors have made Spain an astoundingly rich country in terms of the variety of its cuisine.

The variety of Spanish cuisine

Several Spanish dishes have gained international fame: paella, sangría (wine punch) and tortilla de patatas (potato omelette) have all become part of the essential vocabulary of tourists even before they arrive in Spain.

When it comes to food preparation, it is often said that Spain is divided into three regions: deep-frying in olive oil prevails in the south, roasting is favoured in the centre, and stews are most common in the north. The Mediterranean trio of wheat, vines and olive trees is found throughout the country, so bread, wine and olive oil are enjoyed in all of Spain's regions.

As a rule, typical dishes are based on the most characteristic foods of each region, often the cheapest and easiest to obtain. There is no room here to detail each region's excellence, but we cannot neglect to mention the major regional dishes of Spain, in the hope that our readers will some day be able to enjoy them in their place of origin. All are mere appetizers to the delights awaiting adventurous gastronomic travellers.

Galicia

empanada (a flat pastry), filled with either meat or fish; lacón con grelos (boiled ham with turnip tops); traditional stew or pote; boiled octopus, especially with paprika (pulpo a la gallega); and rolled pancakes (filloas) for dessert.

Asturias

fabada or bean stew, made with beans, lard, pig's ear and blood sausage; followed by casadielles, one of a whole range of sweets.

Cantabria

cocido montañés, a renowned local stew.

Navarre

high-quality vegetables and trout baked with ham.

Aragon

the mountain-cured ham of Teruel; young lamb; and candied frutas de Aragón. Catalonia: a range of stews (escudella, carn d'olla with chickpeas and pork/chicken); romesco (pepper and garlic sauce with almonds and hazelnuts); calçotada (roast spring onions); and pa amb tomaquet (bread with tomatoes and olive oil).

Balearic Islands

the famed ensaimada, a soft spiral pastry.

Basque Country
(boasting the best eating in Spain)

marmitako (tuna cooked with potatoes); multiple variations on cod (bacalao al ajoarriero, bacalao al pil-pil, bacalao a la vizcaína); cocochas (hake barbels); and purrusalda (leek soup).

Valencia

the ubiquitous paella, as well as other rice dishes including arroz a banda and arroz negro (rice with darkened with squid ink); and the fideuá made with pasta instead of rice.

Murcia

zarangollo (marrows, onions and tomatoes fried together); and pipirrana (cucumber and tomato salad).

Northern Castile
(Castilla y León)

garlic soup (sopa de ajo), which accompanies roast suckling pigs or lambs (cochinillo and lechazo).

Southern Castile
(Castilla-La Mancha)

the local vegetable sauté (pisto manchego); fried bread and garlic (migas); and porridge (gachas).

Madrid

cocido madrileño, the local stew; and pig tripe (callos).

La Rioja

excellent vegetables, accompanied by patatas a la riojana (potatoes with onion, pepper and pork ribs).

Extremadura

stuffed pork sausages (embutidos) from the local pig herds; and the unique cheese of Torta del Casar.

Andalusia

cold soups (gazpacho and salmorejo) and fried fish.

Canary Islands

spicy mojo picón sauce, which accompanies papas arrugás (small potatoes boiled whole); also sancocho canario (steamed fish with potatoes) and rabbit.

Special mention must also be made of the wines abundant in almost every region

white wines from Rueda and Catalonia and albariños from Galicia; rosés from Navarre and the Cigales region of Valladolid; red wines from La Rioja and Ribera del Duero. All have earned worldwide renown along with the fino sherries and brandies of Andalusia; the cider of Asturias; the champagne-like cava of Catalonia; the strong spirits (orujos) of Galicia and Potes; and sundry other liqueurs and distillations. Each region treasures its liquid jewels, which command their own rituals.

Spain

The food calendar

Apart from the specialities mentioned above, several dishes are limited to certain times of year. Thanks to refrigeration and efficient transportation, nowadays it is possible to obtain almost any foodstuff in any season. But traditional cooking had more regard for natural cycles and celebrated the changing seasons with specific dishes. The religious calendar also had its own special days on which particular meals were served.

The start of a new season was often celebrated with festivities that reflect ancient propitiatory rites of pagan times. One such occasion still celebrated today is the feast of the "magosto", when the first chestnuts of the year are roasted. Harvest festivals are common in all of the grape-growing regions to mark the first pressings, as wine is the ritual drink *par excellence* in Spain, and the most common accompaniment to any meal. Wine cellars serve as both gathering places and sites of great festivity. In Asturias, where cider is king, popular festivities or espichas are held in the apple pressing barns.

Seasonal changes also have influenced eating habits. In Valencia, the refreshing drink horchata de chufa is particularly welcome in summer, as is that great favourite of foreign visitors, sangría. Anisette mixed with water, known as a paloma (dove), is a summertime drink, while its winter equivalent is carajillo (coffee with a dash of brandy or liqueur). Limitations on hunting curtail the availability of certain foods, and mushrooms are highly appreciated during their short lifespan. Traditionally, the best seafood is harvested from September through April. In the long, hot summers, Andalusia's famous cold tomato soup spreads to every table in the land, while the heavy stews and roasts from Castile and the Cantabrian coast, perfect for fighting off winter chills, are ill-advised in the heat of August.

Without a doubt, however, it is the religious calendar that is responsible for the greatest variations in cooking styles. The prohibition against eating meat during Lent led to the potaje de vigilia, prepared with chickpeas, spinach and a helping of egg and cod. Various regional specialities refer to patron saints, such as the panecillos de San Antón (bread rolls eaten in mid-January), the rosquillas de San Blas (doughnuts served in early February), the rosquillas de Santa Clara (those served from mid-August), or the delicious yemas de Santa Teresa (egg and sugar balls available all year round in Avila). Nuns are considered specialists in sweets and biscuits, and it is not unusual to see people queuing outside the shutters of a cloistered convent to receive their highly regarded delicacies.

Desserts and sweets are especially strongly marked by seasonality. Spring brings torrijas (bread soaked in wine or milk) during Carnival and Lent, while

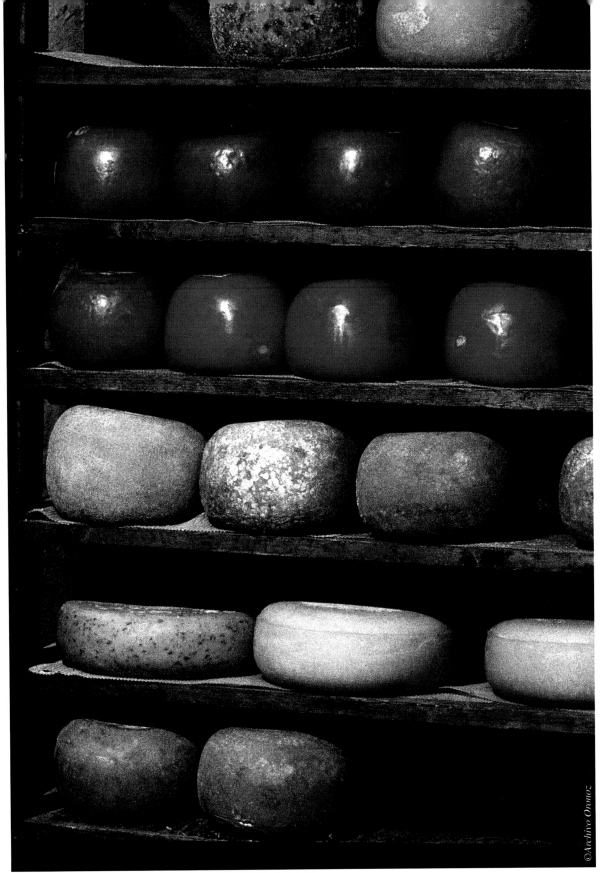

©Archivo Oronoz

Spanish cheeses

buñuelos and huesos de santo are mandatory for All Saints Day in early November. The Yuletide offers the greatest range of seasonal desserts. No Christmas meal is complete without almond pastries from La Estepa (polvorones), candied frutas de Aragón, almond soup and many other delicacies. The undisputed kings of the season are marzipan and various types of almond nougat (turrón). The best marzipan (mazapán) comes from the area around Toledo, while the most famous producers of turrón are in two towns on the eastern seaboard, Jijona (for the softer variety) and Alicante (for the harder type).

Even within the Christmas season special foods mark certain days. Red cabbage (lombarda) is typically eaten on New Year's Eve, while marzipan eels must wait until the Feast of the Epiphany (6 January, Día de Reyes) to be enjoyed alongside the traditional Roscón cake. The arrival of a new year is traditionally welcomed with a glass of cava and twelve grapes. Curiously, this custom of eating grapes at the stroke of midnight does not hark back to any pagan or ancestral festivity, but rather to a skilful marketing campaign from the beginning of the twentieth century, when people were encouraged to eat grapes because of an unexpected glut on the market.

Spain and America, Spain and Europe

In order to appreciate the culinary traditions of Spain to the fullest, we must also take a brief tour of Spanish America.

With his habitual sense of humour, the great Spanish gourmet and writer Julio Camba once remarked that cooking was responsible for the discovery of America, since it was the desire to eat well that led European mariners to seek a new trade route for spices from the Orient. Europe is indebted to America, by way of Spain, for many culinary marvels besides spices. The humble papa, originally from the Viceroyalty of Peru (with more than 200 varieties of potato), has made it possible for Spain to create its emblematic tortilla de patatas (potato omelette). American maize is at the heart of the borona and other cornbreads eaten along the Cantabrian coast. Without the tomatoes of the Americas, there would be no gazpacho, and without the chocolate of Mexico it would be impossible to enjoy the traditional breakfast ritual of dunking churros (fritters).

The Spaniards, in turn, brought their cooking habits to the Americas. Various renditions of Spanish stews can be recognized in their American equivalents. Just as we refer to guinea pigs as conejos de Indias (rabbits from the Indies), in America it is common to refer to the European rabbit as conejo de Castilla (rabbit from Castile).

But beyond the mere exchange of foodstuffs and cooking styles, Spain left in America its traditional

Wine cellar in Córdoba

culinary culture. And just as the forms of the Spanish language that have been preserved in America are much closer to a flowery Baroque style than the Spanish currently spoken in Spain, culinary traditions have been retained much more closely in America than in their homeland.

In Spanish America, the custom of reserving a series of dishes exclusively for certain times of the year is much more deeply rooted. As in Spain, some of these are Christmas dishes, but there are also others eaten only for St John's Day (in June), to celebrate the Virgin's Assumption in August, for Easter, All Saints Day, Lent or Carnival – and not just desserts. Thus America retains some culinary traditions that have

already disappeared in Spain, although cooks have incorporated many seasonings typical of the New World into their dishes.

A blend of Christianity with earlier religions is particularly evident in seasonal foods. Throughout America, the feast of All Saints provides an enormous range of dishes that, besides being eaten at home, are taken to cemeteries to be shared with the dead. Life and death come together as Mexican children nibble sugar skulls with delight, and Bolivians commemorate the day with bread figures shaped like children.

Spain's condition as a land of passage, a hinge between Europe, Africa and America, made it an

417

especially propitious place for culinary legacies from around the world to accumulate. Even as far back as Roman times, writers were singing the praises of the garum in Cádiz, a much-appreciated sauce of Phoenician origin. The same monks who brought the Cistercian style of architecture from the lands of the French and spread it all along the Way of St James also brought the Carthusian and Benedictine liqueurs. These liqueurs are still made today in Silos and other abbeys according to the original 1 000-year-old recipe. The monks also brought the vines that gave rise to Spain's majestic wines.

Meal-time rituals

"No-one cooks better than a devout believer", says the illustrious Julio Camba in *La casa de Lúculo*, a gem of culinary literature. Until not so long ago, it was customary for recipes to contain instructions for timing in the form of a prayer: a lord's prayer, a Salve Regina or a creed represented the time needed for an egg to be boiled just right, or for a sauce to take on the right consistency.

It is easy to see how important religion is to meals. Regardless of what we might believe in or what we do in our daily lives, Spaniards are imbued with the Catholic cultural tradition, which is reflected in our way of eating. In general, we remain reluctant to eat horse flesh, as this was a pagan tradition; and there is no way we will sit down to a plate of dog, considered an exquisite dish in other cultures. However, the pig

The successive groups of Muslims who crossed the Straits of Gibraltar also brought us their agricultural advances – new crops, techniques, and fruits. They also brought, directly or indirectly, new culinary customs. Alongside Arabian-style sweets stands the cocido maragato, a typical stew from the ancient kingdom of León that is eaten in reverse, starting with the meat, followed by the chickpeas and finally the broth. According to tradition, the reason for this peculiar order lies in the need to be well fed in case the Saracens – Al-Mansur and other warlords – launched a surprise attack, a razzia.

is a very important part of our diet. Apart from the nutritional values that pork provides, the Spanish love of this meat has to do with the mediaeval need to prove oneself a "long-time Christian," as opposed to a convert from Judaism, who might still feel repugnance toward an animal considered impure in Jewish tradition.

Nevertheless, when it comes to eating and drinking Spaniards are rather lax in terms of religion. Judging from the poems handed down by Ibn Quzmān and other poets of Al-Andalus, the Muslims of Andalusia were the most permissive in the entire Muslim world regarding the drinking of wine.

The very act of eating is a religious event, and not only in the Christian tradition based on commemorating the last supper. Banquets are always associated with communal life, and there is an unwritten taboo about eating with enemies, as food is strongly tied to friendship and camaraderie. In his treatise on friendship, *De amicitia*, Cicero himself tells us that it is necessary to eat "many measures of salt" with someone to be able to consider him a friend. Indeed, one of the words referring to camaraderie is "companion", etymologically derived from the Latin for sharing bread in company (cum pane).

Eating in company may also be viewed as a social achievement. According to J. G. Frazer in *The golden bough*, public eating is taboo in certain primitive tribes; it is not considered socially acceptable to see anyone eating, especially the head of the tribe. Thus some peoples commonly cover the mouth with

a hand or a veil to avoid being seen. For Spaniards, however, eating is one of the greatest expressions of confraternity. The term agape, from the Greek verb agapao meaning "to love", was originally applied to "love feasts". Now it refers to a copious banquet. From eating as a private, almost animal, act required for survival, the development of society has led us to the shared pleasures of gastronomy.

The Spanish language has retained many expressions deriving from the great importance accorded food as a symbol of agreement. Alifara, a term used in Aragon as a synonym for an early evening snack, originally referred to the meal at which buyers and sellers celebrated the sealing of a deal. One etymology of the Catalan liqueur ratafía traces it to the Latin expression rata fiat, in other words "let the deal be

Spanish paella

Manufacturing cheese in El Paular Monastery, Madrid

made". And an alboloque or alboroque is a small banquet arranged to formalise a deal.

Despite the continuous levelling of customs, certain peculiar culinary customs are still retained today. Festive gatherings and nuptial meals have always called for special food. In León and Salamanca, it is still possible to eat a sweet bun called bollo maimón, distributed during the interval between the religious ceremony and the wedding banquet. And any transition into a new life or a new status requires some culinary rite; baptisms, first communions and jubilees require communal celebrations.

Like other aspects of life, culinary traditions have been retained much more in small towns than in large cities, and more in Spanish America than in Spain itself. Weddings in Spanish America, especially in villages, may require a banquet lasting two or three days. On these occasions an honoured guest is put in charge of the wedding cake and another in charge of drinks. Food and drink augur fertility and good fortune for the newlyweds, while the great festive gathering frightens away bad spirits and attracts good ones.

Meals constitute a community ritual of prime importance. Like religion, they are both ceremonial and syncretist. Just as earlier religions have left their traces on Christianity, so too have culinary practices merged to give us a cuisine rich in both flavours and meanings. For instance, although eating fish on

420

Fridays is a traditional Catholic precept, over the centuries diners have also unwittingly honoured the memory of the goddess Venus (Friday is Venus's day in Romance languages such as Spanish), since fish shared with her an origin in the sea.

Throughout its history, Spain has been fortunate to have been visited by many peoples and cultures. All have left behind something of their culinary traditions, which have gradually been adapted to the local soil and climate. These, in turn, have given rise to a succulent variety of foods, including a long list of regional specialities. All of these influences have converged in a cuisine that is tasty, healthy and extremely varied, always ready to surprise us with new flavours and enliven our day-to-day life.

We trust that these words have conveyed to our readers a taste of the excellent variety of Spanish cuisine. We suggest that readers dip into the culinary writings of some of Spain's great authors, such as Emilia Pardo Bazán, Julio Camba, Álvaro Cunqueiro, Néstor Luján and Juan Perucho, to mention only a few. And, of course, you must come to Spain and enjoy the wonders of our art and our landscape; but be sure not to overlook the other marvels on every stove and in every casserole, which await the traveller willing to seek them out.

Spain

Richard Tellström

Sweden

From crispbread to ciabatta

Swedish culinary art has been moulded by two seemingly contradictory forces – the traditional and the modern. Sweden is situated in the far north, but the softening warmth of the Gulf Stream brings distinct seasonal changes. The climate has set limits on what can be cultivated, which is why hunting and fishing have been important for the way in which our cuisine has developed. Cultural and social aspirations have also moulded cooking techniques and the flavours of the meal. Come with me on a culinary trip through three Swedish epochs: peasant society's food culture until around 1850; the culinary arts of the industrial society from around 1850 to 1950; and modern cuisine from 1950 until today. The framed texts offer examples of the major importance of bread in Swedish cuisine. Welcome to the table!

The flavours of the storehouse economy

A barter economy permeated our food culture until the breakthrough of industrialisation in the late nineteenth century. Historically, the diet of the storehouse economy was based on the vital importance of preserving the fresh foodstuffs of the summer months so that they would last over the winter season in the form, for example, of dried peas, dry bread, fermented milk products, smoked ham and salted fish, or a mixture of different preservation methods. These food processes, often based on the skills and knowledge of women, gave rise to flavours and dishes that in many cases live on even today, such as pea-soup with pork (a dried – salted – boiled dish) or souvas stew (dried – smoked – boiled reindeer meat). The flavour of the dish was always subordinate to the problem of getting enough food to go round. Knowledge of the techniques of the storehouse economy was vital for survival, but food shortages and famine still occurred until as recently as the end of the nineteenth century. The use of dried and conserved foodstuffs led to the dominance of boiled food in the daily diet of the last millennium. Fried and fresh foods were reserved for festive occasions.

The relatively short summer meant that agriculture was intensive, which is why men, women and children alike took part in outdoor work until as recently as the early twentieth century. The types of grain that could be cultivated were limited by the climate. In early history barley was important, and still is in the northern parts of the country. In recent centuries, rye dominated in the south while oats were important in the west. Wheat was grown only to a limited extent and was primarily used for the different types of bread eaten on festive occasions, since white bread was considered special compared with the grey types of bread eaten daily.

In southern Sweden, rye flour was baked into soft loaves and in the central regions it was made into crispbread. Rye flour was sometimes mixed with pea flour and grated potatoes to make it last longer; in times of famine it was mixed with bark. Bark bread has returned in recent years, this time as health bread. In the north of Sweden, a thin bread is baked with barley flour. Tornedalians, a minority group in Tornedalen, bake a soft everyday bread called rieska. Quite unlike other types of bread in the surrounding northern region, rieska does not keep, which is why it is baked several times a week.

Even today, these traditional types of bread are eaten, but new breads like ciabatta and bagels are now popular. Porridge has always been a major dietary staple and is still common, particularly among older people and as food for small children. In recent years, a cold,

sweet rice porridge eaten with jam has become a popular industrially processed snack.

Grain was also important for the drinking culture. In peasant society, small beer was popular with meals, while strong beer had the status of a beverage to be drunk on festive occasions and more recently, at restaurants. The word for beer in Swedish also lent its name to different festivities. Children's beer was drunk at a christening, Christmas beer at Christmas, and even today you may be offered roof-truss beer when people raise the roof truss of a new house. Beer and schnapps were the most common drinks on festive occasions; it was not until the 1970s that wine became more common at dinner parties. Today beer and schnapps are drunk with appetisers at parties, although this has become somewhat rare. International wine trends are also noticeable in Sweden, even in everyday life.

Historically, milk was important in Sweden, and the storeroom economy gave rise to a taste for fermented and matured dairy products. Fermented milk products are still eaten today, with cornflakes for example, and butter remains fairly salty compared to that of the rest of Europe. Cheese was an important part of diet, particularly as daily food. Although sour-milk cheeses previously existed, they were eclipsed after the 1850s by the hard yellow Swiss or Dutch type cheeses. Since the mid-twentieth century, milk has been served with schoolchildren's hot lunches as part of state public-health efforts. Even among the adult population, milk with lunch and dinner remains a common choice.

The open sandwich, a slice of buttered bread with a topping, is a central element of our cuisine, both historically and today. Try a practical Swedish culinary history lesson: Butter a slice of crispbread and put a slice of cheese on top. This is the simplest way to summarise the basis of the traditional Swedish diet – the storehouse economy.

Until the mid-twentieth century, Swedish culinary art was moulded first by German, and later by French culinary ideals. However, these foreign dishes were modified to Swedish taste and when for preparation with the products of the Swedish storehouse economy. Although Swedish cuisine has been dominated by the culinary practices of southern and central Sweden, a distinctive culinary tradition may be found among the ethnic minorities. Among the Sami people, hunting and fishing – for grouse and char, for example – were important, as was reindeer husbandry; reindeer continue to be a vital source of meat even today. Reindeer milk was also a staple of the Sami diet. Until the early-1800s, when Finland, which then represented half of Sweden, was annexed by Russia, the food culture of the Tornedalians was influenced both by agriculture and by the confluence of Swedish, Finnish, Russian and continental trade. For several hundreds of years, Sweden has had a large Swedish-Finnish minority, which in various ways has retained its food culture, as, for example, in

Democratic cooking since the 1950s. With the use of standard units of measure, everyone can succeed in cooking.

Pawel Flato, © Ministry of Culture, Sweden.

Sweden

its use of somewhat sour soft rye bread and wild mushrooms pickled in salt. The Roma minority and travelling people have been marginalised from normative society and were usually prohibited from engaging in agriculture or work in the storehouse economy. Their food culture was based on the fresh food they were able to obtain and shows great variety. Dishes with chicken are common, but there are also recipes with many vegetables, often very spicy.

European explorers in the Americas and Asia in the seventeenth and eighteenth centuries brought back new foods, and East Indian spices became fashion, first in more prosperous homes and then as a general ideal. Even today, the heritage of East Indian spices is strong, and the liberal use of cloves, nutmeg and cardamom in Swedish cooking is striking. Seasoning with these spices can be seen in many traditional dishes as well as in many of the dishes found on the smörgåsbord.

Until the mid-1800s, a more refined Swedish meal began with the schnapps table. This consisted of rye bread, butter, cheese, perhaps a small amount of smoked meat, and pickled herring and schnapps to accompany it. The schnapps table, mainly intended for men, was partaken of while standing, and often in a room separate from the one in which dinner would later be served. The schnapps table was considered old-fashioned when industrialism introduced a new culinary trend – the Swedish smörgåsbord.

During the nineteenth century, sugar-beet refinement began, and sugar, previously precious and desirable, became cheap. This gave rise to a greater sweetening of food in the Swedish kitchen. Today's tastes in cuisine continue to be characterised by sweet flavours that contrast with the sour and salty. Roast meats are served with boiled potatoes, cream sauce and trimmings like sweet and sour pickled vegetables and sweet and sour jelly.

The industrial culinary revolution

Canals, railways and, later asphalt roads rapidly altered the food culture; technical innovations in agriculture were also an important force for reform. In the nation-building process of the latter half of the nineteenth century, newspapers helped to spread novel culinary ideals, and the food culture of the bourgeoisie became the model for the aspirations of the new working and middle classes. When the rural population moved into towns, they wanted to eat modern foods and to test the new flavours of the times, not the traditional foods of the storehouse economy.

The Swedish smörgåsbord emerged in the latter half of the nineteenth century. The inauguration of railways and national monuments by the bourgeoisie and more public modes of social relations formed the basis for this new culinary trend. The new tinned goods industry, together with novel cooking techniques, produced modern dishes, such as different types of pickled fish, meat balls and Jansons frestelse (potatoes and anchovies au gratin). Initially, the smörgåsbord was a first course, accompanying the main dish. In time, the dishes making up the smörgåsbord increased, and in connection with the Stockholm Olympic Games in 1912, the smörgåsbord began to be widely offered as a meal in itself. Today the classical smörgåsbord is rare, but it can still be enjoyed on the ferries between Sweden and Finland.

Between the two world wars, the government began work on strengthening public health. Its campaigns focused on a diet that was richer in minerals, contained more green and root vegetables, and more milk. An important policy goal was to use new technologies and industrial processes to ensure sufficient food for everyone, and to secure domestic food production that was independent of the surrounding world. To reduce alcohol consumption, rationing and a state sales monopoly were introduced.

The cinnamon bun has been a popular coffee bun, both at home and in cafés for eighty years. In the Swedish version, the dough is spiced with cardamom, and the buns are coiled together with a filling of butter, sugar and cinnamon. The best buns are considered to be those that are oven-fresh, home-baked and eaten while still warm with a glass of milk. This meal combines the old heritage of East Indian spices with the Swedish tradition of drinking milk.

The modern dish

Women were once responsible for daily cooking, but after the Second World War, a gender equality programme was initiated. Women once more returned to the labour market, and housewives became rare. Cooking was inspired by developments in the USA, and the food industry produced ready-made and semi-cooked food. Tinned and frozen foods, freeze-dried products and ready-made dishes quickly gained ground. Political campaigns and the marketing of food companies focused on these foods, with the explicit aim of relieving and simplifying women's work in the kitchen.

Consumer co-operatives reformed cooking techniques and created a new type of cookery book in which recipes were standardised. A new measuring unit was introduced so that everyone could succeed in cooking, regardless of how experienced they were in the kitchen. The concept of a democratic food culture was born, the idea being that both men and women should be able to cook. However, even today, men's cooking is limited to more festive holiday cooking at the weekends and to barbecues in summer gardens.

Traditionally, and as a result of public health campaigns, Swedes enjoy going out into the forest to pick

Sweden

427

their own food, such as bilberries, lingonberries and wild mushrooms. These berries and mushrooms are preserved and used later during the winter months both in daily cooking and as an ingredient on festive occasions. Home conservation of garden products still takes place today, despite the fact that time pressure leads many to prefer buying industrially manufactured fruit and vegetable preserves.

The restaurant sector was strictly regulated from the end of the nineteenth century until the 1980s, which is why the development of restaurant cuisine has been relatively modest by international standards. Reasons of public health have guided these regulations, especially the prevention of alcohol-related damage. Over the last fifteen to twenty years, however, restaurant culture in Sweden has begun increasingly to resemble its continental equivalents, and global food and drink trends have changed the restaurant habits of the Swedes. Swedish successes in international culinary competitions have also created interest in more advanced cuisine, both in restaurants and in weekend cooking at home. Today, in the larger cities, there is a wide variety of restaurants to choose from. When Swedes go out in the evening to eat, they want to have something different, such as French, American, Chinese or Italian food experiences.

A pizza in Sweden is of the thin, Italian type, although its base is somewhat thicker. At ordinary pizzerias around the country, tinned mushrooms, pressed ham and other cheap ingredients are used. The cheese is

Swedish cheese made from cream. At special pizzerias you may find reindeer pizzas, pizzas with fillet of pork and béarnaise sauce, or taco pizzas.

Swedes generally eat their mid-day lunch at a restaurant with their work colleagues, although lunch boxes brought to work are also common. Lunches are usually hot, and unlike evening restaurant food, are close to the Swedish daily diet. At lunch restaurants, dishes are sometimes served from the more traditional Swedish cuisine and its former storehouse economy, such as pea soup with pork, or mashed swede with salted beef brisket or hash. These dishes are seldom prepared at home as they are considered too time-consuming for modern city dwellers who work full-time.

The coffee break, or what is called fika, is an institution in Sweden. Work is briefly discontinued as employees gather in the staffroom to drink coffee and perhaps eat a bun or a biscuit. It is also common for companies to offer their employees fruit as part of their health care programmes.

Since the Second World War, Sweden has had a great deal of immigration, and today just over 1 million people (from a total of 9 million) are immigrants or refugees. But these new citizens have had only a limited impact on the dominant, normative Swedish cuisine. The factors for influence and change have instead been international culinary fashion trends. New taste ideals were discovered by Swedish tourists when charter travel to Italy and Spain gained momentum in the

1960s and 1970s and trips to Asia in the 1990s. This can be seen today in the use of tomato sauces, herbs and Thai spices, wok dishes and Tex-Mex food, all of which have evolved from exotic party food to every-day food and everyday flavours.

Historically speaking, Sweden was Catholic and later Protestant, with a Jewish minority. Today, once again, there is a large Catholic population, as well as a growing number of Muslims. For people in dias-pora, the foods and flavours of their country of origin play an important role and are a means of keeping alive their native cultural identity. To be able to prepare the foods important for this identity,

immigrants prepare their dishes using Swedish sub-stitutes or foodstuffs imported from their countries of origin. Many immigrants also start small garage or cellar shops with food products from their home-lands, so as to be able to offer their immigrant group the products and flavours they miss.

Practically all children aged 1 to 18 attend pre-schools or schools where they come into contact with a lunch-food culture organised by public authorities. When immigrant and refugee children come to school they are served dishes from the nor-mative Swedish food culture. These dishes are often prepared according to more traditional Swedish

The "fika" (coffee break) is a Swedish institution. Here members of the Swedish government enjoy a break during their weekly meeting.

ideals, both in taste and structure, but contemporary street food and food adapted to religious dietary rules is also served. Food prepared in public kitchens changes taste preferences, and children bring home new culinary ideals and ask for food at home that tastes as it does at pre-school or school. In this way the food culture of those immigrants who are at home is slowly assimilated into the dominant, normative food culture. In school home economics courses, children also come into contact with "Swedish" cooking; both its techniques and flavours. Assimilation may also be an aspiration. For many immigrants, eating "Swedish" means that they also feel more "Swedish".

Conferences, meetings and discussions are an important part of the Swedish democratic tradition. At these meetings, coffee is traditionally served and often an open sandwich, either before the meeting, in a break, or afterwards, as a reward for a successful meeting. The typical meeting sandwich is an open cheese sandwich, garnished with cucumber or green pepper. The selection of cakes at a meeting may consist of buns, cinnamon buns or, if it is a more festive meeting, Danish pastries and even gâteaux.

Sweden has an increasingly ageing population. Many people live in service accommodation, and here meals play an important role. Elderly people are cautious about new, unusual flavours. Instead they prefer the older food culture they recognise. For those suffering from senile dementia, the food culture in which they grew up plays an important role in their well-being and may stimulate memories, in terms of scents and flavours. As the large immigrant population grows older, there will be a greater need for public institutions to serve food and flavours that older immigrants recognise from their childhood.

The affluent illnesses of the western world, such as being overweight and obesity, are apparent in Sweden, too. The new food culture's ready-made foods, food-stuffs that are often industrially processed, and dishes full of sugar and fat cause the population to gain weight. Meals and eating have also become an anxiety-ridden sphere, and many young girls and boys are affected by anorexia and bulimia. Famine no longer occurs in Sweden, but among the oldest population groups cases of malnutrition have been discovered, often in connection with people losing their partners, and thus losing their appetites for both food and life.

An important characteristic of the modern food culture is that it is no longer just a means of expressing membership in a group but is also an expression of a person's own chosen identity. Ethical rules on eating have begun to play an important role, for example for vegetarians and vegans. New views on what is edible or not in food culture sometimes cause tension between modern and traditional culinary ideas.

Imported fast food and street food trends are naturally also found in Sweden, such as hot dogs, kebabs

Young children enjoying a meal. Preschools offer children their first encounter with the normative Swedish food culture and are one place where children begin to develop their taste preferences.

and hamburgers. A Swedish version of street food is the thin, flat bread roll. It is sold in grill bars throughout the country and has no counterpart in food culture at home. Historically, thin, flat bread is a northern Swedish tradition and is usually baked with barley flour into large, thin, flat cakes, either soft or hard. Mashed potatoes and a boiled or grilled hot dog, pickled gherkins, perhaps shrimp salad, mustard and ketchup are placed on soft, thin, flat bread. The thin, flat bread is folded into a packet and eaten with a fork or held in the hand.

During the course of the year there are many different festivities and holidays of which food and meals are a major element. Herring is a recurring festive food and is prepared in a range of flavours. Historically, herring was everyday food. The most important family occasion is the celebration of Christmas, and particularly the meal eaten on Christmas Eve. It is usually served in the form of a Christmas smörgåsbord with many different dishes. Twenty to thirty dishes are not uncommon, and the dishes are eaten in a special order. The meal consists of many traditional types of dishes based on the ancient storehouse economy, such as salted ham, herring and stockfish, but health campaigns have encouraged more vegetable dishes on the menu. Magazines at Christmas often suggest different ways of revitalising the Christmas table. The Christmas meal is usually eaten at home with one's family, sisters and brothers and the older generation. Sometime in December it is also common for employers to invite their employees to a Christmas smörgåsbord as thanks for their efforts during the year.

In the last few decades, the celebration of Easter has developed from a religious family celebration to a more secularised party for friends, when the first spring vegetables are served with lamb, herring and egg dishes. Midsummer is celebrated when the day is at its longest at the summer solstice. It is the most important social festival, when Swedes like to go out into the country or to the archipelago to party together with their families, relatives, friends, and sometimes their colleagues from work. Specific dishes are associated with midsummer celebrations, and if herring, new potatoes and sour cream are not served along with the requisite beer and schnapps – not to mention the longed-for strawberries – many would not consider it a real midsummer party.

Towards the end of the 1990s, the celebration of Halloween has made a breakthrough as a new festive occasion for children and young people, with various pumpkin dishes previously little known in Swedish cuisine. Birthdays are celebrated more than name days, and then coffee, cake and, preferably, biscuits are served.

A savoury "sandwich" layer cake is a common dish at receptions in connection with student graduation, engagement parties and funerals. It is regarded as festive but is also practical when the number of guests is uncertain. A sandwich cake consists of several layers of bread, sometimes of different types, with filling in between. The cake can be up to 40x50 cm in

Tunnbröd (a thin, flat roll) is a favorite Swedish street food.

Julbord. The Christmas smörgåsbord is served both at home and in restaurants and is a way for employers to thank employees for their efforts over the past year.

size and may be square or round in shape. The filling varies depending on how expensive it is to be, but salmon, liver pâté, sausage and smoked meats are common. The sandwich cake is garnished with cream, mayonnaise, sliced lemon, shrimps and dill. It is accompanied by beer or wine.

The three most common everyday dishes at home are Falun sausage (a lightly smoked and boiled sausage), spaghetti with meat sauce and pizza, and those Swedes who do not observe religious dietary rules also eat a great deal of pork. When used to display Swedish cuisine to foreign guests, the food is of a completely different type. Not infrequently, guests are offered a meal characterised by wild and natural foodstuffs, both meat and fish such as moose, grouse and char, and wild berries such as lingonberries, cloudberries and sea buckthorn. This food can be served at Swedish parties for relatives, at wedding receptions and at 50th, 60th and 70th birthday parties. Festive food in the countryside is often of a more traditional type, where greater use is made of cultivated produce, such as potatoes and vegetables in roasts and brown sauce. Party food in the cities, both at home and in restaurants, more closely follows international culinary trends, and the special food shops of immigrant groups can offer a choice that cannot be found in rural areas. Party food also changes in character as a result of the domestic breeding of, for example, ostriches and turkeys; new vegetables and types of edible fungi are now also cultivated.

Some foods and dishes are less frequently offered to foreign guests, and this applies particularly to food in connection with two festivals in August. At the first, most common in the south of Sweden, cold, dill-boiled crayfish are served and eaten out of hand. These are inevitably accompanied by beer, schnapps, spiced cheese and crispbread. The other festival is the northern Swedish fermented Baltic herring feast,

433

The Nobel Foundation banquet, "the party of all parties", is a major event each year. Its menu and content are much commented upon.

where an ancient preserving method has given rise to a herring dish with a singular aroma and pungent taste. Fermented herring is eaten together with potatoes and thin, flat bread; schnapps, beer and sometimes milk alone are drunk with it.

The Nobel Foundation banquet for the Nobel laureates attracts great attention in Sweden. The banquet is generally commented upon, as the contents of the menu are a well-kept secret until the Nobel festivities begin in the evening of 10 December. The menu consists of modern dishes in which traditional but exclusive home-grown produce is combined with foreign seasonings and modern products that are in fashion. The banquet is also staged in an artistic, spectacular manner.

Swedish culinary art today combines traditional products and cooking methods with global culinary ideals. Flavours, textures and shapes are juxtaposed with one another, creating dishes that give rise to conversation and the exchange of ideas. And perhaps, apart from the feeling of satisfaction after a meal, this may well be its most important function, a place to meet and discuss the world we live in, and the world we would like to live in.

Dusan Matic

"The former Yugoslav Republic of Macedonia"

A new regime of nutrition

Macedonia*, standing as it does at the crossroads of Europe and the Orient, has been visited by many different conquerors (Turks, Austro-Hungarians, Germans, and Bulgarians). All have left their mark, and outside influences are still visible in our culture today, especially in our food culture. Even so, Macedonia has managed to retain its own distinctive dishes, and our national cuisine stands apart from the cuisines of our Balkan neighbours.

Potato moussaka

The use of the terms "Macedonia" and "Macedonian" solely represent the view of the author.

Macedonia is also a place where the Mediterranean and continental climates meet. Winters are long and cold, summers hot. The high humidity and dense vegetation, especially in the north-west, result from the fact that Mount Sar Planina has the highest precipitation levels in Europe. Yet only around 100 kilometres to the east lies the Ovce Pole, which has Europe's lowest levels of precipitation. Both extremes permit a wide range of growing conditions for various grains, vegetables, legumes and fruits. Macedonia grows some of the highest-quality fruit in Europe, particularly peaches, cherries and apples. Macedonian honey is also excellent. Artichokes, experimentally produced in various locations, are generally considered to be of high quality, but unfortunately this vegetable is neither well known nor appreciated in Macedonia. The same is true of many other vegetables that are used in central and northern Europe, where the growing conditions are less favourable. The food cultures of these countries are simply more refined.

This was not always the case. During the fourteenth and the beginning of the fifteenth century, before the onset of Ottoman rule, Macedonian food culture was at quite a high level in relation to the food cultures of other European countries, as is evident from frescoes in medieval monasteries. The fresco "The secret dinner", showing Jesus Christ dining with his apostles, depicts knives, forks and spoons, which means that our ancestors were using eating utensils as early as the fourteenth century – well before the rest of Europe.

At that time, in order to gain certain social benefits, part of the population converted to Islam, either willingly or by force. Thus, as in the other Balkan regions under Ottoman occupation, there were in addition to the Orthodox population people who did not profess Christianity, as well as Islamic converts. These regions were multi-denominational and multi-national, even though the Turks succeeded in imposing many of their habits on the population. Under difficult conditions, the exploited and impoverished population had no choice but to cope with the situation.

Families were large, with many mouths to feed, and therefore the daily meals were mainly vegetarian. Over time, in order to improve the taste of these meatless meals, Macedonian housewives developed a specific way of thickening and enriching their food. Fat was heated to a temperature over 100ºC. The Orthodox population used lard (pig fat), while the Muslim population used suet (the fat from cows). Chopped onions were fried in the hot fat until golden,

then flour was stirred in until it turned brown. Finally, ground red pepper was added, and the mixture was mixed in to the meatless dish to continue cooking. This mixture, called zaprška (browned flour), gave the food a specific taste.

The addition of browned flour to food before it finished cooking became standard, even ritual practice. However, heating the oil to such a high temperature and eating foods made with browned flour caused many people to have gastric problems. Nevertheless, browned flour is still omnipresent in the diet of an insufficiently educated populace, Orthodox and Muslim alike. According to medical statistics, gastric disorders are the number one medical problem for the Macedonian population, followed by cardiovascular ones.

After the Ottoman period and up until the First World War, the rural population, due to continuing poverty, prepared and consumed food under very primitive conditions. During and immediately after the Ottoman occupation villagers prepared their meals on a hearth located in the same room where they lived; they warmed themselves by the fire and slept near it on cattails. According to historical and ethnological data, yeastless baked bread or yeast bread in vršnik (which means "to thresh"); boiled cow's, sheep's or goat's milk; bakrdanik (polenta); various baked goods; wild green and vegetable pies; pastrma (beans with cured mutton) or pork were prepared by the villagers at these hearths.

The rural population at that time prepared a unique vegetarian dish known as day labourers' soup or harvesters' salad, which was not known in other countries. Designed for farmers working in the fields during the hot summer days, it was prepared from diluted vinegar, salt, diced cucumber, chopped and pressed garlic, and minced parsley. This dish not only refreshed the farmer's organism, it also lessened his thirst and kept him from perspiring so heavily in the extreme heat. In the winter months especially, both farmers and others drank hot diluted rakija (brandy) and heated wine.

Fruit juices are still an important part of the Macedonian food culture, as they are very nutritious. Juices from forest berries were well known (bilberries, dogberries, raspberries, rose hips, blackberries, and strawberries). Brine (salted water from the preparation of sauerkraut) was used as a traditional non-alcoholic drink in the winter. This brine contains more vitamin C than the cabbage and is a great scurvy preventative. Different teas were also prepared from the abundant aromatic and medicinal herbs growing in the Macedonian mountains: Klamath weed, wild thyme, yarrow, etc. Dairy products such as sour milk, yoghurt and whey were also well known.

Stuffed peppers

A traditional and refreshing drink is bosa/boza, made from millet, which is, due to the yeast present in it, an excellent source of B vitamins.

Over the last few years the basic diet in Macedonia has improved, largely as a result of information reaped from the media and the Internet, as well as from the experiences of Macedonians living abroad. Unfortunately, it is not yet possible for everyone living in Macedonia to improve their food culture. Informed members of society seek to reduce their intake of carbohydrates (pasta/dough, bread, corn, sugar and sugar concentrates), replacing the classic browned flour used for thickening and enriching meals with Béchamel sauce, dry-fried flour, or cold-pressed olive oil. They are trying to follow the

"The former Yugoslav Republic of Macedonia"

dietary guidelines of the Mediterranean countries, which are considered the healthiest in the world.

Extended cooking, which reduces the nutritional value of food, is still widely practiced in Macedonia. However, informed people have lately begun to cook intensively with steam, following Italian methods. The prepared food should be consumed al dente instead of being overcooked. As far as changes in our eating habits are concerned, we are trying in part to adopt French manners, as we greatly respect the French contribution to world cuisine.

Ajvar (a dish of chopped aubergine and peppers)

Given our fertile soil and propitious climate, people here should be very healthy. Instead, our eating habits brought us close to becoming a sick nation. Even though the old Slavic people were farmers, their daily diet consisted mainly of carbohydrates (various forms of dough, pastries, pies, polenta, bread, etc.). This was not always the case. The Turkish traveler Evlija Celebi

wrote in 1660-1668 about the dietary habits of the urban population and the monks during the period of Ottoman rule in Macedonia. He noted that the Macedonian diet consisted mainly of mutton, lamb and chicken; pigeon and goose were also eaten. Bean soups were ubiquitous. People drank sherbet, mead, raspberry juice and grape juice (must). Celebi was particularly interested in the diet of the small, picturesque town of Struga, where the river Crn Drim flows into Ohrid Lake. There people ate fish, eels, pike, Ohrid trout, carp and Belvica fish. Celebi notes that people ate eel to cure headaches. He visited six Christian monasteries in Ohrid, where the priests were preparing excellent traditional specialities and giving away the surplus food to the Muslim population. He also mentions that while in Macedonia he tried twenty-six types of compotes made from different stewed fruits, each with its own excellent taste and aroma.

It should be stressed that the new foods brought to Europe after the discovery of America were introduced into Macedonia much later than in the European countries not under Turkish domination. For instance, Macedonians did not eat fresh red tomatoes until 1918, after seeing French soldiers on the Thessalonica front enjoy them. Even today, eastern Macedonians from Strumica and Radovis refer to fresh tomatoes as "frenki".

Under Turkish rule traditional foods included polenta (cooked corn meal), bungur (crumbled corn meal), tarana – dough pellets (dried and grated dough), pit-ulici – doughnuts (fried dough), vitkalnik – pie (baked coiled layers of cornmeal dough); pastrmajli-ja – pie (baked dough with cured mutton), zelnik – pie (wild green and vegetable pie), popara (bread soaked in warm milk), meatless beans (bean stew), tavce-gravce (beans baked in an earthenware dish), pastrma (cured mutton), different types of pickled foods (vegetables preserved with vinegar), and coun-try-style meat (various cuts of red meat). Some of the specialities of Macedonian cuisine feature their place of origin: Ohrid-style trout, Struga-style eel, Prespa-style carp, Pestani-style trout, Doyran-style carp, Ovce Pole-style pastrmajlija, Strumica-style pastrma-jlija, Vardar-style pot, Bitola-style tripe.

As for traditional alcoholic drinks, there is wine and rakija (brandy). Quality wines may be white or red, dry or semi-dry, depending on the sugar content and whether or not it has fermented into alcohol. Rakija (brandy) is a native product from the Macedonian wine regions. It can be a grape wine or thin wine dis-tillate, or a fermented fruit distillate (plum, apple, pear, cherry, etc.). Examples of outstanding brandies from Macedonia include Strumica mastika, Veles yellow rakija (brandy), Ohrid komova (grape) and Velgosti cherry rakija (brandy).

Macedonia has many religious rituals: domestic fam-ily feasts, feasts for the whole village, guild feasts (each craft has its own patron), promise to a saint for wishes granted, calendar religious holidays,

Zaoruvanje (Plowing Day), Zadusnica (All Soul's Day), Procka (Forgiveness Day), Todor's Saturday, weddings and others. The Muslim population cele-brates Bairam and Kurban Bairam, while the Roma/Gypsies have Gjurgjovden (St George's Day), celebrated for three days during which lamb must be consumed.

"Princess" doughnuts

During the holidays people organise lavish feasts to which they invite relatives and friends. It is impor-tant to mention that both Muslim and Orthodox feasts welcome uninvited guests as well. Entertaining uninvited guests is a characteristic fea-ture of both Christian and the Muslim feasts in Macedonia and a sign of their special hospitality.

Since the fourteenth century our people have pre-pared their meals in earthenware (terracotta) dishes of different shapes; they are often ornately decorated. Some of these earthenware dishes are pots for cook-ing the food, pans or small pans for preparing the unique Macedonian speciality tavce-gravce (beans baked in an earthenware dish) and other types of

439

baked foods. Crepnja was an earthenware dish used for baking bread, pies or other dishes. It had a metal vrsnik or handle. In order for the food to bake properly, the dish was covered with embers and ash. In addition to earthenware, tin-coated copper pans were also used, such as the djum, a dish for water, and cups, which could also be made of ceramic. A bakarnik (tin-covered kettle) was often used to heat water.

Both Christianity and Islam have rules for temporary fasting. The Orthodox fasts and the Muslim fast of Ramadan are very strict and therefore not recommended for children or for those who are elderly or ill. Orthodox fasts forbid meat, all products of animal origin and, on certain days, even all fats and oils. The Catholic fasts are easier to endure since they preclude only the consumption of meat. The spiritual aspect is most important for all types of religious fasts, while the secular aspect – the purification of the organism – may be achieved through appropriate diet.

At Macedonian feasts the manner of serving abundant food is very interesting. Unlike elsewhere in Europe, all of the food is set out on the table at once so that each guest may take whatever he or she wants and eat it freely. Our well-served guests are eager to return to the table and try some of the specialities we offer for fast days and feast days. Sveti Nikole is meatless sarma (stuffed rolls) made of leek, rice and leaves of soured cabbage; meatless tavce-gravce is made with dry peppers, mint and fried fish. During the holidays, when meat-eating is allowed, roast pork, veal, lamb and chicken are most often served with different cooked vegetables and salads on the side. The Macedonian dish turlitava, made from three types of roasted meat (lamb, veal and pork) and several different vegetables, primarily okra, is also worthy of mention.

For family feasts a special type of pie is prepared from sourdough, which is specially decorated with figures of fresh dough that express the wishes and fantasies of the hostess. For the holiday Badnik (Christmas Eve) a different sort of pie is made. Thin coils of fresh dough are browned on a hot burner, then layered with oil, sugar, nuts and water. This pie is covered with a thin layer of dough and baked in the oven. On Christmas Eve the whole family gathers to enjoy a meatless meal including nuts, figs, chestnuts and almonds. Before dinner, a small loaf of bread

Country-style meat

©State Caterer High School "Lazar Tanev"

baked with a coin inside is divided among the family members; whoever gets the coin hopes for good fortune throughout the coming year. In some parts of Macedonia this bread is prepared for the 14 January holiday of Vasilica, the Orthodox New Year.

Even though Macedonians have retained their traditional holiday diet, our country is ready to embrace the new science of nutrition. Today, the average Macedonian family tries to avoid fast food, and home cooks are learning to shorten cooking times to preserve vitamins, to cook with steam, not to heat fats to such high temperatures, and to use cold-pressed olive oil. They also try to start the day with fresh fruits, not skip daily meals, to balance cooked foods with fresh (salads), and to avoid large quantities of white bread in favour of smaller amounts of wholegrain bread. All of these steps are an effort to improve the dietary standards of our people, and thereby to improve the quality of life.

Fahriye Hazer Sancar

T u r k e y

The tastes of a splendid heritage

"Do not dismiss the dish saying that it is just food. The blessed thing is an entire civilisation in itself!"

Abdulhak Şinasi

The variety of dishes that make up Turkish cuisine, the ways they all come together, and their evident intricacy offer enough material for lifelong study and enjoyment. It is not always easy to discern a basic element or a single dominant feature – like Italian pasta or French sauce – but whether in a humble home, at a famous restaurant, or at dinner in a Bey's mansion, familiar patterns are always present. Turkish cuisine is a rare art which satisfies the senses while reconfirming the higher order of society, community and culture.

A practical-minded child watching mother cook cabbage dolma on a lazy, grey winter day is bound to wonder: "Who on earth discovered this peculiar combination of sautéed rice, pine nuts, currants, spices, and herbs all tightly wrapped in translucent leaves of cabbage, each roll exactly half an inch thick? How was it possible to transform this humble vegetable to such heights with so few additional ingredients? And how can such a yummy dish possibly also be good for you?"

The modern mind, in a moment of contemplation, has similar thoughts upon entering a modest shop where baklava is the generic cousin of a dozen or so sophisticated sweet pastries with names like twisted turban, sultan, saray (palace), lady's navel, or nightingale's nest. The same experience awaits you at a muhallebici (pudding shop) where a dozen different types of milk puddings are served.

One can only conclude that the evolution of this glorious cuisine was not an accident, but rather, as with the other grand cuisines of the world, a result of the combination of three key elements: a nurturing environment, an imperial kitchen, and a long social tradition. A nurturing environment is key. Turkey is known for an abundance of foodstuffs due to its rich flora, fauna and diverse geographic regions. Secondly, the legacy of the imperial kitchen is inescapable. Hundreds of cooks, all specialising in different types of dishes, influenced the cuisine as we know it today. The palace kitchen – supported by a complex social organisation, a vibrant urban life, specialised labour, worldwide trade, and total control of the Spice Road – reflected the flourishing of culture in the capital of a mighty empire. Finally, the longevity of social organisation must also be taken into account. The Turkish state of Anatolia is a millennium old and so, naturally, is its cuisine. As Ibn'i Haldun wrote, "The religion of the king, in time, becomes that of the people," which also holds true for the king's food. Thus, the 600-year reign of the Ottoman dynasty and the exceptional cultural transition into modern Turkey led to the evolution of a grand cuisine through differentiation, the refinement and perfection of dishes, and the sequence and combination of the meals at which they are served.

It is quite rare when all three of the above conditions are met, as they are in French, Chinese and Turkish cuisine. Turkey has the added benefit of being at the crossroads of the Far East and the Mediterranean, resulting in a long and complex history of migration from the steppes of Central Asia (where the Turks mingled with the Chinese) to Europe (where their influence was felt all the way to Vienna).

Such unique characteristics and extensive history have bestowed upon Turkish cuisine a rich selection of dishes, all of which can be prepared and combined with others to create meals of almost infinite variety, but always in a non-arbitrary way. This has led to a cuisine that is open to improvisation through development of regional styles while still retaining its deep structure, as all great works of art do. Turkish cuisine is also an integral aspect of our culture. It is a part of the rituals of everyday life and reflects spirituality through symbolism and practice.

Lamb kebab

© Ministry of Tourism

A nurturing environment

Early historical documents show that the basic structure of Turkish cuisine was already established during the Nomadic Period and in the first settled Turkish States of Asia. Attitudes towards meat, dairy products, vegetables and grains that characterised this early period still make up the core of Turkish culinary thinking. Early Turks cultivated wheat and used it liberally in several types of leavened and unleavened breads, either baked in clay ovens, fried on a griddle, or buried in embers. Mantı (dumplings) and buğra (the ancestor of börek, or filled pastries, named after Buğra Khan of Türkestan) were already among the much-coveted dishes of the time. Stuffing not only the pastry, but also all kinds of vegetables, was common practice, and still is, as evidenced by dozens of different types of dolma. Convenient staples of the pastoral Turks included meat that was skewered and grilled in other ways (later known to us as varieties of kebab) and dairy products such as cheeses and yogurt. These practices were introduced into Anatolia in the eleventh century. There the Turks encountered rice, local fruits and vegetables, and hundreds of varieties of fish in the three seas surrounding the Anatolian Peninsula. These wonderful new ingredients were assimilated into the basic cuisine in the millennium that followed.

Anatolia is known as the "bread basket of the world"; even today, Turkey is one of the seven countries in the world that produces enough food to feed its own populace and still has plenty to export. Turkey encompasses such a wide variety of geographic zones that for every two to four hours of driving, you will find yourself in a different landscape, temperature, altitude, humidity, vegetation and weather. The Turkish landscape combines characteristics of the world's three oldest continents (Europe, Africa, and Asia) and has an ecological diversity surpassing that of any other country along the 40th latitude. The cuisine of Turkey is as diverse as its landscape, with as many regional variations.

In the eastern region, you will encounter rugged, snow-capped mountains, where the winters are long and cold. In the highlands, where spring with its abundant wildflowers and rushing creeks extends into long, cool summers, livestock farming is prevalent. Here, butter, yoghurt, cheese, honey, meat and cereals are the local foods. Long winters are best endured with the help of yoghurt soup and meatballs flavoured with aromatic mountain herbs, followed by endless servings of tea.

The heartland is dry steppe with rolling hills and endless stretches of wheat fields and barren bedrock that take on the most incredible shades of gold, violet, and grey as the sun moves through the sky. Along the trade routes were ancient cities with lush cultivated orchards and gardens. Among these, Konya, the capital of the Selçuk Empire (the first

Turkey

Turkish State in Anatolia), distinguished itself in the thirteenth century as the centre of a culture that attracted scholars, mystics and poets from all over the world. The lavish cuisine that is enjoyed in Konya today, with its clay-oven (tandır) kebabs, böreks, meat and vegetable dishes and helva desserts, dates back to the feasts given by Sultan Alaaddin Keykubad in AD 1237.

Towards the west, one eventually reaches warm, fertile valleys between cultivated mountainsides, and the lacy shores of the Aegean where nature is friendly and life has always been relaxed. Fruits and vegetables of all kinds are abundant; best of all is the seafood. Here, olive oil is a staple, used in both hot and cold dishes.

To the north, the temperate zone of the Black Sea coast is protected by the high Caucasus mountains; it abounds in hazelnuts, corn and tea. The Black Sea people are fishermen and identify with the shimmering hamsi, a small fish similar to the anchovy. There are at least forty different dishes made with hamsi, including desserts! Many poems, anecdotes and folk dances have been inspired by this delicious fish.

The south-eastern part of Turkey is hot and desert-like, offering the greatest variety of kebabs and sweet pastries. Dishes here are spicier compared to all other regions, possibly to retard spoilage in hot weather – or, as the natives say, to equalise the heat inside the body and out.

The culinary centre of the country is the Marmara region, including Thrace, with Istanbul as its queen city. This temperate, fertile region boasts a wide variety of fruits and vegetables, as well as the most delicately flavoured lamb. The variety of fish that travel the Bosphorus surpasses that of other seas. Bolu, a city in the mountains, once supplied the greatest cooks for the Sultan's palace, and even now the best chefs in the country come from Bolu.

The Imperial palace kitchen

The importance of the culinary art to the Ottoman sultans is evident to every visitor to Topkapı Palace. The sultans' huge kitchens were housed in several buildings under ten domes. By the seventeenth century some 1300 kitchen staff lived in the palace. Hundreds of cooks, specialising in different categories, such as soups, pilafs, kebabs, vegetables, fish, breads, pastries, beverages, candy and helva, and syrups and jams, fed as many as 10 000 people a day, and additional trays of food were sent to other city dwellers as a royal favour.

The importance of food is also evident in the structure of the Ottoman military elite, the Janissaries. The commanders of the main divisions were known as the Soupmen. Other high-ranking officers included the

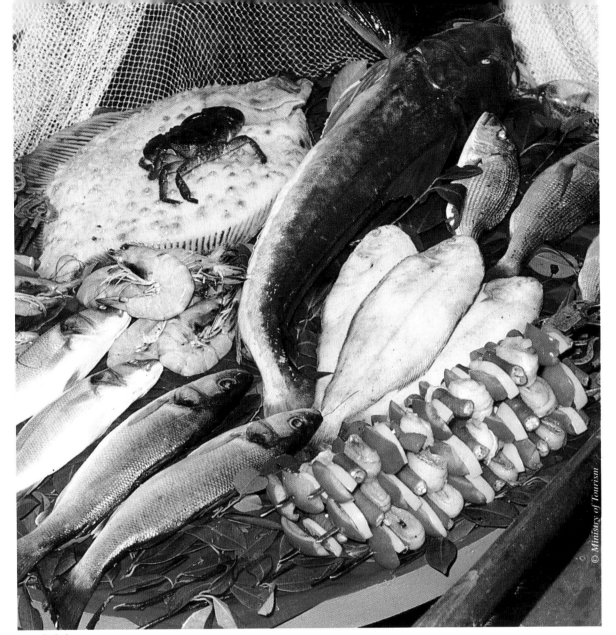

Fresh fish

chief cook, the scullion, the baker, and the pancake maker, though their duties had little to do with food. The huge cauldron used to make pilaf had a special, symbolic significance for the Janissaries, and was the focal point of each division. The kitchen was, at the same time, the centre of politics, for whenever the Janissaries demanded a change in the sultan's cabinet, or the head of a grand vizier, they would overturn their pilaf cauldron. "Overturning the cauldron" is an expression still used today to indicate a rebellion in the ranks.

It was in this environment that hundreds of the sultans' chefs, who dedicated their lives to their profession, developed and perfected the dishes of Turkish cuisine, which were then adopted in areas stretching from the Balkans to southern Russia, and even as far as North Africa. Because Istanbul was at that time the

447

capital of the world, with great prestige, its ways were widely imitated. It was also supported by an enormous infrastructure, which enabled all the treasures of the world to flow into the city. The provinces of the vast Ottoman Empire were integrated by a system of trade routes with caravanserais to refresh the weary merchants and security forces. The Spice Road, an important factor in culinary history, was under the full control of the Sultan. Only the best ingredients were allowed to be traded according to strict standards established by the courts.

Guilds played an important role in the development and maintenance of Turkish cuisine. These included hunters, fishermen, cooks, kebab cooks, bakers, butchers, cheese makers and yoghurt merchants, pastry chefs, pickle makers, and sausage merchants. All of the principal trades were believed to be sacred, and each guild traced its patronage to the saints. The guilds set price and quality controls. On special occasions, such as the circumcision festivities for the crown prince or religious holidays, they displayed their products and talents in spectacular parades through the Istanbul streets.

Following the example of the palace, all of the grand Ottoman houses boasted elaborate kitchens and competed to prepare feasts for one another as well as for the general public. In fact, in each neighbourhood, at least one household would open its doors to anyone who happened to stop by for dinner during the holy month of Ramadan, or during other festive occasions. In this way the traditional cuisine evolved and spread, even to the most modest corners of the country.

Great food places

Without a systematic approach, the wide variety of dishes in Turkish cuisine – each with its unique combination of ingredients and its own methods of preparation and presentation – might appear overwhelming. Grains (rice and wheat) and vegetables are the foundation of Turkish cuisine. However, all Turkish dishes can conveniently be placed in the following categories: grain-based foods; grilled meat; vegetables; seafood; desserts; and beverages.

Each category of dishes contains only one or two types of main ingredients. Turks are purists in their culinary taste; that is, each dish is supposed to bring out the flavor of the main ingredient rather than hiding it under sauces or spices. Thus, aubergine should taste like aubergine, lamb like lamb, pumpkin like pumpkin, and so on. Contrary to the prevalent western impression of Turkish food, spices and herbs are used very simply and sparingly. For example, either mint or dill is used with

Borek (cooked dough)

courgette; parsley is used with aubergine; a few cloves of garlic have their place in some cold vegetable dishes; and cumin is sprinkled over red lentil soup or mixed into ground meat when making köfte (meatballs). Lemon and yoghurt are used to complement both meat and vegetable dishes, as well as to balance the taste of olive oil or meat. Most desserts and fruit dishes do not call for any spices, so their flavours are refined and subtle.

There are major classes of meatless dishes. When meat is used, it is used sparingly. Even with the meat kebabs, the pide or flat bread is the largest part of the dish, alongside vegetables or yoghurt. Turkish cuisine also boasts a variety of authentic desserts and beverages.

For the Turks, the setting is as important as the food itself. Among the great food places are the weekly neighbourhood markets (pazar) and the permanent markets, the most famous of which is Istanbul's Spice Market, where ever since pre-Ottoman times every conceivable type of food item has been found. This is a truly exotic place, with hundreds of scents rising from stalls located within an ancient domed building, which was the terminus for the Spice Road. More modest markets can be found in every city centre, with permanent stalls for fish and vegetables.

The weekly markets are where sleepy neighbourhoods come to life, with the villagers setting up their stalls before dawn to sell their products. On these days, handicrafts, textiles, glassware and other household items are also displayed at the most affordable prices. What makes these places unique is the cacophony of sounds, sights, smells and activity, as well as the high quality of fresh foods obtainable only at the pazar. There is plenty of haggling and jostling as people make their way through the narrow isles while vendors compete for their attention.

Food protocol for the culturally correct

© Ministry of Tourism

Eating is taken very seriously in Turkey. It is inconceivable for household members to eat alone, raid the refrigerator, or eat on the go while others are at home. It is customary to have three sit-down meals a day. Breakfast or kahvaltı (literally, "under the coffee") typically consists of bread, feta cheese, black olives and tea. Many workplaces have lunch served as a fringe benefit. Dinner starts when all the family members get together and share the events of the day at the table. The menu consists of three or more types of dishes that are eaten sequentially, accompanied by salad. In summer, dinner is served at about 8 p.m.

449

Close relatives, best friends or neighbours may unexpectedly join in on meals. Others are invited ahead of time, as elaborate preparations are expected. The menu depends on whether alcoholic drinks will be served or not. In the former case, the guests will find the meze spread ready on the table, frequently set up either in the garden or on the balcony. The main course is served several hours later. Otherwise, the dinner starts with a soup, followed by the main meat and vegetable course accompanied by the salad. Then the olive-oil dishes such as dolmas are served, followed by dessert and fruit. While the table is cleared, the guests retire to the living room to have tea and Turkish coffee.

Women get together for afternoon tea at regular intervals (referred to as the "7-17 days") with their school friends and neighbours. These are very elaborate occasions with at least a dozen types of cakes, pastries, finger foods and böreks prepared by the hostess. The main purpose of these gatherings is to gossip and share experiences about all aspects of life, both public and private. Naturally, one very important function is the sharing of recipes. Diligent exchanges occur while women consult one another on their innovations and solutions to culinary challenges.

By now it should be clear that the concept of having a "pot-luck" at someone's house is entirely foreign to the Turks. The responsibility of supplying all the food rests squarely on the host, who expects to be treated the same way in return. There are two occasions where the notion of host does not apply. One is when neighbours collaborate to make large quantities of food for the winter, such as tarhana (dried yoghurt and tomato soup) or noodles. Another is when families get together to go on a day's excursion into the countryside. Arrangements are made ahead of time as to who will make the köfte, dolma, salads and pilafs, and who will supply the meat, the beverages and the fruits. The mangal (a copper charcoal burner), kilims, hammocks, pillows, musical instruments such as saz, ud, or violin, and samovars are also loaded up for the day trip.

These occasions, often referred to as "stealing a day from fate", are much more than a simple picnic. As numerous songs tell us, Küçüksu, Kalamış, and Heybeli in old Istanbul used to be typical locations for such outings. Other memorable locations include the Meram vineyards in Konya, Lake Hazar in Elazığ, and Bozcaada off the shores of Çanakkale. The 5 May spring festival (Hıdırellez) commemorating Saints Hızır and Ilyas (representing immortality and abundance) marks the beginning of the pleasure season (safa) with lots of poetry, songs and, naturally, good food.

A similar safa used to be the weekly trip to the Turkish bath. Food prepared the day before would be packed on horse-drawn carts along with fresh clothing and scented soaps. After spending the morning at the marble washbasins and steam hall, people would retire to wooden settees to rest, eat and dry off before returning home.

Nowadays such leisurely affairs are all but gone, spoiled by modern life. Yet families still attempt to steal at least one day from fate every year, even though fate often triumphs. Packing food for trips is so traditional that even now, it is common for mothers to pack some köfte, dolma and börek for an airplane flight, especially on long trips, much to the bemusement of other passengers and the irritation of flight attendants. But, seriously, given the quality of airline food, who can blame them?

Weddings, circumcision ceremonies, and holidays are celebrated with feasts. At a wedding feast in Konya, a seven-course meal is served to the guests. The sit-down meal starts with a soup, followed by pilaf and roast meat, meat dolma, and saffron rice, a traditional wedding dessert. Börek is served before the second dessert, which is typically semolina helva. The meal ends with okra cooked with tomatoes, onions and butter, with lots of lemon juice. This wedding feast is typical of Anatolia, with slight regional variations.

Sofra (main course)

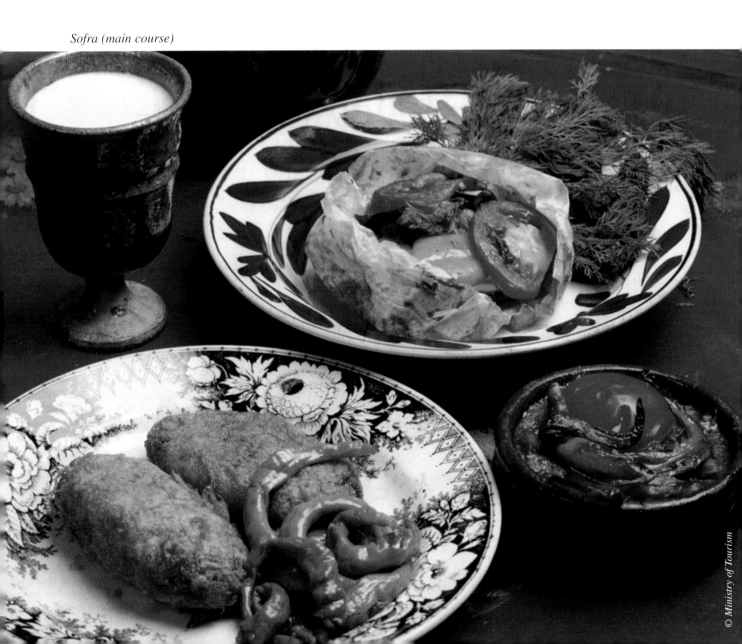

The morning after the wedding the groom's family sends trays of baklava to the bride's family.

During the holidays, people are expected to pay short visits to each and every friend within the city, which are immediately reciprocated. Three or four days are spent going from house to house, so enough food needs to be prepared and put aside to last throughout the visits. During the holidays, kitchens and pantries burst at the seams with böreks, rice dolmas, puddings and desserts that can be put on the table without much preparation.

Death is also an occasion for cooking and sharing food. In this case, neighbours prepare and send dishes to the bereaved household for three days following the death. The only dish prepared by the household of the deceased is helva, which is sent to the neighbours and served to visitors. In some areas, it is customary for a good friend of the deceased to begin

Nar Suyu (pomegranate juice)

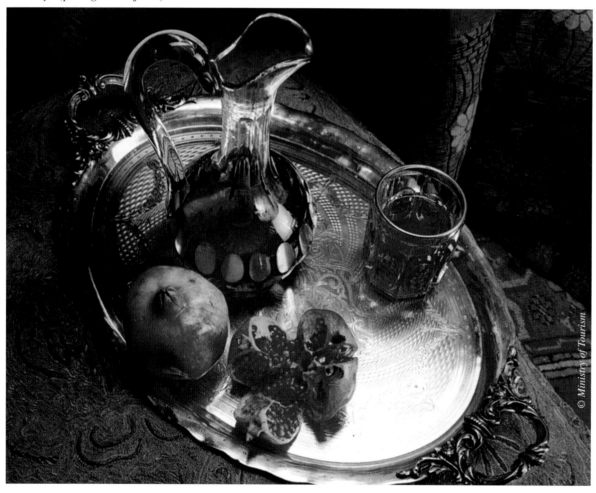

preparing the helva while recounting fond memories and events. Then the spoon is passed to the next person, who takes up the stirring and continues to reminisce. Usually the helva is done by the time everyone in the room has had a chance to speak. This wonderfully simple ceremony allows the people left behind to speak about happier times; it lightens their grief momentarily, strengthening the bond between them.

Food and spirituality

Food and dietary practices have always played an important part in religion. Among the world's religions, Islam perhaps imposes the most elaborate and strict rules regarding food. In practice, these rules have been reinterpreted in regional adaptations, particularly in Turkey, where it is harder to find strict Muslims. In Anatolia, where a variety of Sufi orders once flourished, food gained a spiritual dimension beyond dry religious requirements, as can be seen in the poetry, music, and local practices.

Paradoxically, the month of Ramadan, when all Muslims are expected to fast from dawn to dusk, is also a month of feasting and charitable feeding of those who are in need. Fasting is meant to purify the body and the soul and, at the same time, to nurture a reverence for all blessings bestowed by nature and cooked by a skillful chef. The days are spent preparing food for the breaking of the fast at sunset. It is customary to break the fast by eating a bite of "heavenly" food, such as olives or dates, and by nibbling lightly on a variety of cheeses, sausages, jams and pide. Then come the evening prayers, followed by the main meal. In the old days, the rest of the night would be occupied by games and conversation, or by going into town to attend various concerts and plays, until it was time to eat again just before the firing of the cannon or the beating of the drums that marked the beginning of the next day's fast. People would rest until noon, when shops and workplaces opened and food preparation began.

The other major religious holiday is the Sacrifice Festival commemorating Abraham's readiness to sacrifice his son to God. But God sent Abraham a ram instead, sparing his son's life. The sheep is revered as the creature of God that gives its life for a higher purpose. The henna colouring on the sheep is a symbolic way of showing this respect, as are the strict instructions for its slaughter. Some of the butchered animal's meat is sent to neighbours and to the needy.

Several occasions commemorating prophets also involve food. The six holy nights marking events in Mohammed's life are celebrated by baking special pastries, breads and lokma. The month of Muharrem occurred when the floodwaters receded and Noah and his family were able to land. It is believed that they then cooked a meal using whatever remained in their supplies. This event is celebrated by cooking aşure, or Noah's pudding, made of wheat berries, dried legumes, rice, raisins, currants, dried figs, dates and nuts. You can also taste this most nourishing pudding at certain muhallebi shops.

The feast of Zachariah is prepared whenever one's wish is granted. It consists of a spread of forty-one different types of dried fruits and nuts. Prayers are read, and all of the guests taste all forty-one foods. A guest can then burn a candle and make a wish. If the wish comes true, that person is obligated to prepare a similar Zachariah table for others.

Beyond these practices, examples of religious tradition imbued with food metaphors are found in Sufism in general, and in the poetry of Mevlana Celaleddin Rumi in particular, as well as in the verses of classical Turkish poetry and music. In fact, understanding the full meaning of this spiritual tradition is impossible without deciphering the references to food and wine, cooking, eating, and intoxication. Mevlana, who lived in Konya in the thirteenth century AD, represents an approach to Sufism that follows the way of love to divine reality, rather than knowledge, or gnosis. As mentioned earlier, the food-related guilds and the Janissaries also followed the Sufi Order. A clash of philosophies about food is told in a story about Empress Eugenie's French chef, who was sent to the Sultan's kitchen to learn how to cook an aubergine dish. He soon begged to be excused from this impossible task, saying that when he took his books and scales with him, the Turkish chef threw them out the window, because "an Imperial chef must learn to cook with his feelings, his eyes and his nose" – in other words, with love!

Asceticism, rather than hedonistic gluttony, is associated with Sufism, and yet food occupies an important place. Followers of the order began with the simplest menial duties in dervish lodges, which always included huge kitchens. After 1 001 days of service, the novice would become fully "cooked", a full member of the brotherhood. In other woods, being "cooked" refers to spiritual maturity. One wonders if the Turkish tradition of cooking everything until it is soft and well-done has anything to do with this association (cooking al dente has no meaning to Turks).

The story of the chickpea told by Mevlana in his *Mathnawi* is a superb example of this idea. When the tough legume is cooked in boiling water, it complains to the woman cooking it. She explains that the cooking is necessary so that it can be eaten by human beings, become part of human life, and thus be elevated to a higher form. The fable of the chickpea describes the suffering of the soul before its arrival at divine love. The peasant eating helva for the first time symbolizes the discovery of divine love by the dervish. There is also the image of Allah preparing helva for the true dervishes. In this particular verse, the whole universe, as it were, is pictured as a huge pan with the stars as cooks! In other verses, the beloved is described as being as tasty as salt, or as a friend who has "lips of sugar". Wine also rep-

Tatli Sofrasi (mixed dairy sweets)

resents the maturation of the human soul, similar to the ordeal the sour grape endures. So many mystical meanings are attributed to wine that the word "tavern" stands for the Sufi hospice, and experiencing divine love is described by the metaphor of intoxication.

These mystical ideas are still very much alive in present-day Turkey, where food and liquor are enjoyed with recitations of mystical poetry and dignified conversation. Often these gatherings provide an occasion for people to distance themselves from earthly matters and transcend into mysticism and promises of a better life hereafter.

Contemporary concerns: diet and health

Yet, as modernity takes hold, traditions are falling by the wayside. Spirituality as a guide for conduct in everyday life is something of the past; now we turn to science for answers. Ironically, however, even as McDonald's and Pizza Huts are popping up

everywhere, the traditional way of eating is making a comeback. What our grandmothers knew all the time is now being confirmed by modern science: a diet fundamentally based on grains, vegetables and fruits with meat and dairy products used sparingly is a

455

healthy one. Furthermore, some combinations are better than others for balanced nutrition. The Food Pyramid endorsed by the United States Department of Agriculture resembles age-old practices in ordinary Turkish households. Even the well-known menus of boarding schools or army kitchens, hardly known for their gourmet characteristics, provide excellent nutrition that can be justified by the best of today's scientific knowledge. One such combination, jokingly referred to as "our national food," is beans and pilaf, accompanied by pickles and quince compote – a perfectly nourishing combination which provides essential proteins, carbohydrates and minerals. Another curious practice is combining spinach with yoghurt. Now we know that the body needs the calcium found in the yoghurt to assimilate the iron found in the spinach.

Yoghurt, which the Turks contributed to the world, has also become a popular health food. A staple in the Turkish diet, it has been known all along for its detoxifying properties. Other beliefs about Turkish food, not yet supported by modern science, include the role of the onion, used liberally in all dishes, in strengthening the immune system; the benefits of garlic for high blood pressure; and olive oil as a remedy for forty-one ailments. Given what we know about health food today, one might envy the typical lunch fare of the Turkish construction worker who eats bread, feta cheese and fresh grapes in the summer and bread and tahini helva in the winter. The variety of pastry turnovers with cheese or ground meat, meat pide, or kebabs is fast food for millions of working people. These foods are all prepared fresh, using age-old practices.

One of the main culprits in the modern-day diet is the snack – junk food designed to give a quick sugar high. Again, modern science has come to the rescue, and healthy snacks are now being discovered. Some of these are amazingly familiar to the Turks. Take, for example, fruit roll-ups. Visit any dried-food store that sells nuts and fruits, and you will see the authentic version, sheets of mashed and dried apricots and grapes. These stores carry many other items that await the discovery of some pioneering entrepreneur from western markets.

Another wholesome snack, known as trail mix or "gorp," is well-known to all Turkish mothers, who traditionally stuff a handful of mixed nuts and raisins into the pockets of their children's school uniform to snack on before exams. This practice can be traced to ancient fables, where the hero goes on a diet of hazelnuts and raisins before fighting with the giants and dragons, or before weaving the king a golden smock. The prince always loads onto the mythological bird, the Zümrüt Anka, forty sacks of nuts and raisins for himself, and water and meat for the bird that takes him over the high Caucasus Mountains.

As far as food goes, it is reassuring to know that we are rediscovering what is good for our bodies. Nevertheless, one is left with the nagging feeling that such knowledge will always be incomplete as long as it is divorced from its cultural context and metaphysical traditions. The challenge facing modern Turkey is to achieve such continuity in a time of genetic engineering, high-tech mass production and the growing number of convenience-oriented households. But for now, the markets are vibrant and the dishes are tastier than ever, so enjoy!

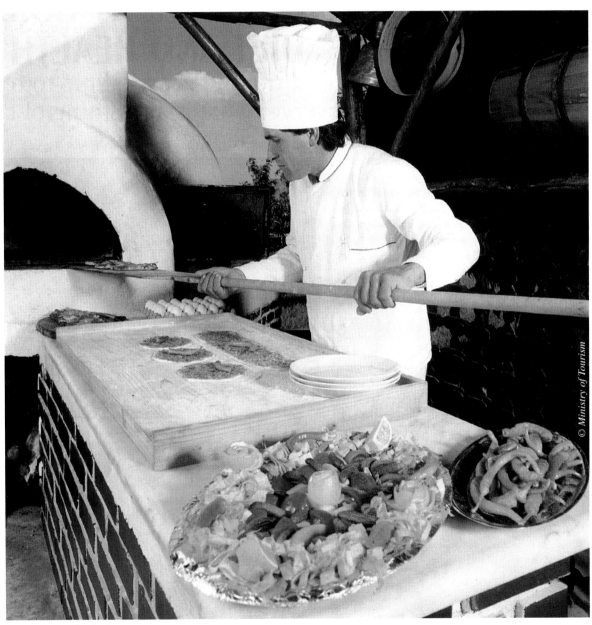

Special dough chef

Turkey

Oksana Y. Vassyl'ieva

Ukraine

The pleasures of good food

Located in the very heart of Europe (Europe's geographical centre is situated near the town of Rakhiv in the Transcarpathian region), Ukraine has long been famous as the breadbasket of Europe, thanks to its fertile black soil, the so-called "chornozem". The history of our land dates back to the fourth to third millennia BC, when the Trypillya civilisation developed an extremely rich culture of grain farmers. Because of its fertile lands and advantageous geographical position, Ukraine has frequently been the object of foreign invasions and devastation. Even in the twentieth century the Ukrainian people endured a devastating man-made famine caused by Stalin's collectivisation programme, which in 1932-1933 killed 8 to 10 million people.

Despite historical hardships, Ukrainians remain open-hearted and hospitable, and our country continues to attract visitors by offering one the most delicious cuisines in the world, famous for its diversity, high nutritional value and excellent taste.

For ages Ukrainians led a settled way of life on their farmlands, growing grains, fruit and vegetables. So it

Young Ukrainian woman enjoying vegetables from a traditional pot

is no wonder that various cereals and their by-products, fruits, vegetables, milk and meat became the traditional ingredients of Ukrainian cuisine.

Each region of Ukraine practices its own way of cooking and boasts its own local produce, fish, meat and dairy products. Each also has its own food. For a Galician this might include milk-and-noodle soup or string-bean zatyranka; for a Poltavian – buckwheat flour halushky (dumplings) with sour cream; for a Volynian – nalysnyky (thin pancakes stuffed with farmer's cheese); and for a Polissyan – deruny (potato pancakes). Such Ukrainian specialities as varenyky (boiled filled dumplings) and borshch are universal.

With its ancient history, Ukraine is a treasure house of old recipes. These include our famous varenyky – half-moon-shaped boiled dumplings that can be filled with potatoes, cheese, meat, fruit, or berries. Each region has its own special type. Hutsulian varenyky are usually filled with berries and mushrooms from the local forests, or with garden fruits and vegetables. Varenyky from the Poltava region are steamed rather than boiled, and they are as large as a fist.

Borshch is the national soup, made from up to twenty ingredients, including beetroots, cabbage, carrots, onions, red pepper, and potatoes. There are more than 100 known borshch recipes, including variations with mushrooms and assorted produce. Each housewife has a special recipe of her own: some add beans, while others use halushky, chicken or corned meat.

Most Ukrainian cooking is based on sophisticated recipes and mixed methods. Stuffing and oven-baking are widely practiced. Ukrainians make holubtsi (baked cabbage rolls stuffed with meat and rice), kruchenyky,

Ukrainian vegetarian borshch

Ingredients
1 cabbage, finely chopped – 1.5 litres water
1 tablespoon oil – 1 onion, finely chopped
2 carrots, chopped – 2 beetroots, chopped or grated – 1 red pepper, chopped
2 potatoes, cut into cubes – 1 can red or white beans in water – 3-5 tablespoons tomato sauce
1 bay leaf – 3-5 black peppercorns
1/4 cup chopped fresh parsley or 2 teaspoons dried parsley – 1/2 cup chopped fresh dill – Salt and ground black pepper to taste.

Method
Cook cabbage in a pot of water on low heat for 15 to 20 minutes.

Meanwhile, heat oil in a large pan and cook the onion until soft. Add carrots and cook for 3 to 5 minutes. Add beetroot and just enough water to cover the vegetables. Cook for 5 to 7 minutes.
Transfer onions, carrots and beetroots into the cabbage pot and cook for 3 to 5 minutes.
Add red pepper, potatoes and beans. Simmer for 5 minutes. Add tomato sauce, bay leaf and black peppercorns. Simmer for 7 to 10 minutes. Add parsley and dill.
Add salt and ground black pepper to taste.
Serve hot with sour cream, chives, garlic or onion, and with rye or black bread.

baked and roasted meat and delicious sausage. A substantial part of the daily Ukrainian diet is devoted to fish. If sauces are used, sour ones such as vinegar and sour cream are favoured.

To prepare for the cold season, meat and fish are pickled, while vegetables and fruits are pickled, dried or made into preserves.

Traditional desserts include uzvar (a dried fruit drink), various kyssils (soft jellies made of berries, milk or oats), compotes and cakes. There are countless recipes for uzvar, as well as for kvas, which in this part of the world is made of birch sap mixed with dried fruit, mint or oregano, unlike the Russian kvas usually made of rye bread.

Alcohol for a Ukrainian normally mean various local horilkas (vodkas) and nalyvkas (berry or fruit liqueurs), the most popular being Ukrainian hot red pepper horilka. Beer is also a favorite drink. Ukraine has its own delicious wines, made from grapes grown in the country's southern and Transcarpathian regions.

To understand a lot about the Ukrainian character, just try the recipe opposite for Ukrainian borshch.

Beetroot soup

United Kingdom

A flavourful adventure

Over the last fifty years the United Kingdom has rediscovered its passion for food: a renewed focus on fresh, locally grown ingredients matched with a fascination for different styles of cooking, celebrity chefs and our heritage of regional specialities.

The past flavours our present. The great kitchen at Hampton Court comes to life when lavish dishes of medieval origin are prepared in themed

demonstrations. Meanwhile, hog roasts on spits are still popular at country fairs and festivals. Seventeenth-century coffee houses were frequented by gentlemen of leisure; in today's versions all ages and genders are welcome, and the language of latte and espresso is universal.

Our food and drink history is based on the fertility, or otherwise, of the land and the passage of invaders.

Whisky barrels

English Saxon farmsteads of the eleventh century revolved around the seasons. Livestock bred for their meat, wool and leather were precious commodities, and animals were slaughtered to fit in with the annual cycle. In contrast, the conquering Normans expected dishes of the finest quality at all times. Alongside their rigorous protection of the New Forest game they demanded prime meat all year round – a source of conflict with the Saxon farming community.

The French style of cooking is still visible in Scotland, where butchers offer gigot chops – a legacy of the days of the French-born Mary of Guise and her daughter Mary Queen of Scots. Many of the traditional dishes of Wales, such as cawl, a warming soup, originated in the Hafods – the mountainous hill farms. Northern Ireland has some of the freshest, finest foods available in these islands. Highlights are the seafood, prime beef and pork, and excellent root vegetables. Make sure you try an Ulster fry, the celebrated local fried breakfast of sausage, bacon, egg, mushrooms, soda farls and potato bread. Colcannon, a tasty mix of mashed potato, cabbage and onions, reflects this green and fertile land.

Food for celebrations, such as Christmas, has changed over time. The Tudor boar's head was replaced by the Victorian turkey and today may well be a piece of prime beef, a whole salmon, or even a nut roast!

Organic food has become the norm for many households and farmers' markets have reappeared. Before the Industrial Revolution markets were part of everyday life. Pannier markets, where the farmer's wife took pats of butter, farmhouse cheeses, and the occasional hen, were where she bought essential goods that couldn't be made on the farm. At hiring fairs, annual events when labourers found new masters, a young man could buy his sweetheart a gilded gingerbread. Similar "fairing" biscuits are still produced in the West Country.

Today, at farmers' markets all over the United Kingdom, growers and producers sell direct to locals and tourists, sharing their knowledge and developing businesses within the community. Local and organic fruit and vegetables are re-introducing us to the tastes of homegrown varieties and the specialities of the seasons. The desire for quality and traceability is leading to interest in rare breeds. Herdwick sheep, raised on the Cumbrian Fells, are sold as lamb and mutton at Borough Market in London, opposite a stand offering beef from longhorn cattle and pork from Tamworth pigs. Welsh Black Beef, too, is enjoying huge popularity and is a favourite with top chefs.

The link between the countryside and the food we eat is increasingly appreciated. Chefs in both Michelin-starred restaurants and cosy country pubs demand to know where their ingredients come from. Government initiatives are promoting quality producers. Food from Britain's website www.regional-foodanddrink.co.uk has helped boost the sector's

British cheeses

earnings, and a joint initiative with VisitBritain, www.visitbritain.com/taste, focuses on producers who welcome consumers to contact them directly. For example, Wensleydale Creamery produces a range of cheeses based on their original recipe and made with local milk. You can watch their cheese-makers at work and see a collection of old cheese-making implements, then taste the varieties and buy some to take home, including the distinctively packaged Wallace and Grommit cheeses.

Tastes have changed from the 1950s explosion of deep-fried dishes, based on the post-rationing fancy for recipes with a lot of fat, to lighter, modern takes on traditional fare. Modern British culinary tastes reflect the growing awareness of the importance of healthier eating, and menus increasingly include light, tasty salads and low-calorie choices in addition to the old fattening favourites of the 1950s. Today's innovative chefs often make a healthier version of old favourites, for example serving black pudding and eggs as a brunch salad, with the pudding dry-fried and crumbly, with delicate quail's eggs on spicy rocket leaves and a balsamic dressing. Fish and chips is a long-term favourite; many pubs now offer it with beer batter, especially light and crisp. In the north of England "mushy peas" is a must-have accompaniment.

Good food is an essential part of UK leisure activities. Strawberries and tennis at Wimbledon are inseparable; Fortnum and Mason, grocers to the Queen, provide sumptuous hampers for sporting and social events all year round. Rugby at Twickenham, cricket at Lords, racing at Ascot and rowing at Henley are just a few of the places where the art of eating out is celebrated.

Food and drink trails are inspiring exploration of regional flavours. The Taste of Anglia food group has a sausage trail, the south-east group a vineyard trail. The Scottish whisky trail has long attracted visitors, and the many cheeses of Wales often have regional names and are an added reason to travel in the glorious scenery. Linking the view to the taste, Strangford Lough shellfish feature on Northern Ireland's top menus, and the many lakes and rivers provide an abundance of salmon, trout, pike, perch and eels. Toomebridge is home to the largest eel fishery in Europe. This extraction has been going on since the Bronze Age. Nowadays, most of the 4 000 eels extracted each night from Lough Neagh are exported to Germany and Holland.

Over 2 000 different real ales are currently produced in the UK. Many breweries offer tours where they demonstrate the blend of tradition and passion that goes into their distinctive brews. Plymouth Gin's distillery is the oldest in the UK and has a brand new visitor centre. Similarly, Old Bushmills Distillery on the rugged, untamed beautiful coast of Northern Ireland also has a visitors centre. The Old Bushmills Distillery is the world's oldest licensed whiskey distillery, with a licence to distil from 1608. Wine

Fishmonger at Borough Market, London

United Kingdom

production is another revival. The Romans planted vines in the Cotswolds. Today's sparkling and still whites, rosés and, increasingly, reds are winning prizes and satisfying a market at home and abroad.

A visit to a supermarket reflects increasing interest in local produce. Bags of potatoes carry the union jack alongside seasonal vegetables and fruits, often from named farms. Aisles of ingredients for cuisines from all over the world bear testimony to a fascination with foreign flavours. Bustling city Chinatowns, such as those of Newcastle and London, the famous Balti Mile in Birmingham, and a multitude of Thai restaurants and tapas bars help satisfy the UK taste for the exotic.

The voyaging, trading and colonising of succeeding generations brought spices and exotic fruits and vegetables to the royal court, tastes that permeated society. Recipes enjoyed abroad were adapted to local ingredients. From earliest times human migration has shaped the UK's food and the way it is eaten. Today's quality food and drink producers enjoy an increasingly interested and knowledgeable marketplace to the benefit of both themselves and the consumer. The best way to appreciate the UK's cuisine is to taste it!

Further information at:
http://www.visitbritain.com/taste

Conclusions

Culinary transitions in Europe: an overview

Stephen Mennell

As this book has helped to demonstrate, for sheer variety the pleasures of eating are unrivalled among the pleasures of the flesh. People's tastes vary widely and, according to the old adage, *de gustibus non est disputandum*. No disputing, perhaps, but there is much to explain about taste.

In everyday usage, we often use the word "taste" as though it denoted some objective qualities of the food – how it "tastes". But when we think more closely about it, we know that what we principally mean is how people perceive the "objective" qualities of the food, using their taste buds and their noses. Psychologists receive large grants from food manufacturers to study the perception of tastes.

But in this book we have been concerned with taste as something more social than physiological or psychological. The entries from the member states of the Council of Europe have depicted both strong continuities and often-dramatic changes in national tastes.

In this case we are using "taste" in the metaphorical sense in which it has come to apply to aesthetic preferences in the fields of music or pictorial art, and then returning the metaphor to the field of food and eating whence it came in the first place. We are speaking of people's food preferences, and their capacity to discriminate aesthetically among different ingredients, dishes and cuisines. "Taste" in this sense is a part of what is now fashionably called "habitus" – that is, it is learned, not innate, but deeply habituated so that it seems to us like "second nature". Although our tastes have been learned or moulded since childhood, they have come to feel "natural" or innate to us – we often find it difficult to imagine feeling different about our likes and dislikes. Although individuals may have idiosyncratic personal preferences, the broad shape of their habituated taste is likely to be shared with many other people, and it is likely to vary considerably between one culture and another – or more concretely between different groups of people. This constitutes what we may call "culinary culture".

Conclusions

If "taste" in this sense is so deeply habituated and socially rooted, how does it come to change? For change it certainly does. It was only in 1964 that I ate my first Indian meal, in an Indian restaurant in Leeds, when Indian cuisine was unknown in my nearby home town of Huddersfield in the north of England; now there is an Indian restaurant in most large villages, not to mention towns, and a politician recently said that chicken tikka masala (rather than roast beef) was now the British national dish. It used to be said that a society's taste in food was one of the most slowly changing, most conservative, aspects of its culture. That may, at a deep level, still be true of some underlying attitudes towards eating and its pleasures; but on the surface, eating seems to have become a part of fashion, which not only changes but changes at an accelerating rate.

One reason why the study of culinary cultures and their history is so fascinating – indeed, I would say intellectually important – is that changes in the food people eat and the way they cook and enjoy it appear to serve as a highly sensitive marker for much broader social, political and economic changes in societies. The sheer social and historic diversity of the member states of the Council of Europe has allowed us glimpses in this book of how food mirrors transitions of many kinds through which European societies have passed, in both the distant and the recent past. Among the significant transitions implicitly documented here are the following:

1. The formation of local peasant cuisines and their gradual emancipation from climate and locality.

2. The formation of more socially stratified cuisines in pre-industrial agrarian societies, and the role that courts and aristocracies played in that process.

3. The process of national culinary integration in the course of nation-building, the growth of associated emotions, and culinary nationalism.

4. The shifting balance of power between men and women in the kitchen.

5. The industrialisation first of food production and then of cooking.

6. The beginnings of conscious and collective direction of diet, through *de haut en bas* cookery lessons, and later the emergence of diet as a social problem, with particular reference to obesity and anorexia and similar eating disorders, health promotion campaigns, and national and international food policies.

7. The advent of cultural and ethnic diversity in the new age of great migrations, with culinary multiculturalism as part of much wider processes of globalisation at the present day.

8. The democratisation of eating, which is linked to a broader social democratisation, and thus an aspect of the commitment to democracy that all member states of the Council of Europe make.

In the beginning ...

Can we say that all human groups have had shared "tastes" in food? Has the capacity to discriminate among foods on the basis of social preferences always existed ever since the emergence of *Homo sapiens*, when the human species was not numerous and existed only in small foraging bands? Yes, probably, in one sense. It has been noted that no human group in normal times eats everything of potential nutritional value that is available to it in its environment. Earthworms, for instance, must be among the most widely distributed of edible fauna, but in no human group do they seem to be a normal and preferred item of diet. Mary Douglas was probably right in arguing that "each individual, by cultural training, enters a sensory world that is pre-segmented and pre-judged for him".[1] The propensity for humans to make patterned classifications of foods is probably universal, and of course Claude Lévi-Strauss sought to show that distinctions between the raw, the cooked and the rotten played a fundamental part in the structure of thought.[2] The rejection of some available foods and preference for others may have been all the more possible if for early humankind, as Marshall Sahlins famously argued in *Stone age economics*, food was relatively abundant and gathering it left plenty of time for leisure and reflection.[3] On the other hand, it can be pointed out that early humans also endured levels of vulnerability and unpredictable danger – from disease, accident, natural disasters, other animals – that are almost inconceivable to modern people; high levels of danger are associated with correspondingly high levels of fear, and in turn high levels of fear and danger are not conducive to foresight, to taking the long view. Not to eat something nutritious that is immediately available, in favour of eating something that may – with care and preparation and perhaps good luck – be available in the future, involves foresight. And thus it is likely that a good measure of security and safety is necessary for a highly developed "taste".

Whether or not early humans had well developed systems for classifying what they ate and did not eat, it should not be forgotten that these were small, local and self-sufficient bands who could eat only what was immediately available to them in their immediate environment. They may have rejected some of what they could have eaten, but the range of comestibles would always have been far smaller than in the modern world, where foods of diverse ecological and economic provenance are traded across the whole globe, so that everything is available all the time in the great world cities for those who can afford it. The diet of most pre-industrial groups was rather monotonous. By the standards of today, it would most likely seem boring.

Transitions in taste and culinary culture are not necessarily very easy. To see how they happen, let us return to our list.

1. The formation of local peasant cuisines and their gradual emancipation from climate and locality

The bedrock of culinary culture in most countries is a tradition of peasant food, the food of farmers – who grew and reared and ate their own products, which they traded locally but generally over no great distance. Many countries, in their contributions to this book, celebrate traditions of this kind that can be traced back over several centuries. The main common features of peasant cuisines are freshness and simplicity, derived from their dependence on locally grown or gathered produce. Dependence on the locality also meant dependence on climate and season. In consequence, despite underlying structural similarities, peasant cuisines differ greatly from each other in ingredients. Lithuania mentions the importance of mushrooms, Bulgaria of fruit. The hard conditions of survival in northerly latitudes, evident for example in the contributions of Estonia, Iceland, and Norway, contrast strongly with the abundance recollected by those who lived in warmer climes – in Azerbaijan, Bulgaria, Slovakia, and Ukraine for instance. And the further north one lived, the more rigorously did the seasons impose constraints on the rhythms of eating. Where the winters were long and freezing, stock had to be slaughtered and the meat salted down; and where the summers were short and their days long, the hours of labour and of meals were all the more determined by the rhythms of farm work, as again Estonia notes.

Peasant traditions are easily romanticised. Yet other things – including climate – being equal, the smaller the locality on which a particular cuisine was dependent the greater the potential monotony of the peasant diet. True, people who had not experienced the vast diversity of modern eating may not have felt their diet to be boring. But to later observers it may appear so: note the prominence of staples such as grains, bread, milk and root vegetables. Over much of Europe, meat was not abundant for ordinary people, although it became more so in the period following the Black Death, when about a third of Europe's population died. Afterwards, the pace of change in the countryside reverted to its normal slow pace and, at least across much of western Europe, the peasant diet appears to have remained virtually unaltered for centuries.[4] In rural France the pot au feu permanently simmering in the peasant kitchen – by no means always with Henri IV's poule cooking in it – for many people provided soupe for breakfast, lunch and dinner; and the same went, pari passu, for much of the rest of Europe.

The monotony, more or less, of the peasant diet is easily forgotten. The cookery books of each nation tend to celebrate the great peasant dishes of the past. These were generally the exciting high spots of a generally unexciting diet, the special dishes for special occasions. Many, perhaps even a majority, of the chapters in this book mention the traditional feasts that in the past marked the year in agrarian societies, and which often continue today even in very different societies. The entries of Estonia, Georgia, Greece, Latvia, Lithuania, Moldova, Monaco, Russia, Slovenia, and Sweden are among those that dwell upon these festive recipes. But occasions for feasting originally stood out against the background of many periods of fasting. Sometimes the fasting was given a veneer of religious justification, but such religious rationalisations mostly helped people feel better about the pressing need to eke out stocks of food through frequent seasons and indeed whole years of dearth. It is not that "rich peasant traditions" did not exist, but that the wonderful masterpieces served at Christmas, harvest, or weddings were not eaten all the time. Nor were they all part of the repertoire across a vast area. So, for example, it has been said that the French peasant cuisine was "invented" in the early twentieth century by Curnonsky and his circle,[5] whose work was sponsored by tyre manufacturers interested in promoting tourism among the new generation of car-owners. What they actually did – and their achievement should never be belittled – was to collect the *trésors gastronomiques de France* in numerous volumes, with the consequence that these dishes became available more or less all the time and everywhere for those able to pay for them. It is perhaps a mark of France's distinctive place in the culinary history of Europe that these collectors of gastronomic folklore

became quite so famous; but such initiatives were by no means confined to France. In Britain, for instance, Florence White explicitly modelled her English Folk Cookery Association on the more famous English Folk Song and Dance Association led by Cecil Sharp.[6] It was in the same era that Bela Bartok was collecting folk music in Hungary, and it seems probable that collections of traditional recipes were being collected, even rescued, around the same time in many countries. We must not romanticise the past, nor imagine that a huge diversity of the best dishes were being eaten every day. Nor should we depict our forefathers as living in the Land of Cockaygne. Indeed the prevalence in European folklore of *mythes de ripaille* – roughly "myths about having a good blow-out" – is symptomatic of the dreams of people who frequently experienced the opposite, in times of scarcity.

Yet, at the same time, we must celebrate the rich heritage of European culinary traditions. The recipes have been collected, and the dishes continue to be cooked, because the tastes and smells of a country's traditional table are the royal route to a part of its collective memory that is accessible to everyone. In a famous essay, Roland Barthes showed long ago how powerfully historical and rural themes are deployed in creating a sense of nostalgia that is a key part of the enjoyment of food in France.[7] For a country like Britain, too, where manufactured food forms a large part of what people eat every day, and where people eat out upon a diversity of cuisines that reflect the ethnic diversity of society today, the entry in this book shows how the traditional dishes of the past are still cherished and celebrated. (Poland shows great realism in pointing out that its great traditional dishes may now be cooked more for visitors than for residents.)

One component of a definition of a peasant cuisine is its dependence on, its relatedness to, a "locality". But what is a "locality"? Plainly, it is an elastic concept. For one thing, self-sufficiency was always relative, and there would always have been some essential ingredients that had to be sought through trade beyond the local community. Salt is an example: the historic shortage of salt is mentioned in the case of Iceland, and Azerbaijan mentions that it was the principal supplier of salt throughout the Caucasus region. Localities grow as trade grows, and as the distance over which trade takes place increases. The spreading web of trade in food in early modern Europe can be plotted quite precisely through the peaks and troughs of grain prices. As trade and transport improved, there was a diminution of the enormously high steeples of food prices when harvests failed in limited regions, and the risk of localised famine declined. The same spreading web of trade also tended to increase the diversity of ingredients, and thus of dishes, in a particular locality. Local differences do not necessarily disappear, of course: Georgia mentions that "food remains an important marker of cultural differences" among the five main sub-groups of its

population. Some countries acknowledge that they were always situated on major trade routes, and that this always had a bearing on what they ate: Estonia makes this point, while Croatia emphasises both local traditions and the intermingling of traditions in the ethnic cockpit of the Balkans. Croatia, indeed, introduces a brave note into the often-cosy world of food history: that the intermingling of food traditions results from war as well as from peaceful trade.

Lest cosiness also permeate a picture of inevitable progress from localised and restricted peasant cuisines, through the development of trade, to the modern diversity of eating, we should also recognise that Europe has experienced bad times in which the trend was reversed. War again, most obviously, has occasioned reversions in the direction of self-sufficiency. Several of the new member states of the Council of Europe also mention the hard times they experienced under the former communist regimes. As the Polish entry remarks: "under authoritarian rule, tradition is … used for political purposes, to compensate for privileges lost to the people. But cuisine usually loses in this process …". In the 1980s, as the communist economy began to collapse, Poles resorted to something that might be called "emergency peasantisation", when town-dwellers went out into the countryside to strike deals, sometimes bartering, with farmers – returning home perhaps with the whole carcase of a pig that would be shared among a few families.

2. The stratification of cuisines: courts, aristocrats and bourgeois

Peasant farmers constituted the great majority of the European population in the past – the more remote past in some parts of the continent than in others. Yet eating was always socially stratified. We know, for instance, that before the Black Death nutrition was very unequally distributed among members of the various estates – and that was especially true of meat, with the peasantry's diet dominated by vegetable and dairy products. The upper strata may have been less likely actually to go hungry in times of dearth, but it would appear that even the warrior aristocracy ate essentially the seasonal produce of their own land, and did not generally have it cooked by means much more elaborate than roasting and boiling. To generalise, when the social divisions between strata are very deep and the interdependence between them is very unequal – when the power that they have over each other is very asymmetrical – then the power and status of the upper strata is more likely to find expression in quantity rather than quality, in periodical displays of indiscriminate heaps of food at ceremonial banquets, for instance, rather than through the quality and labour-intensiveness that are among the marks of a true haute cuisine.[8]

Now it is true, of course, that the manuscript recipes from a very few major courts towards the end of the Middle Ages – the *Forme of Cury* (a manuscript from the late fourteenth-century court of King Richard II of England) and *Taillevent* (a similar manuscript from the late-medieval court of France), for instance – show something more complicated, characterised by the use of spices and flavourings that could have reached these courts only via very long trade routes.[9] But, significantly, there is an old debate about whether this late medieval haute cuisine for the very few represents a debased form, a remote echo, of the cuisine of ancient Rome, when the chains of social and economic interdependence were indeed longer and denser than they were for many centuries afterwards. In any case, this haute cuisine appears to have been confined to a few major European princely courts and – from relatively scanty documentary sources – does not seem to have changed rapidly at all in response to fashion, as later hautes cuisines were to do.

A large body of modern research on European food history suggests that the rate of change in "taste" accelerates when the strata of society become more closely and more equally interdependent, and when social competition becomes more intense. Thus, as far as we can tell, courtly cuisine did not change very quickly when an only partially pacified warrior nobility's reference groups were other courts at a great distance. Hautes cuisines – which can be defined by their typical dishes requiring complex sequences of

Conclusions

475

stages, considerable division of labour among kitchen staff, and thus by their costliness – have tended to emerge in court societies from Ancient Egypt onwards. That appears to be true to varying degrees of several of the national traditions that are now influential throughout the world: the traditions of China and India, and from Europe, of France, Italy and Turkey.

The case of France is especially significant, because from the late seventeenth century onwards, and especially in the nineteenth, French cuisine "conquered the world", in the sense that it came to set the models and standards for upper-class eating throughout much of Europe (and beyond, for instance in North America).[10] The rapid elaboration of French cookery was connected with the consolidation of the absolutist monarchy of the *ancien regime*, in the course of which the court aristocracy became a "two-front stratum", defunctionalised and squeezed between the monarchy and the "pressure from below" of an expanding merchant and professional bourgeois class. Their whole social identity became bound up with virtuoso display, in their manners, clothes, houses, pastimes and eating. Although some of the same trends were present in Britain, there were subtle differences. The development of royal absolutism in England was nipped in the bud a century and half before the revolution in France, and English nobility and gentry retained more of their old social functions – including their ties and influence in the provinces where they still lived for much of the year on their country estates – so that virtuoso consumption became less essential to their social identity and the marks of rural life endured more clearly in their tastes.

In their contributions, both Austria and Turkey explicitly refer to the culinary legacy of imperial courts and the nobility – Habsburg and Ottoman respectively. Courtly cuisine is of course always essentially an urban phenomenon, because the elaboration of a great variety of dishes requires a great variety of ingredients, which are brought together in the markets of the great cities, not in the countryside. The Turkish chapter shows a proper consciousness of the great Spice Road in bringing ingredients from afar, but also recognises how a courtly elite cuisine affected the food of the peasants in the countryside by skimming off the finest produce: the best fish, for instance, found its way from the Black Sea directly to Istanbul. Where a great royal court was associated with an empire, its tastes in food could be a model over great distances. Azerbaijan, Bulgaria and Serbia and Montenegro all mention the influence on their culinary traditions of once having belonged to the Ottoman Empire. Greek and Turkish cuisines show broad similarities, although the two countries are also proud of their differences. Austria appears to take wry pride in contending that Wiener Schnitzel is not distinctively Viennese at all, but derives from Byzantium via Italy; on the other hand, Austrian influence is acknowledged by Croatia, Poland and again Serbia and Montenegro, and Habsburg influence is no doubt evident in other former provinces of the empire such as Slovenia, despite its not being explicitly stated. Spain, the home of Europe's other great Habsburg court, comments upon the variety of new ingredients that arrived from its vast overseas empire – after all, how would a Spanish omelette be possible if potatoes had never been discovered in South America? – but courtly influence is not much stressed, either in the entry in this book or in Spanish cookery books. If the Spanish aristocracy did not have so great a modelling influence on Spanish cookery as did their counterparts in France on French cuisine, it may be because of the greater social distance between the nobility and the bourgeoisie, and the weakness of any pressure from below on the part of an aspirant upwardly mobile middle class in eighteenth and nineteenth-century Spain.

Two countries, Norway and The Netherlands, explicitly draw attention to their food having been shaped by the absence of a royal and aristocratic court society.[11] Norway claims good, but not great, cuisine, while the Dutch are characteristically modest about the plainness of their food.

Although courts historically laid the foundations of grandes cuisines, the pace of culinary change accelerated markedly when, for whatever reason, the competitive virtuoso consumption among courtiers was supplanted by the commercial competition that takes place among restaurateurs using product differentiation to attract customers. In the culinary history of western Europe we tend to point to the proliferation of restaurants in Paris after the French Revolution as a decisive step in the process. An important part of the story of how culinary innovations and fashions in taste spread from the high-class restaurants to the less prestigious establishments and into the domestic kitchen can broadly be described as the "trickle down" model. Aron depicted in some detail the culinary ladder linking the high and the low in nineteenth-century Paris.[12] Not every country was like France, however. Even though the London taverns served as models for the first Paris restaurants in the eighteenth century, Britain later fell far behind France in the abundance and variety of its eating places, and "eating out" remained an exceptional experience for all but the fairly well to do until roughly the last four decades. Several other countries mention that the mass of the people have been attracted only quite recently to eat frequently in what is now the great variety of restaurants in all parts of Europe.

3. National culinary integration

Some countries have placed emphasis on the strongly persisting regional variations within their borders, while others tend to express pride in an overall national style of cookery. In fact these are not necessarily incompatible: it is partly a matter of the focal length of the lens through which one is looking. There are always local variants on a national style where that exists. Croatia, Germany, Serbia and Montenegro and Slovak Republic are among those countries which stress the regional variants. It is especially interesting that the chapters from Croatia and Serbia and Montenegro draw such attention to the culinary influences of ethnic minorities at one of the cultural crossroads of Europe, something to celebrate in view of the difficult and complex history of the Balkans. Germany similarly mentions Polish influences, such as pierogi in its north-eastern border areas, but it also recognises the more important *kleindeutsch* inheritance (to which Austria refers when distinguishing itself as a formerly large state from the mass of tiny principalities that composed Germany to its north until the second half of the nineteenth century). Late national unification is probably correlated with the strength of distinctive regional dishes, which one can observe everywhere in Germany. The same is probably true of Italy, where the *Risorgimento* only very slightly antedated the establishment of the *Kaiserreich*. Most people would agree that both in Germany and Italy, the regional specialisms belong within a broad national style. Within such an overall style, however, there is great diversity and change, something that the Italian entry demonstrates in a novel way, showing social change through the prism of art, and especially through the cinema as the quintessentially modern visual art.

National culinary styles do not necessarily change abruptly when one walks across an international border in Europe. Transitions are often more gradual, just as linguistic transitions used to be more gradual than they

are today. In Strasbourg, home of the Council of Europe, one hears French; in Kehl, across the bridge over the Rhine, one hears German. True, if one listens carefully, one can still hear the Alsatian dialect, but it is less common than it was. But in the restaurant alternatively known as *Aux armes de Strasbourg* or *Stadtwappe* (not -*waffe*), the food shows both German and French traits. Elsewhere the culinary transitions are still more gradual, with strong similarities, for example, among the various Slavic countries. Poland refers to its eastern "borderlands" with Lithuania, Belarus and Ukraine, associated with a "joint supper", consumed by many peoples. For the Poles, culinary traditions played their part (along, obviously, with Catholicism) in preserving the strong sense of national pride and identity through the tribulations of Polish history. Three times at the end of the eighteenth century the national territory was partitioned between the three neighbouring great powers, a partition that endured until 1918, when the Polish state was resurrected, only to undergo radical changes in its boundaries, immense movements of population, and subsumption into the Soviet empire after the Second World War.[13]

One of the most encouraging conclusions from the story of Poland, and many other countries too, is that however much food and culinary tradition can serve as a badge of national pride and identity, they do not necessarily have to serve an exclusionary function. A history as complex as Poland's has promoted culinary diversity, and continuing influence from neighbouring countries – east as well as west – is welcomed.

4. From women to men and back in the kitchen

Most countries focused in their entries mainly on "traditional" dishes and recipes, which in this context tends to mean "domestic", and most often it is simply taken for granted that women do the cooking in the home. Hungary and Cyprus make it clear that they are indeed aware that they are speaking of women's roles in food preparation, while Georgia comments that economic development privileges the men in Georgian communities, with the women left having to walk further and further to collect clean water. What is taken for granted here is justifiably taken for granted: factually, most cooking in the home in almost every society past and present has been done by women. There is another strand to the history of food, however: that of professional cookery in courts and great houses, in restaurants and in a great range of modern catering establishments. At its higher – that is, more prestigious – levels, this has tended to be dominated by men. There are some exceptions; just to give one instance, Lyon, in contrast to Paris, was noted in the nineteenth century for having some great restaurants operated by celebrated women cooks. But, on the whole, the pattern holds. Cookery books setting out the most elaborate, diverse, complicated and costly dishes served at the pinnacle of society are written by men. Those which simplify such dishes and show how something resembling them can be served in the home are written by women. In the history of French culinary art – the tradition that came to dominate European elite cookery – the line of famous male chefs runs back from Bocuse through Escoffier, Carême, La Chapelle and La Varenne to Taillevent in the Middle Ages. Quite how this pattern originated in unclear. The most likely explanation lies in the origin of the social institution of the court not as a "private" or "domestic" household, but as a military establishment. It is probable that men always served as cooks with armies (and by extension on fighting ships), and that their function in the kitchens of the court began as an extension of that role. There is no reason to suppose that the food cooked by male cooks was in origin any more sophisticated than that cooked by women, but men having established their monopoly in courtly kitchens, they became the instruments of the refinement of cooking as the court itself developed as the locus of the arts of consumption.[14]

It is possible that the male monopoly over hautes cuisines is now weakening, although it appears to be far from broken. A disproportionate number of the "celebrity chefs" who now appear on television would appear still to be men, although it would be interesting to know whether that is true of every country.

Meanwhile, back in the home, there is little sign of any decisive shift in the burden of housework from women to men. Several countries mention the much higher rate of female participation in the workforce

479

Conclusions

today than in previous generations, and Finland refers to the proliferation of mass catering services – such as school and works canteens – saying that as many as one-third of Finns use them every day. Most sociological research, however, shows that women continue to work a "second shift" at home even when they have been out at work all day just like their husbands.[15] What is probably true is that in food manufacturing and mass catering the gender balance is more nearly equal.

5. The industrialisation of eating

Finland states the unvarnished truth that its people have today been transformed from food producers into food consumers. That is the outcome of the industrialisation of eating, which is now evident everywhere. It impinges even on traditional food production: Georgia, listing some of its local specialities, casually mentions "beer locally made from barley … *in plastic bottles*" (my italics). But industrialisation of food production is not a particularly new process. Its roots lie back in the nineteenth century, and the effects of industrial production of food are not easy to separate from the effects of industrialisation more generally. Sweden mentions the impact of canals, railways and later asphalt roads upon the country's food culture. In what is perhaps an implicit allusion to what Benedict Anderson called "print capitalism" and to the role that it played in the construction of "imagined communities",[16] the Swedish chapter also points out that as part of processes of nation-building in the nineteenth century, "novel culinary ideals were spread with the help of newspapers, and the food culture of the bourgeoisie became the model for the aspirations of the new working and middle classes". The new urban foods were what migrants from the countryside wanted to eat too. A century later, according to Slovakia's chapter, industrialisation had a very similar effect in reducing the contrasts between the diets of the people of the lowlands and uplands in that country. It is as well to remember that the industrialisation of eating has had beneficial effects, for (without doubting what Poland says about low-quality industrial food under communism), it is too easy to dwell upon the aesthetic downside of mass-produced food. It is again necessary not to romanticise the past. When judged by the finest culinary creations once consumed by a tiny privileged minority, the chilled and frozen foods from the supermarket and the hamburgers and pizzas from the chain eating-places may look like decline. When viewed from the perspective of the often-monotonous diets of poor people in the past, such food may seem a veritable cornucopia.

6. Eating as a problem: the beginnings of dietary advice and food policy

A cornucopia gives rise to its own problems. The last few paragraphs of Turkey's chapter are devoted to the health problems that have arisen with the transformation of its traditional diet, which from a nutritional point of view had many virtues. Where food has become so much more diverse and abundant – and also more secure and regular – as it has across most of Europe, control of the appetite has become problematic in a way that it rarely was in the past. Farm labourers often wolfed down prodigious quantities of food at harvest suppers. Their way of life was extremely strenuous, and they often went hungry, so why worry when the opportunity came for a blowout? Very often, being plump was a source of prestige, and that attitude has not entirely disappeared from Europe today: the Austrian entry slightly gloatingly dwells upon its people's perception of themselves as "informed by unbridled gluttony, the preference for being gourmand rather than gourmet, and the partiality for large quantities of food of the fatty or sugar-laden variety", a point of view that would be regarded as politically incorrect in many other countries. Iceland suggests that it could easily have gone in the same direction, had not poverty and taxation prevented it: instead it went down the route of very heavy consumption of sugar – something else that is not exactly in line with modern dietetic opinion. In fact, that route of adaptation was not unique

to Iceland; it was common among working-class people in the late nineteenth and early twentieth centuries, the age of bread and jam.[17] From the same period in several countries – Britain, the Netherlands, Scandinavia, and also the USA – date middle-class initiatives to provide cookery lessons for housewives, and cookery schools for domestic servants. While welfare was one motive, it is clear that another was, *de haut en bas*, to "improve", to "refine", and to "civilise" the "lower orders" – in other words, the teachers' mixed motives often included the satisfaction of manifesting their own social superiority.[18] Cookery lessons also found their way into the curriculum for schoolgirls. Interestingly, such initiatives were far less evident in France, where it seems to have been taken more granted that an interest in food and some skill in its preparation would be encountered within the home.

It is significant that, again a little more than a century ago, what are now called "eating disorders" first became a concern, mainly in the better-off ranks of society where food was never in short supply.[19] It was then that anorexia nervosa was first described and named by clinicians, and that cookery books began to have sections on how to cope with obesity. The two disorders, apparently opposites, in fact have something in common in their aetiology – both

Conclusions

481

represent the failure of a steady and even self-control over appetite capable of maintaining a normally healthy body weight. As for instance Sweden and Finland remark, the fear of fatness is now widespread – both on the part of individuals and governments. People are, in many countries, on average becoming steadily plumper, yet the cultural ideal of the sexually attractive body is becoming steadily slimmer. So for individuals, being fat causes anxieties about attractiveness as well as healthiness. For governments, the increasing prevalence of fatness is a public health and even an economic problem. Campaigns to persuade people to take more exercise, as well as to eat more sensibly, are prevalent – although their effectiveness is debatable.[20]

7. Globalisation and multicultural eating

Today, the diversity of ethnic influences found in the cooking and taste of all the richer countries of the world, enmeshed as they are in worldwide food chains, makes it more difficult of speak of separate national culinary cultures. In one way we may even have reverted to a pattern reminiscent of the medieval world. The separate strata are now at a global level, with the rich countries looking towards each other to make sure that they are not too far out of step, while a huge gap divides them from the large part of the world's people who form the nutritional underclass. Those are people who often go hungry, or, even when they are not hungry, live somewhat monotonously off the product of their own labours; they are (sadly) irrelevant to the culinary cultural consciousness of the west and of Europe.

One consequence of this pattern of global stratification is that we are living through a second *Volkerwanderungszeit* – a second great age of the migration of peoples – that dwarfs in scale those of the previous two millennia. There is nothing new in the principle of ethnic migrations and diasporas. Over much of Europe, but especially in central and eastern Europe, cuisine was significantly enriched by the traditions of the Jews. This is specifically mentioned in the entry from Poland, to which the Jews were invited as an oppressed minority by the enlightened Casimir the Great, many centuries before Poland was, as its entry remarks, turned into a "Jewish cemetery". The Roma, or Gypsies as they are more familiarly known, are also represented in the lexicon of European cookery: many dishes are described as being *in der Zigeuner Art* (although whether real Roma would recognise them is another question – like all recipes, those of minorities change over time and are adapted by host communities).

But the scale of mass migration since the second half of the twentieth century is unprecedented; it has had,

482

and is continuing to have, huge effects on how people eat in most of the countries of Europe. Of course, as Georgia comments, "the impact of migration is centuries old"; nor, as Serbia and Montenegro notes, does ethnic diversity have any absolute beginning. Sweden illustrates the culinary impact of its recent immigrant population in a striking comparison of recipes for meatballs in 1938 and 1999. Yet old traditions are typically not overwhelmed by new ethnic influences; Sweden also reports that for its new migrants, "eating Swedish" is one important means of assimilation to Swedish society. There are many puzzles concerning which new culinary influences are adopted and which old traditions stand their ground. The Netherlands remarks how curious it is that the Dutch dominated world trade for a century and a half in and after their Golden Age, yet their one contribution to world cuisine was the doughnut. That is all the more puzzling when, having lost its empire and suffered surprisingly little collective trauma through its loss, the Netherlands now has a strikingly multicultural eating scene. There is much here that merits further investigation and reflection.

There is an overall trend towards "diminishing contrasts, increasing varieties".[21] Economic inequality has not disappeared – indeed, in many western societies it has increased over the last quarter of a century – but old-style class inequalities crosscut with ethnicity to an extent inconceivable in Europe half a century ago. Above all, they cross-cut with many different kinds of status groups which are defined as much by their patterns of consumption and taste as by their disposable income. This has led to a culinary pluralism that is the counterpart of something which is more familiar in the arts: the loss of a single dominant style. Styles like the Baroque and Rococo enjoyed virtually unchallenged dominance in their age, more unchallenged indeed than the aristocratic upper classes with which they were associated. In a more problematic way so did Romanticism dominate an age and spread across the range of the arts. During the last hundred years or more, however, this stylistic unity has been lost. There is a greater diversity of tastes coexisting and competing at one time – competing more equally, again like classes and interests in society. There is a rapid succession of fashions in artistic styles. And the mixture of elements deriving from several styles is common: the label "kitsch" often applied to incongruous mixtures of style in other aspects of culture, can also be used about the domain of food.[22]

One such mixture is the modern so-called "fusion food". In 1998 in the Netherlands I was served *kipfilet* (chicken breast) surmounted by a slice of Brie, accompanied by sauerkraut mixed with mangoes and lychees. Such a mixing of traditions is made possible not only by long chains of interdependence, but also by a loosening of the model-setting centres for taste which would previously have judged such a combination to be incongruous. But I would also add that the sheer pace of change itself probably means that incongruity appears and disappears before the arbiters of taste – such as they still are – have a chance to label it incongruous. We shall never again see the codification of high culinary taste in coherent systems such as those represented by, say, Carême, Escoffier or (to a lesser extent) the nouvelle cuisiniers of the 1960s – which is not to say that there will not be fashions that spread internationally and last for a longer or shorter period. One example of the last decade or so is the fashion adopted by many restaurants for the "tian", in which the fish or meat is piled on top of vegetables and potatoes in the middle of the plate, surrounded by sauce.

8. The democratisation of eating

Three decades ago the Council of Europe sponsored an intense discussion of the rival merits of the notions of the "democratisation of culture" on the one hand, and "cultural democracy" on the other.[23] The first phrase was used to denote traditional attempts to spread knowledge and enjoyment of "elite culture" – whether drama, music, literature or art – to the masses, those who by reason of socio-economic condition or lack of education had not had access to it. In the wake of *les événements de mai* 1968 – the student protests of May 1968 in Paris – a certain loss of nerve was apparent. At any rate, there was no denying *le refus ouvrier*: the workers, or most of them, did not much care for Sophocles, Shakespeare or Schoenberg. The ideology of "cultural democracy" was a response to that, and meant that equal value should be accorded to the "cultural expression" of all social groups. Since it was unclear how "cultural democracy" was to be distinguished from the mass culture provided by the mass media – which commercial interests justify by saying that they are giving people "what they want", even though "the people" may still have little knowledge of or access to anything different – one could be sceptical about whether this conceptual dichotomy represented real policy alternatives.[24]

These issues play themselves out in curious ways in the specific field of food culture. The democratisation of eating has been under way for a long time. It can be seen two centuries ago, with the shifting of the locus of culinary innovation and leadership from the kitchens of great houses to the restaurants where cooks competed for the favour of the eating public. Also associated in France with the aftermath of the revolution was the emergence of the knowledgeable gastronome, men like Grimod de la Reynière and Brillat-Savarin, who wrote the precursors of the restaurant guides – *Michelin, Gault-Millau*, the *Good Food Guide* – and of the cookery columns in newspapers and magazines. At first glance they, and their successors, can appear to be snobbishly decreeing for the ignorant populace what their betters consider to be good and bad food. But in broader perspective they can also be seen to have democratised good eating, working along with cooks to educate the palates of diners, spreading knowledge over great distances through print and later the electronic media.

Still, the democratisation of eating does not involve only the trickle down of tastes and dishes that once may have been known only to the wealthy, privileged and well travelled. "Trickle up" also occurs, when tastes and dishes that once belonged to the lower strata of society are adopted by higher strata. The activities of collectors of old recipes and promoters of the romantic image of peasant cuisines have already been mentioned. Also active in effecting the upward social mobility of simple farmers' fare, however, have been some of the most famous chefs. Elizabeth David described what she called the "butterisation" of simple Provençal recipes by the great Escoffier himself; he might take a dish of artichokes and potatoes baked in olive oil and transform it by adding truffles (very expensive) and using this as the bed on which to serve a choice cut of lamb to his rich customers.[25] That would represent long-range upward social mobility for the humble vegetarian dish from Provence, and probably – as in the social ascent of people – the upward social mobility of foods is more likely to be over a shorter than a longer range. Examples abound: cases include both the humble pizza and eating with the fingers in the street. Across much of Europe today, the eating scene is reminiscent of Peter Burke's description of popular culture in the late Middle Ages.[26] Then, all ranks of society participated in popular culture, and it was only with printing and more widespread literacy that the upper classes withdrew into a more exclusive high culture. Today, one might argue that all ranks participate in the fast food and manufactured food cultures, even if only the better-off come to sample elite cuisines and search for new ways of distinguishing themselves.[27] The use they make of food and eating to symbolise their styles of life is now well recognised. Above all, however, interest in and the enjoyment of food – and, moreover, the opportunity to enjoy it, appears to be spread more widely through the ranks of society than ever it was before. Estonia observes that "staggering innovations and changes in society have created strong undercurrents which have raised eating … to the status of unflagging public interest". This is true not only of the "transition democracies" of the post-communist countries but also of most of the member states of the Council of Europe. And perhaps this is as good a case as one may find of the "cultural democracy" that the Council has advocated.

Can any conclusions and recommendations be drawn from the entries in this book, for governments, local authorities, and people at large? Perhaps. It used to be a truism that people's tastes in food were among the most conservative aspects of cultures, the most resistant to change. And yet today it is probably the speed of change and the burgeoning diversity of eating across Europe that most strikes the reader. The two statements may not be so incompatible as they appear at first glance. Undoubtedly, the development of food manufacturing, transport and distribution since the Second World War has filled the supermarket shelves with an abundance of new products and exotic flavours which must occasionally tempt even the most conservative shopper. Can we now imagine life without the supermarkets – even though they have spread across Europe only since about the 1960s or later? Can we remember that in northern Europe most people in the 1960s had never seen a pepper [capsicum] or aubergine? That mangos became a familiar fruit far more recently than that? Or, indeed, that bananas were almost unobtainable in parts of eastern Europe in the 1980s? At the same time, it is too simple to say that the old conservatism has vanished. The entries in this book show the extent to which people in most countries still enjoy, celebrate and take pride in their traditional foods and recipes. But it does not prevent them from enjoying a change. This facet of modern European culinary culture may be seen as one manifestation of what has been called a "quest for excitement" that is characteristic of modern society.[28] People do not need just to "relax" from the strains and stresses of work; they need the pleasurable arousal and excitement, and the pleasurable catharsis that follows, from playing a hard-fought game of tennis, watching a fast-moving game of soccer, reading a thriller or great literature, being in the audience at a good play or concert. Or eating out, maybe sampling food from an unfamiliar country or culture.

It follows that sampling other people's foods is one of the simplest and most direct ways to promote multi-cultural understanding. It should not, however, be promoted heavy-handedly. There is a certain tension – albeit an often pleasurable and exciting tension – for most people between their attachment to the old ways of eating in their country and their interest in the new foods they encounter when travelling abroad, or in new ethnic restaurants or among newcomers in their own country. It would most likely be disastrous were officials to decree that "Thou shalt enjoy rogan josh/moussaka/baklava/pirozhki/bryndza" (delete as appropriate). That would obviously provoke the reaction "why shouldn't we just carry on eating our fish and chips/Bratkartoffeln/lasagne/paella" (or whatever). If adventurous eating is encouraged with a gentle touch from schooldays onwards, however, what more directly enjoyable way is there of coming to know, to understand, and to like other cultures?

Notes

1. Mary Douglas, "Culture", *Annual report 1977-78 of the Russell Sage Foundation*, New York, 1978, p. 62.
2. Claude Lévi-Strauss, *The raw and the cooked*, London: Jonathan Cape, 1969.
3. Marshall Sahlins, *Stone age economics*, Chicago: Aldine–Atherton, 1972.
4. Marc Bloch, "Les aliments de l'ancienne France", J.J. Hémardinquer, ed., *Pour une histoire de l'alimentation*, Paris: A. Colin, 1970, p. 231.
5. Curnonsky (pseud. of Maurice-Edmond Sailland) and Austin de Croze, *Le Trésor gastronomique de France*, Paris: Librairie Delagrave, 1933; Curnonsky and Marcel Rouff, *La France gastronomique: Guide des merveilleuses culinaires et des bonnes auberges françaises*, Paris: F. Rouff, 1921-6.
6. Florence White, *Good things in England*, London: Jonathan Cape, 1932.
7. Roland Barthes, "Pour une psychosociologie de l'alimentation contemporaine", *Annales E-S-C*, 16 (5) 1961: 977–86. [English translation: "Toward a Psycho-sociology of contemporary food consumption", pp. 166–73 in R. Forster and O. Ranum, eds, *Food and drink in history*, Baltimore, MD: Johns Hopkins University Press, 1979].
8. See Stephen Mennell, *All manners of food: eating and taste in England and France from the Middle Ages to the present* (Rev. edn, Champaign, IL: University of Illinois Press, 1996. [First edition published 1985, by Blackwell, Oxford.]), pp. 30-34 and passim for a more detailed exposition of this argument.
9. Pegge, Samuel, ed., *The forme of cury*, London: J. Nichols, printer to the Society of Antiquaries,1780; Guillaume Tirel dit Taillevent, [*c*. 1380] *The cookery book*, Oxford: D. Atkinson, 1992.
10. Mennell, *All manners*; Priscilla Parkhurst Ferguson, *Accounting for taste: the triumph of French cuisine*, Chicago: University of Chicago Press, 2004.
11. Strictly speaking, there was a court society around the Stadhouder – who became king only after 1815 – at Den Haag (with a subsidiary branch at Leeuwarden), but the political and economic power, and thus most of the cultural model-setting power, rested with the mercantile Regenten elite in the towns of the Randstad.
12. Jean-Paul Aron, *Le mangeur du 19ᵉ siècle*, Paris: Laffont, 1973.
13. Davis, Norman 1981 *God's playground: a history of Poland* (2 vols, Oxford: Oxford University Press).
14. Mennell, *All manners*, p. 201.
15. Arlie Russell Hochschild, *The second shift: working parents and the revolution at home*, New York: Viking, 1989.
16. Benedict Anderson, *Imagined communities: reflections on the origina and spread of nationalism*, London: Verso, 1983.
17. On the economic, political and social forces that shaped the exponential rise in the consumption of sugar in Europe and North American from the eighteenth century onwards, see Sidney Mintz's classic *Sweetness and power*, New York: Viking, 1985.
18. Mennell, *All manners*, pp. 226-8.
19. Mennell, Stephen "On the civilising of appetite", *Theory, culture and society*, 4 (2–3) 1987: 373–403.
20. For more than thirty years, the Council of Europe has promoted exercise under its slogan of "Sport for All"; it is less easy to think of such a straightforward and effective slogan for promoting sensible eating. The message would have to cut two ways: too many people in the world are still going hungry, while others are eating far too much.
21. Mennell, *All manners*, pp. 318-32.
22. Norbert Elias, "The kitsch style and the age of kitsch", pp. 26–35 Johan Goudsblom and Stephen Mennell, eds, *The Norbert Elias reader*, Oxford: Blackwell, 1996; essay originally published in 1935.
23. Stephen Mennell, *Cultural policy in towns*, Strasbourg: Council of Europe, 1976; James A Simpson, *Towards cultural democracy*, Strasbourg: Council of Europe, 1976.
24. Stephen Mennell, "Theoretical considerations on the study of cultural 'needs'", *Sociology*, 13 (2) 1979: 235–57.
25. Elizabeth David, 1964 "French provincial cooking", *Wine and food*, 121, 28-31.
26. Peter Burke, *Popular culture in early modern Europe*, London: Temple Smith, 1978.
27. Pierre Bourdieu, *La distinction*. Paris: Minuit, 1979; Joanne Finkelstein, *Eating out: a sociology of modern manners*, Cambridge: polity press, 1989.
28. Norbert Elias and Eric Dunning, *Quest for excitement: sport and leisure in the civilising process*, Oxford: Blackwell, 1986.

References

Anderson, Benedict 1983 *Imagined communities: reflections on the origina and spread of nationalism.* London: Verso.

Aron, Jean-Paul 1973 *Le mangeur du 19ᵉ siècle.* Paris: Laffont.

Barthes, Roland 1961 "Pour une psychosociologie de l'alimentation contemporaine", *Annales E-S-C,* 16 (5): 977–86. [English translation: "Toward a psycho-sociology of contemporary food consumption", pp. 166–73 R. Forster and O. Ranum, eds, *Food and drink in history.* Baltimore, MD: Johns Hopkins University Press, 1979]

Bloch, Marc 1970 "Les aliments de l'ancienne France", in J.J. Hémardinquer, ed., *Pour une histoire de l'alimentation.* Paris: A. Colin, pp. 231-5.

Bourdieu, Pierre 1979 *La distinction.* Paris: Minuit.

Burke, Peter, 1978 *Popular culture in early modern Europe.* London: Temple Smith.

Curnonsky (pseud. of Maurice-Edmond Sailland) and de Croze, Austin, 1933 *Le trésor gastronomique de France.* Paris: Librairie Delagrave.

Curnonsky and Rouff, Marcel, 1921-6 *La France gastronomique: Guide des merveilles culinaires et des bonnes auberges françaises.* Paris: F. Rouff.

Elias, Norbert, 1996 [originally 1935], "The kitsch style and the age of kitsch", pp. 26–35 in Johan Goudsblom and Stephen Mennell, eds, *The Norbert Elias Reader.* Oxford: Blackwell.

Elias, Norbert, and Eric Dunning 1986 *Quest for excitement: sport and leisure in the civilising process.* Oxford: Blackwell.

David, Elizabeth 1964 "French provincial cooking", *Wine and food*, 121, 28-31.

Davis, Norman 1981 *God's playground: a history of Poland.* 2 vols, Oxford: Oxford University Press.

Douglas, Mary 1978 "Culture", *Annual report 1977-78 of the Russell Sage Foundation*, New York, pp. 55-81.

Ferguson, Priscilla Parkhurst 2004 *Accounting for taste: the triumph of French cuisine.* Chicago: University of Chicago Press.

Finkelstein, Joanne 1989 *Eating out: a sociology of modern manners.* Cambridge: Polity Press.

Hochschild, Arlie Russell 1989 *The second shift: working parents and the revolution at home.* New York: Viking.

Lévi-Strauss, Claude 1969 *The raw and the cooked.* London: Jonathan Cape.

Mennell, Stephen 1976 *Cultural policy in towns.* Strasbourg: Council of Europe.

Mennell, Stephen 1987 "On the civilising of appetite", *Theory, culture and society*, 4 (2–3): 373–403.

Mennell, Stephen 1979 "Theoretical considerations on the study of cultural 'needs'", *Sociology*, 13 (2): 235–57.

Mennell, Stephen 1996 *All manners of food: eating and taste in England and France from the Middle Ages to the present.* Rev. ed., Champaign, IL: University of Illinois Press. [First edition published 1985, by Blackwell, Oxford.]

Mintz, Sidney 1985 *Sweetness and power: the place of sugar in modern history.* New York: Viking.

Pegge, Samuel, ed., 1780 *The forme of cury.* London: J. Nichols, printer to the Society of Antiquaries.

Sahlins, Marshall 1972 *Stone age economics.* Chicago: Aldine–Atherton.

Simpson, James A. 1976 *Towards cultural democracy.* Strasbourg: Council of Europe.

Taillevent, Guillaume Tirel dit, 1992 [c. 1380] *The cookery book.* Oxford: D. Atkinson.

White, Florence, 1932 *Good things in England.* London: Jonathan Cape.

Conclusions

Biographical notes

Darra Goldstein

Darra Goldstein is Professor of Russian at Williams College and Founding Editor of *Gastronomica: the journal of food and culture*. Since earning her Ph.D. in Slavic languages and literature from Stanford University, she has published numerous books and articles on Russian literature, culture, art, and cuisine, and has organised several exhibitions, including "Graphic design in the Mechanical Age" and the forthcoming "Feeding desire: design and the tools of the table" for the Cooper-Hewitt National Design Museum, Smithsonian Institution. She is also the author of three cookbooks, *A taste of Russia* (nominated for a Tastemaker Award), *The Georgian feast* (winner of the 1994 IACP Julia Child Award for Cookbook of the Year), and *The winter vegetarian*. Goldstein is currently Food Editor of *Russian Life* magazine and General Editor of the book series *California studies in food and culture* (University of California Press).

Kathrin Merkle

Kathrin Merkle is in charge of cultural policy research and development at the Council of Europe. She co-ordinated the present publication with the support of the Steering Committee for Culture as part of the European Cultural Convention's fiftieth anniversary celebrations. In recent years her work focused on policy information systems, the development of standards and indicators and best practice collections. She edited several Council of Europe publications in the cultural policy field, and as a sociologist, takes an interest in all manifestations of everyday culture and their inherent societal potential.

Fabio Parasecoli

Fabio Parasecoli lives in Rome, where he is a journalist for the magazine *Gambero rosso*. After working as a correspondent in foreign affairs and political issues, focusing on Islam and the Far East, he concentrated his research on the interactions among food, culture, politics and history. He teaches courses in the History of Food and Food and Culture in the programme for Communication and Journalism in Food and Wine at the Città del Gusto School in Rome. He also teaches in the Department of Nutrition, Food Studies, and Public Health at New York University. His book *Food culture in Italy* has been published by Greenwood Press.

Stephen Mennell

Stephen Mennell's book *All manners of food: eating and taste in England and France from the Middle Ages to the present* (1985) was the first book in English to win the *Grand prix internationale de littérature gastronomique*; the French translation, *Français et anglais à table*, was awarded the Prix Marco Polo in 1988. He has been Professor of Sociology at University College Dublin (the National University of Ireland, Dublin) since 1993; previously, he held the chair at Monash University, Australia, and before that taught at the University of Exeter, UK. He was a student at Cambridge and Harvard Universities, and took his doctorate from the University of Amsterdam. For the Council of Europe, in the 1970s he wrote the book *Cultural policy in towns*. His many other books include *Norbert Elias: civilisation and the human self-image* (1988), and he is one of Elias's literary executors. He is currently completing a book on *The American civilising process* (forthcoming from Polity Press). He has served as a member of the Irish Research Council for the Humanities and Social Sciences, was founding Director of the Institute for the Study of Social Change at UCD, and is founding Chairman of UCD Press. In 2004 he was elected a foreign member of the Royal Netherlands Academy of Arts and Sciences.

Armenia

Svetlana Haik Poghosyan, an historian, has been carrying out a comparative ethnosociological study of the Armenians in Yerevan and the Moscow diaspora since 1998. She is the author of nearly fifty scientific publications and presentations in scientific journals and international conferences. In 2001 she became one of founding chairpersons of "Kamurj", a non-governmental organisation of female anthropologists in Armenia. Her recent interests focus mainly on the reformation of scientific and presentation work of the National Museum of Ethnography of Armenia.

Austria

Rainer Metzger, an art historian and author, lives in Vienna. He is a substitute professor for art history at the Academy of Art in Karlsruhe and a corresponding member of the Viennese Secession. His publications include *Kunst in der Postmoderne – Dan Graham* (1996), 2003 *Der Tod bei der Arbeit. Bilder der Gewalt/Gewalt der Bilder – ein Führer für Wien und Buchstäblichkeit. Bild und Kunst in der Moderne* (2004).

Azerbaijan

Tahir I. Amiraslanov, himself a chef, is the General Director of the Azerbaijan National Cookery Centre, a member of the International Judging Board, and Vice President of the Russian Cookery Experts Association. He is also a member of the World Culinary Congress, of the Presidium of Unesco International Jury of Folk Art Food and Drink Committee, an honourable member of the French Culinary Academy and a correspondent for the magazine *Nutrition and society.*

Belgium

Marc Jacobs, an historian, is the Director of the Flemish Centre for the Study of Popular Culture in Brussels. He has worked on the tradition of charivari in Europe, cultural and social history, popular culture, cultural policy and intangible heritage. Together with Peter Scholliers, he published the book *Eating out in Europe. Picnics, gourmet dining and snacks since the late eighteenth century* (2003).

Jean Fraikin is the author of many books and articles on popular traditions in the fifteenth century. He serves as Director of the collection *Tradition wallonne* and as policy officer and administrator of the Ethnology Service at the Ministry of the French Community "Wallons-Brussels".

Bosnia and Herzegovina

Nenad Tanović, a professor of electronics and of informatics, has published several scientific notes and manuals in the field of physics and electronics in foreign and national journals. He has also published a book on Bosnian history, *Vitezi kulina bana,* (1996), a collection of poems, *The shapes of Bosnian souls,* as well as poems and tales in periodicals in Albania, Denmark, Canada and Sweden.

Bulgaria

Rayna Gavrilova is an Associate Professor of History in Sofia University and Visiting Associate Professor at Macalester College, Minnesota, USA. She was the Deputy Minister of Culture in 2000, and since 2001 she has been the Executive Director of the Open Society Foundation in Sofia. Among her publications are: *Everyday life in Bulgarian renaissance towns* (1995), *The history of civil organisations in Bulgaria* (1998), *Bulgaria: history retold in brief* (with V. Fol, N. Ovcharov and B. Gavrilov), (1999), and *Bulgarian urban culture during the eighteenth and nineteenth centuries* (1999).

Croatia

Veljko Barbieri, a fiction writer, is the author of numerous novels, short stories, essay collections, theatre, radio and television plays, in which his predominant interest is European and Mediterranean heritage. His bestknown novel is *Epitaph of an imperial gourmand* (1983), and his collection of short stories *134 short stories on food* (2003) was nominated for the best book prize at the Barcelona Book Fair. Since the 1980s, Barbieri has been writing for numerous Croatian and Italian weeklies as a culinary author. His *Cooking canzoniere* (2003), a compilation of articles, has been published in several volumes and languages. Barbieri has also hosted a Croatian TV programme on history.

Cyprus

Savvas Sakkadas is the head of Food and Beverage Studies at the Higher Hotel Institute in Cyprus. Previously he was the Hospitality, Travel and Tourism Co-ordinator at the Intercollege in Cyprus. He has worked at the Hotel Pierre, the Four Seasons and for hotels within the Leading Hotels of the World organisation in New York.

Denmark

Else-Marie Boyhus, an historian, is currently working as a freelance researcher and writer on the history of food and cooking. She is a former museum director and president of the Danish Board of Museums. She is also a member of the Danish Gastronomic Academy/L'Académie Gastronomique du Danemark.

Estonia

Maire Suitsu is the food editor of the magazine *Estonian Woman*. She has published *Home cook's book of wisdom, Maire Suitsu's recipe book,* and *For the beginner cook*, among others, and has co-authored several books. She has also presented a cooking programme on Estonian television.

Finland

Johanna Mäkelä, a sociologist, has studied, lectured and written about the social and cultural dimensions of food and eating since the beginning of the 1990s. Today she is the head of Food Research at the National Consumer Research Centre in Helsinki. Recently she has studied the cultural acceptability of functional foods in Finland and the role of trust in the food chain. She is currently working on research projects that explore consumers' food choice and food classifications in an everyday context.

France

Jean-Pierre Poulain is a socio-anthropologist at Toulouse University, Director of the Interdisciplinary Research Unit on Tourism (ERIT) and of the Centre of Studies on Tourism and Hospitality (CETIA). He co-ordinates the Research Committee on the Sociology and Anthropology of Nutrition at the International Association of French speaking Sociologists (AISLF).

Poulain is the author of *Histoire de la cuisine et des cuisiniers* (1988) and of *Sociologies de l'alimentation* (2002), for which he was respectively awarded the Grand Prix of the French Culinary Academy and the Jean Trémolières prize.

Georgia

Zaal Kikodze is a lecturer in Stone Age archaeology, human origins, and the anthropology of borders at the State University of Tbilisi.

Mary Ellen Chatwin is a socio-cultural anthropologist from Switzerland who works in the Caucasus and especially Georgia. Her principal activities are community and organisational development, and writing and lecturing in foodways, gender and development. Currently she is a social policy advisor for two international organisations in Tbilisi.

Germany

Gunther Hirschfelder studied history and ethnology in Bonn and received a doctorate from the University of Trier on European long-distance trade in the late Middle Ages. He completed his postdoctoral thesis on the consumption of alcohol on the threshold to the industrial age. Since 2000 he has held a temporary professorship in the Ethnology Department of the University of Bonn.

Gesa U. Schönberger has headed the Dr Rainer Wild-Stiftung für gesunde Ernährung (Foundation for Healthy Nutrition), Heidelberg, and has been Director of the International Association for Research on the Culture of Eating since 1998. Following her training as a dietician she studied Ecotrophology at the University of Giessen. Her main areas of research are healthy nutrition from a holistic viewpoint and the integration of various disciplinary approaches in the field of nutrition.

Greece

Eleonora Skouteri-Didaskalou is a lecturer in social anthropology at the Aristotle University of Thessaloniki. She has done research, taught and published works on a number of subjects including the anthropology of food. Her most recent book is *Distinctions* (2003).

Evie Voutsina is a professional cook and author of eleven books and many publications on Greek cuisine and cooking. Her most recent books are *Greek bourgeois cooking* (2003) and *The simple cooking of Saint Quotidianity* v. 1-3 (2004).

Hungary

Zsuzsanna Tátrai, an ethnologist and historian, is the Executive Secretary to the Hungarian Society of Ethnography. She also works as a researcher in the Research Group of Ethnography at the Hungarian Academy of Sciences. Her primary research interests lie in folk festivities, traditional festival customs and the special customs of different age groups. She has published two books and many essays on these topics.

Iceland

Örn D. Jónsson is Professor of Innovation and Entrepreneurship at the Business and Economics faculty of the University of Iceland, Reykjavik. He is the Vice-Director of the Technological Institute of Iceland, Head of the Fisheries Research Institute of the Icelandic University and has had a long standing interest in culinary history, theory and practice.

Ireland

Regina Sexton is a food historian, food writer and cook based in county Cork, Ireland. She has published widely at both the academic and popular levels. She is the author of *A little history of Irish food* (1998) which was made into an eight-part television series by the national broadcaster RTÉ in 2002. Currently she is a weekly food writer with the *Irish examiner*. Her main research interests are food patterns in eighteenth- and nineteenth-century Ireland.

Italy

Viviana Lapertosa graduated in history of cinema from the University of Bologna, winning the Filippo Sacchi award promoted by the Sindacato Nazionale Giornalisti Cinematografici Italiani.

She has published *Dalla fame all'abbondanza. Gli italiani e il cibo nel cinema italiano dal dopoguerra a oggi (2002)* [*From Hunger to abundance. Italians and their food in Italian cinema postwar to today*]. She is currently working as a food writer.

Latvia

Ieva Pīgozne-Brinkmane is an editor at the Latvian Institute that promotes knowledge of Latvia abroad. Earlier she studied in Norway and Ireland, where she graduated from Trinity College in Dublin. She is currently a post-graduate student at the Latvian Academy of Culture doing research on the ancient Latvian lifestyle and world-view. Her interests focus on folklore, mythology, and experimental archaeology.

Lithuania

Birutė Imbrasienė is a culinary publicist. Since 2000 she has been the director of the public organisation Culinary Heritage Fund. She has published *Lithuanian traditional foods* (1998), *Lithuanian calendar feasts* (1990), *Easter eggs* (1990), and *Family traditions, rituals and feasts* (1987).

Luxembourg

Georges Hausemer is a writer, translator and editor living in Esch/Alzette, Luxembourg. He has published novels, short stories, and travel reports as well as articles on food and drink, books on Andalucia and Thailand, and *Culinary Luxembourg. Country, people and cuisine* (1997).

Malta

Kenneth Gambin studied at the University of Malta and graduated in history after having conducted research in the Vatican Archives. His two theses focus on the popular culture of the populace in seventeenth-century Malta, especially as influenced by the Inquisition Tribunal. He currently holds the post of Curator of Ethnography with Heritage Malta, the national agency for museums and heritage sites, and has authored a number of monographs on the subject. He co-authored *Storja tal-Kultura ta' l-Ikel f'Malta* [A history of Maltese culinary culture] (2003).

Moldova

Varvara Buzilă, a philologist, is the Scientific Director of the National Museum of Ethnography and Natural History as well as President of the Society of Ethnology of the Republic of Moldova. She has carried out field research in the Republic of Moldova, Romania and Ukraine. Varvara Buzilă has published the book *Bread: food and symbol. The sacred experience* (1999) and has written many articles on traditional culture. She is a university teacher of ethnology, traditional culture and the semiotics of culture.

Teodorina Bâzgu, a student at the Lyceum "Prometheus", works as a translator at the Society of Ethnology. She is the author of the book *Pluie sur le chevalet* (1996) and co-author of radio programmes for teenagers. She is currently doing research on traditional nutrition systems.

Monaco

Françoise Gamerdinger graduated in humanities at the University of Nice, taught for fifteen years in Monaco, and now works for the Ministry of Culture. She is in charge of international cultural policies and the organisation of the European Heritage Days in Monaco.

René Novella, after completing his studies, including humanities, has held various key positions in cultural and educational institutions in Monaco, such as Conservator of the National Library of Monaco, Secretary General of Cultural Affairs, Director of National Education, Youth and Sports and, since 2000, State Secretary. He has represented his country internationally (Unesco, etc.) and nationally as president of cultural associations, foundations and agencies. Novella has published extensively on Monaco and its history, including *Histoire de Monaco* in collaboration with Jacques Freu, Jean Pastorelli and Jean Baptiste Robert (E.G.C.) and *La Principauté de Monaco,* (Bonechi) and *Seigneurs et princes de Monaco* (Arts et Couleurs).

Netherlands

Bert Natter is a freelance journalist who writes about arts, Dutch culture and history. In 2004 he published *The Rijksmuseum cookbook, great chefs draw inspiration from the Dutch Masters.*

Norway

Henry Notaker is a writer and journalist for the NRK (Norwegian national TV network). After studies in Norway and Mexico he worked as a foreign news reporter in Spain, Italy, Portugal, Central America, Poland and Iraq and as a permanent foreign correspondent in Paris. Notaker has hosted several art and food history series. Since 1997 he has mainly been involved with documentaries.

Poland

Kazimierz Krzysztofek is professor of sociology at the University of Bialystok and at the Warsaw School of Advanced Social Psychology. His fields of research include the sociology of the media and the Internet, human development, the impact of information technology on arts and society, cultural industries, community cultures and civil society. Krzysztofek is the author of a vast number of works and co-author of *Understanding human development: from traditional to information societies* (2002). He has received numerous awards and honours.

Portugal

Ana Pessoa e Costa began her career as a Marketing Account Executive, followed by work in national television and radio. She took several cookery courses in Lisbon and London, in particular with chef Sobral. Her work also involved public relations to VS – Food Consultancy.

Romania

House of Guides is a Romanian publisher specialising in thematic guides of Romanian tourism, cuisine, religious sites, and culture, among other topics. Many of the titles appear in both Romanian and English to aid foreign visitors coming to Romania. These include *City guide Bucharest top 30, Moldavia and Bucovina monasteries, Romanian cookery, Romanian seaside, Danube delta guide, Famous Romanian monasteries,* etc.

Russian Federation

Alexandra Grigorieva studied at Moscow State University (Classics, Ph.D.) where she developed an interest in food history. The focus of her research is Latin culinary terminology. Currently she teaches Latin and Medieval Latin in the Department of Byzantine and Neo-Hellenistic Studies, writes books and articles on food and wine, and is the menu expert in the Russian Guild of Chefs.

Serbia and Montenegro

Vesna Bizić-Omčikus, an ethnologist, is a senior curator of the Ethnographic Museum in Belgrade. She is a member of the Executive Council of YU NC ICOM and has been a member of its editorial board bulletin since

1999. Bizić-Omčikus is the creator of the Serbian Museum Information System and has organized numerous exhibitions and written extensively on the protection of ethnographic heritage.

Slovak Republic

Rastislava Stoličná, an ethnologist, is a researcher at the Ethnological Institute of the Slovak Academy of Sciences in Bratislava and lecturer at the Faculty of Ethnology and Educational Sciences at Unywerstytet Âlaski, Poland. She has dealt with traditional culinary culture in several publications, including *Jedlá a nápoje našich predkov* [Our ancestors' food and beverages] (1991), *Tradiãná strava Slovenska* [Traditional food of Slovakia] (2000), and *Jedlo ako kᵒúã ku kultúre* [Food as a key to culture] (2004). Rastislava Stoličná is a member of the International Commission for Ethnological Food Research.

Slovenia

Janez Bogataj is an ethnologist and professor of art history. In his teaching and research work he covers the ethnology of the Slovenes. He is involved in research on cultural heritage and its relationship to modern society, arts and crafts, food, gastronomy, culinary arts and tourism. Bogataj has published 18 monographs, more than 150 papers and articles, over 250 popular articles and 60 reviews. He is a member of the Slovene Ethnological Society and several other professional associations.

Spain

Diego Valverde Villena, a poet and writer, currently works for literary journals and as a literary translator. He has published numerous books on literature and art in which he describes his experiences with different traditions and folklore gained from his travels in Spain and South America.

Sweden

Richard Tellström is an ethnologist and a scholar at Örebro University, Department of Restaurant and Culinary Arts. He has done research in the fields of local and regional food and meal culture and on the commercialisation and politicisation of the culinary heritage in our time. Of import are his studies on food and meal culture as a tool for economic development in the new regions of Europe and as an expression of the economy in new forms such as culinary tourism and meal exhibitions. Tellström has also worked as a political analyst.

"The former Yugoslav Republic of Macedonia"

Dusan Matic is considered the founder of nutritionism in "the former Yugoslav Republic of Macedonia". Until recently he worked as a food nutrition counsellor. He has written many expert articles on nutrition for the Macedonian public media and abroad. Matic regularly lectures on "Food as a cure" in south-east Europe. Currently he is working on several books that are to be published in the near future.

Turkey

Fahriye Hazer Sancar is a professor in the College of Architecture and Planning at the University of Colorado. Her current research focuses on developing and testing collaborative approaches to environment, landscape, and urban planning and design. Other research interests include environmental aesthetics, politics of urban design, and vernacular/traditional settlements in the context of tourism development.

Ukraine

Oksana Y. Vassyl'ieva graduated in Romano-Germanic Studies at Kiev State University in 1982. She worked as an interpreter guide at the State Tourist Company Intourist in Kiev before joining the Ministry of Foreign Affairs in 1992. There, in addition to other duties, she headed the division of cultural cooperation. Since 2003, she has been the First Secretary (humanitarian issues) at the Embassy of Ukraine in Moldova.

United Kingdom

VisitBritain, the tourism authority for Britain, markets Britain to the rest of the world and England to the British, building the value of tourism by creating world-class destination brands and marketing campaigns.

Heather Hay Ffrench's in-depth knowledge of British regional food and drink is reflected in the many articles and books she has written, including the award winning *Great British food*. Her interest in social history and the evolution of national "tastes" has developed alongside farming rare breed sheep. Together with her family, Heather Hay Ffrench makes mustards and preserves as "The merchant farmer" in a converted apple store in the beautiful Weald of Kent, sourcing quality local produce from like-minded growers.

Sponsors

Boutari Foundation

The Stellios & Fany Boutari Foundation was created by the Boutari family in 1991 and approved by presidential decree on 30 September of that year. It has been operating since January 1992 and is chaired by Mr Yiannis Boutari, with other members of the family serving as board members. The foundation reflects the Boutari family's sense of public duty and is only one of the charitable activities in which they have long been involved. The location of the foundation's headquarters in Thessaloniki reflects the family's activities in Greek Macedonia during their first 100 years of contributing to the country's economic life. This location also emphasises the decentralisation of the foundation's scientific work.

The goal of the foundation is to promote scientific research on Greek wine (viticulture, viniculture, and surrounding issues). To this end it engages in numerous activities. It is of great importance to the foundation that links and co-operation on both the national and international levels be pursued. In this way it hopes to increase its expertise and effectiveness in order to be even more successful in its pursuits.

Ursula Lübbe Foundation

Books are the foundation of education and culture and reading opens the way to both. In 2003, Ursula Lübbe took the initiative to consolidate the efforts by Lübbe Publishing in this spirit by setting up the Ursula Lübbe Foundation.

The encouragement in the field of education, art and culture for young people is the prime objective of the foundation. It aims at providing effective support by connecting people and media. The focus is on encouraging children and young adults to interact with the key medium of "the book" and audiovisual media in a responsible way.

Making culture accessible to the generations to come also takes place on the stage and in museums, through the works of the Old Masters or the activities of today's "young wild artists". For the development of new cultural projects, the foundation has found competent partners such as the Foundation of Prussian Cultural Heritage with the Berlin Museum Island and the Vienna State Opera.

Further activities of the foundation include seminars, workshops, performances and other events, always with the aim of facilitating access to education and culture for the young.

For more information see:
http://www.ursula-luebbe-stiftung.de

Sales agents for publications of the Council of Europe
Agents de vente des publications du Conseil de l'Europe

BELGIUM/BELGIQUE
La Librairie européenne SA
50, avenue A. Jonnart
B-1200 BRUXELLES 20
Tel.: (32) 2 734 0281
Fax: (32) 2 735 0860
E-mail: info@libeurop.be
http://www.libeurop.be

Jean de Lannoy
202, avenue du Roi
B-1190 BRUXELLES
Tel.: (32) 2 538 4308
Fax: (32) 2 538 0841
E-mail: jean.de.lannoy@euronet.be
http://www.jean-de-lannoy.be

CANADA
Renouf Publishing Company Limited
5369 Chemin Canotek Road
CDN-OTTAWA, Ontario, K1J 9J3
Tel.: (1) 613 745 2665
Fax: (1) 613 745 7660
E-mail: order.dept@renoufbooks.com
http://www.renoufbooks.com

CZECH REPUBLIC/RÉPUBLIQUE TCHÈQUE
Suweco Cz Dovoz Tisku Praha
Ceskomoravska 21
CZ-18021 PRAHA 9
Tel.: (420) 2 660 35 364
Fax: (420) 2 683 30 42
E-mail: import@suweco.cz

DENMARK/DANEMARK
GAD Direct
Fiolstaede 31-33
DK-1171 COPENHAGEN K
Tel.: (45) 33 13 72 33
Fax: (45) 33 12 54 94
E-mail: info@gaddirect.dk

FINLAND/FINLANDE
Akateeminen Kirjakauppa
Keskuskatu 1, PO Box 218
FIN-00381 HELSINKI
Tel.: (358) 9 121 41
Fax: (358) 9 121 4450
E-mail: akatilaus@stockmann.fi
http://www.akatilaus.akateeminen.com

FRANCE
La Documentation française
(Diffusion/Vente France entière)
124, rue H. Barbusse
F-93308 AUBERVILLIERS Cedex
Tel.: (33) 01 40 15 70 00
Fax: (33) 01 40 15 68 00
E-mail: commandes.vel@ladocfrancaise.gouv.fr
http://www.ladocfrancaise.gouv.fr

Librairie Kléber (Vente Strasbourg)
Palais de l'Europe
F-67075 Strasbourg Cedex
Fax: (33) 03 88 52 91 21
E-mail: librairie.kleber@coe.int

GERMANY/ALLEMAGNE
AUSTRIA/AUTRICHE
UNO Verlag
August Bebel Allee 6
D-53175 BONN
Tel.: (49) 2 28 94 90 20
Fax: (49) 2 28 94 90 222
E-mail: bestellung@uno-verlag.de
http://www.uno-verlag.de

GREECE/GRÈCE
Librairie Kauffmann
28, rue Stadiou
GR-ATHINAI 10564
Tel.: (30) 1 32 22 160
Fax: (30) 1 32 30 320
E-mail: ord@otenet.gr

HUNGARY/HONGRIE
Euro Info Service
Hungexpo Europa Kozpont ter 1
H-1101 BUDAPEST
Tel.: (361) 264 8270
Fax: (361) 264 8271
E-mail: euroinfo@euroinfo.hu
http://www.euroinfo.hu

ITALY/ITALIE
Libreria Commissionaria Sansoni
Via Duca di Calabria 1/1, CP 552
I-50125 FIRENZE
Tel.: (39) 556 4831
Fax: (39) 556 41257
E-mail: licosa@licosa.com
http://www.licosa.com

NETHERLANDS/PAYS-BAS
De Lindeboom Internationale Publikaties
PO Box 202, MA de Ruyterstraat 20 A
NL-7480 AE HAAKSBERGEN
Tel.: (31) 53 574 0004
Fax: (31) 53 572 9296
E-mail: books@delindeboom.com
http://home-1-worldonline.nl/~lindeboo/

NORWAY/NORVÈGE
Akademika, A/S Universitetsbokhandel
PO Box 84, Blindern
N-0314 OSLO
Tel.: (47) 22 85 30 30
Fax: (47) 23 12 24 20

POLAND/POLOGNE
Głowna Księgarnia Naukowa
im. B. Prusa
Krakowskie Przedmiescie 7
PL-00-068 WARSZAWA
Tel.: (48) 29 22 66
Fax: (48) 22 26 64 49
E-mail: inter@internews.com.pl
http://www.internews.com.pl

PORTUGAL
Livraria Portugal
Rua do Carmo, 70
P-1200 LISBOA
Tel.: (351) 13 47 49 82
Fax: (351) 13 47 02 64
E-mail: liv.portugal@mail.telepac.pt

SPAIN/ESPAGNE
Mundi-Prensa Libros SA
Castelló 37
E-28001 MADRID
Tel.: (34) 914 36 37 00
Fax: (34) 915 75 39 98
E-mail: libreria@mundiprensa.es
http://www.mundiprensa.com

SWITZERLAND/SUISSE
Adeco – Van Diermen
Chemin du Lacuez 41
CH-1807 BLONAY
Tel.: (41) 21 943 26 73
Fax: (41) 21 943 36 05
E-mail: info@adeco.org

UNITED KINGDOM/ROYAUME-UNI
TSO (formerly HMSO)
51 Nine Elms Lane
GB-LONDON SW8 5DR
Tel.: (44) 207 873 8372
Fax: (44) 207 873 8200
E-mail: customer.services@theso.co.uk
http://www.the-stationery-office.co.uk
http://www.itsofficial.net

UNITED STATES and CANADA/ ÉTATS-UNIS et CANADA
Manhattan Publishing Company
2036 Albany Post Road
CROTON-ON-HUDSON,
NY 10520, USA
Tel.: (1) 914 271 5194
Fax: (1) 914 271 5856
E-mail: Info@manhattanpublishing.com
http://www.manhattanpublishing.com

Council of Europe Publishing/Editions du Conseil de l'Europe
F-67075 Strasbourg Cedex
Tel.: (33) 03 88 41 25 81 – Fax: (33) 03 88 41 39 10 – E-mail: publishing@coe.int – Website: http://book.coe.int